P9-CLU-170

347.7324
Sch32

Phillips Library
Bethany College
Bethany, W. Va. 26032

DISCARD

Learned Hand's
Court

Learned Hand's Court

MARVIN SCHICK

THE JOHNS HOPKINS PRESS
BALTIMORE AND LONDON

Copyright © 1970 by The Johns Hopkins Press
All rights reserved
Manufactured in the United States of America

The Johns Hopkins Press, Baltimore, Maryland 21218
The Johns Hopkins Press Ltd., London

Library of Congress Catalog Card Number 73-97491

ISBN 0-8018-1214-3

FOR MY MOTHER

347.7324
Sch 32 l

Contents

List of Tables
viii

List of Abbreviations
x

Preface
xi

Acknowledgments
xv

Introduction
1

1. Learned Hand's Court
5

2. A Brief History
39

3. The Decision-Making Process
73

4. Judicial Relations
123

5. The Obedient Judge
154

6. Three Quiet and Sometimes Conservative Judges
192

7. The Battling New Dealers
219

8. Judges Frank and Clark and the Law of the Second Circuit
247

9. The Business of the Court
305

10. The Second Circuit and the Supreme Court: 1942–51
328

11. The Stature of a Court
348

Bibliography
356

Index
365

Index of Cases
369

LIST OF TABLES

1 The Business of the Second Circuit, 1845–69 45
2 The Business of the Second Circuit, 1869–79 49
3 Distribution of Opinions—Second Circuit, 1893 56
4 The Business of the Circuit Courts of Appeals and the Second Circuit, 1892–1915 58
5 The Business of the Circuit Courts of Appeals and the Second Circuit, 1916–39 65
6 The Business of the Courts of Appeals and the Second Circuit, 1940–69 68
7 The Business of the Second Circuit, Fiscal Years 1942–51 306
8 Second Circuit's Share of Business of Courts of Appeals.............307
9 The Second Circuit and Its Docket, 1942–51 308
10 Time Taken to Dispose Cases, Second Circuit and All Circuits 1942–51 308
11 Sources of Cases Commenced in the Second Circuit, 1942–51.........309
12 Distribution of Cases from the District Courts, Second Circuit, 1942–51 311

13 Nature of Cases Terminated, Second Circuit, 1942–51 311

14 Opinions of the Second Circuit Included in the *Federal Reporter 2d*, Volumes 120–89 313

15 Writers of Opinions in the Second Circuit, 1941–51 315

16 Action of Second Circuit Judges, Cases with Dissent 321

17 Interactions of Judges in Cases with Dissent 321

18 Total Disagreements of the Judges 322

19 Supportive Interactions of Judges in Cases with Dissent 323

20 Rate of Agreement of Judges in Cases with Dissent 323

21 Solidarity of Judges According to Pairs 323

22 Subject Matter of Dissents 324

23 Dissents of Judges According to Subject Matter .326

24 Terminations and Petitions for Certiorari Filed and Granted, All Courts of Appeals and Second Circuit 330

25 Termination–Certiorari Relationship According to Subject Matter, Second Circuit 330

26 Memorandum Decisions of the Supreme Court in Cases from the Second Circuit 334

27 Supreme Court Actions in Cases from the Courts of Appeals Decided by Full Opinion, 1941–51 334

28 Supreme Court Decisions in Cases with Full Opinion from the Second Circuit, According to Subject Matter 337

29 Outcome of Dissents by Second Circuit Judges in the Supreme Court after Certiorari Was Granted 339

30 Supreme Court Interaction with Judge Learned Hand 341

31 Supreme Court Justices' Interactions with Judge Swan 341

32 Supreme Court Justices' Interactions with Judge Augustus Hand 342

33 Supreme Court Justices' Interactions with Judge Chase 342

34 Supreme Court Justices' Interactions with Judge Clark 343

35 Supreme Court Justices' Interactions with Judge Frank 343

36 Supreme Court Justices' Percentage of Agreement with Second Circuit Judges 345

37 Percentages of Support of Second Circuit Judges by Supreme Court Justices, According to Group 346

38 Second Circuit Judges' Interactions with the Supreme Court, All Justices 347

List of Abbreviations

LH Learned Hand
TWS Thomas Walter Swan
ANH Augustus Noble Hand
HBC Harrie Brigham Chase
CEC Charles Edward Clark
JNF Jerome New Frank

Preface

THE SUGGESTION FOR A STUDY OF THE UNITED STATES COURT OF APPEALS
for the Second Circuit came from Professor Joseph Tanenhaus, who
introduced me to the subject of judicial behavior at New York University. At the time, political scientists seemed to think that the federal
courts of appeals or, for that matter, any American court below the
Supreme Court, were unfit for study by the profession. Courses on the
judiciary dealt exclusively with the Supreme Court and the constitutional decisions that it made. About the only mention made of lower
courts in political science literature was the brief (and insipid) sketches
usually included in introductory course textbooks.

Of course there have been many changes and improvements in our
approach to courts and judges. We have learned that the Supreme
Court alone does not make the American judicial system, nor do legal
opinions a court make. Sophisticated analytical techniques have been
developed or borrowed from other fields to permit us to probe more
deeply into the judicial process. Whether quantitative or verbal, and
no matter what their defects, we cannot deny that these techniques
have made clear the inadequacy of the old Supreme Court-constitu-
tional law tradition.

The behavioral thrust has extended the boundaries of political science beyond—or below—the Supreme Court and its justices. Professors Kenneth Vines, Sheldon Goldman, Sidney Ulmer, Stuart Nagel, Louis Loeb, Joel Grossman, Herbert Jacob, and Kenneth Dolbeare, among many others, have examined state and inferior federal courts. They have produced a significant body of work. Still, their studies have been directed to special aspects of the operations of these courts and, in any case, the bulk of recent research is Supreme Court oriented. If I have not relied specifically on the methodology and research of others who have worked in this field, I can say with all sincerity that the mood within the discipline that they have created has sparked this and other research on courts.

This book is an effort to present a comprehensive picture of a lower federal court. It is aimed at both lawyers and those political scientists who are interested in the legal process. The dearth of knowledge about the Second Circuit and the courts of appeals made it necessary to include in this study historical and biographical material that would introduce the reader to the subject. Beyond this, the dual audience made even more difficult the problem of which approaches to take toward the Second Circuit.

It is no secret that many lawyers, and not a few political scientists, have deprecated quantitative and other behavioral approaches to the judicial process. On the other hand, a good deal of scorn has been directed at the case method that has dominated legal education and scholarship for so long. I do not believe it necessary to take sides in the debate, for the separation of the two disciplines implies distinct approaches. I do feel strongly, though, that we political scientists who study courts must do more than imitate lawyers, if only because we cannot do as good a job as they do in analyzing case law. Since I am writing for lawyers and political scientists both, I have tried to employ techniques familiar to each. I confess to having doubts as to whether I have succeeded to the satisfaction of either; after all, I have been told by a couple of lawyers that the statistical approach is overdone in Chapters 9 and 10, while a colleague has found the same material a bit on the primitive side (that is, from a behavioral point of view).

I also have had to face several substantive problems and these ought to be briefly discussed here. This book is principally about ten years (1941–51) in the history of the Second Circuit. The selection of this period is easily justified on grounds of court membership. The source of the difficulty is that no matter how significant and worthy of the study is the period of Learned Hand's chief judgeship, these years hardly constitute a neat analytical unit. After all, the court existed prior to 1941 and many of the decisions handed down during 1941–51 had precedential roots in earlier years. On an individual level, Learned Hand and Judges Swan, Augustus Hand, and Chase sat on the court as far back as the 1920's, so that their definitions of the judicial role and approaches to many legal problems were already shaped before the years studied here.

The point is that I have deliberately selected a single decade out of the much larger context of Second Circuit history, law, and behavior. Study of these years is apt to be somewhat distorted, if only because so little is known of all the other years that the court has been sitting. I also recognize that even with regard to 1941–51 the Second Circuit functioned within judicial frameworks that are not the principal concern of this book. In the first place, it shared intermediate appellate status in the federal judiciary with ten other courts of appeals. Secondly, as an inferior court, the Second Circuit is affected by the actions of the Supreme Court.

Each of the contextual limitations imposed by the ten-year scope of this study has been considered in the preparation of *Learned Hand's Court*. A great deal of time has been spent examining Second Circuit rulings to learn of their decisional origins and future impact and also to trace their relationship to Supreme Court decisions. The effect of this research has been to extend the study to at least some appeals heard by the Second Circuit outside of the Learned Hand years. Of course, overwhelmingly, attention is paid to 1941–51 decisions. With respect to this decade, I believe that for the most part the rulings that gave vigor to the court and provoked the greatest effort by the judges were those that had either no roots prior to 1941, or weak ones. In short, I believe that it makes sense to study a single decade.

With regard to the work of the other courts of appeals during 1941–51, it is sufficient to note here that I argue in the text (Chapter 4) that these courts are not much influenced by the actions of tribunals of the same rank.

But obviously the Supreme Court does affect lower court activity, and for this reason what the Supreme Court did during the period, particularly in appeals from the Second Circuit, is very much a part of this study.

Of all the major institutions of our government, the appellate courts are unique in the degree to which their actions are hidden from the public. We know more about the internal discussions preceding decision-making of various national security agencies than we do of the private discussions of the justices of the Supreme Court. Most of what we know and study about courts concerns their rulings. From the standpoint of law, this limited view is adequate, though barely so. After all, many important decisions are compromises of the differing views of judges, arrived at after considerable bargaining; the decision that is published and then studied and applied often obscures the conflict and bargaining that took place in conference and elsewhere.

Courts as agencies of policy-making ought to be studied as systems with social and psychological characteristics relevant to the rulings they render. We must examine as deeply as we can their modes of operation. Because for the most part their business is conducted privately, we should be grateful for such opportunities as are available for learning about those features of their operations which traditionally are never publicized. For this study of the Learned Hand court I have been fortunate in securing access to the papers of Judge Charles E. Clark, which are at the library of the Yale Law School. I am deeply grateful to Mrs. Dorothy Clark and Professor Elias Clark for making available to me the papers of their late husband and father. Their willingness to allow me to use the Clark Papers has contributed importantly to this study. While they or others may at times disagree with the way I have used or interpreted some of the material, I can say with confidence that these papers have advanced significantly our understanding of the Second Circuit and the way appellate courts function.

The Clark Papers principally consist of the memoranda of Judge Clark and his colleagues in the cases that he heard, judicial correspondence involving Judge Clark, and other material relating to the work of the Second Circuit. Because it is an important matter, I have reserved discussion of my approach to the use of these papers for a place in the text (note at the beginning of Chapter 7) where I feel more assured that it will catch the eye of the reader.

I recognize that reliance on the papers of a single judge might well lead to the overemphasis of certain events in which this judge was involved and an underemphasis of some of the things that his colleagues did. The danger is real and I suppose that I have erred in some places. But it is not without importance that Judge Clark heard approximately one-half of the appeals that were decided by the Learned Hand court, and for these cases I have used the memoranda and other material prepared by the sitting judges. The most important feature of the Second Circuit during these years was the relationship between Judges Frank and Clark, and on this subject the Clark Papers contain a great deal of documentation.

Acknowledgments

MANY PEOPLE HAVE HELPED ME SIGNIFICANTLY IN THE PREPARATION OF this book. The judges and other persons who have been associated with the Second Circuit who granted me interviews, and friends and colleagues who gave me advice and encouragement, all have my sincere appreciation even if their names are not included in these few lines.

In addition to access to the Clark Papers, Mrs. Clark and her son granted me permission to use the quotes from Judge Clark's letters that appear in the text. Similar permission for Judge Frank's letters was obtained from Mrs. Florence Kiper Frank and for those of Judge Learned Hand from Mr. Norris Darrell. Happily, the preparation of this book afforded me the opportunity to make the acquaintance of Mrs. Frank, a fine and gracious lady.

I wish to express my gratitude to the Walter E. Meyer Research Institute of Law, and to its Director, Professor Maurice Rosenberg, for the financial support that enabled me to take advantage of the opportunity to use the Clark Papers. Harvey Arfa and Judith Milone served splendidly as research assistants on these papers.

There is no way that I can adequately write about my debt to my teacher Professor Joseph Tanenhaus. His criticism when he felt that I had not met the standards that he set and his guidance are the sources from which this work has sprung. Years after I last sat in his classroom I feel pride that I am a student of this good scholar and gentleman.

In my freshman years at Brooklyn College Professor Samuel J. Konefsky first taught me about the Supreme Court. He remained my dear teacher until his recent death. I am deeply saddened that he did not live to see the completion of this book, which we often discussed. *Learned Hand's Court,* and the many other books written by Professor Konefsky's students, are tributes to the memory of a great teacher. Professors Jacob Landynski and Alan Rosenthal are friends who happen to be scholars. They read the manuscript and provided numerous suggestions. This is only part of the invaluable help that they gave me. The manuscript was also read by Professors Gerald Gunther and Allen Schick and Mr. Julius Berman. Their comments and criticisms saved me from many errors and resulted in a great deal of improvement in the text.

Much of the research on the book was done in the library of the Association of the Bar of the City of New York. I am in debt to the staff of the library for countless services rendered to me.

In somewhat different form, Chapter 4 of the book appeared in the November 1969 issue of the *New York University Law Review.*

For a goodly number of years most of my time has been devoted to a variety of communal activities that deserve no mention here except to say that they have required that work on the book go on at the expense of the too little time that I reserved for my wife and children. Malka has been encouraging and she has known when to get me back to this task. She has done editing and typing and sundry other things and I have never adequately expressed my appreciation. Rabos banos asu chayil, v'at alise al kulana.

Introduction

Very little has been written about the United States Court of Appeals for the Second Circuit or, indeed, about any of the federal courts of appeals. These eleven courts occupy positions of central importance in the federal judicial system, yet most of their work and decisions go unnoticed. Far greater attention is paid not only to the Supreme Court but also to much of what goes on in the district courts. In part the neglect is due to the total absence of glamor and drama in the operations of the intermediate courts. There is nothing exciting about their decisional processes. On the other hand, there is often great drama in the Supreme Court in the announcement of new constitutional doctrine or in the clash of justices. And, in the trial court there is frequently an air of excitement and expectancy, particularly during a well-publicized criminal prosecution.

The neglect of the courts of appeals may also be the result of a lack of appreciation of the degree of finality of their rulings. Although the result is final in well over 90 per cent of the appeals they decide, the notion persists in the minds of some that what these courts do is of minor importance because an appeal will be taken to the nation's highest court.

While these explanations account for the lack of public interest, they do not tell us why lawyers and political scientists have contributed little to our understanding of the functions and operations of these courts. However, the reasons why scholars concentrate almost exclusively on the Supreme Court are not hard to find. An obvious reason is that the Supreme Court plays such a vital role in the American scheme of government. Never in history has any court had as high and permanent a position in the governmental process as the Supreme Court. It is not unreasonable that we have a proliferation of histories, biographies, critiques, and law review articles centering around the High Court.

Actually, courts of appeals cases are not dissimilar to those coming to the Supreme Court. At both levels, statutory interpretation is a major, and perhaps dominant, aspect of the judges' work, although of late a substantial percentage of cases disposed of with full opinion by the Supreme Court are constitutional cases. Still, the Supreme Court is faced with considerable antitrust, tax, bankruptcy, and other commercial litigation. In the law schools, special courses are devoted to these fields and the casebooks include lower court decisions. In the law journals, however, with the exception of student case notes, the tendency is to concentrate on Supreme Court action. Generally, political scientists do not study these specialized public law fields, even at the Supreme Court level. A noteworthy exception to this tendency, political scientist Martin Shapiro, asks,

> Why do Constitutional scholars keep the flame of an unsuccessful 1896 antitrust prosecution[1] and a New Deal marketing restriction[2] alive while hiding [United States v.] Du Pont[3] under a bushel? Because they are Constitutional scholars. The antitrust cases do not raise Constitutional questions. Indeed we owe the one incursion of antitrust questions into traditional courses and texts on the Supreme Court, the E. C. Knight case, to the by now fortuitous circumstance that the opinion formulated the since repudiated rule that production is not commerce. Study of the Constitutional Supreme Court thus often leads us to either legal archaeology or triviality, while major areas of the Court's activity escape us.[4]

Obviously, if constitutional scholars do not pay much attention to major public law areas in the Supreme Court, they will even more readily ignore lower court decisions in these areas.

[1] United States v. E. C. Knight, 156 U.S. 1.
[2] Wickard v. Filburn, 317 U.S. 111 (1942).
[3] 353 U.S. 586 (1957), a very important antitrust case.
[4] Shapiro, *Law and Politics in the Supreme Court* (Glencoe, Ill.: Free Press, 1964), p. 253.

Even in areas where Supreme Court law is examined, courts of appeals decisions receive little attention. This may be so because it is relatively easy to study most Supreme Court decisions, particularly those in the constitutional law field. While many Supreme Court decisions may be subjected to different interpretations, it is unlikely that more than one or two readings will be needed to reveal what each case is about.

The same is not true of the courts of appeals, although it is generally conceded that a majority of the cases brought to these courts are frivolous and not difficult to decide.[5] At the same time, trivial (and some important) appeals are denied review by the High Court, which reserves argument and written opinions for the most important and contentious cases. Thus it might be thought that of the two judicial levels, cases at the intermediate court level are easier to follow. This is not true. To nonlawyers, and also to many lawyers, the decisions of the lower courts are more difficult to comprehend. What is difficult about Supreme Court cases is analytical, not factual, and is inherent in the complex problems that arise out of the judicial function; what is difficult about lower appellate litigation is often due to the subject matter of the cases. Supreme Court decision-making is an arduous process not because the facts of the cases confronting the justices are too technical or very complex, but because the justices are required to choose between competing social and political values which have legitimacy. In many areas they must spell out their attitudes on the judicial function itself. The analyst of Supreme Court decisions has a task which parallels that of the justices. He, too, is little troubled by the factual aspects of the litigation (although he may make different use of the facts than do the justices) and devotes most of his attention to philosophical and normative issues. He accepts or rejects what the Supreme Court has done and his judgment springs from his norms about freedom of speech, criminal justice, and the like.

Unfortunately, the business of the lower courts does not open up as many avenues that are amenable to philosophical analysis, and, in any case, inferior judges are bound to accept the prevailing norms as well as the law of the Supreme Court. So much of the work of the courts of appeals is factual, involving technical matters on which

---

[5] "Judge Clark, in a subjective test covering 300 appeals on which he has sat during the last two years, found clear one-way cases comprised at least 70 per cent, while around 10 per cent were highly original cases giving scope to the methods of social values. In the remaining 20 per cent, the outcome actually proved certain, but counsel might be forgiven for thinking they had a bare chance of success" (Charles E. Clark and David M. Trubek, "The Creative Role of the Judge: Restraint and Freedom in the Common Law Tradition," *Yale Law Journal,* 71 [1961], 256, n. 7).

many judges, most lawyers, and almost all political scientists are not well trained. The Second Circuit—and this is true to a lesser extent of the other courts of appeals—decides a large number of admiralty, patent, bankruptcy, corporate reorganization, antitrust, and tax cases. This litigation is beyond the pale of easy comprehension for most people who are concerned with judicial affairs.

Whatever the difficulties, continued neglect of the business and procedures of lower courts cannot be justified. The relationships between these courts and the Supreme Court, the decisional processes of all courts, federal and state, and the impact of lower court decisions on political and social institutions are subjects worthy of scholarly concern. What a leader of the political science profession wrote a decade ago remains valid today:

> Our literature does not provide a full account of the organizational structure for deciding constitutional issues. Political scientists have not given us a thorough report of the general structure of the federal courts or of any state court system, or of the nationwide judicial structure which filters out issues and assigns to different courts particular roles in deciding constitutional issues. . . .
> We have made little exploration of the relationships of lower federal courts to constitutionality of legislation . . . control of judges in lower courts by judges in higher courts seems to have been passed by. It may be that political scientists have purposely limited their attention to some of these matters on the supposition that lawyers will provide better descriptions than political scientists can supply; if this be the case, it must be admitted that a charting of what political scientists write about and what they pass over gives little clue to what they consider a proper division of labor between the two professions.[6]

This study of the Learned Hand court by a political scientist is an attempt to reduce the gap in our understanding of the lower federal courts. The Second Circuit is only one of eleven federal courts of appeals. Much of what is included in this study is relevant to the other ten courts. For example, both the history and the procedures of the Second Circuit parallel those of all these courts. But obviously every court has had its own personalities and body of decisions, and until these are studied for more of the courts of appeals we cannot say how much of the behavior of the Second Circuit is common to the other courts at its level.

[6] Charles S. Hyneman, *The Study of Politics* (Urbana, Ill.: University of Illinois Press, 1959), pp. 42–43.

1

Learned Hand's Court

IN EARLY 1939, WHEN LEARNED HAND BECAME SENIOR CIRCUIT JUDGE
(in effect, chief judge) of the United States Circuit Court of Appeals
for the Second Circuit,[1] conditions on the court did not augur particularly well for the emergence of a judicial body that would come to be
rated as one of the top appellate courts in the history of the country.
After almost a decade of rumors of misconduct, Martin T. Manton,
Hand's predecessor as senior circuit judge, resigned his position amid
charges that he had accepted bribes and corrupted his judicial office.
Shortly thereafter, Manton was indicted, tried, and convicted. On
appeal, his conviction was unanimously affirmed by a special panel of
judges of his former court. Manton was the first federal judge to be
prosecuted for selling his vote.[2]

The federal courts of appeals are small groups; in almost all cases
decisions are made by panels composed of three judges. When the

[1] From the time of their creation in 1891 until 1948, the federal intermediate courts were called "circuit courts of appeals." In 1948 their name
was changed to "courts of appeals." At the same time, the term "senior circuit judge" was replaced by "chief judge."

[2] The Manton case is described in journalistic style in Joseph Borkin,
The Corrupt Judge (New York: Clarkson N. Potter, 1962), pp. 25–93.

Manton case broke, the Second Circuit consisted of five judges. In a way, Manton's corruption involved his colleagues and could have tainted the reputation of the entire court. In order to guarantee at least temporary success to those who purchased his vote,[3] it was necessary for Manton to receive the supporting vote of one of his colleagues. In each case where there was evidence that Manton had been bought, he was on the winning side, and in all but two of these the decision was unanimous. Judge Manton's efforts on behalf of his "clients" also required him to tamper with the panel and case schedules to insure that he would be sitting when their cases were argued. These panel maneuverings were highly irregular and could not have gone completely unnoticed by the other Second Circuit judges. Yet, all of his colleagues testified for Manton's defense at the trial.[4] Clearly there was good reason to expect in 1939 that the Manton case, which received considerable attention from the newspapers, would undermine public confidence in the Second Circuit.

Other factors were present at the time which also might have contributed to a feeling that the court under Learned Hand could not attain judicial eminence. Hand was sixty-seven years old when he became senior circuit judge; had the present statute governing chief judgeships of federal courts of appeals and district courts been in effect during the 1940's he would have had to relinquish his senior position on the court at the age of seventy.[5] Interestingly, in 1942 when Hand was seventy, President Roosevelt refused, despite great pressure, to elevate him to the Supreme Court, primarily because he thought him

[3] There was always the prospect that the Supreme Court would grant certiorari and reverse the lower court.

[4] Without the papers of the judges who served with him, it is almost impossible to determine what Manton's colleagues felt about his misdeeds. In what seemed a clear reference to the Manton case, Learned Hand once intimated that he knew much more than was ever made public. The following exchange occurred in 1951 in testimony before a Senate subcommittee considering proposals to improve morality in public affairs:

Judge Hand: "There linger in the back of my memory some things that happened very close at home, but they shall not be mentioned."

Senator Fulbright: "If there is anything wrong, it has been better concealed, at least. I am not aware of anything wrong."

Judge Hand: "All right, then, I will not bring it to your attention. I could a tale unfold."

Senator Douglas: "There is a former judge from New York who is serving in the penitentiary."

Judge Hand: "He has gone now. I would not say to a greater penitentiary."

From Irving Dilliard (ed.), *The Spirit of Liberty; Papers and Addresses of Learned Hand* (New York: Vintage Press, 1959), pp. 171–72.

[5] Although he would have been able to remain on the court.

too old; this ended the possibility that Learned Hand would obtain a seat on the nation's highest court.[6]

With the exception of Judge Harrie B. Chase, who was fifty, the other members of the court in 1939 were also rather old and could not have been expected to continue in active judicial service for too many years. Judge Thomas W. Swan, second in seniority on the Second Circuit, was sixty-two. His good friend—and Learned Hand's first cousin—Judge Augustus Hand, was a few months short of his seventieth birthday. The age factor was also important because during the 1930's the Second Circuit was by far the busiest court of appeals in number of cases docketed and disposed of. While the volume of business slackened somewhat in the next decade, the Second Circuit still had the heaviest case load of the eleven courts of appeals. The burden on the court was considerable, a condition not made any lighter by the fact that while he was senior circuit judge Manton had been the opinion writer for the court in more cases than any of his colleagues.

Qualitatively, as well, there may have been some question of the ability of the Learned Hand court to perform its judicial responsibilities in a superior fashion. The entire nucleus of the court—the two Hands, Swan, and Chase—had been appointed to the appellate bench by President Coolidge; three of the four were Republicans, and Augustus Hand, who was the sole Democrat, definitely leaned toward the more conservative wing of the party. Although not always conclusive or even meaningful in terms of future conduct on the bench, party affiliation and political and social attitudes usually determine judicial appointments (particularly to the lower federal courts) and influence the actions taken by judges after their appointment.[7] How would a court dominated by Coolidge appointees react to the fundamental changes in Supreme Court policy that resulted from the revolution of 1937–38? What would its attitude be toward the rulings of New Deal administrative agencies, such as the National Labor Relations Board, which generally had adopted an antibusiness posture? Moreover, important New Deal legislation—the Fair Labor Standards Act of 1938, for example—would come before the court for interpretation, challenging the willingness of the judges to make decisions which might be contrary to their personal predilections. What the Second Circuit would do in these cases was of special importance by virtue of its location in the financial and commercial capital of the nation.

In other areas, too, difficult litigation would confront the court presided over by Learned Hand. Reversals by the Supreme Court and

[6] Francis Biddle, *In Brief Authority* (Garden City, N.Y.: Doubleday and Company, 1962), p. 194.

[7] Jack W. Peltason, *Federal Courts in the Political Process* (Garden City, N.Y.: Doubleday and Co., 1955).

new legislation by Congress would test the Second Circuit. The Roosevelt court was beginning to expand the rights of criminal defendants under the Bill of Rights. The newly adopted Federal Rules of Civil Procedure had radically altered practice in the United States district courts and also had a significant impact on the handling of appeals. The rights of aliens were of increasing concern to the judiciary. In 1938 in *Erie v. Tompkins*[8] the Supreme Court rejected more than a century of precedent and ruled against accepted notions of a federal common law, necessitating a new approach to diversity of citizenship cases in the lower federal courts. In the area of patent law, in which the Second Circuit (particularly Learned Hand) had made an immense contribution, the Supreme Court in the middle 1930's began to formulate a new antimonopolistic approach that would force the Second Circuit to re-examine its own case law. In addition to all of this, the Second World War would create novel problems such as appeals from Selective Service Boards and the determination of the job rights of returning servicemen. Finally, the major revision of the Internal Revenue Code in the late 1930's added a flood of tax law cases involving the interpretation of the esoteric language of a most complex statute.

Learned Hand had the increased difficulty of statutory interpretation in mind when, in 1947, he complained about the Internal Revenue Code, the words of which

> merely dance before my eyes in a meaningless procession. Cross-reference to cross-reference, exception upon exception—couched in abstract terms that offer no handle to seize hold of—leave in my mind only a confused sense of some vitally important, but successfully concealed, purport, which it is my duty to extract, but which is within my power, if at all, only after the most inordinate expenditure of time. I know that these monsters are the result of fabulous industry and ingenuity, plugging up this hole and casting out that net, against all possible evasion. . . . Much of the law is now as difficult to fathom, and more and more of it is likely to be so; for there is little doubt that we are entering a period of increasingly detailed regulation, and it will be the duty of judges to thread the path—for path there is— through these fabulous labyrinths.[9]

Possibly the most serious source of impending difficulty for the Second Circuit when Learned Hand became its senior circuit judge was the President of the United States. By 1939 Roosevelt's appointees to the Supreme Court had transformed it into a staunch upholder of New Deal legislation; might not his appointments to the Second Circuit substantially affect the operations of that body? In 1938 Congress had created a sixth judgeship for the Second Circuit, giving the Presi-

8 304 U.S. 64 (1938).
9 L. Hand, "Thomas Walter Swan," in Dilliard, *Spirit of Liberty*, p. 161.

dent his first opportunity to put a New Dealer on that court. Manton's departure gave him another.

For the new seat Roosevelt selected an ardent New Dealer who had "long been noted for his liberalism," Charles E. Clark, the Dean of the Yale Law School. Clark was the only law school dean to testify publicly in favor of Roosevelt's 1937 proposal to enlarge the Supreme Court.[10] He could be expected to bring a more liberal point of view and, perhaps, also a different style to the court.

Robert P. Patterson was the President's choice for the other vacancy. A Republican, Patterson had served with great distinction as a judge on the Southern District court since 1930 and had gained the respect of bench and bar alike, particularly that of his "superiors" on the court of appeals. His promotion, although he was a Republican, was dictated by two factors. Learned Hand held him in very high regard and wanted him on the appellate court,[11] and, more important, the President felt it was necessary that Manton's successor be a person of great integrity, irrespective of party affiliation. Patterson's experience as a trial judge and the warm relationship he had developed through the years with his new colleagues insured that he would fit in well with the Coolidge appointees.

So it was for a year. Clark's freshman year was uneventful, as he did nothing to upset the tranquility of the court. However, in the middle of 1940, with war imminent, Patterson resigned at the request of the President and accepted appointment as Assistant Secretary of War.[12] This gave Roosevelt a new opportunity to increase New Deal strength on the important Second Circuit; he responded with the appointment of a "super liberal,"[13] Jerome N. Frank.

[10] *New York Times,* January 6, 1939, p. 1.

[11] Hand's warm feeling for Patterson is evident in the memorial address he made in 1952, L. Hand, "Robert P. Patterson" in Dilliard, *Spirit of Liberty,* pp. 201–8.

[12] The Second Circuit was unwilling to let Patterson go; his colleagues wanted him to take a leave of absence. At the request of his brethren, particularly Learned Hand, Judge Clark twice wrote to Attorney General Robert Jackson (on August 7, and December 4, 1940) asking that no successor be named so long as there remained a possibility that Patterson would return to the bench. The probable explanation for the junior member of the court representing all the judges on this matter is that only Clark had personal relations with the national administration and it was thought that a request from him would have a better chance of success than one coming from any of the other judges.

[13] In the first of the two letters mentioned in the preceding note, Clark wrote that if the return of Patterson "appears to be an impossibility," he would hope and know that the Attorney General would do his "best to insure that we get a new member who is at once able and liberal in viewpoint."

9

In 1943 a reviewer of Frank's book *If Men Were Angels* described the President's action as "perhaps his happiest appointment" and a "coup d'etat," and likened it "to the choice of a heretic to be a bishop of the Church of Rome."[14] The analogy was occasioned by the fact that since the publication of *Law and the Modern Mind* in 1930 Frank was regarded as perhaps the most critical and abrasive of the legal realists who had vociferously attacked many of the foundations of American jurisprudence. He had also had a stormy public career in several key New Deal positions. Inevitably, his presence on the court would substantially affect what it did and the manner in which it went about its business, more so if he and Judge Clark, the other New Dealer, would share a common philosophy and approach in the cases coming before the Second Circuit.

Frank assumed his judicial office on May 5, 1941, and this study of "Learned Hand's court" begins with that date.[15] As we have seen, a number of factors—recent scandal, the age of the judges, predominance of Coolidge appointees, the addition of two New Dealers, and important legislative and judicial innovations affecting the cases coming to the court—were present which undermined prospects that the Second Circuit would achieve legal fame. Yet, none of these conditions had the effect that might have been expected. In the words of Karl Llewellyn, "even the continued self-will and corruption and final public disgrace of a Manton left the Second Circuit still for decades the most distinguished and admired Bench in the United States."[16] The composition of the court remained intact until Learned Hand's retirement in the middle of 1951. Ironically, Hand, who continued to serve on the court until shortly before his death in 1961, outlived Justice Wiley Rutledge by a dozen years. It was Rutledge who was the President's choice to fill the Supreme Court vacancy in 1942—when Learned Hand was too old. During the 1940's the Second Circuit, busiest of any of the courts of appeals, had the best record in terms of the expeditious handling of appeals. Moreover, whatever private doubts the judges had about the wisdom of legislation and administrative rulings—and at times these were substantial—their decisions accepted the New Deal revolution, so much so that a study of appellate court review of National Labor Relations Board decisions shows that the Second Circuit was the most pro Labor Board circuit in

[14] William Seagle, Book Review, *Virginia Law Review* (1943), 664.

[15] Because Patterson's tenure as an appellate judge was so brief, I have not covered him or his period on the court in this study. His contribution to the work of the court was too limited for purposes of discerning patterns in his opinions or relations with the other judges.

[16] Llewellyn, *The Common Law Tradition* (Boston: Little, Brown & Co., 1960), p. 48.

the nation.[17] Finally, Judges Clark and Frank spent more time fighting one another than challenging the views of the Coolidge judges.

Even before Learned Hand stepped down from "active judicial service," Judge Charles E. Wyzanski, Jr., of the Federal District Court of Massachusetts, one of America's outstanding jurists, characterized the Second Circuit as the "ablest court now sitting."[18] Similar expressions came from John Frank, a noted legal writer, in a 1951 article[19] and Professor Philip B. Kurland in 1957, shortly after the death of Jerome Frank.[20] According to a competent foreign observer, the

[17] Rondal G. Downing, "The Courts, Congress and Labor Relations," unpublished paper delivered at the 1962 Annual Meeting of the American Political Science Association. The author speculates as to the reasons for this record: "One traditional explanation that is sometimes invoked to account for the differences in behavior of courts is that the benches of the courts vary in terms of the ability of their judges. . . . The Second [Circuit] Court of Appeals, for example, has for years had the reputation of being one of the truly outstanding benches in the country. . . . The stature of . . . [its] judges— and the role which the Second Circuit long has played in the Federal court system—may well have an important bearing upon the decisional processes of that circuit. Whether they would account for the Second Circuit's being consistently the most pro-labor circuit in the country is another matter" (p. 5).

[18] Wyzanski, "Augustus Noble Hand," Harvard Law Review, 61 (1948), 573.

[19] John P. Frank, "The Top U. S. Commercial Court," Fortune, January 1951, p. 92.

[20] Kurland, "Jerome N. Frank: Some Reflections and Recollections of a Law Clerk," University of Chicago Law Review, 24 (1957), 661. Kurland's words bear quotation: "Once upon a time, but not so long ago, there was a great appellate court in this country. It sat not in Washington but in New York. . . .

"The Second Circuit was a strange court. Every member of the court respected every other member of the court. Although disagreements in judgment were frequent, no one accused another of treachery to a cause, intellectual dishonesty, chicanery or venality. None was jealous to occupy the middle chair, nor ambitious for high political office, nor anxious to lead a faction because he could not lead the whole. If some were hopeful of appointment to the Supreme Court, the chosen path was by proof of capacity to fill the post and not by appeal to the electorate through the instrument of judicial opinions or public speeches. . . . Of the judges of this Second Circuit, vintage 1941–51, some were brilliant, and some were sound, and some were wise, and, at times, some were foolish. But they all measured up to a high standard of judicial capacity and they were all dedicated to the job which each had undertaken to perform: to administer justice under law. It was indeed a strange court, and we are not likely to see its equal for many a year."

Not all of Professor Kurland's recollections and reflections should be accepted uncritically, particularly his description of relations among the judges. As we shall see, throughout this period the relations between judges Frank and Clark were strained and, at times, each of these judges bitterly attacked other colleagues.

Second Circuit under Learned Hand was "the strongest tribunal in the English-speaking world."[21]

These accolades say much about the stature of the judges who made up the Second Circuit during these years. Learned Hand is commonly regarded as being among the great figures of American jurisprudence, but he was "not alone in adding to . . . [the Second Circuit's] luster."[22] In order to understand how and why the court reached the pinnacle of judicial repute we must know more about the careers of its members. Their attitudes and performance on the bench will be discussed in subsequent chapters; here the description will be limited to brief biographical sketches.

The great reputation enjoyed by Learned Hand during his lifetime, and which continues undiminished after his death, is not easily explained. The difficulty arises not so much from the fact that he did not serve on the Supreme Court—although this contributes to the mystery—as from the clearcut discordance between Hand's view of the judicial function (and the implementation of this view as a judge) and the contrary and more popular activist attitude that has gained considerable acceptance in the Supreme Court and in many law schools over the past thirty years. Some of Hand's most notable enthusiasts are also libertarian activists.[23] This is the central question that dominates any study of Learned Hand.

[21] Edward McWhinney, "A Legal Realist and a Humanist—Crosscurrents in the Legal Philosophy of Judge Jerome Frank," *Indiana Law Review*, 33 (1957), 115.

[22] Whitney North Seymour, in *Proceedings of a Special Session of the United States Court of Appeals for the Second Circuit to Commemorate Fifty Years of Federal Judicial Service, by the Honorable Learned Hand*, April 10, 1959, published as a special section in 264 F. 2d (p. 34).

[23] Unlike Justice Frankfurter, who also achieved great esteem, Hand was barely subjected to any strong adverse criticism until he gave a series of lectures on the Bill of Rights at the Harvard Law School only a few years before his death. Until then he was virtually immune from attack, although for a half century he had espoused a philosophy that was always controversial and since 1937 or so had been rejected by judicial liberals. An illustration of this anomaly is the writings of Irving Dilliard, whose collection of Learned Hand's papers, *The Spirit of Liberty*, contributed handsomely to the fame of the Second Circuit judge. Dilliard praises Hand extravagantly. Some years after the publication of *The Spirit of Liberty*, Dilliard edited a collection of judicial opinions of Justice Black. In a long introductory essay, he speaks glowingly of this noted civil libertarian. Yet, it is just not possible to reconcile Hand's views on the Bill of Rights with those of Black.

In Chapter 5 I attempt to show that Judge Hand's reputation is, as Justice Frankfurter sadly pointed out, mostly myth; that is, it is not based (except in rare instances and then in limited circles) on an examination of what he did or said as a judge.

While he was chief judge, Hand virtually dominated the public image of the Second Circuit, even if he could not dominate the decisions emanating from his court. His reputation easily transcended the inferior court he sat on. Judge Clark once noted that Hand's relationship to the Second Circuit was analogous to that enjoyed by Justice Oliver Wendell Holmes, Jr., in his relations with the Supreme Court.[24] There was a tendency on the Supreme Court to cite Learned Hand opinions specifically, whereas normally the High Court refers to lower court opinions without mentioning the name of the writer.

Like his great friend Justice Holmes, Hand has become a legend. Justice Felix Frankfurter, who was not happy about it, recognized this phenomenon as early as 1947.[25] We shall see that Frankfurter's concern over the legend of Learned Hand affords a penetrating insight into the places occupied by Holmes, Hand, and Frankfurter in the American judicial hall of fame. Of course, the Hand legend is far more remarkable than the legend of Holmes. Jerome Frank, Learned Hand's almost worshipful colleague, said of his chief judge's failure to be appointed to the Supreme Court: "I think of Cervantes' advice: 'Try to win the second prize. For the first is always by favor. The second goes for pure merit.' The praises of Judge Hand have been earned, not by occupying the highest bench, but by pure merit."[26]

Billings Learned Hand was born in Albany, New York, on January 27, 1872, into "the most distinguished legal family in northern New York."[27] ("Billings" was dropped at about the age of thirty because it was "vastly formidable" and "pompous."[28] Many of his close friends called him B. Hand.) His paternal grandfather, Augustus Hand—after whom his first cousin, lifelong companion, and colleague, Augustus N. Hand, was named—achieved some fame in upstate New York as a lawyer active in the Democratic Party and an associate justice of the New York Supreme Court. His father distinguished himself at the bar in Albany.

[24] Interview, November 26, 1962.

[25] Frankfurter, "Judge Learned Hand," Harvard Law Review, 60 (1947), 325.

[26] Jerome N. Frank, "Some Reflections on Judge Learned Hand," University of Chicago Law Review, 24 (1957), 668. To the extent that they suggest an iron rule, neither Cervantes nor Frank can be taken too seriously. Ironically, too, had Hand "won" the first prize, unquestionably he would have been subjected to a great deal of criticism and there would have been dissenters from the chorus of praise.

[27] Charles E. Wyzanski, Jr., "Learned Hand," Atlantic Monthly, 208 (December 1961), 54.

[28] I have relied on several sources for this sketch, notably, Dilliard's introduction to The Spirit of Liberty.

Hand's education was marked by success and honor. He had an outstanding record at Albany Academy, a private school. In 1889 he followed his cousin Augustus to Harvard College, where he majored in philosophy under a brilliant faculty that included William James, Josiah Royce, and George Santayana. At Harvard he excelled as an editor, speaker, and scholar, and, upon graduation summa cum laude in 1893, he was chosen class orator for Commencement Day. Hand next attended the Harvard Law School and studied under Langdell, Ames, Thayer, and Gray. He was an editor of the *Law Review* and was graduated with honors in 1896.

After admission to the New York bar Hand spent five years in Albany practicing law. In 1902 he moved to New York City and for the next seven years was engaged in private practice, which he found dull and petty. Fortunately, President Taft had a keen interest in improving the quality of federal judges and, acting upon the recommendation of his Attorney General, George W. Wickersham, he appointed Learned Hand to the Southern District Court. Almost forty years later, Charles C. Burlingham, a leader of the New York City bar who had suggested Hand's name to Wickersham and "did what he could"[29] to get Hand named to the Supreme Court, hailed his friend as "unquestionably first among American judges."[30]

While Taft's action was amply rewarded by Hand's performance on the bench, it did not reap any political dividends for the President or the Republican Party, for in 1912 Hand supported the Bull Moose candidacy of Theodore Roosevelt. A year later, for the first and last time, he sought elective office and ran for chief judge of the New York Court of Appeals on the Progressive ticket. Although not eager to run, he did so because he "felt that he could not flinch." However, he refused to campaign, because, as he put it later, "I was already on the bench and the thought of harassing the electorate was more than I could bear."[31]

Although Hand was resoundingly defeated, Taft did not forgive him for his betrayal. During the 1920's, particularly when Harding was in the White House—years when there was an unusually large number of openings on the Supreme Court—Taft, as chief justice, exercised great power over appointments to the federal judiciary. In 1922 Hand

[29] Alpheus Thomas Mason, *Harlan Fiske Stone: Pillar of the Law* (New York: Viking Press, 1956), 592.

[30] Burlingham, "Judge Learned Hand," *Harvard Law Review,* 60 (1947), 331.

[31] Herbert Mitgang, *The Man Who Rode the Tiger* (New York: J. P. Lippincott Co., 1963), p. 106.

was under consideration as successor to Justice Mahlon Pitney. Taft, conceding that Hand was "of proper age, . . . an able judge and a hard worker," strongly objected. In a letter to President Harding he recalled that Hand "turned out to be a wild Roosevelt man and a Progressive, and though on the bench, he went into the campaign." He continued, "If promoted to our Bench, he would almost certainly herd with Brandeis and be a dissenter. I think it would be risking too much to appoint him."[32]

For fifteen years Hand served as a district judge. In 1924 President Coolidge, with the reluctant approval of the chief justice, promoted him to the Second Circuit to succeed Judge Julius M. Mayer, and there he served until his death on August 18, 1961.[33] Retirement in 1951 did not free him of judicial responsibilities and in the final decade of his life he often sat on the Second Circuit, at times to his consternation.[34]

Learned Hand's conduct on the bench was long a subject of considerable interest. John Frank once wrote that he "has a reputation as the most irritable man on the C.A. 2d Bench."[35] Counsel and colleagues were the victims of his explosive temper. The present chief judge of the Second Circuit noted after Hand's death,

> Many of us have seen and felt the force of his judicial wrath. His thunder terrified the boldest counsel and his lightning questions and comments could short-circuit any argument. Afterwards, he was penitent for any pain or suffering he may have caused. Sometimes he apologized from the bench, but always he begged forgiveness from his colleagues and he usually found some way of making amends to counsel. He always took great

[32] Alpheus Thomas Mason, *William Howard Taft: Chief Justice* (New York: Simon and Shuster, 1964), p. 171.

[33] In a brief address in 1958 commemorating Hand's fiftieth year as a federal judge, Attorney General William P. Rogers revealed that in 1917 Hand was considered for a vacancy on the Second Circuit. He also disclosed that C. C. Burlingham helped in securing Hand's promotion in 1924.

[34] Only six weeks after retiring, in the summer of 1951, Hand granted bail to a group of second-string Communist leaders under indictment. After a sharp exchange with the prosecutor, he remarked, "I thought I was going to get some relief when I retired, but all my colleagues have left me and I'm here alone" (*New York Times,* July 13, 1951, p. 8). In Hand's eighty-eighth year, the Second Circuit's chief judge, Charles E. Clark, said that Hand "still carries an unusual work load as a judge. During the current year he has already participated in some thirty appeals in three different judicial weeks. He will be sitting again in about ten days and probably yet once more during the spring" (in *Proceedings of a Special Session,* p. 26).

[35] John P. Frank, "Top U.S. Commercial Court," p. 95.

care to seek out any possible merit in points which he had summarily brushed aside in the courtroom.[36]

"Above all he was tolerant," writes former Attorney General Francis Biddle. "Yet his tolerance never touched indifference, and he was passionate in his beliefs as well as his feelings."[37]

For most of his life, until he was about seventy-five, Learned Hand was little known to the general public. Familiarity with Learned Hand was limited to the elite of the legal profession: judges, professors at law schools, lawyers who were active in the affairs of the American Law Institute (of which Learned Hand was a founder) and other professional organizations, as well as the lawyers who argued before the Second Circuit. He had written a number of articles for law journals, especially the *Harvard Law Review*, and received a handful of prestigious honorary degrees. Because of his oratorical ability, he was often invited to address legal societies, but his speeches did not receive wide circulation.

Yet, the legend of Learned Hand was already in the making. In 1944 he was invited to speak to a very large gathering at an "I Am an American Day" ceremony in New York City's Central Park. His brief and eloquent address—"The Spirit of Liberty"—was published in many newspapers and received an unusually wide circulation. It contributed much to his spreading fame. In 1946 *Life* published a long article on Learned Hand called "The Great Judge." A year later, an issue of the *Harvard Law Review* was dedicated to him on the occasion of his seventy-fifth birthday. At the same time, and four years later when he retired, leading newspapers and popular magazines printed articles and editorials in praise of him. In 1952 a collection of his papers and addresses was published under the title of *The Spirit of Liberty;* this brought Learn Hand's words to additional thousands of persons throughout the world and substantially enlarged the company of his admirers. The final ten years of his life saw Learned

---

[36] J. Edward Lumbard, in the "Learned Hand Memorial Issue" of the *New York State Bar Journal,* 33 (December 1961), 410. Justice Harlan recounts that as a young lawyer he once submitted a lengthy brief to the Second Circuit in a case in which Hand was on the panel. Hand took the brief and threw it onto the counsel table, saying that he would not read it. Yet, when the decision came down, Hand voted to uphold the position taken by Harlan (in *Proceedings of a Special Session,* p. 23).

When it came to the dignity and decorum of courts he was strict: in 1927 he had the owner of a radio store located near the old federal court building in lower Manhattan arrested on a charge of disorderly conduct because music coming from a loudspeaker in front of the store disturbed the equanimity and dignity of the court of appeals (*New York Times,* February 17, 1927, p. 23).

[37] Biddle, *In Brief Authority,* p. 95.

Hand honored and recognized by public, bench and bar, and government. Even the Oliver Wendell Holmes Lectures in 1958 at the Harvard Law School on "The Bill of Rights," in which Learned Hand criticized quite directly Supreme Court decisions in civil liberties and school segregation cases, did not disturb the public and professional acclaim. Nothing illustrates more clearly than the response to these lectures that Learned Hand was a legend.

Most of the attention paid to Learned Hand concerns his legal philosophy and not the opinions he wrote as a judge. As a district court and intermediate appellate judge, he was isolated from the final determination of the great political and constitutional issues of this century.[38] For half a century he was concerned with the daily operation and decisions of two courts that are not in the public eye. His own philosophy favored even greater restraints on the political and constitutional role of courts. Conflict in the Second Circuit was left behind in the conference room, or was submerged in opinions read by relatively few people or in memoranda that were not made public.

A puzzling facet of Learned Hand's career is his failure to be appointed to the Supreme Court. Charles C. Burlingham wrote in 1947 that "Judge Hand should have been on the Supreme Court of the United States years ago, but the stars in their course fought against him.[39] This explanation—luck, or the lack of it—seems close to the truth. Hand was under active consideration for promotion to the High Court a number of times from the early 1920's through 1942. During these two decades some of the most important names in American law supported his appointment. Among these were Justice Holmes, who wanted Hand on the Supreme Court while the latter was still a district judge;[40] Justice Harlan Fiske Stone, who recommended Hand (and two others) as successor to Holmes when he was consulted by President Hoover;[41] and Justice Frankfurter, who "spent not a little part" of his life promoting Hand's advancement.[42] It appears that at one time or another, geography, politics, and age

[38] On February 6, 1934, Hand wrote to Justice Stone: "The most futile job I have to do is to pass on Constitutional questions. Who in hell cares what anybody says about them but the Final Five of the August Nine of whom you are one?" (Mason, *Harlan Fiske Stone*, p. 384).

[39] Burlingham, "Judge Learned Hand," p. 330.

[40] In a February 24, 1923, letter to Pollock, Holmes characterized Hand as "a good U. S. District Judge, who I should like to see on our bench" (Mark DeWolfe Howe [ed.], *Holmes-Pollock Letters* [Cambridge: Harvard University Press, Belknap Press, 1961], vol. 2, p. 114).

[41] Mason, *Harlan Fiske Stone*, p. 335.

[42] Frankfurter, in *Proceedings of a Special Session*, p. 21.

worked against Hand's promotion, although we may never learn the exact reasons for his unsuccessful candidacies.[43] Chief Justice Taft, as we have seen, blocked him throughout the 1920's. After 1930 "President Hoover was said to have been twice about to nominate Hand and was then persuaded to offer the opportunity to another in the expectation on each occasion that he would turn it down. The first of these was Chief Judge Hughes and the second Cardozo himself."[44] Hughes's biographer reports this story but vigorously disputes its authenticity.[45]

In 1942, after Justice James Byrnes resigned from the Supreme Court to direct the Office of Economic Stabilization at President Roosevelt's request, Justice Frankfurter began a campaign to have Hand appointed to fill the vacancy. Frankfurter almost succeeded, for at the President's direction he prepared a statement announcing Learned Hand's nomination. In it the President was to say:

> In time of national emergency when each must serve where he can be most useful, it is fitting that in replacing a member of the Court who has been drafted into the war effort, considerations of age and geography—which in normal days might well be controlling—should not yield to the paramount considerations of national need.
>
> Judge Learned Hand enjoys a place of pre-eminence in our federal judiciary. His long experience as a judge, his deep knowledge of all phases of law, especially of federal law, make him uniquely qualified for the Supreme Bench. His choice at this time is clearly indicated. He will bring to the Court a youthful vigor of mind and a tested understanding of the national needs within the general framework of the Constitution.[46]

However, as Roosevelt put it in a private note to Justice Frankfurter, "Sometimes a fellow gets estopped by his own words and his own deeds."[47] The President could not escape from the rigid position he had taken on age during the "Court packing" fight years earlier. Learned Hand's name was not sent to the Senate.

[43] The Justice Department's file on Judge Hand contains "a good many things" that if disclosed would shed considerable light on the subject. See the remarks of Attorney General Rogers in *Proceedings of a Special Session,* p. 14.

[44] D. W. M. Waters, "Judge Learned Hand," *Solicitor Quarterly,* 1 (1962), 38.

[45] Merlo J. Pusey, *Charles Evans Hughes* (New York: Macmillan Co., 1951), p. 653.

[46] Max Freedman, *Roosevelt and Frankfurter* (Boston: Little, Brown & Co., 1967), p. 673. The story of Frankfurter's efforts on Hand's behalf and the correspondence between him and the President are in Freedman's important book, pp. 671–76.

[47] *Ibid.,* p. 674.

Judge Swan believes that Learned Hand was much happier on the Second Circuit than he would have been on the Supreme Court because the atmosphere on the lower court was so much more pleasant.[48] Whether Judge Hand actually was happy over the turn of events is another matter. Judge Wyzanski in his memorial alludes to the feeling "that, while Learned Hand outwardly accepted his situation with calm, the 'trophy of Miltiades would not let him sleep.' "[49] Hand himself, shortly before he died, may have given a clue to his attitude in a letter he wrote to President Kennedy. In support of the efforts of District Judge Irving Kaufman to win promotion to the Second Circuit, he urged the President to promote "those best qualified in the lower levels" and he concluded with the admonition, "Promote when you can."[50]

Still, Justice Frankfurter called Hand "lucky" because "in the first place, down there his views would have been diluted eight-ninths and here only two-thirds. In the second place, I think almost inevitably, though certainly as authenticated by history, the controversies down there are more strident than they are in the quietude of Foley Square."[51] And, "It is extremely doubtful whether on the Supreme Court, with its confined area of litigation, he would have influenced the course of law in its widest reaches as much as he did from the Second Circuit and through the Law Institute."[52]

Justice Frankfurter may have been right when he spoke of his friend's luck; he failed to say, or did not say explicitly, that Judge Hand's fortune in not being on the Supreme Court bench, is part of the Learned Hand legend which he called dangerous. Had Hand been on the Supreme Court it is doubtful that he would have become a legend.

Judge Swan has been on the Second Circuit since early 1927; for all these years of judicial service, however, there is only a single article of tribute or evaluation in the law journals, and but scarce mention of his name in the annual index of the *New York Times*. This dearth of material—not counting, of course, the hundreds of opinions in the *Federal Reporter*—is more the result of Swan's humility and quiet style than of a lack of appreciation of his talents and accomplishments. The lone article is by Learned Hand and it conveys more effectively than could a dozen tributes the high regard in which Swan was held by his colleagues and members of the bar. Other testaments are also

[48] Interview, November 16, 1962. This view is shared by Judge Wyzanski, "Judge Learned Hand," *Atlantic Monthly*, p. 58.

[49] *Ibid.*

[50] *New York Times*, June 18, 1961, p. 41.

[51] Frankfurter, in *Proceedings of a Special Session*, p. 21.

[52] Frankfurter, "Learned Hand," *Harvard Law Review*, 75 (1961), 4.

available: Professor Arthur Corbin would have appointed Learned Hand and Swan as the first two members of Hand's (unwanted and mythical) Committee of Platonic Philosophers that would be given governmental powers.[53] Karl Llewellyn considered Swan to be one of the very best commercial law judges in the history of the English-speaking world.[54] Invariably, Justice Frankfurter linked Swan to the two Hands when he spoke of the greatness of the Second Circuit.

Thomas Walter Swan was born on December 20, 1877, in Norwich, Connecticut, to Thomas Walter and Jane Adelaide Swan. Except for about a dozen years in Chicago, he has always lived in Connecticut. His parents were prosperous and Swan was given an excellent education, attending Williston Academy in Easthampton, Massachusetts, and Yale College. Upon graduation from Yale in 1900 he went to the Harvard Law School, which at the time was generally considered far superior to that of Yale. At Harvard he was chairman of the Editorial Board of the *Law Review* and the first non-Harvard College graduate to be elected class marshal. After graduation he moved to Chicago, where he lived until 1916. During these years he was engaged in private law practice, largely corporate in nature and highly lucrative. In 1919 he married Mabel Eleanor Dick, the daughter of A. B. Dick of the duplicating machine company.

Intermittently, while living in Chicago, Swan lectured at the University of Chicago Law School. In 1916, after a long search, a faculty committee succeeded in getting Swan appointed Dean of the Yale Law School. He was not well known in academic circles and his selection came as a surprise. As Dean he contributed significantly to the tremendous growth in stature of the Law School in the early decades of this century. In late 1926, after ten years at Yale and "after rejecting a district court judgeship . . . [he] accepted a call to sit among the mighty, alongside of Gus and Learned Hand."[55] Although Swan had been a lifelong Republican (who never held or sought elective office), his appointment by President Coolidge was in Learned Hand's words "an act of faith." This was because "it would have been easy . . . to assume that such a man, put on an appellate court, would prove to be more a scholar remote from practical affairs and given to

[53] Corbin, "The Yale Law School and Tom Swan," *Yale Law Report*, 4 (Spring 1958), 27.

[54] Llewellyn, *Common Law Tradition*, p. 334.

[55] Corbin, "Yale Law School and Tom Swan," p. 26. Interestingly, Judge Charles E. Clark also served as dean of the Yale Law School for ten years. Corbin writes: "Probably a sensitive man cannot endure more than a decade of managing a live school of law, riding its wild horses, bearing with their bucks and snorts, and always nourishing their wants. An insensitive dean may have a longer life, while his school remains in the old groove."

speculation, than a judge who would be interested primarily in the just dispatch of causes, and who would make no further excursions into the realm of theory than was necessary to support his decisions." However, "it at once became evident" that President Coolidge "had made no mistake, and that his act of faith had been justified."[56]

On the bench, Swan's closest friend and the judge whose philosophy was nearest to his own was Augustus Hand. They frequently consulted one another regarding the cases they were working on, even when one of them was not a panel member. They shared a distrust for New Deal legislation and administrative agencies. In the 1941–51 period, with Judge Chase, they formed the only viable voting bloc on the court. For two years following Learned Hand's retirement Swan was chief judge of the Second Circuit. In mid-1953, at the age of seventy-five, Swan, along with Judge Augustus Hand, retired from active judicial service. Judge Swan continued to sit a number of weeks each term as a senior judge to help the busy Second Circuit meet its docket. He last sat in April 1965; in his ninety-third year, he is now fully retired from judicial activity.

In an interview several years ago, Judge Swan accepted the description of himself as a conservative. But while he was obviously not in sympathy with much of the social and economic legislation since the advent of the New Deal, he was not a conservative activist of the type that dominated the Supreme Court prior to 1937. As was usually true of the other conservatives on the Second Circuit, he generally did not permit his own views to seriously influence his decisions. Swan, however, was less reluctant than his colleagues to reverse federal administrative agencies. In particular he did not like what he believed to be the pro-labor bias of the National Labor Relations Board. Still, he was far less antilabor than many judges in other circuits.

Judge Swan's demeanor reinforced the view that he was a conservative. John Frank wrote of him in 1951: "The aristocrat of the bench, reserved and unemotional, he has given the impression to one observer of 'the Lord speaking to his retainers.' He is nowise a snob, but he is a most dignified man. His dominant quality is a kindly, contained courtesy."[57] Swan's opinions were short and subdued, as were the memoranda he sent to his colleagues. His writing was not exuberant and no more than a very few of his opinions will be read in years to come. However, his place as one of the finest judges to serve on any of the courts of appeals seems secure, as does his contribution to the development of law in the Second Circuit.

[56] L. Hand, "Thomas Walter Swan," in Dilliard, *Spirit of Liberty,* pp. 158–59.
[57] John P. Frank, "Top U.S. Commercial Court," p. 110.

In 1947 the *Yale Law Journal* celebrated the twentieth anniversary of Swan's appointment with a dedicatory issue. Learned Hand wrote a tribute that more than a decade later still made Swan "squirm with warm feelings of embarrassment."[58] Because it so beautifully expresses how his colleagues felt about him and because many people interested in legal affairs know little of Thomas Swan, it merits quotation at length.

> His urbanity is almost always unruffled; never, in an experience with him of over twenty years, have I known him to hector a lawyer, or abuse the advantage of his position which denies any retort in kind. He has as little of the bully as of the showman, and he has reaped from the bar the harvest which his courteous and considerate nature has sown. Not that he suffers fools gladly, or is ready to let those wander along who think that they shall be heard for their much speaking. To direct, and if necessary to curtail, argument seems to him as much a part of the judge's duty, as to listen; and listen he always does; or, at least he gives the appearance of listening, for he never adopts the not uncommon device of discouraging prosy advocates by a real, or assumed, show of contemptuous inattention. In conference he is open minded, until he has heard what his brothers have to say, which he considers with respect and at times with too much deference; but, after he has once come to a conclusion, he is tenacious and very seldom yields. He is little given to dissent, being wholly without vanity, and—as it seems to me—not conscious enough of the importance of weakening the force of a wrong decision as a precedent. He is readier than most judges to take seriously petitions for rehearing (especially if he has written the opinion himself) ; not indeed, because of vacillation or of any shrinking from responsibility, but from an over tender scruple, coupled with entire absence of any pride of opinion. Incidentally, I have, however, never observed that he, more often than other judges, votes to change the original result. On the other hand he is always ready to accept suggestion from his brothers in amending or even in rewriting his opinions, before they are handed down, if he agrees with the substance of the proposal. He will not overrule a precedent, unless he can be satisfied beyond peradventure that it was untenable when made; and not even then, if it has gathered around it the support of a substantial body of decisions based upon it. As a corollary, he is not given to wide commitments when he writes, for he distrusts the guidance which the present evidence and the present argument give, if the issues be amplified beyond what is necessary to dispose of the controversy. He believes that the industry of other suitors to whom they may become vital, if expanded, is likely farther to explore and illuminate them. Consistently with this, he does not seek to support his conclusions by resort to broad or speculative general principles; but, like an

[58] Corbin, "Yale Law School and Tom Swan," p. 4.

English judge, looks to the precedents or to the text for his warrant.[59]

Hand concluded:

> It is well that we should seize upon a moment, in itself irrelevant, on which to celebrate an anniversary of such a public servant. We are aware that today the foundations of all that we hold dear are in the balance; and we live in just apprehension. Without such servants no society can prosper; without such servants no society can in the end even endure. Let us pause then to acclaim one, who—himself all unaware of his deserts—has so richly earned our gratitude, and whose presence helps us to take heart against our forebodings.[60]

The qualities that make for greatness in judges are elusive and the subject of debate. One thing that is certain is that there is no strong correlation between judicial eminence and the ability to win support from colleagues on the bench; on the contrary, many of the ablest and most renowned judges are frequent dissenters.[61] Usually, the great judge's impact on law is a long-range one because he is an innovator challenging the legal status quo.

Judge Augustus Hand's claim to judicial stature—which has long been advanced by other outstanding jurists—is supported almost exclusively by his performance on the bench. Few judges have been as highly thought of by members of their own court as was Hand on the Second Circuit. Over a long period he influenced what the Second Circuit did, a remarkable feat in view of his unwillingness to insist, except rarely, on his point of view. On a court with a liberal attitude toward dissent and judges of strong mind and will, it was often his vote that determined the decision in close cases. Yet he was little concerned with such matters as securing a reputation, writing quotable opinions, or doing anything that was extraneous to the decision that had to be made. "He did little to draw the crowd and contented himself in performing his judicial task with a competence that was the envy and delight of the profession." This from a colleague of fifteen years who lamented, "As I look back upon it, I wish that he might

---

[59] L. Hand, "Thomas Walter Swan," in Dilliard, *Spirit of Liberty*, pp. 160–61.

[60] *Ibid.*, p. 166.

[61] Notable examples in this century are Holmes, Brandeis, Stone, Frankfurter, Black, Learned Hand, Jerome Frank, and Judge Henry W. Edgerton of the Court of Appeals for the District of Columbia. All these men were federal judges; it may be that on state courts the best judges—for example, Cardozo and Vanderbilt—are men who are able to forge a consensus on their courts.

have let himself soar more often to the end that others beyond his professional intimates might have known the glories of expression of which he was capable."[62]

Augustus Noble Hand was born in Elizabethtown, New York, on July 26, 1869, to Richard Lockhart and Mary Elizabeth Hand. His father and paternal grandfather (Learned Hand's uncle and grand-father) had practiced law in Elizabethtown, and throughout his life Augustus Hand returned each summer to this small village in the Adirondacks. It was almost inevitable that the third generation (Augustus and Learned Hand) would pursue legal careers. Augustus attended Phillips Exeter Academy, from which he graduated in 1886. He entered Harvard College and compiled an excellent academic record, graduating magna cum laude in 1890. Postgraduate study and law school followed and in 1894 he received a Master of Arts degree and graduated from the Harvard Law School. He then moved to New York City, where from 1897 to 1914 he practiced law.

A lifelong Democrat, although never active in politics, Hand was appointed to the Southern District of New York court by President Wilson in 1914, joining a bench that included Learned Hand and Charles Merrill Hough, one of the most respected federal judges of the first quarter of this century. During the years that these men were on the Southern District it was the outstanding federal trial court in the country. According to Judge Wyzanski, cases were diverted to the district "not by necessity but by the choice of lawyers who were free to go to any of several tribunals and selected the Southern District as their preference because of the quality of its bench."[63] Of the three district judges, Augustus Hand was by temperament probably best suited for trial work; neither Learned Hand nor Hough made a better trial judge. Max Eastman, a defendant in the *Masses* case, which was presided over by Judge Augustus Hand, described him as "a judge who could have upheld in a hurricane the dignity of the law. He was less genial and less patriarchal than his cousin, Learned Hand, but he had a like unshakeable integrity."[64] The *New York Times* celebrated Hand's eightieth birthday with an editorial that said in part, "No appointment to a United States District Court has ever been happier than Judge Hand's appointment by President Wilson."[65]

Judge Hough had been elevated to the Court of Appeals during the Wilson administration and, when he died in 1927, President

[62] Charles E. Clark, "Augustus Noble Hand," *Harvard Law Review*, 68 (1955), 1115.

[63] Wyzanski, "Augustus Noble Hand," *Harvard Law Review*, p. 578.

[64] Eastman, *Love and Revolution* (New York: Random House, 1964), p. 85.

[65] July 26, 1949, p. 26.

Coolidge, "in accordance with Hough's frequently expressed wish,"[66] named Augustus Hand to succeed him. The appointment was unusual because of the divergent party affiliations of the President and the appointee. The *New York Times* reported that "it is understood that members of the United States Supreme Court had expressed themselves in favor of his appointment."[67] In an editorial the newspaper said, "There has been nothing but praise from the Bench, the Bar and the public for President Coolidge's appointment of Judge Augustus N. Hand. . . . The promotion was indicated by every sign of judicial fitness, proved by long service, and is admirable in every way."[68]

Almost the only person who was not especially happy with the appointment was Judge Hand. In response to a congratulatory note from Justice Louis D. Brandeis he wrote: "I am almost abundantly without ambition and I am by no means sure that I am not better fitted to administer an important trial court, full of interest to me, than to sit in appeals."[69] Judge Wyzanski wrote in 1948 that "it is doubtful whether Judge Hand would say that the transfer was a promotion that he welcomed. He liked the work in the district court better than the work in the circuit court of appeals."[70] However, he was by no means unhappy with the work in the Second Circuit. When Benjamin Cardozo was appointed to the Supreme Court, Hand refused to be considered for a position on the New York Court of Appeals because he didn't want to be out of a job at seventy—the retirement age for New York judges—and hated to leave Learned Hand and Swan.[71]

Judge Hand continued in active service on the Second Circuit until he was almost eighty-four. Then, on June 30, 1953, he retired. Like Learned Hand and Swan he continued to serve as a senior judge, but only briefly. He died on October 28, 1954. At his death, Judge Swan wrote, "A mighty oak has fallen,"[72]

[66] Wyzanski, "Augustus Noble Hand," *Harvard Law Review,* p. 581.

[67] May 21, 1927, p. 19. Chief Justice Taft played a key role in securing the appointment. In addition to his support he got Charles Evans Hughes and Justice Stone to contact Coolidge in Hand's behalf (Mason, *William Howard Taft,* p. 187).

[68] May 27, 1927, p. 22.

[69] Quoted by Judge Wyzanski in "Augustus Noble Hand," An Address before a Special Memorial Meeting of the New York County Lawyers' Association and the Association of the Bar of the City of New York, May 4, 1955, p. 15.

[70] Wyzanski, "Augustus Noble Hand," *Harvard Law Review,* p. 582.

[71] Wyzanski, "Augustus Noble Hand," "Special Memorial Meeting," p. 17.

[72] Swan, "Augustus Noble Hand," *Memorial Book, 1955,* Association of the Bar of the City of New York, p. 39.

One of the remarkable aspects of Judge Hand's appellate career was the infrequency of dissenting opinions from him. In the ten years 1941–51 he dissented only eleven times. In part this was because "he was absolutely without vanity" and had no "desire to shine."[73] But it was also a manifestation of the confidence which his colleagues had in him. Because the other judges would usually go along with him, he had less need to dissent. When in 1948 the *Harvard Law Review* paid tribute to Judge Hand, one of his former law clerks, Judge Wyzanski, wrote:

> Every law clerk who has watched him in chambers knows how often, even after memoranda have been distributed, a conference has been held, a tentative vote taken and a preliminary opinion written, Judge Hand has been able to swing the court to an unforeseen result. Quite justifiably, the law clerks have come to look upon him as often the key judge in determining the final conclusion. It is not that Augustus N. Hand has the richest mind or the strongest will of the judges of the Second Circuit. The secret lies in the respect his steadiness of character inspires. He avoids petty squabbles with his brethren; he does not fuss about their foibles or try to restrain their exuberance. He cannot be led into a controversy in terms of personalities. Eschewing exhibitionism in any form, he remains disinterested and detached.[74]

Judge Swan summed up his friend's career in these words:

> In the opinion of the writer Judge Hand's distinction as a judge stems as much from his noble character as from his wide legal learning and his great wisdom in practical affairs, which is often called "common sense." No one could know Judge Hand intimately without acquiring the maximum of confidence, respect and admiration for him. He cared nothing for his own aggrandizement; his philosophy of the judicial process was that of English common law judges; he realized that a judge should not attempt to construe statutes or extend accepted judicial rules in order to carry out his own predilections of what justice required. As a member of the federal Court of Appeals he regarded the court as an institution where team-play was essential and dissent was justified only in rare instances where his own judgment could not yield to the argument of his brothers; his integrity and steadfastness of purpose were beyond question. . . . With such character, supplemented by a fine education and a remarkable memory it is no wonder that he achieved a judicial career of magnificent worth.[75]

Those who believe that a judge should take pains to remain out of the limelight have much to applaud in Judge Chase's long career.

[73] *Ibid.*, p. 38.
[74] Wyzanski, "Augustus Noble Hand," *Harvard Law Review*, p. 583.
[75] Swan, "Augustus Noble Hand," *Memorial Book*, pp. 38–39.

During his twenty-five years on the Second Circuit, his name never appeared in the newspapers except in connection with court opinions; he was not the subject of a critical study in any law journal; and there is no record of any address or article of his on a judicial topic or a statement of his philosophy. It is difficult to conceive of a judicial career of comparable length and importance cloaked in a greater degree of anonymity.

Not that Judge Chase, who lived in quiet and comfortable retirement in Brattleboro, Vermont, until his recent death, looked back on the quarter of a century as one of lost or unused opportunities; he did not regret the lack of publicity and acknowledgment. He regarded himself as a New Englander and strongly preferred the virtues of a quiet and private life.[76]

Harrie Brigham Chase was born in Whitingham, Vermont, on August 9, 1889, to Charles Sumner and Carrie Emily (Brigham) Chase. The elder Chase was a lawyer, and father and son practiced law together for about six years in Brattleboro, where the family moved not many years after Harrie was born. He was educated in public schools and at Phillips Exeter Academy in nearby New Hampshire. Chase went to Dartmouth College but left before graduation to attend Boston University Law School. He later received an honorary degree from Dartmouth in 1939. Upon graduation from law school in 1912, until early 1919, he was engaged in private practice. During these years he had many opportunities to meet some of the state's leading lawyers and to argue before the important state courts, including the Supreme Court.

In 1919 he was elected state's attorney for Windham County on the Republican ticket. A lifelong Republican, Judge Chase was never active in political affairs. After four months as state's attorney, he was appointed a judge of the Superior Court of the state; Chase was then only thirty years old and one of the youngest judges in the nation. In 1926 he was made chief judge of the court. About a year later he was made an associate judge of the Supreme Court of Vermont. Two years later President Coolidge appointed him to the United States Circuit Court of Appeals for the Second Circuit.

Judge Chase readily conceded that this appointment was the result of the fortuitous combination of a number of circumstances. From 1869 to 1929 the judges of the Second Circuit were exclusively from New York and Connecticut. Although Vermont had always been the third state forming the second judicial circuit, it was ignored because of the lack of prominence of its bar and judiciary as compared

[76] Much of the information on Judge Chase was provided by him in an interview in Brattleboro on September 3, 1963.

with those of New York and the faculty of the Yale University Law School, and because only a handful of cases decided by the appellate court originated in the federal District Court for Vermont. However, at least as far back as the mid-1920's, the small congressional delegation from the state has insisted that a Vermonter be on the Second Circuit. When in 1927 a vacancy on the court occurred upon the death of Judge Hough, a delegation from the state, including Judge Chase, went to Washington to ask the President to appoint someone from Vermont. The President, himself a native Vermonter, was sympathetic, but pressure from New York City led to the selection of Judge Augustus N. Hand. In 1929 Congress provided for an additional judge for the Second Circuit and President Coolidge and Attorney General John C. Sargent (also from Vermont) were immediately agreed that the new seat belonged to Vermont. Judge Chase was appointed. In John Frank's words, this was partly "the product of the close affection of Coolidge's Attorney General Sargent for the Chase family."[77]

Judge Chase remained on the Second Circuit until September 1, 1954. Then, shortly after his sixty-fifth birthday, because of poor health and on the advice of his doctor, he took advantage of a newly liberalized retirement statute and retired at full pay. For about a year prior to his retirement he was chief judge of the court. Unlike many of the other retired federal judges, Judge Chase decided not to remain in active judicial service. Once in the late 1950's, when the Second Circuit was badly undermanned, he consented to sit on several panels for a few weeks. But that experience convinced him that he no longer had any desire to sit as a judge or to undergo the rigors of regular travel to New York City.

John Frank, in his 1951 analysis of the Second Circuit, said of Chase:

> Far less colorful than the New Dealers is Harrie Brigham Chase of Vermont . . . the least known member of the Court. He comes to New York for sessions but usually returns to Brattleboro to write his opinions, and takes a great interest in bar activities in his home state. . . . Chase is strong in patent law, clear in style, orthodox in thinking, shy and diffident on the bench. His greatest skill is analysis of complicated facts. As one leader of the New York Bar says, this Vermonter "will never wear himself out in loose talk." Attorneys practicing in the C.A. 2 say that if it had been Chase's fortune to be on a court where he was surrounded with less color he would be outstanding.[78]

The view that Chase's reputation suffered because he sat alongside such illustrious judges is supported by a reading of the opinions he

[77] John P. Frank, "Top U.S. Commercial Court," p. 110.
[78] *Ibid.*

wrote between 1941 and 1951. They are remarkable for their clarity in outlining difficult situations and legal principles. They show that he was a first-rate craftsman and a much underrated judge.

The opinions also indicate that Chase was the most conservative member of the court. This was especially true of the small number of civil liberties cases that came before the Second Circuit. Chase made no excuses for his conservatism and admitted that he did not like much of what the New Deal was doing; still, he believed that he was reasonably willing to enforce the legislation of the 1930's and that he did not allow his predilections to lead to reactionary opinions. In this respect he was in line with the prevalent view on the Second Circuit.

Of the six members of the Learned Hand court, Judge Clark was the last to remain in regular service on the Second Circuit. He died on December 13, 1963, shortly after his seventy-fourth birthday and in his twenty-fifth year on the bench. In his final years he was one of the busiest judges in the country, keeping up with his share of the court's workload and remaining active in the struggle for improvements in the efficiency of courts. At his death, after a half-century of important work, he was respected as one of the leading men of American law and jurisprudence.

Charles Edward Clark was born on December 9, 1889, in Woodbridge, Connecticut, to Samuel Orman and Pauline Caroline Clark. His father was a farmer and the agrarian background may have contributed to his strong individualism. He attended New Haven High School and Yale College, from which he received an A.B. in 1911. Upon graduation he was elected a member of Phi Beta Kappa. He next attended the Yale University Law School, receiving his L.L.B. in 1913, summa cum laude; that same year he was admitted to the Connecticut bar.

While at law school he worked in the law office of Judge Livingston W. Cleaveland of New Haven. He continued in this office until 1915, when he joined another firm in that city. Clark was moderately active in political affairs in and around New Haven and for two years (1917–18) he represented the town of Woodbridge in the Connecticut House of Representatives as a Republican. In 1932 he supported the candidacy of Franklin D. Roosevelt and from then on was a consistent and enthusiastic supporter of the Democratic Party and New Deal programs.

In 1919 Clark began a career at the Yale Law School that was to last virtually to the end of his life. He was appointed an Assistant Professor of Law by Dean Swan, as part of a program of revitalizing the school. Three years later he was made an Associate Professor and in 1924 he was promoted to Professor of Law. His rapid rise at Yale continued when in 1926 he was selected as the Arthur E. Lines Professor of Law. In 1929 he succeeded Robert Maynard Hutchins as Dean of the Law School. His deanship was marked by important innovations in legal education such as the emphasis on the inter-disciplinary approach and the introduction of courses on procedure. The Yale Law School grew greatly in prestige. In a recent book of re-flections, Thurman Arnold called Clark "the greatest educator I have ever known"[79] and credited him with many advances in legal education and practice. In a 1960 tribute, Second Circuit Judge Harold Medina said that in his view Clark "did as much, if not more, for Yale Law School as any other man in its history."[80]

While he was active at Yale, Clark was involved in Connecticut judicial affairs. From 1927 to 1931 he was a deputy judge in the town of Hamden. He participated in the work of the Connecticut Judicial Council. Between 1931 and 1939 he was a member of the State Legislative Commission on Jails. In the middle 1930's he served as Vice-Chairman of the Connecticut Commission on the Reorganization of State Departments. In addition to these activities and other state reform work, in 1931 he drafted the Uniform Principal and Income Act for the National Conference of Commissioners on Uniform State Laws.

Clark was a frequent contributor to professional journals and the author or editor of a number of standard law school texts and case-books on pleading, procedure, and commercial law. Of a very sub-stantial output over an almost fifty-year period, perhaps his outstand-ing work was the pioneering study of judicial administration, *Law Administration in Connecticut,* which he co-authored in 1937 with Professor Harry Shulman of Yale.

He was one of the first to recognize the importance of judicial statistics to judicial administration. Throughout most of his career on the Second Circuit, he was Chairman of the Committee on Statistics of the Judicial Conference of the United States.

Clark's reputation as one of the giants of the judicial reform movement of the first half of the century, along with Chief Justices Taft and Hughes, Roscoe Pound, and Arthur Vanderbilt, is based primarily on the role that he played in the adoption of the Federal Rules of Civil Procedure in the 30's. The rules are widely regarded as the single greatest procedural improvement of the twentieth century in the federal judicial system. They were drafted by the Advisory

[79] Arnold, *Fair Fights and Foul* (New York: Harcourt, Brace & World, 1965), p. 35. For a discussion of Clark's contributions to legal education, see pp. 63–67.

[80] Medina, "Remarks," *Record of the Association of the Bar of the City of New York,* 15 (1960), 17.

Committee on Civil Procedure of the Supreme Court, which Clark served as Reporter from 1935 to 1956, and he has been called their "father."[81] Henry F. Chandler, the first director of the Administrative Office of United States Courts and himself a leading judicial reform figure, described Clark's contribution in these words:

> It was he who first publicly opposed a partial reform by the abolition of rules for cases at law only and urged that the rules for law and equity should be united. . . . But the great contribution of Judge Clark was in his capacity as Reporter. He was responsible for the preparation of the drafts of rules and the notes on them. The comprehensiveness and accuracy of the research conducted by him and his staff, their celerity and skill in preparing drafts and altering them to conform with the decision from time to time of the Advisory Committee, and his flexibility in loosening hard knots and adjusting difficulties were highly important factors in the collective functioning of the Committee.[82]

It is ironic that many of Judge Clark's sharpest dissents and battles with his colleagues were over the Federal Rules. As we shall see, his reform activities at Yale and his work as Reporter to the Advisory Committee significantly influenced his performance on the bench and limited his ability to creatively confront litigation which presented procedural questions.

Twice while at Yale he was offered a seat on the United States Court of Appeals for the District of Columbia, first by President Hoover shortly after becoming Dean and then in 1937 by President Roosevelt. Each time Clark demurred, because he preferred to stay at Yale; he also believed that the Second Circuit was a more important court than the District of Columbia tribunal. Therefore, when Roosevelt proffered appointment to the Second Circuit after Clark had turned down a position on the National Labor Relations Board, he could no longer decline.[83]

Throughout his first fifteen years on the bench Clark was eclipsed in seniority by Coolidge appointees. As late as 1951 he was still fifth on the court in years of service. Three years later, on September 1, 1954, he became chief judge of the Second Circuit and he remained in this position until late 1959, when he reached the statutory retirement age for chief judges of the inferior federal courts (seventy) and reluctantly stepped down. However, he continued as a regular member of the court until his death.

[81] *Ibid.*

[82] Chandler, "Some Major Advances in the Federal Judicial System: 1922–1947," 31 *Federal Rules Decisions* 513.

[83] Like Judge Swan, he had served ten years as dean; see n. 55 above.

Clark's chief judgeship is noteworthy because he refused to be rigidly bound to court traditions espoused by Learned Hand. He revitalized the Judicial Conference and the Judicial Council of the circuit, put into effect new court rules that he had prepared prior to becoming chief judge, and departed from the Hand-imposed refusal to permit the Second Circuit to hear cases en banc. His tenure as chief judge was also a trying one because of the many changes in membership that occurred in the middle and late 1950's.

Over the years, Clark was involved in numerous disputes with colleagues, often over matters that were regarded as petty by the other judges. Between 1941 and 1951 (and for several years thereafter) there was incessant conflict between him and Jerome Frank, much of which was hidden from the readers of the *Federal Reporter*. In his final years, Clark bitterly and openly criticized the Second Circuit for what he considered conservative tendencies. This combativeness seems to have been his most distinctive feature. In combination with his fierce, unrelenting promotion of fidelity to certain ideas that he had regarding procedure, it contributed much to the style and the inner dynamics of the Learned Hand court.

The final appointee to the Second Circuit, 1941–51, and the judge with the shortest judicial tenure (sixteen years) is the most difficult to write about. Jerome Frank was a remarkable man who had already had a noteworthy career before his appointment to the bench. He was a leading member of the realist school of jurisprudence that had strongly attacked many aspects of the American judicial system in the first third of this century. This led to the suggestion, noted above, that President Roosevelt's appointment of him to the Second Circuit "might be likened to the choice of a heretic to be a bishop of the Church of Rome." Although the writer observed that it rarely happens that "the heretic long survives the atmosphere of orthodoxy," and he feared Frank might begin "to conform and by more or less imperceptible degrees [become] a veritable pillar of the church,"[84] it is clear that he remained an iconoclast until the end of his life. Wallace Mendelson is far from correct when he intimates that Frank, as a judge, abandoned the positions he had taken earlier: "A generation ago 'legal realists' led by Jerome Frank and Karl Llewellyn dismissed law as a myth—a function of what judges had for breakfast. The important thing, they insisted, was what a court *did,* not what it *said.* Yet, however broad Frank's 1930 language, later on the bench he loyally acknowledged the compulsive force of legal rules. As a lower court judge, he decided

[84] Seagle, Book Review, p. 664.

cases in accordance with what he found the law to be—and on occasion, he made clear in addenda what he thought it ought to be."[85]

The major challenge in any study of Jerome Frank is to correlate his nonjudicial writings—both before and after 1941—with his opinions as a judge. This is an especially difficult undertaking because Frank was a very prolific writer who did not have high regard for consistency. The several studies of Frank that have been made do not attempt an integration of his writings; instead they concentrate on his jurisprudence. These are inadequate because they are primarily concerned with the rationality and internal consistency of Frank's views. But Frank was an explosive writer who often was interested in using shock effect to produce a theory or approach to jurisprudence. Much of what he wrote is vulnerable to sharp attack, but this is almost unimportant. More important, for example, is his impact on judicial reform and criminal law. To dismiss him as a relatively minor legal philosopher, as some have done, is to beg the crucial questions about him. Some day, perhaps, an extensive, scholarly study of Frank will be undertaken. In this book I can do no more than briefly touch upon the highlights of his career and philosophy.

Jerome New Frank was born on September 10, 1889, in New York City to Herman and Clara (New) Frank. He attended public schools in Chicago, where his family moved when he was very young. He studied at the University of Chicago, from which he received a B.A. in 1909. Frank then attended the university's law school, graduating in 1912 with Phi Beta Kappa honors and the degree of Doctor of Jurisprudence. Two years later he married Florence Kiper, who at the time of her marriage was a well-known poet and playwright. The Franks moved in literary circles with such writers as Carl Sandburg, Rebecca West, Sherwood Anderson, and Max Eastman.

Frank was admitted to the Illinois bar and practiced law in Chicago. Much of his work was with corporate reorganization, and he gained some success as a corporation lawyer of liberal tendencies. He was moderately active in political affairs as a member of the famous "Kitchen Cabinet" of William E. Dever, the city's progressive Democratic mayor. In 1929 he moved to New York City and joined a large Wall Street law firm.

With the Roosevelt victory in the 1932 election, Frank "applied" for a federal position to Professor Felix Frankfurter. He had already gained considerable notoriety with the 1930 publication of *Law and the Modern Mind*. On the influential professor's recommendation he

[85] Mendelson, "The Neo-Behavioral Approach to the Judicial Process: A Critique," *American Political Science Review*, 57 (1963), 593.

was appointed by Henry Wallace to the post of general counsel of the Agricultural Adjustment Administration. In the A.A.A. Frank fought in behalf of consumer interests, came into conflict with other officials, and was finally ousted by Wallace. His next government positions were with the Reconstruction Finance Corporation as special counsel, and then with the Public Works Administration, where he helped to win the famed *Alabama Power* case. In late 1937, after a brief return to private practice, where he earned a large income doing railroad reorganization work, Frank reluctantly accepted the President's offer of a commissionership on the Securities and Exchange Commission, which was then headed by his friend and former colleague at the Yale Law School, William O. Douglas. After Douglas' elevation to the Supreme Court in 1939, Frank became chairman of the S.E.C. He was a controversial chairman; after two years in that post he was appointed to the Second Circuit. He remained on the court until his death on January 13, 1957.

In terms of learning and intellect alone, Jerome Frank has to be regarded as one of the great figures of American law. Some excerpts from an unfinished portrait of him written by Richard Rovere for *The New Yorker* give an indication of Frank's uniqueness.

[Frank's friends] nearly always speak of him as an anachronism . . . many of them consider him a species of universal genius, and since it is well known that they hardly ever make them that way any more, they find it necessary to set him down in more hospitable and constructive centuries. Some think of him as an ancient Greek, some as Roman. One friend . . . puts Frank astride the sixteenth and seventeenth centuries. "Jerry's a man of the Renaissance," he says. "There are no barriers in his mind. He's like Leonardo."

[Rebecca West] thinks Frank too large a figure to have been comfortable with the smallminded British and American talkers of the Enlightenment. "As for his conversations," she has written, "what can one possibly say of them? He is like Voltaire, who covered contemporary life so completely and with such unfailing brilliance that you can't write a life of him—the stream's too full."

He has a quicksilver mind. It works at about top speed for about twenty out of every twenty-four hours. "He is in perpetual cerebration," Judge Learned Hand has said. He can read, write, talk, and think faster than anybody.

The law is Frank's profession and he has worked in every department of it. He is also an authority of recognized competence on finance, pedagogy, diabolism, moral philosophy, transportation, economics, the history of religions, and several literatures.

His most spectacular gift is for reading. It is, of course, pure myth that any human being can take in a page of a book at a single focusing of the eyes, as several prodigies are said to be able to do. Frank, however, has come as near to doing it as any human being. It is difficult to imagine that even the fastest reader in history could have beaten Frank who does anywhere between one hundred and two hundred pages an hour, depending on the specific gravity of the text.

It seems entirely possible that he has read more than anyone else alive today. He has not yet exhausted New York's library facilities, but the day when he will have done so cannot be too far off.[86]

In two important ways Judge Frank was an extraordinary judge: in his use of his judicial opinions as a sounding board for his views on courts and law, and in his knowledge and use of social science literature.

With regard to the first of these, Frank quite often ignored the unwritten rule—one that is invariably heeded by intermediate appellate judges—that opinions should be short and contain only the facts and points of law that are necessary for the decision. But Judge Frank

> was firmly wedded . . . to the view that a judge in his decisions is under obligation to lay bare the fullness of his thought as far as he can himself understand it—the complex of his biases, his predispositions, his intellectual premises, his social views, his economic predilections. A judicial opinion to him was more than a brief and dry appendage to a settled issue. It was more than an epitaph to an ended case. . . . The judge's opinion was an instrument for clarifying, for the perennial reexamination of legal principles in ever-changing context, and thus for furthering the progress of the law. . . .
>
> On occasion, when a case fired his imagination and kindled his enthusiasm, his opinion became a literary essay, written in his characteristically strong, clear and argumentative style, brimming with the exceptionally broad range of his learning, laced with his wit, and eloquent with the deep compassion stirred in him by the human beings involved in the disputes before him. He enlivened law with the breath of life.[87]

In these essay-like opinions Frank wrote about the subjects that had occupied his brilliant mind for two decades and more: the deficiencies in the jury system, the need for special (as opposed to general) verdicts, the weaknesses of trial court fact-finding, the role of the trial court judge, improvements in criminal law, the myth of legal certainty, and suggested reforms in legal education. This is only a partial list.[88] Frank did not use these opinions only as a forum for

[86] Rovere, "Jerome N. Frank," An Address at Special Memorial Meeting of the New York County Lawyers' Association and the Association of the Bar of the City of New York, May 23, 1957.

[87] Sidney M. Davis, "Jerome Frank—Portrait of a Personality," *University of Chicago Law Review*, 24 (1957), 628.

[88] Julius Paul, in *The Legal Realism of Jerome N. Frank* (The Hague, Netherlands: Martinus Nijhoff, 1959), has listed Frank's major opinions according to these subject matters (pp. 154–56).

his ideas, but also as a device for introducing into legal literature information that had been culled from his readings in psychology, anthropology, biography, literature, sociology, the daily newspaper, and almost every other source of written material.[89]

Apparently Judge Frank's lengthy opinions were not always welcomed by the legal profession and some of his brethren on the Second Circuit. No one openly attacked Frank on this point, but that there was criticism is implicit in Frank's defense of the practice. He once wrote to Justice Douglas:

> "My aims, so far as I can articulate them, in writing opinions, when they are essayistic are these: a) To stimulate the bar into some reflective thinking about the history of legal doctrines, so that they will go beyond the citator perspective of doctrinal evolution; b) To induce them to reflect on the techniques of legal reasoning (e.g., to consider the nature and value of stare decisis, or the use and value and limitations on the proper employment of fictions); c) To recognize that the judicial process is inescapably human, necessarily never flawless, but capable of improvement; d) To perceive the diverse 'forces' operative in decision-making, and the limited function of the courts as part of government.
>
> "And, underlying it all, is a strong desire, not easily curbed, to be pedagogic—not in a didactic manner but in a way that will provoke intelligent questioning as to the worth of accepted practices in the interest of bettering these practices. . . . In my clumsy way,

[89] Edmond Cahn, an admirer of Frank, wrote in tribute: "To many of his friends, Jerome Frank's most impressive attribute consisted in his matchless command of humanistic studies and social sciences. He seemed to have read almost everything in these fields, and remembered all that he had read; what is more important—his brain was so richly provided with active synapses that the thought currents moved like lightning from one area to another, from law to philosophy, from economics to ethics, from theory of knowledge to sociology to semantics and back to law" ("Fact-Skepticism and Fundamental Law," *New York University Law Review*, 33 [1958], 10).

In a memorial address, Justice Douglas said: "The contribution of Frank was unique in another way. His exploration of a legal problem left a treasure-house for the lawyer. His mind led even the prosaic student into fields quite new and often startling to him. Frank opened wide vistas that lawyers did not often explore. He was at home in most fields of literature. Psychoanalysis and psychiatry were fascinating tools for him. His mastery of philosophy placed at his finger tips the wisdom of the ages. The allied field of mathematics helped him discover new worlds. His interest in the humanities and in social sciences often put him in possession of data, statistics and surveys which illuminated shadowy ideas of the law. One who comes to these essay-like opinions in search of knowledge, discovers more leads to answers to legal problems than he ever dreamed existed" ("Jerome N. Frank," An Address at a Special Memorial Meeting of the New York County Lawyers' Association and the Association of the Bar of the City of New York, May 23, 1957, p. 8).

I've tried to indicate the limited utility of generalization uttered by me in my opinions. I doubt whether I've given birth to many dicta."[90]

There can be little argument with Judge Frank's defense of his technique. However, at least some of the criticism was not motivated by the belief that a judge has no business writing essays, but by the way in which Frank went about refuting the opinions and arguments that he did not accept. While the other judges never said so in their opinions, some of them resented, at times, the sharpness of Frank's attacks on their positions. It is noteworthy that Judges Learned Hand and Clark spoke of Frank's aggressive style in their memorial tributes to him.[91]

Jerome Frank was a complex individual with a seemingly ambivalent personality. He appears in a sympathetic light in his wholly sincere and often single-handed fights in behalf of judicial reform and criminal justice. His remarkable tribute to Learned Hand shows his modesty and the depth of his feeling for others.[92] The published statements about him by former law clerks, colleagues, and friends reveal countless admirable qualities. Yet, there is also the Jerome Frank of the written word—the books and articles and legal opinions— who emerges as an abrasive, even disagreeable, individual. Judging by what others said of him, he certainly was not nasty; judging by what he said in his writings, he appears to have been so. Perhaps, as he insisted,

[90] *Ibid.,* pp. 6–7.

[91] Judge Hand said, "I am sure you have all felt his passionate resentment on any occasion in which the defenseless or the weak were oppressed, especially if they were accused of crime" ("Tribute from the Bench," *Yale Law Report,* 3 [1957], 9). Judge Clark remarked, "Recollection brings back incidents often humorous, at times grim, of problems and responsibilities shared or divided, of battles serious and absorbing. These intellectual combats must loom large in retrospect, for the inner life of a vigorous appellate court is that of controversy." He added, "Judge Frank, although a gladiator of unusual power and adroitness, never seemed to harbor permanent spite of any form whatsoever, indeed, I doubt if he realized how heavy was the impact of his intellectual blows" ("Jerome N. Frank," *Yale Law Journal,* 66 [1957], 817, 818).

The view of Judge Clark is of special interest, since he and Judge Frank provided much of "the inner life" of the Second Circuit. However they loom in retrospect, at the time the combats were often more personal than intellectual, though it is true that Judge Frank, who was stronger and more adept in debate than his New Deal adversary, did not bear a grudge after battle. But it is questionable whether the same can be said of Judge Clark, who had a penchant for reviving old disputes with Frank, at times many years later.

[92] Jerome N. Frank, "Some Reflections on Judge Learned Hand," p. 668. This posthumously published article is based on lectures given by Frank at the Yale Law School in 1955.

the extralegal sallies in the essay-opinions were not dicta; beyond a doubt, many were gratuitous.[93] When he disagreed with others, it was almost as if he could not attack or criticize men and ideas short of all-out, no-holds-barred war. An extreme example of this is his pseudonymous attack on Cardozo, who was then already dead. Not only was this an unfavorable critique of Cardozo's much praised style, which is all that Frank probably intended it to be, but also a tasteless and almost repellent attack against a much respected judge.[94]

Justice Frankfurter touched on this dualism in Frank's personality and presented a balanced judgment. In a memorial tribute he wrote:

> To have known Jerome Frank only through his writings was not to have known him. On paper he appeared prickly and pugilistic; in personal relations he was warm-hearted and generous. His combatative curiosity gave battle at the drop of a word, so that those who encounterd him only on paper were apt to be surprised when they found in him a devoted, uncritical friend and a compassionate observer of the human scene. . . . While he somehow managed to envelop himself in an atmosphere of dogmatism, he was singularly free of bias or imprisoning doctrine. His seeming iconoclasm was rooted in his zealous loyalty to the realization that the history of thought, particularly sociological thought, is the history of continuous displacement of erroneous dogma.[95]

Jerome Frank's philosophy (which will be discussed at greater length later) is vulnerable to effective criticism; it could hardly have turned out otherwise once he set as his primary goal an onslaught against many of the accepted notions of the existing legal order. His remedies are usually found defective—is it not common that those who throw stones live in glass houses? Frank's importance barely rests on the positive aspects of his jurisprudence, for it was "as a legal publicist [that he] . . . reached his highest intellectual permanence."[96]

[93] For example, Frank did not care much for Sir Edward Coke, the man or his views. In one opinion Frank labeled him "an antique dealer in obsolescent medieval ideas" (United States v. Forness, 125 F.2d 938 [2d Cir. 1942]. In another case, decided at about the same time, Frank was even sharper: "Unscrupulous and unreliable in his life, Coke should not govern us from the grave" (Commissioner of Internal Revenue v. Marshall, 125 F.2d 945 [2d Cir. 1942]).

[94] Anon Y. Mous, [Jerome N. Frank], "The Speech of Judges: A Dissenting Opinion," *Virginia Law Review*, 29 (1943), 625.

[95] Frankfurter, "Jerome N. Frank," *University of Chicago Law Review*, 24 (1957), 625.

[96] Edward McWhinney, "Judge Jerome Frank and Legal Realism: An Appraisal," *New York Law Forum*, 3 (1957), 114.

2

A Brief History[1]

WHEN THE CONSTITUTION WAS WRITTEN IN THE SUMMER OF 1787, disagreement over the question of mandatory establishment of inferior federal courts was resolved by a compromise that left the creation of such tribunals to the discretion of Congress.[2] In what Felix Frankfurter and James Landis regarded as the "transcendent achievement" of the Judiciary Act of 1789, Congress immediately exercised the constitutional option to "ordain and establish" courts below the Supreme Court level and established a two-tiered system of lower federal courts consisting of district and circuit courts.

The intermediate courts of appeals of today are quite unlike those set up by the first Congress, either in terms of composition or of

[1] In the parts of this chapter dealing with the one hundred years prior to the creation of the circuit courts of appeals, I have relied heavily on three works: Henry M. Hart, Jr., and Herbert Wechsler, *The Federal Courts and the Federal System* (Brooklyn: Foundation Press, 1953); Charles Merrill Hough, *The United States District Court for the Southern District of New York* (New York: Maritime Law Association, 1934); and, Felix Frankfurter and James M. Landis, *The Business of the Supreme Court* (New York: Macmillan Co., 1927).

[2] Hart and Wechsler, *Federal Courts*, pp. 17–18.

jurisdiction. The modern appellate courts trace their existence directly to 1891; yet the hybrid circuit court system that existed for one hundred years had some enduring influence on the shape of the federal judiciary.

Charles M. Hough, a distinguished member of the Second Circuit in the first quarter of this century, described the new circuit court system as immature,[3] a point of view echoed more recently by Professors Hart and Wechsler, who called it "a curious one."[4] This is because it provided for two distinct types of trial courts. The first consisted of thirteen district courts, roughly along state lines, each with one judge. These formed the basis for the federal courts of original jurisdiction still in existence today. The second type was made up of three circuit courts, cutting across state boundaries and with no judges assigned exclusively to them. Each circuit court was to have three judges, two of them Supreme Court justices riding circuit and the third a district judge. There were to be two sessions a year in each of the districts within the circuit.[5]

One of the reasons for this system was that Congress believed that the Supreme Court would not have enough work to occupy it full time. "The Circuit Court, as the act clearly shows, was the tribunal in which the Supreme Court justices were expected to do most of their work. At a time when in no city on the continent were courts continuously open, it was assumed that the officers of the Supreme Court could not find enough work at the Capitol for more than a few weeks a year."[6] However, the failure to staff the circuit courts adequately was a recurring and growing headache for the federal judiciary throughout the nineteenth century.

The circuit courts had both original and appellate jurisdiction. They were authorized to review on appeal from the district courts final decrees in admiralty and maritime cases in which the sum in controversy exceeded three hundred dollars and decisions in civil cases in which the sum in controversy exceeded fifty dollars.

From the available evidence it appears that appeals constituted the smaller part of the business of the circuit courts. Using figures in an 1820 Senate Report as a guide, Frankfurter and Landis concluded that the appellate work of the circuit courts "could not have been very

---

[3] Hough, *District Court*, p. 3.

[4] Hart and Wechsler, *Federal Courts*, p. 38.

[5] Under this system a district judge sitting in the circuit court in a case on appeal could sit in review of his own decisions.

[6] Hough, *District Court*, p. 5. Judge Hough points out that the term "circuit judge" was used frequently to describe the Supreme Court justices and that at least until Jackson's time this is how they were described in presidential messages p. 6).

considerable."[7] In the Southern District of New York, lawyers were accustomed to taking their appeals directly to the Supreme Court.[8] Samuel R. Betts served on that court for more than forty years, 1826 to 1867, and "during his first twenty years on the bench it is said that no appeal was taken from any of his decisions."[9] But in the second half of the nineteenth century appeals to the Second Circuit became more frequent. The circuit courts retained their appellate jurisdiction until 1891, when the circuit courts of appeals were established, and their original jurisdiction until 1914 when they were abolished.[10]

From the beginning, "the circuit courts were the weak spot"[11] in the federal court system. The requirement for circuit riding put a considerable physical burden on the Supreme Court justices, who protested continuously against it. Judge Hough writes that "the system is commonly believed to have been fatal to Justices Wilson and Iredell."[12] Congress reacted to the protests by gradually reducing the circuit responsibilities of the justices; the practice persisted well into the nineteenth century, however.

The abolition of circuit riding was one of the secondary features of the Judiciary Act of 1801, popularly called the "Law of the Midnight Judges," because, as is well known, it was passed in the closing "lame duck" days of the administration of John Adams. While the motivation for the law was largely political—to perpetuate Federalist power in the judiciary—the balanced view of Frankfurter and Landis is that it "combined thoughtful concern for the federal judiciary with selfish concern for the Federalist Party."[13]

The Federalist law provided for twenty-three district courts, which in turn were divided into six circuits, each of which was staffed with three judges except the sixth (the Western Circuit), which had only one. The Second Circuit was comprised of New York, Connecticut, and Vermont, and this has remained unchanged for more than a century and a half.

Not surprisingly, all sixteen new circuit judges were Federalists, a factor that increased Jeffersonian distaste for the law; upon taking office the Jeffersonians quickly undid the work of the Federalists by repealing the Act of 1801 and abolishing the circuit court judgeships.

[7] Frankfurter and Landis, *Business of the Supreme Court*, pp. 12–13, n. 36.

[8] Hough, *District Court*, p. 31.

[9] 30 *Federal Cases* 1, 363.

[10] This brief description of the jurisdiction of the circuit courts is based on the provisions of the First Judiciary Act. Later statutes made substantial changes which are beyond the scope of this review.

[11] Hart and Wechsler, *Federal Courts*, p. 38.

[12] Hough, *District Court*, p. 13.

[13] Frankfurter and Landis, *Business of the Supreme Court*, p. 25.

Later, this proved to be harmful to the development of the federal judicial system and the administration of justice in the federal courts; but from the perspective of 1801 there was insufficient business to justify three-judge circuit courts. This was also true of the Second Circuit, about which Judge Hough writes:

> There was really nothing for three resident circuit judges to do, and the inference is strong that such men as the three who served on the Second Circuit soon found out that no court could make business, but must wait for business to grow out of the community, and they were not indisposed to be legislated out of offices whose emoluments were but $2,000 a year, especially as the offices were also abolished, and they were not troubled by the sight of political opponents as successors.[14]

Thus, the repeal of the Judiciary Act of 1801 did not, at first, create any hardship. There were no heavy workloads and overcrowded dockets to contend with. "To modern ears the whole amount of work done by all the courts, state and federal, in the City of New York about the beginning of the nineteenth century seems ridiculously small."[15] This situation seems to have prevailed at least until the decade of 1810, when "really begins the history of the circuit court as a growingly important metropolitan tribunal."[16] Even then, however, it can not be said that the Second Circuit was busy.

The act replacing the "Law of the Midnight Judges" retained the status quo ante. Six circuit courts were established, composed of one Supreme Court justice[17] and one district judge. To mitigate the hardships resulting from circuit riding, Congress authorized the holding of the circuit court by a single district judge. "Circuit riding thus became a duty of imperfect obligation. . . . As the country grew the privilege of non-attendance came increasingly to be used. Correspondingly, circuit court review of district court decisions became more and more frequently futile."[18] Nevertheless, Frankfurter and Landis present conclusive evidence that at least as late as 1838 circuit duties occupied much of the time of the Supreme Court justices.[19]

[14] Hough, *District Court*, p. 16. See also Frankfurter and Landis, *Business of the Supreme Court*, pp. 12–13, n. 35, for data showing that from the establishment of the circuit courts through 1801 the New York circuit was one of the least busy of the circuit courts.

[15] Hough, *District Court*, p. 12.

[16] *Ibid.*, p. 17.

[17] There were then six justices on the Supreme Court and each was assigned to one circuit. Thus began the practice, which lasted until 1866, of tying the size of the Supreme Court to the number of circuits.

[18] Hart and Wechsler, *Federal Courts*, p. 43.

[19] Frankfurter and Landis, *Business of the Supreme Court*, pp. 49–50.

The justices assigned to the Second Circuit apparently took their circuit riding responsibilities seriously, at least in the district in which New York City was located.[20] Between 1806 and 1872 three justices served as circuit justice for the Second Circuit: Brockholst Livingston, 1806–23; Smith Thompson, 1823–43; and Samuel Nelson, 1845–72. Each of these men regarded New York City as home and devoted much time to the business of the circuit court in the district. Then, as now, most of the work of the Second Circuit came from New York City. The interest of these justices "made the circuit court a tribunal attractive to a growing bar in a growing city."[21] When Justice Nelson retired, the press of work in Washington was too great to permit the justices to devote much time to circuit work. Moreover, in 1869 Congress for the first time provided for judges assigned exclusively to the circuit courts. But Nelson's successor, Ward Hunt (1872–82), did not completely ignore the circuit responsibilities.

The earliest published report of any case from the Second Circuit was in 1814. It was not until 1827 that the business of the court was sufficient to justify the labors of a Reporter who published for profit. In that year the first volume of *Paine's Reports* appeared. Paine attempted to gather only a small number of the cases decided in the circuit and it is doubtful that he could have done a very competent job since in his time opinions were not filed but remained the private property of the judges.[22] Sixty-two cases are included in volume one of *Paine's Reports;* the earliest is from Vermont in 1808 [23] and the latest was decided in 1826. All of the opinions were written either by Justice Livingston or Justice Thompson.[24]

[20] A note about the district courts within the Second Circuit: the circuit courts were required to meet in each district within the circuit. At first, no state comprised more than one district. In New York, with the gradual, and later rapid, increase in cases, the state was divided. The first division came in 1812 with the formation of the Southern District (essentially all of what is now New York City) and the Northern District for the upper and interior parts of the state. The Western District was formed in 1900 out of the Northern District. In 1865 the Eastern District was created in Brooklyn. Connecticut and Vermont, the other states in the Second Circuit, to this day are each a single district. It was not until the beginning of this century that any of the districts had more than a single judge. At present, the Southern District of New York alone has twenty-four judges, which plainly illustrates the tremendous growth in litigation before the federal courts in New York City.

[21] Hough, *District Court,* p. 17, n. 30.

[22] *Ibid.,* p. 21.

[23] Hough erroneously writes that the earliest case was decided in 1840 (*ibid.,* p. 20, n. 40).

[24] A number of the opinions are actually charges to the jury. This is also true of the later reports from the circuit court. This indicates the importance of the circuit courts as tribunals of original jurisdiction.

The second volume of *Paine's Reports* appeared in 1860 after the death of the Reporter. Included are sixty-six cases from the years 1827 to 1840. In fifty-eight of these Justice Thompson wrote the court's opinion. From both volumes it appears that in most of the cases court was held by one judge and that the largest single category of cases was admiralty appeals from district court decisions.

Gradually, as New York became the commercial center of the nation, the workloads of the federal courts in the city grew considerably and commercial litigation other than admiralty law cases became more frequent. In the five years 1840–45 the circuit court in the Southern District considered 676 motions or cases and the district court 1,645, increases of about 300 per cent since the 1820's.[25] This, of course, does not include the cases in the other districts within the circuit. When we remember that the circuit work was done by two men, one of whom owed his primary duty to the Supreme Court, and the other occupied with the affairs of the district court, it becomes apparent that the circuit court was in need of additional manpower.

By the middle of the nineteenth century the Second Circuit was important and busy enough to merit a full-time Reporter, and in 1852 Samuel Blatchford published his first volume of reports. Blatchford appeared regularly before the courts in the circuit and was later a judge on the district and circuit courts and a Supreme Court justice. "By judicious selection of cases and syllabi evidencing a legal breadth which he also proved at the bar and on the bench," Blatchford "distinctly advanced the reputation of the Circuit."[26] *Blatchford's Circuit Court Reports* are in twenty-four volumes and cover the years 1845 through 1887. Their cessation was occasioned by the publication beginning in 1880 of the *Federal Reporter* by the West Publishing Company.[27]

As the years passed, it was no longer possible for Justice Nelson to handle most of the circuit work. By 1850 New York was the first city in the nation in both population and business volume, and the dockets of the city's courts were becoming more crowded. From the 1850's to the present the story of the Second Circuit has been one of overcrowded calendars, shortage of judicial manpower, and legislative attempts to ease the burden on the court's judges. In 1850 and 1852 Congress provided that district judges could serve in other districts within the circuit upon designation by the circuit justice. This laid the foundation

[25] Hough, *District Court*, p. 26.

[26] See the memorial tribute to Justice Blatchford at 150 U.S. 701–12.

[27] The Blatchfords tried unsuccessfully to continue their reports in rivalry with the *Federal Reporter*, which they regarded as undignified.

for the present system of intracircuit and intercircuit assignment of judges. The district judges of Connecticut, Vermont, and northern New York became regular visitors to New York City. They devoted most of their time in the city to the district court. This enabled the Southern District judge to spend more time on circuit court work. The out-of-town judges also helped out in the circuit court. In practice, until 1869 the major responsibility of the circuit justice was appeals (admiralty and bankruptcy cases), while the district judges conducted most of the original business of the court. Additional help came in 1865, when the Eastern District of New York was created out of the Southern District. This meant an additional district judge to participate in the work of the circuit court.

Table 1 shows the trend of business in the Second Circuit from 1845 to 1869, based on the first six volumes of *Blatchford's Reports*.

Table 1. The Business of the Second Circuit, 1845–69

	1	2	3	4	5	6
Volume of reports	1	2	3	4	5	6
Years covered	1845–50	1845–53	1853–57	1857–61	1861–67	1867–69
No. of cases reported	86	89	121	126	123	99
Cases from						
Southern District	56	70	105	103	87	69
Northern District	24	15	7	11	17	9
Eastern District					16	8
Connecticut	3	1	6	10	2	13
Vermont	3	3	3	2	1	0
Two-judge courts		46	44	10	17	5
Opinions[a] by						
Circuit Justice	68	28	48	74	66	27
Southern District Judge	6	51	38	3	4	38
Northern District Judge	2	1	6	15	9	7
Eastern District Judge					14	11
Connecticut District Judge	0	0	17	31	27	15
Vermont District Judge	3	3	3	2	4	2
No judge given	11	7	10	1	0	0
Subject of cases						
Patent[b]	31	30	22	30	22	26
Admiralty	18	10	36	40	21	17
Diversity	13	12	11	15	17	25
Customs	15	22	37	20	15	6
Bankruptcy	2	0	0	0	3	9
Criminal	0	7	5	7	17	7
Tax	0	0	0	0	12	2
Miscellaneous[c]	7	8	10	14	16	7

[a] Includes charges to the jury.
[b] Includes a small number of copyright and trademark cases.
[c] Includes jurisdiction and procedure; U.S. civil cases.

These data are not complete because not all decisions during this period were reported. We have no way of knowing what percentage of all cases decided in the circuit court during these years is represented by the reported cases, though it is virtually certain that the figure is below 50 per cent. However, this does not detract greatly from the significance of the information contained in these volumes. The data verify the preponderant position within the circuit of the Southern District and the important role played by the circuit justice. There is a discrepancy between the number of cases and the number of opinions due to the fact that in a handful of cases two judges wrote opinions. However, for that quarter of a century we have reports of only two dissenting opinions.

The period from 1869 to 1891 marks the "nadir of federal judicial administration."[28] The great economic expansion following the Civil War unloosed a flood of litigation which swamped the federal courts. Advances in transportation and communications further stimulated economic growth. Congress, instead of giving meaningful relief to the already overworked courts and judges, expanded the jurisdiction of federal courts. The Bankruptcy Act of 1867 added considerably to the business of the district courts in particular, and also to that of the circuit courts and the Supreme Court. This law was repealed in 1878; by then Congress had in the Removal Act of 1875 opened up an even greater source of litigation. Frankfurter and Landis, in discussing the effect of this statute, say:

> In the Act of March 3, 1875, Congress gave the federal courts the vast range of power which had lain dormant in the Constitution since 1789. These courts ceased to be restricted tribunals of fair dealing between citizens of different states and became the primary and powerful reliances for vindicating every right given by the Constitution, the laws, and treaties of the United States. Thereafter, any suit asserting such a right could be begun in the federal courts; any such action begun in a state court could be removed to the federal courts for disposition. The old jurisdiction in cases of diverse citizenship was retained. It had been enormously extended through the developing doctrine of corporate citizenship, as well as by legislation prior to 1875. To the increasing volume of litigation due to diversity of citizenship, the Act of 1875 opened wide a flood of totally new business for the federal courts.[29]

The Judiciary Act of 1869, which authorized the appointment of one circuit judge for each of the nine circuits then in existence, did not

---

[28] Hart and Wechsler, *Federal Courts,* p. 45.
[29] Frankfurter and Landis, *Business of the Supreme Court,* p. 65.

do much to alleviate this situation. It further reduced the circuit-riding responsibilities of the justices of the Supreme Court and provided that circuit court could be held by either the circuit judge or the district judge alone. Until 1891 circuit court was almost always conducted by a single judge.

The ineffectiveness of the Act of 1869 is shown by the state of the dockets of the lower federal courts in the years after its passage. "In 1873 the number of cases pending in the circuit and district courts was twenty-nine thousand and thirteen, of which five thousand one hundred and eight were bankruptcy cases. In 1880, despite the fact that the repeal of the Bankruptcy Act had dried up that source of business, the number had increased to thirty-eight thousand and forty-five. The year 1890 brings the total to fifty-four thousand one hundred and ninety-four."[30]

In the Second Circuit the situation was no better, though Judge Hough writes that "for more than 25 years after the first circuit judge was appointed under the Act of 1869, the two Courts of the [Southern] District remained, if not fully manned, not absurdly undermanned."[31] The evidence, however, does not support this evaluation. Even before the post-Civil War economic boom, patent cases and other difficult commercial litigation were increasingly occupying the attention of the city's federal courts. Justice Nelson, who retired in 1872 at the age of eighty, said of the workload of the Second Circuit during the years that he served as its circuit justice: "The calendar was large, and many of the causes important, involving great labor and responsibility. As an evidence of the magnitude of the business for many years, the Court was held three months in the Spring and three in the Autumn of the year, and still left an unfinished calendar."[32]

In 1869 President Grant appointed Lewis B. Woodruff, a judge on the Court of Appeals of New York, circuit judge for the Second Circuit. He served in this position until his death in 1875. During his years on the court, the Second Circuit was easily the busiest circuit in the number of United States government civil suits terminated. In 1870, of 3,347 such suits disposed of in all federal district and circuit courts, 1,620 of these were in the courts of the Second Circuit. At the end of the same year, fully three-fourths (6,043 out of 8,150) of all United States civil suits pending in the lower federal courts were in

[30] *Ibid.*, p. 60.

[31] Hough, *District Court*, p. 28.

[32] "Proceedings by the Bar of the United States Courts for the Second Circuit, on the Retirement of Mr. Justice Nelson from the Supreme Court of the United States," 10 *Blatchford's Circuit Court Reports*, 555.

the Second Circuit.[33] Other circuits and districts had more criminal cases, but then, as now, this type of case did not cause much difficulty since most of the accused pleaded guilty. The Second Circuit usually did not dispose of as many private civil suits as some of the other busy circuits. However, it always had a tremendous backlog of these cases. Moreover, while it is not possible to document this point, it is probable that the private litigation disposed of by the Second Circuit was of a more difficult type than that terminated elsewhere in the country. The Second Circuit was certainly a busy court.

Woodruff's successor as circuit judge was Alexander Smith Johnson, a former chief judge of the New York Court of Appeals. Johnson was even more burdened than Woodruff and it became obvious that one circuit judge was not sufficient to handle the business in the Second Circuit. The circuit justice heard few cases and the district judges were needed in their own districts and in the Southern District. It was commonly accepted that Johnson's death after three years as circuit judge "was hastened by the undue pressure of judicial labors and

[33] *Report of the Attorney General, 1871.* This was the first such report of the business of the federal courts. Starting in 1873 statistics of non-U.S. government civil suits were also reported. The years in the Attorney General's reports correspond with the fiscal year. Thus in 1873, the year began on July 1, 1872, and ended on June 30, 1873. On the basis of these reports it is not possible to determine how many of the cases were in the district courts and how many in the circuit courts. Most of the business was, of course, in the district courts. Although the statistics reported by the Attorney General are used in this study, I must emphasize that at least until the beginning of this century the *Reports of the Attorney General* were not completely accurate. At best, they indicate the business of the courts that reported. In the early years it was not infrequent for even a considerable number of districts not to report. It is also significant that no uniform coding and reporting system was employed. The clerk of each district counted in whatever manner suited him best. There was no way for the Attorney General to know whether the figures sent to him were accurate. The statistics given for the courts in the Second Circuit illustrate the point. In 1881 the Attorney General reported 3,041 non-U.S. civil suits were pending in the Northern District of New York. The Northern District did not even bother to report in 1882. In 1883 only 350 non-U.S. civil suits were pending upstate, but in 1884 the number had risen to the phenomenal figure of 4,761. These statistics must be inaccurate because in no year was the number of non-U.S. civil suits commenced or terminated in the Northern District large enough to allow for such sensational drops and rises. In 1884 only 356 non-U.S. civil suits were commenced in the Northern District. Even if none of the 350 that were pending nor the 356 new cases was disposed of, it is not possible to account for 4,761 cases. The statistics of the Southern District are also open to question. In 1888, 7,306 non-U.S. civil suits were pending in this district. A year later the number was 12,167. Since only 2,483 such suits were commenced in the period from July 1, 1888, to June 30, 1889, there must be some mistake in the reports.

Table 2. The Business of the Second Circuit, 1869–79

Volume of reports	7	8	9	10	11	12	13	14	15
No. of cases reported	79	79	72	71	65	71	98	134	66
Cases from									
Southern District	57	49	41	48	47	42	54	84	34
Northern District	12	17	11	4	9	16	15	14	22
Eastern District	7	8	8	15	7	7	16	18	5
Connecticut	3	4	10	2	2	5	8	13	4
Vermont	0	1	2	2	0	1	5	5	1
Two-judge courts	9	4	4	3	4[a]	4	2	0	1
Opinions by									
Circuit Justice	5	1	0	1	6	9	18	15[b]	13[c]
Circuit Judge	36	47	37	37	34	26	24	41	27
Southern District Judge	31	24	25	20	15	18	7	11	0
Northern District Judge	3	1	1	0	3	8	10	10	8
Eastern District Judge	3	6	5	8	4	7	15	26	6
Connecticut District Judge	1	2	14	5	3	3	23	20	6
Vermont District Judge	0	0	0	0	1	0	0	11	6
No judge given	1	0	0	0	0	0	1	0	0
Subject of cases									
Patent[d]	25	21	34	25	19	23	24	38	26
Admiralty	20	17	5	14	17	4	11	21	7
Diversity	7	12	14	12	6	11	11	24	5
U.S. civil[e]	8	13	3	7	8	6	8	10	9
Bankruptcy	11	7	15	8	6	15	10	14	8
Criminal	3	6	0	2	5	6	10	14	2
Miscellaneous[f]	5	3	1	3	4	6	24	13	9

[a] Including one case decided by a three-judge court.
[b] Because of the incapacitation of Justice Hunt, Chief Justice Morrison R. Waite served as circuit judge on the Second Circuit. Ten of the fifteen opinions are by him.
[c] All by Chief Justice Waite.
[d] Includes a small number of copyright and trademark cases.
[e] Includes customs and U.S. tax cases.
[f] Includes jurisdiction and procedure and cases in which the subject cannot be determined.

responsibilities against which he struggled with self-sacrificing toil."[34] In 1879 Charles Devens, the Attorney General, reported to Congress that "for several years there has been a most pressing want of an additional judge in the Second Circuit, and it is now doubtful whether one such judge would enable that Court, even if there is no increase in the duties to be performed by its judges, to transact its regular business."[35]

Table 2, based on the cases recorded in *Blatchford's Reports*, indicates the distribution of cases in the Second Circuit from 1869 to 1879.

[34] "Proceedings of the Members of the Bar in the City of New York, on the Death of the Honorable Alexander S. Johnson, Circuit Judge of the Second Circuit," 14 *Blatchford's Circuit Court Reports*, 557.
[35] *Report of the Attorney General, 1879*, p. 8.

Again it must be stressed that these reports contain only some of the cases decided in the circuit. Through most of this period Blatchford served as judge in the Southern District, and it is a good guess that, as a result, a relatively large number of opinions written by the Southern District judge were reported. The figures clearly show the importance of patent cases. It is also noteworthy that the circuit court was composed of more than one judge in only a small handful of cases. Finally, any discrepancy between total number of cases and number of opinions written is due to the cases in which more than one opinion was written. Each volume of reports covers approximately one year.

Upon Johnson's death President Hayes elevated the Southern District judge, Samuel Blatchford, to the circuit court. Of course this did not involve much change, since Blatchford as district judge had previously served on the circuit court and, in any event, he was the Second Circuit's Reporter.

The decade of the 1880's was one of the most difficult for the Second Circuit and its judges; they were almost swamped by private civil litigation. Judge Hough thinks that "the ordinary business of the Circuit Court appeared to be sufficiently cared for by a resident Circuit Judge with the aid of district judges from other parts of the Circuit" and that whatever difficulty there was was due to a "customs calendar" made up of suits to recover from the Collector of Customs import duties that he had exacted.[36] Judge Hough is in error. First, while it is true that there was a considerable backlog of customs cases in the 1870's, by 1880 many of these had been disposed of. Second, in the 1880's United States civil suits made up only a relatively small percentage of the cases pending in the federal courts. While there were 8,150 civil suits pending at the end of 1870, by July 1, 1883, there were only 4,432. This number was further reduced in subsequent years. In contrast, in 1883, 27,791 non-United States government civil suits were pending, 7,589 of which were in the courts of the Second Circuit.[37] It is beyond dispute that in the 1880's the burden on the Second Circuit was caused by private civil litigation. Judge William James Wallace, who became circuit judge upon Blatchford's promotion to the Supreme Court in 1882,[38] thus described the Second Circuit from 1882 to 1891:

> The office of Circuit Judge at that time was a place of great responsibility and great labor. . . . Although many of these

[36] Hough, *District Court,* p. 30.

[37] The statistics are from the *Report of the Attorney General* for these years.

[38] Blatchford was the first—and perhaps the only—man to have served on all three federal courts.

[circuits] were larger territorially, and were composed of a larger number of states, there was none whose business, in magnitude and intrinsic importance, exceeded that of the Second Judicial Circuit. . . . The judge of the Circuit was expected to sit more or less frequently in Connecticut and Vermont, and in the three districts of New York; but the business of the Federal Courts in this city alone which devolved upon the Circuit Judge was, in my deliberate judgment, as extensive, as important, and as various as was allotted to any single judge in this country or in England to undertake. The business was certainly too onerous to be properly disposed of by any single judge. . . . In this Circuit so many foreign corporations, and citizens of different states, doing business in this city, and having their principal place of business here, habitually brought their controversies to the Federal Courts, that from this source alone these courts were burdened beyond their capacity with common law and equity litigations of every kind. Of course, the ordinary common law and equity litigations were but a part of the general business which occupied the Federal Courts. There were probably more patent cases, and more admiralty causes, than were in any other single jurisdiction in the United States, and perhaps in the world. Besides there were the numerous controversies arising under the various statutes of the United States.[39]

Congress took its time providing additional judges for the over-burdened courts. By 1884, 30,372 private civil cases were pending in the circuit and district courts; 12,776 of these were in the courts of the Second Circuit. By 1886 the figures were 31,455 and 13,885, respectively.[40] It was obvious already that a major overhaul of the judicial system was necessary to restore order to the administration of justice in the country. But Congress was not yet ready to act. It did, however, afford some relief for the Second Circuit when in 1887 it authorized a second circuit judge for the court. Almost immediately President Cleveland appointed Emile Henry Lacombe to serve with Wallace. But this did not lead to any reduction in the backlog of cases; to the contrary, the number of cases pending continued to grow. In 1888 there were 34,922 private civil cases pending in the lower federal courts, 14,330 of which were in the Second Circuit. In 1889 it was 38,872 in the country and 19,453 in the Second Circuit; a year later the figures were 42,584 and 21,990, respectively.[41]

Wallace was born in Syracuse, New York, in 1837 and served as mayor of that upstate city. In 1874 he was appointed district judge for the Northern District of New York, where he served until his elevation

[39] William James Wallace, Address at "Dinner in Honor of Judge William J. Wallace on His Retirement from the Bench Given by Members of the Bar of the State of New York, May 29, 1907," pp. 18–19.

[40] From *Report of the Attorney General* for 1884 and 1886.

[41] From *Report of the Attorney General* for these years.

to the circuit bench. In 1891, when Congress created the circuit courts of appeals, he became presiding judge of the Second Circuit, the office he held until he retired in 1907 at the age of seventy.

While no critical study of his twenty-five years as circuit judge is available, a fair estimate of his judicial career is that he was hard-working, respected, and quite conservative in his views. One evaluation of Wallace is that he was "ultra-conservative."[42] Since judges were recruited mostly from the ranks of successful corporation lawyers, and considering the general attitude of the judiciary of this time toward property, it is probable that his views were similar to those held by his brethren. When he retired he was called a "great judge"[43] whose opinions had "enriched for all time the judicial literature of his country,"[44] which should caution us to take all tributes to dead and retired judges with a grain of salt.

By the last decade of the nineteenth century it was abundantly clear that basic structural changes were required to solve the problems of the circuit courts. In the Evarts Act (the Court of Appeals Act of 1891) Congress finally adopted the solution that had been proposed for half a century and established a system of intermediate appellate courts. It thus fixed the outline of the twentieth-century scheme of federal appellate review.

Circuit courts of appeals, consisting of three judges each, were established in each of the nine existing circuits. To man these courts Congress created an additional circuit judgeship in each circuit, thus providing two circuit judges in all of the courts of appeals except the Second Circuit, which now had three.[45] Two judges constituted a quorum and, in the early years, it was not infrequent for the circuit court of appeals to be a two-judge court. The Evarts Act satisfied the wishes of the traditionalists by retaining, at least in theory, the circuit functions of Supreme Court justices[46] and by not abolishing the

---

[42] *Dictionary of American Biography,* vol. 17, p. 378.

[43] "Dinner in Honor of Judge William J. Wallace," p. 13.

[44] *Ibid.,* p. 29.

[45] In the courts of appeals with two circuit judges the third place was ordinarily to be filled by a district judge, but Supreme Court justices were also eligible to sit. However, the long-standing practice of district judges sitting in review of their own judgments was eliminated.

[46] Of course, while each Supreme Court justice is assigned to one or more circuits, the justices only rarely sit on the courts of appeals. The major function of the circuit justice today is to decide whether to grant a temporary stay of the lower court ruling pending decision of the entire Supreme Court on the petition for review. The circuit justice also is called on to allow bail where the lower court has refused it or has set bail at a very high figure.

old circuit courts, although it took away their appellate jurisdiction.[47]

Except where provided by law the circuit courts of appeals were given jurisdiction to review all final decisions of the district and circuit courts. Circuit court of appeals decisions were declared to be "final" in all diversity litigation, in suits under the revenue and patent laws, in criminal prosecutions, and in admiralty suits; but in all such cases the Supreme Court was authorized to order the judgment brought before it for review. In other cases, court of appeals decisions were reviewable by the Supreme Court as of right where the dispute involved more than one thousand dollars besides costs. In addition, as remains true today, each intermediate appellate court was authorized to "certify to the Supreme Court . . . any questions or propositions of law concerning which it desires the instruction of that Court for its proper decision."[48]

Later, when Congress in the Judiciary Act of 1925 further narrowed the scope of review as of right of circuit court of appeals decisions, it used the certiorari device. Today, except in extraordinary cases where the courts of appeals declare federal laws unconstitutional, all review of court of appeals decisions is discretionary.[49]

[47] See Frankfurter and Landis, *Business of the Supreme Court*, pp. 128–35, for the struggle to retain the circuit courts. Another concession to the old tradition was the calling of the new intermediate appellate courts "circuit courts of appeals." The title lasted until 1948 when it was changed to "United States courts of appeals."

[48] The Supreme Court, in recent years, has discouraged certification and, in practice, it has fallen into disuse. See Hart and Wechsler, *Federal Courts*, pp. 1379–81, and James W. Moore and Allan D. Vestal, "Present and Potential Role of Certification in Federal Appellate Procedure," *Virginia Law Review*, 35 (1949), 1.

[49] It is beyond the purpose of this study to examine the development of the jurisdiction of the courts of appeals. On this subject it is helpful to consult Bunn, *A Brief Survey of the Jurisdiction and Practice of the Courts of the United States*, 5th ed., (St. Paul, Minn.: West Publishing Company, 1949) and earlier editions. Of course the pertinent sections of Title 28 (Judiciary) of the United States Code Annotated give the fullest picture of the jurisdiction of the federal courts.

To a large measure, the jurisdiction of the courts of appeals is dependent on the jurisdiction of the district courts. All final judgments of district courts are appealable as of right. Some interlocutory orders are also appealable as a matter of right; in general, most such orders are appealable only by permission of the court of appeals, which permission is predicated upon a finding below that an immediate appeal may substantially advance the termination of the litigation. The courts of appeals are also authorized to review directly the decisions of certain administrative agencies: e.g., the National Labor Relations Board, the Federal Trade Commission, the Securities and Exchange Commission, the Federal Power Commission, and the Tax Court. Finally, the courts of appeals are authorized to issue extraordinary writs, but these constitute a negligible portion of their business.

The Evarts Act authorized two judges to constitute a quorum in the courts of appeals. When the new Second Circuit opened its first session on October 27, 1891, Judges Wallace and Lacombe constituted the court, as the third circuit judge had not yet been appointed. Lacombe is one of the illustrious names in the history of the Second Circuit. Born in New York City in 1846, he was graduated with honors from Columbia College at the age of seventeen, notwithstanding the fact that his studies had been interrupted by service in the Civil War. In 1865 he was an honor graduate of the Columbia Law School, but could not be immediately admitted to the bar because of his age. Prior to becoming a circuit judge in 1887, he was Corporation Counsel of New York City, a prestigious position. In 1907 he became senior judge of the Second Circuit, on which he continued to serve until his retirement in 1916.

According to Judge Charles E. Wyzanski, Jr., Lacombe twice refused appointment to the Supreme Court because he preferred to live in New York City.[50] One of his successors on the Second Circuit said of Lacombe:

> No judge stood higher in the regard of his colleagues or the bar or the general public. His integrity, fair mindedness, and ability were universally recognized. His promptness in the dispatch of business and his ready accessibility made him justly popular with the bar. Few men come to the bench with such natural equipment for the office. . . . He was a master in all of the branches of law which come under the jurisdiction of the National Courts. It was difficult to decide whether his attainments were greater in the Admiralty, in patent law, or in the common law. He had a distinctly original mind and he was fearless in blazing new legal paths. . . . He leaves behind him a permanent record of a great judge and the memory of a lawyer and gentleman highly respected, who had the warm affection of those who knew him well.[51]

In its obituary, the *New York Times* observed that "his decisions were seldom overruled, although critics of modern liberal tendencies were sometimes disposed to find the judge too regularly on the side of property."[52]

In March of 1892 Nathaniel Shipman, a member of the faculty of the Yale Law School, was appointed to fill the third seat on the

[50] Wyzanski, "Augustus Noble Hand," *Harvard Law Review*, 61 (1948), 577.

[51] Julius M. Mayer, "Memorial of E. Henry Lacombe," *Yearbook of the Association of the Bar of the City of New York*, 1925, pp. 505–6.

[52] November 29, 1924, p. 13.

court. Shipman continued to teach at Yale during his decade on the Second Circuit.[53]

The newly established courts of appeals were able to function smoothly. The district courts remained overburdened, but the flow of cases from them to the appellate courts was not yet sufficient to strain the capabilities of the circuit judges. Even the Second Circuit judges found that they could relax. Judge Wallace said fifteen years after the organization of the courts of appeals that "the office of circuit judge, if it has lost much of its former prominence and power, has gained vastly in its attractiveness to a judge who longs occasionally for a breath of liberty, and is willing to share a divided responsibility in deciding important and doubtful controversies."[54]

Admiralty cases made up most of the business of the new court "until the bar at large found out by practical experience how much easier it was to take appeals other than in Admiralty, to another story in the same Court House instead of to Washington."[55]

The new court had to decide what procedures it would require and follow. Its formal rules were not much different from those of the other circuits.[56] A disagreement arose within the court over the form of opinions. Judge Wallace, who was an admirer of the English method of an oral decision at the end of the argument, suggested that the Second Circuit opinions, except in cases of dissent, should be per curiam. Judge Lacombe was willing to go along with this, but it was not adopted because of the opposition of Judge Shipman.[57]

In the first decade following its formation, "the appellate business [of the Second Circuit] while abundant was not oppressive. For the first ten years the yearly crop varied from 120 to 160 cases. There was plenty of time to hear argument, long enough recesses to write in without hurry, and over and above all, opportunity left for eight to ten weeks of first instance work at circuit,—mainly in jury trials."[58]

The early opinions of the Second Circuit are characterized by their brevity. Few cases take more than two pages in the *Reports*. Dissent was infrequent; concurring opinions even rarer. There was a tendency, continued well into the twentieth century, to affirm per curiam on the opinion below or in open court without any opinion.

[53] Edward McWhinney calls Jerome Frank the "pioneer in modern times" of the professor-judge ("Judge Jerome Frank and Legal Realism: An Appraisal," *New York Law Forum,* 3 [1957], 113). At the turn of the century it was not too unusual for judges to lecture regularly at law schools.

[54] "Dinner in Honor of William J. Wallace," p. 20.

[55] Hough, *District Court*, p. 31.

[56] For the rules of the newly established courts, see *United States Circuit Court of Appeals Reports*, vol. 1.

[57] Lacombe, "Dinner in Honor of William J. Wallace," p. 51.

[58] *Ibid.,* p. 50.

Table 3. Distribution of Opinions—Second Circuit, 1893

Number of opinions[a]	112
Opinions by two-judge courts	53[b]
Opinions by	
Wallace	21
Lacombe	18
Shipman	29
Townsend[c]	2
Per curiam[a]	42
Dissenting opinions	3
Wallace	1
Shipman	1
Wheeler[d]	1

[a] Includes a number of memorandum decisions.
[b] Would be higher, but in some memorandum decisions the composition of the court is not given.
[c] Townsend, district judge for Connecticut, sat in three cases.
[d] Wheeler, district judge for Vermont, sat in three cases.

Table 3 gives an idea of how the court functioned in 1893.[59] It is based on volumes 4–7 of the *United States Circuit Court of Appeals Report*.[60] Noteworthy are the abundance of cases decided by two-judge courts and the liberal use of per curiam opinions.

During the court's first ten years its composition was unchanged. Two vacancies occurred in 1902. The first, resulting from the retirement of Judge Shipman, was filled by the appointment of William Townsend, the district judge for Connecticut who had sat occasionally on the appellate court. The second opening came about because Congress provided a fourth judge for the Second Circuit. The business of the court had grown to the point that it was difficult for the three judges to do all the work, although they had retired almost completely from trial court activity. It was not until 1929 that Congress increased the number of judges to five.

The new circuit judge was Alfred Conkling Coxe, who twenty years earlier had succeeded Wallace as the district judge for the Northern District of New York. Like so many of the early members of the Second Circuit, Coxe had sat on the appellate court prior to his appointment to it.

[59] A few of the cases are from late 1892. The selection of 1893 was arbitrary. For purposes of comparison and to trace possible changes throughout the years, I also analyzed cases for the years 1903, 1913, 1923, and 1933.

[60] Until 1933 decisions of the courts of appeals were published in the *United States Circuit Court of Appeals Reports* and the *Federal Reporter*, both put out by the West Publishing Company. The *Federal Reporter* at first also included cases from the district courts and for this reason I have used the *Circuit Reports*. After 1933 courts of appeals cases are reported only in the *Federal Reporter*; district court cases in the *Federal Supplement*.

· Study of the court's work in 1903 reveals little change from ten years earlier, except that there was a significant decrease in the number of cases decided by two-judge courts. Opinions were brief; many were per curiam or in open court, and dissent was infrequent.

The volume of business before the Second Circuit grew steadily. In 1907 Judge Lacombe complained that "the court used to begin the fourth week in October, holding three-week sessions, with a recess of two weeks 'to write opinions.' This last year we began the first week in October; the session for argument remained 'three-week,' but the recesses (all save one) shrank from two weeks to one." Judge Lacombe concluded, "We have reached the limit of the tether."[61]

If we consider the number of weeks in which a judge hears argument as a reliable indicator of how busy he is, the conclusion must be that the early judges of the Second Circuit were busier than their present-day counterparts. Today, judges on the Second Circuit usually hear arguments in no more than one week out of four.

Table 4 shows the business of the courts of appeals and the Second Circuit from 1892 to 1915. The figures are from the annual reports of the Attorney General. The business of the Court of Appeals for the District of Columbia was then reported separately and is not included in the totals for all the circuits. However, in each of the years the Second Circuit was busier than the District of Columbia court. It should be noted that before 1902 the Eighth Circuit had more work than the Second; after 1902 the Second Circuit was the busiest court of appeals. Also, despite its heavy workload, the Second Circuit often had fewer cases pending than some of the less busy courts.

It is difficult to determine whether during this period the Second Circuit was regarded as one of the strongest courts of appeals. It may not have been as highly respected as the Sixth Circuit, which was located in Chicago.[62]

In 1907 the Second Circuit experienced two changes in membership through the resignation of Judge Wallace and the death of Judge Townsend. Their replacements were Henry Galbraith Ward, a railroad attorney from New York City, and Walter Chadwick Noyes of Connecticut.

In the decade of 1910 the court handed down, on the average, more than two hundred opinions each year. While many of the cases were not too difficult to decide, the burden on the judges prevented them from writing lengthy opinions. Even reversals of district court

[61] Lacombe, "Dinner in Honor of William J. Wallace," pp. 50–51.

[62] Judge Wyzanski writes that Judge Augustus Hand regarded the Sixth Circuit during most of its first fifty years as one of the several strongest courts in the English-speaking world ("Augustus Noble Hand," p. 584).

Table 4. The Business of the Circuit Courts of Appeals
and the Second Circuit, 1892–1915

	All Circuits			Second Circuit		
Year	Docketed	Disposed	Pending	Docketed	Disposed	Pending
1892	841	403	438	196[a]	73	123
1893	704	542	431	116[a]	104[a]	87
1894	766	684	510	140[a]	127[a]	100
1895	866	870	510	189	186[a]	103
1896	815	824	501	145[a]	161	87
1897	775	729	547	142[a]	112[a]	117
1898	806	833	521	138	170[a]	85
1899	907	856	572	169[a]	165	89
1900	952	917	607	185	171[a]	103
1901	901	937	571	162[a]	163[a]	102
1902	1,003	907	667	184	179	107
1903	965	1,001	631	193	164[a]	136
1904	1,021	1,009	646	232	240	128
1905	1,126	1,036	725	283	262	149
1906	1,235	1,149	811	348	308	189
1907	1,193	1,243	761	257	318	128
1908	1,277	1,209	833	286	281	133
1909	1,283	1,254	862	319	315	137
1910	1,448	1,314	1,007	378	352	163
1911	1,245	1,388	864	279	333[a]	109
1912	1,241	1,219	881	275	244	140
1913	1,262	1,319	824	288	303	125
1914	1,380	1,243	961	303	309	119
1915	1,452	1,482	931	320	345	94

Note: The caution expressed previously (see n. 33 above) regarding the accuracy of
the statistics included in the yearly reports of the Attorney General pertains also to
the data presented in Table 4. I have no way of knowing whether the numbers given
for the cases docketed and disposed of are accurate. However, it is readily apparent
that there are many errors in the column of cases pending—all circuits. The yearly
increase or decrease in cases pending must correspond with the difference between the
number of cases docketed and disposed of. Yet, this is not true for many of the years,
1892–1915; in fact, there are discrepancies in the annual reports from one year to the
next as to how many cases were pending. For example, the 1893 Report puts the figure
at 431, but the Report for 1894 says that there were 428 cases pending at the end of
the previous year. This is but one of a number of such inconsistencies.

[a] Fewer than the Eighth Circuit.

decisions were brief; and reversals were frequent, averaging around 35
per cent of cases during the decade.[63]

Congress did not think it necessary to provide additional judges
and, interestingly, the reports of the Attorney General do not show
that requests for additional judicial manpower were made. The prevailing atmosphere to keep unchanged the number of judges is
probably linked with the establishment by Congress in 1910 of the

[63] The Attorney General began reporting percentages of reversal by the
courts of appeals in 1910.

ill-fated Commerce Court.[64] This court, which had jurisdiction of cases coming from the Interstate Commerce Commission, was composed of five newly appointed circuit judges. Congress provided that the Chief Justice of the United States could assign the judges of the Commerce Court to serve on any of the circuit courts of appeals or on the district courts. Chief Justice Edward D. White designated Judge Martin A. Knapp, the presiding judge of the Commerce Court, as an additional circuit judge for the Second Circuit. When the Commerce Court was abolished in 1913, Congress maintained the existing judgeships by providing that the Commerce Court judges be assigned to act as judges on the district courts and circuit courts of appeals. However, upon the death or resignation of these judges, the vacancies were not to be filled. Judge Knapp's assignment to the Second Circuit was continued until 1915, when he was transferred to duty in the Fourth Circuit.

Whatever help Judge Knapp may have given to the district courts of the circuit, he was not of much service to the Circuit Court of Appeals for the Second Circuit. In the year 1913 he did not once sit as an appellate judge on the court. Judge William H. Hunt of the Commerce Court, who was assigned to the Ninth Circuit, sat once on the Second Circuit during that year.

Judge Noyes resigned in 1913, giving as his reason his inability to provide comfortably for his family and the education of his children on the salary of $7,000.[65] He was succeeded by Henry Wade Rogers, Dean of the Yale Law School.[66] An analysis of the more than two hundred opinions handed down by the Second Circuit in 1913 reveals that the pattern first set when the court was established was still largely adhered to, though the panels usually were composed of three judges. Opinions continued to be brief, except for those of Judge Rogers, who had a habit of writing extremely long opinions.

[64] See Frankfurter and Landis, *Business of the Supreme Court*, pp. 153–74.

[65] During his less than six years on the bench, Noyes was the Second Circuit's leading dissenter, dissenting in 12 cases out of the 867 in which he participated (H. T. Newcomb, "Memorial of Walter C. Noyes," *Yearbook of the Association of the Bar of the City of New York*, 1927–28, p. 414).

[66] Born in 1853, Rogers was educated at the University of Michigan and was a protégé of Thomas M. Cooley, the great Dean of the Michigan Law School. He became a professor of law at Michigan in 1883 and in 1885, at the age of thirty-two, succeeded his mentor as dean. Five years later he was chosen President of Northwestern University, which he helped to build into one of the great universities in the midwest. In 1900 Rogers left Northwestern to teach at the Yale Law School. In 1903 he became Dean and served in that position until 1916, when he was forced out through faculty pressure and Thomas W. Swan was brought in to replace him. Rogers continued to teach at Yale until 1921.

In the early years of the twentieth century, the judges who served on the Southern District Court were men of exceptional talent. Between 1914 and 1916 four judges sat on this court: Charles M. Hough, Learned Hand, Julius M. Mayer, and Augustus Hand. Together they formed a group of judges seldom, if ever, equaled in ability on any bench in this country. Each of these judges was later to serve on the Circuit Court of Appeals for the Second Circuit.

Charles Merrill Hough, the first of the group to be appointed to the Second Circuit, was born in Philadelphia in 1858. The son of a soldier, he spent his boyhood at an army post; to his death he admired the soldier's life and would have chosen it had his health allowed. After graduating from Dartmouth College in 1879, he studied in a law office in Philadelphia. For twenty years he practiced law in New York City, during which time he attained a leading position in maritime law. In 1906 President Roosevelt appointed him to the Southern District bench despite some opposition because he "was identified too intimately with the Pennsylvania railroad interests."[67] In his ten years as a district judge he conducted 1,200 trials and filed 1,809 written opinions.[68] Although he was a Republican, President Wilson elevated him to the appellate court in 1916. Throughout his judicial career Judge Hough's life was constantly in peril because of very poor health; still, he did at least his share of the work in his courts. He died in 1927 at the age of sixty-eight.

By common consent, Judge Hough was one of the greatest judges in the history of the federal judiciary. Judge Wyzanski calls him "as distinguished a lower court judge as we ever had."[69] To Charles Evans Hughes "he stood in the foremost rank" among all the able judges who have served in New York City federal courts.[70] Chief Justice Taft, in particular, wanted him on the Supreme Court.[71] Holmes referred to Hough as "a good old admiralty judge," in a letter to Sir Frederick Pollock.[72] Hough is one of the nine great commercial law judges of the English-speaking world (three are Americans) to whom Karl Llewellyn dedicated his final book, *The Common Law Tradition.*

Today, Hough is almost completely forgotten and his work is ignored. Llewellyn writes that he "died substantially unknown out-

[67] *New York Times*, June 21, 1906, p. 7.

[68] *Dictionary of American Biography*, vol. 9, p. 249. Other sources for Hough are *The National Cyclopaedia of American Biography*, vol. 20, p. 190; Learned Hand, "Charles M. Hough," *Yearbook of the Association of the Bar of the City of New York, 1928*, p. 399.

[69] Wyzanski, "Augustus Noble Hand," p. 577.

[70] *New York Times*, April 23, 1927, p. 17.

[71] Wyzanski, "Augustus Noble Hand," p. 577.

[72] Mark DeWolfe Howe (ed.), *Holmes-Pollock Letters* (Cambridge: Harvard University Press, Belknap Press, 1961), vol. 2, p. 135.

side of New York City, and embittered. Practically every great opinion he had written had happened to go up, and had been completely superseded in authority and therefore in notice—often enough by a Lorenburnish [meaning an awful] job upstairs."[73] Charles C. Burlingham, on the other hand, said in a memorial that Hough's "life was exceptionally happy," but "he was impatient of irrelevance, incompetence and prolixity and at times presented a formidable and even alarming exterior."[74]

There has been no study of Judge Hough's career on the bench and, given the current ignorance of him, one appears unlikely. It may be well, then, to repeat the evaluation of one of his colleagues:

His mind was swift; his habit, of extraordinary concentration. He could master the contents of a record with a speed and completeness beyond his colleagues' powers. He was considerate in council, tolerant of differences, but inflexible after his own critical point of precipitation had been reached, not because he alone could be right, but because he lacked the discursive habit of mind. Discussion was not to him a part of action, and action must not be clogged. The mood which holds conclusions open, and is led

[73] Llewellyn, *The Common Law Tradition* (Boston: Little, Brown & Company, 1960), p. 318. Llewellyn cites Hough's posthumously published article "Concerning Lawyers," *Ohio State University Law Journal*, 5 (1938), 1, as evidence of this bitterness.

[74] Burlingham, "A Memorial From Bench and Bar to Charles Merrill Hough," (no publisher, 1927), p. 12. According to Judge Augustus Hand, in the years immediately before his death, Judge Hough "often showed a delightful humor that I had not at first realized that he could or would employ" (p. 13).

Hough's sense of humor is apparent in the following devastating remarks on student law review comments. It is from his address at the twenty-fifth anniversary dinner of the *Columbia Law Review* in 1925 and was reproduced in William D. Guthrie, "A Tribute to the United States Circuit Judge Charles M. Hough" (Address at Dinner December 21, 1926 [no publisher, pp. 6–7]). It is reprinted here because of its general interest.

"This well-written decision re-examines in a modern way a difficult subject. It frankly overrules several earlier decisions of the same court (an excellent procedure), and while flatly opposed to the Supreme Court of the United States in Doe v. Roe 360 U.S. 1001, is in accord with the more recent decision of the same court in Roe v. Doe 361 U.S. 1002. There are a few States which still refuse to apply the doctrine, but this decision falls squarely in line with the majority view, which is best expressed in Dives v. Lazarus, 5 New Zealand 25, and more recently set forth in Pharoah v. Moses, 2 Palestine 1. The English rule is somewhat stricter, drawing unwarranted distinction between Stellar and Lunar; but the general tendency in this country is toward liberality in all tender matters. There can be no monopoly in tenderness. Doubt should always be resolved in favor of freedom in exchange (citations from Arizona, Alaska, and Hawaii Reports). The principal case is well reasoned and seems to be correctly decided."

hither and yon as successive aspects arise, was indistinguishable from vacillation. He could not brood.

He was sensitive in his personal relations, given to almost extravagant personal loyalty and confidence, emotional and affectionate. He read widely, and retained an astonishing amount of general historical information. When he died the bar had come to recognize his authority in the admiralty as unequalled anywhere; he is unlikely for long to be followed by a successor comparable in knowledge and capacity. He probably understood the actual administration of the bankruptcy law better than any other judge alive.[75]

The author of the tribute was Judge Learned Hand, a man noted for the care with which he chose his words.

The next vacancy on the Second Circuit occurred in 1918, when Judge Coxe retired. It, too, was filled by a Southern District judge, but not by one of the three former colleagues of Judge Hough. Instead, the promotion went to Martin T. Manton, who only two years before had been appointed to the district court to fill Judge Hough's seat.

Manton was born in New York City in 1880. He was educated in city public schools and at Columbia University Law School, from which he graduated in 1901. He immediately began to practice law in Brooklyn and later formed a partnership with W. Bourke Cochran, a powerful leader in the Democratic Party in the city. His political connections advanced his career. When President Wilson appointed him to the district court he was only thirty-six, the youngest federal judge in the United States. When Judge Hough died in 1927, Manton became senior judge of the Second Circuit and participated actively in the work of the Conference of Senior Circuit Judges. In the years in which he served as the presiding judge, the Second Circuit was by far the busiest of the federal courts of appeals.

Manton's corruption and downfall were the result of his decision to remain active in business after his accession to the bench. By his own estimates, Manton had amassed more than a million dollars at the time of his appointment as district judge, much of it in real estate. His interests suffered considerably from the Depression, and in order to protect his investments he borrowed heavily from litigants and accepted outright payments from them.[76]

[75] Learned Hand, "Charles M. Hough," Yearbook, pp. 400–401.

[76] Manton's corruption could not have come as a complete surprise. In 1932 his actions in the I.R.T. Receivership case was a clear instance in which a judge was acting in a way to gain benefits for a particular party (Joseph Borkin, The Corrupt Judge [New York: Clarkson N. Potter, 1962], pp. 34–38). Even before this, on February 2, 1931, the New York Times, in a story on the bankruptcy of the Bank of the United States, reported that Manton had made very large unsecured personal loans from the Bank. In

Before he resigned, Manton was frequently honored by law schools and groups of lawyers. He was a gifted speaker and was often invited to address gatherings of lawyers. In August of 1938, several months before his case broke, Manton gave a speech in which he attributed the strength and stability of the American government to the independence of the judiciary.[77]

Using his political connections, Manton endeavored to win appointment to the Supreme Court. Surprisingly, in view of his party affiliation, during the 1920's he received serious consideration for the High Court. In 1922 he was one of three leading candidates to succeed Justice William R. Day. Manton received the strong backing of the Catholic Church in New York. Chief Justice Taft vigorously opposed Manton, whose appointment he thought would be a disaster, and the Judiciary Committee of the prestigious Association of the Bar of the City of New York "voted unanimously to do all in its power to stop Manton's drive for the Court."[78] Following this failure, Manton continued his efforts in the 1920's and 1930's to gain promotion, but he never again came as close to success as he was in 1922.[79]

Changes in the composition of the Second Circuit came fairly rapidly in the 1920's. Five men were appointed to the court; only the career of the first will be touched on here. The others—Learned Hand, Thomas Swan, Augustus Hand, and Harrie Chase—are subjected to more critical study in other chapters.

Julius Marshuetz Mayer was born in New York City in 1865. He was educated at City College and the Columbia University Law School, receiving his L.L.B. in 1886. For the next fifteen years he practiced law and was active in Republican Party affairs as a member of the "Old Guard."[80] He served for three years as a justice of the Court of Special Sessions in New York City and in 1904 was elected

---

1934, testifying before the Liquidators of the Bank of the United States, Manton disclosed that he had been insolvent since 1931 (Borkin, *Corrupt Judge*, p. 43) , Three years later there were newspaper reports of a Securities and Exchange Commission investigation of loans by one Samuel Ungerleider to Manton totaling $470,000 in 1929 and 1930, most of which was never repaid (*New York Times*, May 5, 1937, p. 37).

[77] *New York Times*, August 25, 1938, p. 13.

[78] See David J. Danelski, *A Supreme Court Justice Is Appointed* (New York: Random House, 1964, p. 74). Chapters 3 and 4 detail Manton's campaign and the Chief Justice's opposition. Danelski quotes Justice Jackson: "Manton had come within an ace of being appointed to the Supreme Court at the time of the appointment of Pierce Butler. I understand that it was only due to the intervention of Chief Justice Taft that this appointment was prevented" (p. 146) .

[79] *Ibid.*, pp. 195–96.

[80] *New York Times*, December 1, 1925, p. 1.

Attorney General for the state on the Republican ticket. He served for two years; a bid for a second term was thwarted. President Taft appointed him to the Southern District Court in 1912 and President Harding promoted him to the appellate bench in 1921. In 1924 he resigned and returned to private practice. He died suddenly in 1925 at the age of sixty.

Judge Mayer was very highly regarded by the bench and bar of his time.[81] By present-day standards, he must certainly be rated as ultra-conservative, if not reactionary, in civil liberty matters. During the world war period, he sustained the emergency measures of the government in every case brought before him. He presided at the famous trials of Alexander Berkman and Emma Goldman, who were prosecuted for conspiracy to violate the Selective Service law, and of Scott Nearing, who was tried under the Espionage Act of 1917. In a speech in 1919 he proclaimed: "There is only one way to deal with the Anarchist, and that is to eliminate all this nonsense about internationalism, and in every case where an Anarchist is not a citizen of the United States—and there are few who are,—send him back from whence he came. Rid the country of them. We do not want them here."[82]

In 1923 the court handed down more than 250 written opinions. The judges, with the exception of Rogers, wrote brief opinions. Manton was the most active judge, writing 55 times for the court and authoring half of the 14 dissents; 4 cases were certified to the Supreme Court. Forty times the judges made use of the time-saving device of handing down a one-sentence memorandum decision. Clearly, the members of the Second Circuit were busy men. The Conference of Senior Circuit Judges repeatedly requested a fifth judge for the court, and in 1929, after much delay, Congress agreed.

The nucleus of the 1941–51 Second Circuit was formed in the middle and final years of the 1920's. Learned Hand succeeded Mayer in 1924 and, two years later, when Judge Rogers died, Thomas Swan joined the court. In 1927 the vacancy caused by the death of Judge Hough was filled by Augustus Hand. Harrie Chase was appointed to the new seat created by Congress.

Table 5 is a continuation of Table 4 and shows the trend of business in the circuit courts of appeals and Second Circuit from 1916 through 1939. From 1935 on, the business of the District of Columbia Court of Appeals is included in the overall totals. It should be noted that there was a substantial rise in 1924 in the totals for all the

---

[81] Charles M. Hough, "Julius M. Mayer," *Yearbook of the Association of the Bar of the City of New York, 1926*, p. 463.

[82] *The Law of Free Speech* (pamphlet issued by the National Security League, 1919).

Table 5. The Business of the Circuit Courts of Appeals
and the Second Circuit, 1916–39

Year	All Circuits			Second Circuit		
	Docketed	Disposed	Pending	Docketed	Disposed	Pending
1916	1,518	1,459	990	349	341	102
1917	1,447	1,487	950	296	298	100
1918	1,320	1,477	793	245	279	66
1919	1,324	1,338	779	272	257	81
1920	1,308	1,242	845	292	265	108
1921	1,471	1,372	944	282[a]	268[a]	122
1922	1,621	1,587	978	378	404	96
1923	1,704	1,731	951	333	322	107
1924	2,131	1,898	1,184	484	441	150
1925	2,156	2,175	1,165	419	441	128
1926	2,278	2,208	1,235	464	435	157
1927	2,212	2,293	1,154	413	428[b]	142
1928	2,204	2,159	1,199	405[a]	417	130
1929	2,501	2,296	1,404	451	444[b]	137
1930	2,549	2,646	1,307	463	458	142
1931	2,649	2,710	1,246	563	552	153
1932	2,950	2,838	1,358	614	608	159
1933	2,771	2,824	1,305	642	638	163
1934	3,076	2,886	1,495	643	635	171
1935	3,514	3,452	1,674[c]	706	691	186
1936	3,521	3,526	1,669	676	646	216
1937	3,231	3,215	1,685	648	714	150
1938	3,218	3,113	1,790	629	605	174
1939	3,318	3,442	1,666	579	614	139

[a] Slightly less than the Court of Appeals for the District of Columbia.
[b] Less than the Eighth Circuit.
[c] Although the excess of cases docketed over dispositions was only 62, the number of cases pending increased by 189 because starting with this year the business of the Court of Appeals for the District of Columbia was included in the totals for all circuits. There were 117 cases pending in the District of Columbia court.

circuits and the Second Circuit. Except for four years, the Second Circuit was the busiest circuit in the number of cases docketed and disposed of. During the 1930's the Second Circuit was by far the busiest circuit. At the same time, it was behind some of the other circuits in the number of cases pending at the end of the year.

An examination of the Second Circuit's opinions in 1933 illustrates how busy the court and its judges were in the 1930's. In that year the court handed down 317 written opinions. As had been true of the previous forty years, opinions were, in general, brief. Manton wrote 70 opinions for the court, Learned Hand 59, Swan 56, Chase 50, Augustus Hand 48, and per curiam opinions numbered 34. Because of the heavy workload, the judges resorted frequently to memorandum decisions. In addition to the written opinions, there were 115 summary dispositions, in most of which the court affirmed without opinion the decision below. There were 21 dissenting opinions, rather low in view of the large case load and by comparison with 1941–51. Learned Hand led in this department with 6 dissents; there were also 7 concurring opinions.

The composition of the Second Circuit remained unchanged for a decade after Chase's appointment. The events of 1939–41—Manton's resignation, the addition of a sixth judgeship, Patterson's brief tenure on the court, and the appointments of Charles Clark and Jerome Frank—were described in the opening chapter. Another decade of stability in membership followed these changes, interrupted by the resignation of Learned Hand in 1951.

In the years since 1951 the Second Circuit has undergone many changes in membership as a total of thirteen judges have been appointed to the court. By way of comparison, in the thirty-year period 1921–51, only eight appointments were made. As a result of this lack of stability, and for other reasons that will be mentioned shortly, the court's reputation has suffered considerably.

The first of the new judges after Learned Hand stepped down was Harold R. Medina, who had presided over the trial of the top leaders of the Communist Party in the Southern District Court. It is widely believed that Medina was selected by President Truman in order to stifle criticism that his administration was soft on communism. Medina retired in 1958, although he has continued to serve as a senior judge.

Judge Swan's replacement was Carroll C. Hincks, a federal district judge in Connecticut, who retired completely from judicial work after six years on the Second Circuit. The tenure of Augustus Hand's successor, John Marshall Harlan—a grandson of the illustrious Supreme Court justice of the same name—lasted only a year, as Harlan became the second judge ever on the Second Circuit to be promoted to the Supreme Court.

The next five of President Eisenhower's seven appointees to the Second Circuit continue to serve on the court. J. Edward Lumbard is now senior in service and since 1960 he has been chief judge of the Second Circuit. Actually, the margin of his seniority is one day, for a day after he was appointed, on July 13, 1955, Sterry R. Waterman of Vermont was named to succeed Judge Chase of the same state, who had retired.

The vacancy caused by the death of Jerome Frank was filled by Leonard P. Moore, perhaps the most conservative member of the Second Circuit today. Eisenhower's most distinguished appointee to the court is Judge Henry J. Friendly, who joined the bench upon Medina's retirement. As a student in the 1920's, Friendly compiled one of the best scholastic records in the history of the Harvard Law School and after graduation served as law clerk to Justice Brandeis. The

Republican President's final appointment was that of J. Joseph Smith of Connecticut, who was promoted from the district court to succeed Judge Hincks.

The size of the Second Circuit remained at six until 1961, despite urgent pleas throughout the 1950's for additional manpower. In that year, Congress in one piece of legislation added close to one hundred new judges to federal courts throughout the country and the Second Circuit was enlarged to nine judges.[83] Almost immediately there was intense competition and "politicking" for the new seats. President Kennedy was also faced with the problem of establishing a new balance among the states comprising the Second Circuit to replace the old one of three seats to New York, two to Connecticut, and one to Vermont. Lawyers' groups in New York City, particularly those in the Southern District, felt strongly that since the large majority of appeals originate in the city, the new judges should come from that area. The President agreed.

One of the three new judges was Irving R. Kaufman, who as a Southern District judge (since 1941) had long conducted an intense and not too secret campaign to secure promotion to the appellate bench. Kaufman had presided over the prosecutions of the Rosenbergs and the "delegates" to the Apalachin "crime convention."

The second seat went to Paul R. Hays, a professor at the Columbia University Law School and former chairman of the Liberal Party in New York State; it is believed that his appointment was a reward for the support given to the Kennedy candidacy by the party in 1960.

The final appointee was Thurgood Marshall, who had gained national prominence as the counsel for the National Association for the Advancement of Colored People. Clearly there were important political considerations in the President's action. After an unusually long delay the Senate approved Marshall, who, however, did not remain on the court very long. In August 1965 he resigned to become Solicitor General of the United States, a post he held for a year and a half before being appointed to the Supreme Court. Marshall's departure created a vacancy on the Second Circuit that was filled by Wilfred Feinberg, who is now its junior member. This was President Johnson's second appointment to the Second Circuit; earlier he had named Robert P. Anderson, the latest of many Connecticut district judges to be promoted to the appellate bench, to succeed Judge Charles Clark.

[83] During most of the 1950's Congress was controlled by the Democrats, who were not eager to create new opportunities for President Eisenhower to appoint Republicans to judgeships. So they ignored the alarms of the Judicial Conference of the United States. Their tune changed quickly when President Kennedy took office and they added more judges than the Judicial Conference requested.

The record of the Second Circuit in the 1920's and 1930's is remarkable when contrasted with the business of the court in recent years. As Table 6 shows, from 1940 to 1960, when the court had six members, the highest number of cases filed in any year was 595; the average for the period was about 420. The ten-year average of cases filed for the 1920–29 court that consisted of four judges was 392; the yearly average of the five-judge 1930–39 court was a phenomenal 616 cases. In view of the persistent complaint of overworked judges voiced during the 1950's by Second Circuit members before meetings of the Judicial Conference of the United States and congressional committees, the question arises, how were the judges of earlier years able to dispose of so large a volume of cases without falling behind in their dockets

Table 6. The Business of the Courts of Appeals and the Second Circuit, 1940–69

Year	All Circuits			Second Circuit		
	Docketed	Disposed	Pending	Docketed	Disposed	Pending
1940	3,446	3,434	1,678	572	554	157
1941	3,213	3,448	1,443[a]	533	548	142
1942	3,228	2,999	1,714[a]	501	471	172
1943	3,093	3,197	1,610	499	504	167
1944	3,072	3,039	1,643	595	547	215
1945	2,730	2,848	1,525	466	520	161
1946	2,627	2,621	1,531	425	450	136
1947	2,615	2,654	1,492	378	386	128
1948	2,758	2,577	1,673	381	378	131
1949	2,989	2,753	1,909	344	351	124
1950	2,830	3,064	1,675	318	355	87
1951	2,982	2,829	1,828	361	319	129
1952	3,079	3,048	1,859	340	349	120
1953	3,226	3,043	1,845[b]	352	359	113
1954	3,481	3,192	2,134	366	325	154
1955	3,695	3,654	2,175	581	453	282
1956	3,588	3,734	2,029	462	480	264
1957	3,701	3,687	2,043	533	459	338
1958	3,694	3,704	2,033	506	506	338
1959	3,754	3,753	2,034	520	511	347
1960	3,899	3,713	2,220	582	554	375
1961	4,204	4,049	2,375	674	663	386
1962	4,823	4,167	3,031	582	553	415
1963	5,437	5,011	3,457	695	697	413
1964	6,023	5,700	3,780	717	660	470
1965	6,766	5,771	4,775	860	798	532
1966	7,183	6,571	5,387	876	791	617
1967	7,903	7,527	5,763	979	959	637
1968	9,116	8,264	6,615	1,072	1,101	608
1969	10,248	9,014	7,849	1,263	932	939

[a] In the 1942 Report, the number of cases pending at the end of the previous year was given as 1,485 and not 1,443.
[b] Obviously there is something wrong in the pending figure for this year.

while the better-manned courts of more recent years invariably fall behind?

Before attempting to answer this question, two points must be made about the data in Table 6. The first is that the source of these data is the Annual Reports of the Director of the Administrative Office of United States Courts, while for pre-1940 years the source is the annual reports of the Attorney General. This may not mean much, but we do know that collection of statistics on the work of the federal courts was not taken as seriously before the creation of the Administrative Office as it was after. Thus, it is possible that the statistics for the years before 1940 are not as reliable as the data reported by the Administrative Office.

A second point to be made is that there is a distinct difference between the performance of the Second Circuit in the 1940's and the court's record after Learned Hand retired in 1951. Later on it will be seen that although under Learned Hand the Second Circuit was the busiest court of appeals, it had the best record of any of these courts with respect to the number of cases pending at the end of each year and the time that was required to dispose of cases. On the other hand, as Table 6 shows, from about 1954 the court has had great difficulty keeping up with its case load. Moreover, since 1951 the court has had one of the poorest records of any of the circuits in the time required for disposition of cases.

Now to return to the question raised by the comparison of the business of the court of the 1920's and 1930's with the record of recent years. Clearly, the answer does not lie in the size of the court, since in the 1920's the Second Circuit had four judges, in the 1930's five judges, and from 1940 to 1961 six judges. Now there are nine judges. Moreover, until Learned Hand retired there were no retired (now called senior) judges to ease the burden. Also, it was not the practice of the Second Circuit to rely much on district judges or judges from other circuits, whereas in the 1950's as much as 40 per cent of the court's work was done by outside judges.[84]

Another explanation—one that I think would be favored by many of the earlier judges—is that present-day judges do not work as hard as the former judges did. Certainly, if we base our judgment on quantitative data, the available evidence supports this view. However, it is at best hazardous (and, at worst, erroneous) to evaluate the workload of judges on such raw statistics as the number of cases filed per judge. Professor Hart's attempted reconstruction of the Supreme Court

[84] Testimony of Chief Judge Lumbard, U.S., Congress, House, Subcommittee No. 5 of the Committee on the Judiciary, 86th Cong., 2d sess., 1960, p. 209.

workday makes at least this much clear.[85] More convincing evidence of how busy judges are is provided by the number of weeks they devote to listening to argument. The present practice is for each judge to hear argument one week each month and to spend the other weeks working on opinions. In the 1920's and 1930's the Second Circuit judges sat two, and at times three, weeks each month to hear argument. Charles A. Horsky, who clerked for Augustus Hand in the mid-1930's, has testified to the burdens of that period: "Indeed, in my day the volume of cases was so great that in a few weeks after the opening of court in the fall the piles of briefs and records in cases assigned to him for opinion would begin to expand along the length of a long table in his chambers, and some . . . would be tentatively earmarked for the next summer at Elizabethtown. Summers were not vacations."[86]

While it is convenient to accept the "judges used to work harder" explanation, as expected, it runs directly counter to the views of the present judges, some of whom are able to point to piles of records in their chambers as imposing as those seen by Horsky. One of these judges said in an interview that in his first five years on the Second Circuit he "worked almost every night and weekend."[87]

Several of the present judges say that cases coming to the court are more complex than in former times and, as a result, they claim that opinions are longer and more difficult to prepare and it takes longer to dispose of the cases on the docket. There is some evidence to support this contention. A significant number of cases come from administrative agencies and these often pose complex and technical questions. Moreover, trials in the district courts take longer than they used to and this means that on review there are voluminous records with which to contend.

However, the increased complexity of litigation alone is not sufficiently pronounced to account for the fact that Second Circuit judges hear fewer cases, write fewer opinions, and take more time doing their work than their predecessors. After all, cases in the 1950's and 1960's are not that much more difficult than those that confronted the Learned Hand court, which had a heavy docket and was able to dispose of its business with reasonable dispatch. Also, judges of the past decades seem agreed that fully two-thirds of appeals are virtually

[85] Henry M. Hart, Jr., "The Time Chart of the Justices," *Harvard Law Review,* 73 (1959), 84; Thurman Arnold, "Professor Hart's Theology," *Harvard Law Review,* 73 (1960), 298; Erwin N. Griswold, "Of Time and Attitudes—Professor Hart and Judge Arnold," *Harvard Law Review,* 74 (1960), 81; William O. Douglas, "The Supreme Court and Its Case Load," *Cornell Law Quarterly,* 45 (1960), 401.

[86] Horsky, "Augustus N. Hand." *Harvard Law Review,* 68 (1955), 1120.

[87] Judge Leonard P. Moore, December 11, 1962.

frivolous and present little difficulty. In the one week a month that they sit, the judges are unlikely to come across more than three or four hard cases.

Much of the difference between the former and the present judges may be in their work habits. Now, as in the past, judges work hard, but for a variety of factors relating to judicial style it now takes longer for Second Circuit judges to dispose of cases. To a limited extent the complexity of a small number of cases and the larger records are responsible; more important, I believe, are such factors as the lack of previous judicial experience of many of the Second Circuit judges since 1951, the intrusion of dicta in opinions, the trend toward longer opinions even in easy cases, the poor quality of advocacy, the frequency of dissent, inability of judges to make up their minds quickly, and, finally, the simple fact that a number of the judges are unable to write with facility or grace.

In the 1920's and 1930's many of these factors were not present. During this period cases were, in general, less complex and records were briefer. So were the opinions and many cases were disposed of summarily. Moreover, the judges in these years wrote few time-consuming concurrent and dissenting opinions.

When Learned Hand was chief judge, dissent was common, issues were contentious, opinions were longer, cases had become more difficult, and the judges made little use of the time-saving device of deciding summarily. That the six judges serving during these years did not fall behind in their work is a tribute to the ability and one measure of the quality of Learned Hand's court.

In the 1950's, five of these six judges died or retired and there were numerous changes in the Second Circuit's personnel. Several judges appointed to the court served only briefly. In the 1950's the court also had three chief judges after Learned Hand. Under the circumstances, it was not easy to integrate the new men effectively—most of them had never served as judges—into the court's work or to establish a pattern that would overcome the pressures for delay. The fact that the Second Circuit relied so heavily on outside judges did not help matters much because, at times, these judges were less determined than the regulars to keep up with the court's docket and they were in little hurry to get their (Second Circuit) opinions written. The total effect of all of these factors has been that after Learned Hand the Second Circuit's efficiency record has been poor.

At present many of the causes of delay remain. Cases are as difficult as ever, the records seem to grow even fatter, and the judges continue to write many dissenting opinions. Moreover, the willingness to hear cases en banc, which will be discussed in the next chapter, can only add to the burden on the judges. On the other hand, there is a growing tendency on the Second Circuit to treat easy cases summarily. Also, the court now consists of nine judges and the rate of turnover has slowed so that the 1970 court has far more experience than the court of the preceding two decades. As a result, there may be reason to believe that in the coming years the performance of the Second Circuit will once more be one of the finest of the courts of appeals. At the same time, the continued increase in the number of appeals might continue to prevent the court from keeping abreast of its docket. When Congress authorized three additional judges for the Second Circuit, it also provided for quite a few new judges for the district courts within the circuit, particularly the Southern District of New York. The added burden on the appellate court is particularly reflected in the large increase in appeals over the last half-dozen years, as shown in Table 6. There were 1,263 appeals docketed in 1969, as compared with 520 a decade earlier. While the number of cases disposed of has also risen sharply, dispositions have not kept pace with filings, so that at the end of fiscal 1969 the Second Circuit had a record 939 cases pending.[88] Clearly, the court is not out of the rough yet.

[88] A record, that is, for the Second Circuit. The situation in several other circuits was even worse.

3

The Decision-Making Process*

ONE TERM OF THE UNITED STATES COURT OF APPEALS FOR THE SECOND
Circuit is held annually in New York City, beginning either on the
last Monday in September or the first Monday in October. Although
the court is authorized to sit anywhere within its circuit, it very rarely
sits elsewhere than at the United States Courthouse at Foley Square in
lower Manhattan.

The courtroom of the Second Circuit is located on the seventeenth
floor of the courthouse. The room is handsome and well furnished,
with more than enough space for counsel, law clerks, and spectators.
On a typical day when the court is hearing argument, the room is
almost empty. As the day progresses, there usually are not more than a
dozen or so persons in the room, including judges, clerks, counsel, and
spectators. When the court meets, there is no feeling in the room of
excitement and importance, of momentous decisions in the making.[1]

---

* In most respects, with some important changes that are detailed in this
chapter, the court functions today in much the same manner as it did from
1941 to 1951. Consequently, the general description set forth here of the
Second Circuit's operations is applicable both to the Learned Hand period
and the present court.

[1] Opinions of the judges are filed and not read in court. Only rulings
on motions and some summary decisions in very easy cases are made in
open court.

To the outsider, the atmosphere is completely relaxed and unhurried; drama, whatever there is of it in the operation of the Second Circuit, is reserved for the private conferences of the judges and other nonpublic aspects of the work of the court. In this setting one of the nation's most important courts goes about its business.

All of the active judges and the senior judges who participate in the court's work have chambers in the courthouse. The judges from Connecticut and Vermont also have chambers in United States government buildings (usually the post office) in the cities in which they live, which they use when they are away from New York. The New York City offices are used when the judges are hearing arguments.

For the Learned Hand court, the use of hometown offices had a significant impact on relations among the judges. Three of its six members—Judges Swan, Chase, and Clark—did not live in New York and were commuters. Judge Jerome Frank spent a good deal of his time in New Haven, though his home was in New York City. This dispersal is not found on the Supreme Court, all of whose members live in the Washington area and are in frequent direct contact with one another.

The physical dispersal of the Second Circuit judges precluded their coalescing into a closely knit social group. Chase preferred to spend as much time as he could in Brattleboro, Vermont, and he never became very friendly with any of his colleagues, including those with whom he served for a quarter of a century. Clark commuted to New York, and usually returned to New Haven the same day. While on the bench, his closest attachments were at Yale. Also, the Hands and Swan were almost a generation older than the others; by the time Clark and Frank came to the Second Circuit the older men had long-established friendships, developed over many years of important activity. In a way, though, a warm relationship came into being between Learned Hand and Frank.

This lack of social cohesion was reflected in an addendum to a memorandum sent by Clark to Learned Hand expressing "some regret that we are not to have our pictures taken as a group. If the Supreme Court can do it once or twice a year, cannot some of us lesser guys have it done at least once in twelve years or perhaps longer? Am I wrong in thinking that it might conceivably be of some historic value to see us together on at least a single occasion?"[2]

Of far greater importance than its social effect was the impact of separation on the court's decisional process. On appellate courts,

---

[2] CEC to LH, October 25, 1950 (see the Preface and List of Abbreviations for list of initials used and location of letters cited).

bargaining is a factor in decision-making. The structure of bargaining, the manner in which judges deal with one another, is determined by personal relations, tradition, formal rules, location of participants, and perhaps other conditions as well. Ideally, bargaining should be direct and verbal, either through regularly scheduled conferences or informal meetings and discussions. Invariably, when judges (or others in a bargaining situation) meet face to face the likelihood for understanding of positions and resolution of conflict is enhanced. On the Second Circuit, as is true of other courts, there are three media for direct contacts among judges. They are the judges' conference scheduled after argument, in chambers when a judge drops in on a colleague to discuss a matter, and in more informal settings such as at lunch. However, except for the conferences—and even these were at times cut short to allow a judge to catch a train home—the opportunities for the Learned Hand court judges to bargain directly were curtailed as a result of the separate locations of half of the court. This led to a reliance on more indirect forms of interaction such as intracourt memoranda and letters.

For Judges Swan and Chase, commuting posed no special problems in their relations with colleagues; both were laconic men, not given to much dissent, and quite willing to resolve differences quickly through direct discussion. But the long distance dealings created communications problems for Judge Clark, particularly in his relations with Jerome Frank.

Clark was the Second Circuit's leading dissenter and an inveterate letter writer. He had more confidence in written communications than conferences; as he once put it: "Since I am not in New York so as to have available personal conference continuously, I find it often rather difficult to get over points and doubts which could be quite easily resolved by direct conference. The one way I could do it, however, is by writing something very definite by way of concurrence or dissent; this brings the point right at issue, and often we can then work out a way of proceeding of some satisfaction to all."[3]

Despite Judge Clark's belief in the efficacy of his form of bargaining, it appears that its major effect was to exacerbate disagreement on the court. There was a tendency for the correspondents to indulge in extended exegetical analysis of collegial letters; certainly, in relations between Clark and Frank this was usually the case. Answer-

[3] CEC to Judge Evan A. Evans of the Seventh Circuit Court of Appeals, March 8, 1945. Evans was one of the few visiting circuit judges to sit on the Second Circuit during Learned Hand's chief judgeship.

ing (and often accusing) letters would go back and forth for weeks and even months before an issue was exhausted, but not settled. Had they talked things over a little more, the history of the Learned Hand period might have turned out differently.[4]

The court sits about twenty-six weeks a year, from early October until the middle or end of June, according to a schedule prepared by the chief judge at the beginning of each term after consultation with the other judges. If necessary, the court also sits during the summer in emergency session to dispose of business that cannot wait.

Actually, the term hardly ends in June, as it does for the Supreme Court, with all argued cases disposed of. Bargaining, opinion-writing and filing, and much of the usual work of the court continue through the summer, although new appeals ordinarily are not heard.

When hearing argument, the court meets Monday through Friday from 10:30 A.M. until about 1:30 P.M. There is no particular reason for the 10:30–1:30 session, which interferes with the accustomed lunch hour of the judges and counsel. However, it does allow commuting judges to get to the courthouse on time without having to rise at a very early hour. It is a small miracle that Second Circuit judges who use the New Haven Railroad have been able to arrive on time. The judges usually try to wind up the session before 1:30 and they generally succeed.

The court sits in panels of three judges, except when it sits en banc. As we shall see, Learned Hand was doggedly opposed to full court hearings, and during his chief judgeship and several years thereafter, only the panel system was employed. For all of the federal courts of appeals, Congress has authorized two judges to constitute a quorum, so that if one of the assigned judges does not participate, his two remaining colleagues decide the appeal.

As a rule, the panels are composed in a manner that equalizes the work of the judges and provides as many combinations of judges as possible. The Second Circuit's present complement of nine judges forms up to eighty-four different combinations. While ordinarily each panel sits for an entire week, it is common for more than three judges to hear argument in any given week. At times, a retired Second Circuit judge or a judge from another federal court serves on the Second Circuit for a portion of a week.

In recent years much of the work of the court has been performed by judges who are not regular members of its bench, by district judges

[4] In the course of one long and sharp Clark-Frank hassle in mid-1942, just a year or so after Frank joined the court, Frank wrote: "I wish you had spoken to me about the matter when you were here the other day. And I wish that we had an opportunity, sometime soon, to chat together" (June 30, 1942).

and by other circuit judges.[5] In 1953 an important criminal appeal was decided by a panel composed of Judges Learned Hand, Thomas Swan, and Augustus Hand, all retired.[6]

Unless the practice is abused, there should be little argument with assignment of district judges to occasional duty on the appellate bench. Virtually all the courts of appeals have at one time or another made use of such judges, although it was a rare occurrence on the Learned Hand court, which tended to rely on its own personnel. These assignments are usually given to trial judges with considerable experience in order to familiarize them with the operations of the appellate court and also as an expression of respect for them by their "superiors." In view of the difficulty that district courts have in keeping up with their case loads, assignment to appellate work ought to be selective and cautious.[7]

Several Second Circuit judges, including the present Chief Judge, have served as trial judges on district courts within the circuit. They believe that this enables them to better appreciate the problems of trial work.[8] Of course, all circuit judges serve once in a while as members of special three-judge district courts which try cases raising important constitutional questions. Federal (as well as state) judges may get involved in time-consuming work that does not evolve out of the responsibilities of their office. Activity of this sort can be for governmental or private agencies; while usually it is strictly voluntary,

[5] After the death of Justice Jackson in 1954, Justice Frankfurter was temporarily assigned circuit justice for the Second Circuit. During his brief tenure of about five months, he briefly revived the practice of circuit-riding and several times served as presiding judge over a panel.

[6] United States v. Remington, 208 F.2d 567 (2d Cir. 1953).

[7] "Although it is recognized that benefits are to be derived from occasional participation by district judges in appellate work, the circuit judges think that the practice should not be availed of as extensively as the Court [Fourth Circuit] has been obliged to do. It unduly interrupts district judges in their own work and it sacrifices a measure of continuity of decision desirable in an appellate court" (Memorandum of Chief Judge Simon E. Sobeloff, U.S., Congress, House, Subcommittee No. 5 of the Committee on the Judiciary, 86th Cong., 2d sess., 1960, p. 316).

[8] Judge Clark apparently was the only one during 1941–51 to sit as a trial judge while on the appellate bench. In fact, a decision of his was reversed by a Second Circuit panel consisting of Learned Hand, Chase, and Frank (Pure Oil Co. v. Puritan Oil Co., 127 F.2d 6 [2d Cir. 1942]). In another case decided at the same time, Clark dissented from a majority decision adhering to Pure Oil and defended his trial court ruling: "The recent decisions in this Circuit on this problem, while disclosing small variations of fact, seem to me irreconcilable on any readily apparent grounds of logic or practical expediency. I can only express the hope that the bar and the district judges are not as mystified as to the law of this Circuit as I am" (Musher Foundation Inc. v. Alba Trading Co. Inc., 127 F.2d 9, 12 [2d Cir. 1942]).

judges are often remunerated for their services. During the Second World War several of the Second Circuit's judges did special work for federal agencies. For a time, Learned Hand—who agreed with Holmes that it was not the judge's job to do "justice"—was chairman of the Advisory Board on Just Compensation, which prompted Judge Clark to ask, "Do you think that it is 'compatible with the judicial function' for judges to be dealing with 'just compensation' or anything at all that must be 'just'? I thought we dealt with the law, not justice."[9] Extrajudicial activity is warranted so long as it does not conflict with judicial responsibilities or impede a court's efficiency. It did not do so for the Learned Hand Court, which compiled an outstanding administrative record. But after a generation of uninterrupted pleas for more judges—both state and federal—to reduce huge case backlogs, it may be that judges should be very cautious before undertaking outside work. The disclosures of Justice Fortas' outside activities have served to bring about a strong reaction against almost all forms of extrajudicial work, including activities which until recently were not questioned seriously.

There is little argument that, where possible, retired judges who wish to continue their judicial service should be allowed to do so.[10] These judges are men of great experience and can aid their colleagues without placing any new burdens on them or the judicial system. In addition, a psychological lift is given to the retired judges, who are made to feel that they still have a role to play, and are needed, in the court where they spent many of their active years.[11]

On the other hand, the assignment of judges from other circuits for limited work on a court of appeals has drawn much criticism from congressmen and even judges. There has been some feeling that the statute providing for such assignments has been abused and that they have been made to satisfy the desires of particular judges rather than to serve the needs of the federal courts.[12] These assignments are often

[9] CEC to LH, November 23, 1943.

[10] For more than a quarter of a century, until Learned Hand stepped down in 1951, the Second Circuit had no retired judges to supplement its regular work force. Since that time, it has had the services of a number of them.

[11] There is also a significant advantage to the retired judge who elects to remain on active duty; he keeps his office and staff. While they sit, these judges exercise full judicial authority, except that they are not members of the judicial council of their circuit and under the present statute are not permitted to sit en banc.

[12] For example, on April 12, 1960, Congressman Frank Bow charged in Congress that intercircuit assignments were made to fit the desires of the judges and not according to the requirements of efficient administration of justice. "I point out to you, however, that one of the most congested districts in the entire United States is the Southern District of New York. They tell

made in conjunction with planned vacations. Chief Judge John Biggs of the Third Circuit, which is located in Philadelphia, testified in 1960 that it was easier to get judges to go to Philadelphia when the Phillies had a better baseball team.[13] A potentially more serious defect in the intercircuit assignment of judges is that when the assigned judge returns to sit on his regular court his attention is directed to the problems and cases confronting that court and he is in no hurry to conclude the business still unfinished from his temporary service elsewhere. In July of 1946, Judge Peter Woodbury of the First Circuit, after a brief assignment to the Second Circuit, wrote to Judge Swan that because he was "rather deeply involved with some elusive problems of Puerto Rican law and application of constitutional principles thereto," he could not get out a draft of an opinion assigned to him before September.[14] A half-dozen years later, Harrie Chase wrote to Clark thanking him for prodding visiting Judge Biggs of the Third Circuit into action. "I had been on the verge of trying to do that for some time but kept putting it off, because he was a visiting judge, in the hope that he would get the work done."[15]

As a result of the criticism of the intercircuit assignment system, the Judicial Conference of the United States in 1960 adopted a plan which restricts assignments to situations "beneficial to the judicial system as a whole."[16]

The question of misuse aside, there are several good reasons why intercircuit assignments should be stopped completely, even if it could be shown (which is doubtful) that they contribute to improved administration in the federal courts. These reasons stem from the circuit system itself, which, as it has developed, leaves each circuit free to operate as it pleases. Even the uniform rules of appellate procedure which have been recently adopted did not bring about a uniform decisional process in the courts of appeals.

This point is readily illustrated by reference to the Second Circuit. Unlike the overwhelming majority of federal and state appellate courts which hold their conferences to discuss argued cases either the same day as argument or shortly thereafter, the Second Circuit's long-stand-

---

us they need more judges there. In our hearings we are told stories about their congested dockets, but let me say to you that they have time to travel to California and try cases out in California; and, lo and behold, around theater season . . . the California judges find time to go to New York to try cases" (U.S., Congress, House, Subcommittee No. 5" of the Committee on the Judiciary, 87th Cong., 1st sess., 1961, p. 425).

[13] Hearings before Subcommittee No. 5, 1960, p. 284.

[14] From the files of Judge Clark.

[15] HBC to CEC, September 12, 1952.

[16] Hearings before Subcommittee No. 5, 1961, pp. 438–39.

ing practice is to hold the conference the week after argument. In the interim, panel members are busy writing memoranda on the cases to be considered at the conference. Visiting judges are not assigned for more than a week, and unless they remain in New York—perhaps reluctantly—there is apt to be some difficulty in disposing the appeals heard by them.

Moreover, many, though not all, of these judges have found the Second Circuit's memorandum system bothersome, if not an outright waste of time and energy. They do not see why it should be necessary for each panel member to write a preliminary opinion in most of the cases he hears. It is rumored, for example, that Calvert Magruder, former chief judge of the First Circuit and a very highly regarded federal judge, refused to prepare memoranda during his period of service on the Second Circuit in the October 1960 term. It is said that this, and his delays in getting out opinions assigned to him, displeased Chief Judge Lumbard, an apparent believer in the adage "When in Rome, do as the Romans do."

A more crucial aspect of the circuit system further undermines the rationality of intercircuit assignment. It is not always sufficiently appreciated, even among lawyers, that the courts of appeals sharply disagree on various legal matters that may not be decided with finality by the Supreme Court. The pages of the *Federal Reporter* are replete with specific rejections by courts of appeals of decisions of other circuits, and in a good percentage of these, probably more than half, the Supreme Court does not quickly resolve the conflict. In addition to overt conflicts, there are numerous differences between circuits which are more subtle, such as the varying approaches to administrative agency rulings; for these, the word of a court of appeals is the law of the circuit.

Obviously, outside judges should not follow the law of their own circuit when it is in open conflict with that of the circuit they are visiting; but do they always adhere to the decisions of their temporary court? At home there is a tendency to follow circuit precedents even when contrary to personal judgment. Should the same be true of intercircuit assignments?

This problem came up several times in the 1940's, although the Learned Hand court made little use of outside judges. One of these, Judge Evan Evans of the Seventh Circuit, made it clear that "when sitting in the 2d Circuit a question arises which has arisen before in that circuit, I will follow the precedents of that circuit even though the decisions of the 7th Circuit are not in accord therewith."[17] In an

17 Judge Evan Evans to CEC and JNF, March 20, 1945.

appeal heard by him and Judges Clark and Frank he became involved in a question that had bitterly divided the Second Circuit: whether defense counsel were entitled to examine notes prepared by F.B.I. agents relating to statements made by defendants while they were questioned. The trial judge had turned down the defense lawyer's request for the documents; the Second Circuit panel affirmed the conviction in a brief per curiam opinion, which said in part: "The majority of this court, for the reasons stated in United States v. Ebeling . . . find no error in the trial judge's action. Judge Frank, for the reasons stated in his dissent in the Ebeling case, is of the opinion. . . ."[18] Evans cast the deciding vote because he adhered to a Second Circuit precedent. However, privately "he was conscious . . . of a leaning toward the views expressed in the dissenting opinion in United States v. Ebeling" and he admitted that "if and when the question arises in the Seventh Circuit Court of Appeals, I believe I will adopt the dissenting opinion."[19]

But this was not the policy of Judge Joseph Hutcheson of the Fifth Circuit, a noted opponent of the New Deal and federal administrative agencies. In *Security Exchange Commission v. Long Island Lighting Co.*,[20] a majority consisting of Judges Hutcheson and Charles C. Simons (Sixth Circuit) —both visiting judges—reversed the S.E.C., over the dissent of Judge Clark. Several years later the Second Circuit specifically rejected the decision in *Long Island Lighting*.[21]

In another case decided at about the same time, *Duquesne Warehouse Co. v. Railroad Retirement Board*,[22] the federal agency was overruled in a decision authored by Judge Hutcheson and joined by Judge Chase, probably the Second Circuit member least sympathetic to governmental agencies. The majority opinion is replete with arguments in favor of judicial control over administrative agencies which are clearly contrary to established Second Circuit policy. Judge Frank wrote a long, caustic dissent in which he discussed judicial review of administrative decisions at some length, "for fear that, unless I do, the views here expressed by Judge Hutcheson may be taken as indicating

[18] United States v. Cohen, 148 F.2d 94 (2d Cir. 1945).

[19] Judge Evans to CEC and JNF, February 17, 1945.

[20] 148 F.2d 252 (2d Cir. 1945).

[21] West India Fruit & Steamship Co. v. Seatrain Lines, Inc., 170 F.2d 775 (2d Cir. 1948). In S.E.C. v. Long Island Lighting Co., the Supreme Court granted certiorari, indicating a strong likelihood of ultimate reversal; later it vacated and remanded because of mootness—a decision which was regarded as tantamount to reversal by Judge Frank, in his opinion in West India, p. 779, n. 2.

[22] 148 F.2d 473 (2d Cir. 1945).

the position of this Circuit."[23] Then Frank lectured the visiting judge with sharp words:

> In this circuit, recognizing the Supreme Court as the authoritative head of the federal judicial hierarchy, we have heretofore felt obligated, as an intermediate tribunal, to follow the rulings of that Court whether or not any members of this court happened to like those rulings. Consequently, I do not feel it necessary to defend the Supreme Court against charges of heresy; for I think we must bow to its determination even if, perchance, we should find Judge Hutcheson's political philosophy and heresiography more attractive.[24]

This "Second Circuit" decision was reversed by the Supreme Court.

The illustrations given here are all from the same period in the 1940's. It may be that after having made some use of outside judges, the Second Circuit decided that it could do well enough without their help. From what we know, during the last half-dozen years of the Learned Hand court, it got along excellently without such assistance.

While it would help to speed up the disposition of cases, the court does not permit the sitting of concurrent panels. Today, with nine judges and a large case backlog, concurrent sittings merit consideration in the interest of increased judicial efficiency.

The chief judge, when he sits, or, in his absence, the judge senior in service, acts as presiding judge. In addition to working out the schedule of time allotted to counsel for argument, the presiding judge speaks for the court in ruling on motions and in handing down summary decisions. He also presides (informally) over the panel's conference the week after argument and has the task of assigning opinions. There may be some tendency for the presiding judge to assign to himself a disproportionate number of important opinions,[25] but there is no pronounced trend in this direction. Chief Judge Lumbard asserts that he does not take the "great" cases for himself and cites as evidence his assignment of opinions in cases decided en banc.[26]

The Second Circuit's chief judge—like those of the other courts of appeals—is faced with important administrative duties.[27] In evaluating all that he must do, it seems surprising that he is able to maintain a

[23] *Ibid.*, p. 481.

[24] *Ibid.*, p. 485. The ruling by Judges Hutcheson and Chase was reversed by the Supreme Court, 326 U.S. 446 (1946).

[25] This is the view of, for example, Charles A. Horsky, "Augustus Noble Hand," *Harvard Law Review*, 68 (1955), 119.

[26] Interview on January 3, 1963.

[27] For a description of the multiple responsibilities of the chief judges, see E. Barrett Prettyman, "The Duties of a Circuit Chief Judge," *American Bar Association Journal*, 46 (1960), 633.

pace of judicial output comparable to that of his less burdened colleagues. A decade ago, Judge Clark spoke of the passing of the day of
"the great Chief Judge" and, in recognition of the fact that currently
the major task of chief judges is to oversee the operations of their
courts, he half seriously proposed that "we might well think of doing
away with the title of Chief Justice . . . and now ought to call the
man in charge of the daily operations of the Court the 'Vice-President
in Charge of Production.' "[28]

Apart from overseeing the work of his court, the administrative
duties of the chief judge consist of service as chairman of the judicial
council of his circuit, which is made up of the active judges of the
court of appeals and is charged with the supervision of the district
courts within the circuit;[29] chairmanship of the judicial conference of

[28] Clark, "The Role of the United States Courts of Appeals in Law
Administration," *Conference on Judicial Administration,* Conference Series
No. 16, The Law School, University of Chicago (Chicago: University of
Chicago Press, 1957), p. 87.

[29] On the judicial councils of the circuits, see J. Edward Lumbard,
"The Place of the Federal Judicial Councils in the Administration of the
Courts," *American Bar Association Journal,* 47 (1961), 169. In recent years
the judiciary committees of both houses of Congress have been sharply
critical of the failure of the councils to exercise the powers granted to them
by Congress (sec. 332 of Title 28 *United States Code*) to oversee the work of
the courts within their circuits. The judicial councils were established in
1939 at the urging of Chief Justice Hughes and the Judicial Conference of
the United States. The rationale for adding a supervisory task to the duties of
the circuit judges was explained by the Chief Justice as follows:

"When you come to the supervision of the work of the judges . . . there
you have the great advantage of the supervision of that work by the men
who know. The circuit judges know the work of the district judges by their
records that they are constantly examining, while the Supreme Court gets
only an occasional one. And the circuit judges know the judges personally
in their districts; they know their capacities. And if complaints are made,
they have immediate resort to the means of ascertaining their validity." (From
Transcript of the Proceedings of the Judicial Conference of the United
States, September, 1938, Session, p. 192. Reprinted in "Report on the Powers
and Responsibilities of the Judicial Councils," A Report of the Judicial
Conference of the United States, Foreword by Congressman Emanuel Celler,
House Document No. 201, 87th Cong., 1st sess., 1961, p. 3.)

Congressman Celler, warning that "there is an urgent need for the
judicial councils in all circuits to recognize their full responsibilities and to
perform more effectively the function originally intended by the Congress,"
hopefully believed that there was "every reason to expect that in the future
the judiciary will undertake to do their job in housekeeping and not leave
these responsibilities to the Congress" (*Ibid.,* p. vi).

The Judicial Council of the Second Circuit has been especially lax. This
is due, in part, to the downgrading of the Council by Judge Learned Hand,
who became chief judge at about the same time that the councils were
established. Another factor, according to Judge Lumbard, has been the

the circuit, which consists of all federal judges within the circuit and serves as an informal gathering of bench and bar;[30] and membership in the Judicial Conference of the United States and service on its committees. Because of his administrative activities, the chief judge has an additional law clerk (two in all) to assist him.

As a result of the burdens on the chief judges and because some of these men were unable to run their courts smoothly, Congress in 1958 adopted a mandatory retirement age of seventy for chief judges of all lower federal courts. Retirement is mandated only from the chief judgeship; after seventy, continuation in active service is discretionary. Thus, at present, the chief judges of inferior federal courts are those members under seventy who have most years of service on their courts.[31]

---

shortage of judges within the Second Circuit (Lumbard, "Place of the Federal Judicial Councils," p. 172).

The courts of appeals are beginning to take their councils more seriously. In the most far-reaching action taken so far by any of the councils, the Judicial Council of the Tenth Circuit, in effect, suspended a district judge pending proceedings before the Council. The Supreme Court, over the vigorous dissent of Justices Black and Douglas, refused to block this action (Chandler v. Judicial Council of the Tenth Circuit, 382 U.S. 1003 [1966]). Judge Chandler persisted in challenging the authority of the judicial council and the Supreme Court agreed to take another look at the case. However, on June 1, 1970, the Supreme Court rejected his suit on the ground that he had not sought relief from either the judicial council or from another tribunal. The Supreme Court did not reach the question of whether the judicial councils had broad disciplinary powers. The vote in the Supreme Court was 5–2, with Justices Black and Douglas dissenting (*United States Law Week,* June 2, 1970, p. 4413).

On the subject of the judicial councils there is a useful recent article, Peter Graham Fish, "The Circuit Councils: Rusty Hinges of Federal Judicial Administration," *University of Chicago Law Review,* 37 (1970), 203.

[30] Judge Learned Hand did not care too much for the Judicial Conference and while he was chief judge the court only went through the motions of holding its conference. When Charles E. Clark became chief judge, the Second Circuit adopted the practice prevalent in some of the other circuits of holding the conference in a city within the circuit other than the one in which the court sits. The Second Circuit conference traditionally is a gathering of the judges of the circuit, leading members of New York, Connecticut, and Vermont bar associations, individuals concerned with the operation of the federal courts, and their wives. Apart from the social activities, a number of papers on judicial administration are read, and there is an executive session of the judges.

[31] Chief Judge Lumbard owes his position to a single day. He was appointed to the Second Circuit on July 12, 1955, one day before the appointment of Judge Waterman. Both took the judicial oath on July 18. Presumably the difference of a day was not accidental.

From the beginning, each court of appeals had the authority to make its own rules of procedure, within bounds set by statute; because of this, some procedural rules varied significantly from circuit to circuit. Although the Federal Rules of Civil Procedure (Rules 72–76) and the Federal Rules of Criminal Procedure (Rules 37–39) required uniformity in those parts of the appellate process that take place in the district court,[32] until recently there were no uniform rules for the courts of appeals.

The freedom given to the courts of appeals with regard to their procedures conflicted with the uniformity of procedure since the late 1930's in the operations of the district courts. As John Parker, the late chief judge of the Fourth Circuit, said in 1950, "Under the modern practice, an appeal is not a new proceeding but a mere continuation of that begun in the trial court."[33] It follows, then, that "if procedural uniformity is a virtue in the district courts there appears to be no good reason why it should not also be a virtue in the courts of appeals."[34] Four arguments were advanced in favor of uniformity:

> In the first place, uniformity will ease the burden of the lawyer who practices in several circuits, and also of the judge who may be a visitor in other circuits. It is quite true that this argument is not as strong in the case of the courts of appeals as it is in the district courts. There are fewer courts of appeals and fewer lawyers who practice in more than one circuit. The problem, however, is not academic, and the chances are that it will increase rather than diminish. In the second place, in order to achieve uniformity the competing rules of the various circuits must be scrutinized, which should result in the elimination of outmoded methods and the adoption of the most up-to-date procedure. In the third place, and this is really a by-product of the second, in the re-evaluation process it is quite likely that new and better procedures will emerge. Finally, the uniform establishment of modern methods in appellate practice will inevitably result in increased efficiency and decreased costs.[35]

In 1960 Chief Justice Earl Warren appointed the Advisory Committee on Appellate Rules. After receiving the views of many interested parties, the Advisory Committee prepared a draft of proposed rules

[32] Even with respect to these civil and criminal rules, different interpretations by courts of appeals may result in different procedures. Moreover, in the Second Circuit, especially during the 1940's, the Federal Rules were a major source of friction.

[33] Parker, "Improving Appellate Methods," *New York University Law Review*, 25 (1950), 4.

[34] Milton D. Green, "The Next Step: Uniform Rules for the Courts of Appeals," *Vanderbilt Law Review*, 14 (1961), 948.

[35] *Ibid.*

for the courts of appeals.[36] These were approved by the Committee on Rules of Practice and Procedure of the Judicial Conference of the United States, the Judicial Conference, and finally the Supreme Court, which is empowered to promulgate rules for the courts of appeals. They went into effect on July 1, 1968.

Although uniform rules of appellate procedure are now in effect, there still is not absolute uniformity in the courts of appeals because there are varying interpretations as to what they require. Moreover, the appellate courts are permitted to make supplementary rules which are not inconsistent with the uniform rules. Finally, Rule 2 provides that "in the interest of expediting decision, or for other cause shown, a court of appeals may, except as otherwise provided . . . suspend the requirements or provisions of any of these rules . . . and may order proceedings in accordance with its direction." The exception is that a court of appeals may not extend the time for taking an appeal or seeking a review.

The present rules of the Court of Appeals for the Second Circuit went into effect on August 1, 1954. In the years since, they have been amended several times. For the most part, they do not have an important impact on the court's decisional process. In any case, the practice of the Second Circuit is to apply the rules flexibly.

The Federal Rules of Appellate Procedure require that any party wishing to appeal a decision of the district court must serve on the other parties and file with the district court a "Notice of Appeal" within thirty days of the decision. When the federal government is a party, the notice must be filed within sixty days.[37] In criminal cases notice has to be filed within ten days of the decision. In cases coming from other sources, such as the Tax Court of the United States and administrative agencies, the time requirement is set by the applicable statute. The notice of appeal has the sole function of indicating that an appeal is to be taken and is not to be confused with the appellant's brief.

Within forty days of the filing of the notice, the clerk of the district court (or the appropriate official of the administrative agency) transmits the record of the proceeding below to the appellate court. As is the case with the other time limits, this requirement is not absolute and additional time may be allowed by the district court, the court of

[36] For a discussion of some of the work of the Advisory Committee by one of its members, see Robert L. Stern, "Changes in the Federal Appellate Rules," 41 *Federal Rules Decisions* 277.

[37] Fourteen days additional after the first notice of appeal are now permitted for cross-appeals.

appeals, or in accordance with provisions of administrative statutes. The record normally consists of the important papers used in the original proceeding and a transcript of the portions of the testimony designated by the parties.

Within thirty days after the record has been transmitted to the court of appeals, the appellant files his brief, in which he describes the nature of the case, the proceedings below, and the questions raised on appeal, and argues that the original decision was erroneous and should be reversed or modified. The brief may not exceed fifty pages of standard typographic printing except upon special permision, which is usually granted when applied for. Printing by other processes of duplication or copying is now permitted. In recent years, the average length of appellants' briefs in the Second Circuit has been thirty pages; the average for appellees' briefs—where a fifty page limit is also mandated—has been twenty-five pages.[38]

Accompanying the appellant's brief, either in a single volume or bound separately, is an appendix, which reproduces "such portions of the record as are relevant to the questions raised on appeal. . . . This is a supporting, reference type of document. The brief describes the proceedings and contains citations to the appendix, wherein the appellate judges may verify for themselves the happenings described."[39] In order to reduce printing costs, or because they do not know what to include, it has been found that, "counsel omit much relevant matter from their appendices."[40]

Appendices are recent innovations, an outgrowth of the movement to streamline appellate procedure and to cut the cost of appeals. They replaced the printing of the entire record. During the 1940's Judge Clark championed the appendix method, while some of his colleagues were cool to it. The Second Circuit required the separate appendix

[38] J. Edward Lumbard, "Appellate Advocacy," mimeographed (New York: Institute of Judicial Administration, 1962), p. 1.

[39] Delmar Karlen, "The United States Court of Appeals for the Second Circuit," *Record of the Association of the Bar of the City of New York,* 17 (1962), 505.

[40] Lumbard, "Appellate Advocacy," p. 7. Occasionally, when the papers submitted by counsel are poorly prepared, the judges will administer a public rebuke while rendering opinion. It is hard to think of more stinging criticism than the following, which was given per curiam by Judges Learned Hand, Clark, and Frank: "We wish further to call attention to the inclusion in the present record of the colloquy of court and counsel. . . . None of the colloquy which was printed can be thought to have been, in the remotest way, 'essential to the decision.' If in the rambling discussion anything 'essential' had appeared, it should have been selected and put in such form as to be comprehensible. We cannot undertake to grope our way through a heap of rubbish on the odd chance of picking up a bit of sound metal here and there" (Royal Petroleum Corp. v. Smith, 127 F.2d 841, 843 [2d Cir. 1942]).

system, whereby the appellee can print his own appendix and include material omitted by the appellant. The question of a suitable appendix system proved to be one of the more difficult problems facing the committee preparing the uniform appellate rules.[41] The new Rules encourage a joint appendix. The appellee's brief must be submitted within thirty days after the filing of the appellant's, who then has an additional fourteen days to submit a reply brief.

If the time limits are observed, no more than 144 days should pass in a civil suit, where the government is not a party, from the decision below to the filing of the last brief:

30 days—Notice of Appeal
40 days—Filing of Record
30 days—Appellant's Brief
30 days—Appellee's Brief
14 days—Reply Brief
———
144 days.

However, the court is likely to grant more time upon request. In an average case, about seven months elapse until argument is heard.

The clerk frequently sets down cases for argument before all the briefs are in. The schedule of cases (ordinarily between fifteen and twenty) to be argued during a particular week is prepared about three weeks in advance. As a result of the Manton scandal, counsel are not informed of the composition of the panel before they will appear until the Thursday of the week prior to argument. In the 1940's the court was sensitive in its relations with counsel[42] and about premature dis-

---

[41] Committee on Rules of Practice and Procedure, "Drafts of Proposed Rule 30," 41 *Federal Rules Decisions* 311.

[42] To a request by Morris Ernst, a noted New York lawyer, for a meeting to discuss a case just decided, Judge Clark responded, "I have found in our Circuit a very strong feeling that the judges should not consider pending cases with counsel except in the presence of, or notice to, the opposing side" (letter of March 22, 1945).
While lawyers had no opportunity to influence the composition of panels, it is difficult to determine whether the judges tried to control cases, in any way, so that they came before certain judges. Of course, in the overwhelming majority of appeals, the judges did not care at all which of them would constitute the panel. Obviously, also, there was some panel "manipulation" brought about by disqualification of a judge for one reason or another. A short while after Judge Clark came to the Second Circuit, his brother was appointed to a high Justice Department position and was in charge of tax appeals. Although, at first, Judge Swan did not regard this as requiring disqualification (TWS to CEC, July 18, 1939), Clark did not hear tax appeals until 1946, when his brother resigned. In one case, the entire regular complement of Second Circuit judges was disqualified because it involved the A. B. Dick Co. and Judge Swan was the son-in-law of the company's founder

closure of decisions. In June of 1941 Clark sent to Learned Hand a clipping from a Connecticut newspaper dealing with a columnist's prediction that the Second Circuit would decide a certain case by a 2–1 vote. Hand replied that he was "a little disturbed about that clipping. . . . I hope it was only because of what we said on the bench. I should hate to think that there was a leak anywhere."[43]

Counsel are asked to indicate by mail how much time they will need to present their cases. In most appeals the rules permit up to thirty minutes of argument for each side, but lawyers often do not use all of their time. On the average, appellant's counsel takes twenty-five to thirty minutes to state his case while appellee's counsel takes twenty-five minutes. Requests for additional time are determined by the presiding judge, who looks over the briefs and decides whether they are justified. Several years ago, the Second Circuit heard five and one-half hours of argument in a single case involving twenty appellants.[44]

Before the judges get to the cases scheduled for the week, they spend time on Monday (at times, on other days) on the motion calendar. This consists of such matters as motions for extension of time, applications for bail, motions to dismiss appeals, and stays. Applications for prohibition and mandamus, arising out of rulings in the trial court in cases still pending, are also included on the motion calendar.

All of these motions are argued orally; they are not submitted. The judges pay close attention to the brief arguments and ask questions, as they do on appeals. Most of the motions are disposed of from the bench immediately after argument. Occasionally, a motion raises novel questions of procedure and the court's ruling may be accompanied by a written opinion. As a rule, three or four cases are heard each day. The present practice is to schedule argument on definite days so that counsel will know when they will be heard. Until a few years

---

and owned company stock. The "Second Circuit" panel consisted of three specially designated judges from other circuits (A. B. Dick Co. v. Marr, 197 F.2d 498 [2. Cir. 1952]).

Apart from disqualifications, there is no evidence of any attempt to assign cases to certain judges and perhaps it was never done. Interestingly, the appeal of the Communist Party leaders (Dennis v. United States) was decided by a panel consisting of Learned Hand, Swan, and Chase. Was there any possibility that Learned Hand would not sit when the Dennis case was argued? The appeal of the contempt conviction of the Dennis trial lawyers came before a panel of Augustus Hand, Clark, and Frank.

[43] LH to CEC, June 30, 1941.

[44] This was the criminal prosecution arising out of the raid on the crime convention at Apalachin, New York.

ago many cases were scheduled for the same time and, at times, lawyers had to wait several days until their cases were called.

Almost everyone agrees that the current practice is preferable, although Learned Hand was said to remark, "I hate it."[45] The main virtue of indefinite scheduling is that it lets the court be flexible in the number of cases it will hear on a given day; the court is not tied down to a maximum of only three or four cases a day. In times gone by, when the Second Circuit had six judges and a crowded calendar, this scheduling procedure helped it to keep up with its docket. Under the new system, there are weeks where the panels have virtually no difficult cases; yet they are unable to add to the appeals they will hear.

On the other hand, counsel are now spared the inconvenience of sitting around for long periods until their cases are called. Far more important, the change in scheduling practice has led directly to a significant change in the judges' reading habits. Their former practice is described in a letter Judge Frank wrote to Frederick Bernays Wiener: "I think that (with me as an occasional exception) the judges of our court (almost) never read the briefs before the argument. With our heavy docket, we don't set a case for a day certain. Wherefore, many a case goes over to another week when a different bench is sitting. If a judge reads the briefs before argument, he may thus be acting futilely."[46] Today, the judges generally read the briefs before argument. But they do not all do so with the same degree of care or interest. Judge Hays, perhaps, reads them the closest; Judge Waterman, only when presiding. Judge Friendly

> will begin reading the briefs toward the end of the preceding week. Most of this has to be done at home, either at night or over the weekend. When I say "read" I mean precisely that. I do not study the briefs and rather endeavor not to come to any

[45] Interview with Judge Clark, who also leaned toward the old method because it kept the court busy.

[46] Wiener, *Effective Appellate Advocacy* (New York: Prentice-Hall, 1950), p. 12.

Not only didn't the earlier judges read the briefs before argument, they almost resented any judge who did. Judge Medina tells of his first day on the Second Circuit: "I could hardly wait to be up there on the Bench listening to the arguments. So I read all the briefs and what we call appendices in the cases coming up for argument, and on the big day I marched up to the Bench from the robing room at the end of the procession, with a pile of briefs and appendices under my arm. To make matters worse, I asked a number of questions during the arguments. At the end of the session we returned to the robing room and one of the older judges said: 'Trying to impress the populace, I see'" (Medina, "Some Reflections on the Judicial Function at the Appellate Level," *Washington University Law Quarterly*, 2 [1961], 148).

conclusions, although it is not always possible to refrain from one. My purpose is to familiarize myself with the facts and issues, with the opinion or charge of the lower court, with the controlling statute, if there be one, and, perhaps with one or two decisions, at least if they are of the Supreme Court or of our own, which seem to be most pertinent.[47]

Whatever additional advantage the new scheduling system has meant for lawyers, it does not appear to have effected any improvement in the quality of advocacy. Chief Judge Lumbard, in particular, is severely critical of the poor arguments made by lawyers. "The quality of arguments and briefs," he once wrote, "is disappointing and in the opinion of most appellate judges it has worsened in recent years. Only about one argument in every five is passable and only one in ten is good. The same grading is also true of the briefs."[48] While Justice Frankfurter once favorably compared Second Circuit arguments with those heard in the Supreme Court,[49] there is almost universal agreement that arguments generally are poor, an opinion that is likely to be confirmed by a visit to the courthouse at Foley Square.

The major cause of the inferior quality of advocacy is, in Judge Clark's words, "the general development of American law that the higher rewards of practice are no longer in the courtroom. Unlike our English brethren, the aristocrats of the Bar are not in the courts but tend to do their work in the law offices." Judge Clark continued:

> On one occasion I asked one of my brilliant students, now a member of a New York law firm, "why is it that the truly great men in the profession such as yourself here in New York don't come down to our court?" His answer, without any repudiation of my soft impeachment and after some careful consideration was: "Well, to tell the truth, I can't afford it. I can't afford to spend my time coming down and wasting it for you fellows." . . . I remember once asking my chief, Learned Hand, the name of a lawyer then addressing us; and he replied in one of those stage whispers for which he is famous: "Well, I don't know his name, but he's the

[47] Henry J. Friendly, "How a Judge of the United States Court of Appeals Works," mimeographed (New York: Institute of Judicial Administration, 1962), p. 1.

[48] Lumbard, "Appellate Advocacy," p. 9. In interviews, six of the nine present members of the court expressed similar views. Judge Hays, a seventh, thought that arguments are not as bad as they are said to be.

[49] Letter to Judge Clark, December 20, 1954: "My dear Chief Judge: I should feel ungrateful if I did not tell you the pleasure it gave me to sit in your court last Friday. The cases were interesting, the arguments not merely brief but good, reflecting the bar's understanding of the standards set by your court for oral arguments. Down here arguments are to a not inconsiderable extent rehashes of briefs instead of an endeavor to focus the attention of the Court to what are deemed to be controlling considerations."

fellow that Messrs, Blank, Blank, Blank, Blank, & Blank (naming one of the great law firms) sends down to talk to boobs like you and me."[50]

A second explanation for the poor quality of advocacy was suggested by Chief Judge Lumbard in an analysis of the October 1960 term, during which 758 arguments were made before the Second Circuit: "Appeals were argued by 625 different counsel and only 97 counsel argued more than one case; thus 528 counsel argued in our court only once during the year. . . . perhaps because they appear more often, Government counsel usually make better oral arguments and write better briefs than their adversaries."[51] With the steady rise in the number of cases begun, it is apparent that no improvement in the quality of arguments will be forthcoming unless minimum standards of appellate advocacy and a specialized appellate bar are established or penalties are directed against lawyers who come to court poorly prepared.[52]

Because most appeals are one-sided, the careless attitude of counsel toward advocacy usually has little effect on their client's chances. In close cases, the presentation may have a bearing on the outcome. Judge Medina echoed the view of most of his colleagues when he said,

[50] Clark, "Role of the United States Courts of Appeals," pp. 90, 91. Learned Hand used to become furious with lawyers who were poorly prepared and occasionally walked out while argument was still in progress. After a Hand performance, Judge Clark wrote, "I only wish that . . . [his] comments during the argument to counsel could have been taken down, for they were quite in character" (letter to Paul Kerins, October 28, 1949). In a painful letter to Justice Frankfurter (September 29, 1954), responding to sharp criticism that he had been rude to Learned Hand, Judge Clark wrote, "I have cringed at times to see him ride lawyers. Some years since, Virginia Howland appealed to me to try to stop Learned from being so harsh on counsel; but who was I to beard or tame a lion."
Judge Frank could also be rough with lawyers. Once he apologized to an Assistant United States Attorney for "some remarks . . . which were harsh and unfair" (JNF to a Mr. Sexton, June 15, 1947). The memoranda of the Learned Hand court contain many unkind references to lawyer performances.
[51] Lumbard, "Appellate Advocacy," p. 9.
[52] The difficulty with the second proposal is that courts are reluctant to punish litigants for the negligence of their counsel. Nor would it help to tell poorly prepared lawyers to come back again better prepared. This would further burden the already overcrowded calendars. In Chief Judge Lumbard's view, it is the job of both bench and bar to take "appropriate measures to raise the standards and quality of advocacy" ("Appellate Advocacy," p. 12; see also J. Edward Lumbard, "The Responsibility of the Bar for the Performance of the Courts," *New York State Bar Journal,* 34 [1962], 169).

"Of course we judges are influenced by the arguments of lawyers."[53] Second Circuit memoranda include references to performances in the seventeenth-floor courtroom, indicating that judges are swayed by what lawyers tell them. "I have changed the opinion that I had of this case upon the argument,"[54] was Learned Hand's admission in one appeal. That the influence of argument is not merely occasional was stressed by Chief Judge Lumbard:

> The importance of oral argument is emphasized by the fact that in about 75% of the arguments the case is finally decided in accordance with the impression which the judges have as they leave the bench. Probably 20% is a fair estimate of the proportion of cases in which our judges have no firm impression one way or the other at the conclusion of the argument. In the remaining 5% of the cases the decision finally arrived at is contrary to the impression after oral argument. While it is quite true that the impression after oral argument derives from the reading of the briefs as well as from the argument, it is also true that the impression from reading the briefs is frequently changed or modified by the oral argument.[55]

The Second Circuit's discouragement of submission of cases without argument is another manifestation of its attitude. "For the appellant to forego oral argument is usually considered by the judges as a confession of the weakness of the appeal. . . . Last year (October 1960 term) only five cases were submitted out of 420 considered, a smaller percentage of submissions than in any court except the Supreme Court."[56]

During argument counsel are interrupted by questions, which by and large deal with the issues of the case and not abstract legal principles. But the questioning does not impart an air of excitement to the proceedings, as it often does in the Supreme Court.

In a small number of appeals—the most frivolous ones—judgment is handed down from the bench immediately after argument is concluded, following a brief consultation among the sitting judges. There is a trend toward more of such summary decisions, which Delmar Karlen attributes to an exchange of visits by English and American

[53] Medina, "The Decisional Process in the United States Court of Appeals, Second Circuit—How the Wheels Go Around Inside—with Commentary," Address at New York County Lawyers' Association Forum Evening, April 26, 1962 (typewritten), p. 22.

[54] Memorandum in Manufacturers Trust Co. v. Kaganowitz, November 6, 1944.

[55] Lumbard, "Appellate Advocacy," p. 9.

[56] Ibid., p. 9.

jurists. "Chief Judge Lumbard was a member of the American team which observed English appellate courts disposing of the great number of their cases orally (and extemporaneously) immediately upon the close of oral argument."[57] There is an important difference between the forms of bench dispositions practiced in the two systems: unlike the English judges, when a Second Circuit panel rules from the bench it does not give the reasons for its decision.

Apart from these bench decisions, about 20 per cent or so of the appeals are decided per curiam without lengthy opinions. What happens in most of these cases is that shortly after the arguments for the day are concluded, the judges informally agree that certain cases do not raise any significant questions and memoranda and detailed opinions on them will not be necessary. These cases are then disposed of in very brief per curiam opinions. At times, the per curiam devices is decided upon at the conference.

As a rule, these opinions are prepared by the presiding judge and are no longer than a few lines; often nothing more is written than "Affirmed on the opinion of Judge . . .," or something to that effect. Some per curiams run to several pages and it is not always possible to know why the court chose this manner to render its decision. Once in a while, a per curiam opinion will occasion a dissent from a member of the panel.

For many years, despite its heavy case load, the Second Circuit relied less on summary disposition[58] than did most of the other courts of appeals. While Learned Hand was chief judge there were relatively few cases so disposed of. In recent years, a greater percentage of appeals have been handled in this fashion. The increase may be attributable to the influence of the present chief judge who believes, "Our Court could readily dispose of more cases immediately after argument and it could write per curiam opinions in a larger percentage of cases heard, especially in personal injury cases and the less complicated criminal appeals."[59] There is considerable concurrence in this attitude among the Second Circuit's other judges. Given the huge growth of business in recent terms, it seems inevitable that in coming years a very significant percentage of appeals will be disposed of without opinion.

While the administrative argument in favor of more per curiam opinions is convincing, there are good reasons for the Second Circuit (and other appellate courts) to be hesitant in making greater use of them. Much of the criticism directed against state supreme courts is based on their abuse of summary disposition. The New York Court of

[57] Karlen, "Court of Appeals for the Second Circuit," p. 507.

[58] By summary disposition is meant bench decisions and very brief per curiams.

[59] Lumbard, "Appellate Advocacy," p. 10.

Appeals is a case in point. Once rated among the very best courts in the country, its reputation has steadily declined. A striking feature of its decisional process is the extraordinary number of cases which are decided with no more than a memorandum opinion; the impression one gets is that it evades more than it decides. The New York Court of Appeals is not worse than other state supreme courts in this respect; as Karl Llewellyn argued, American appellate courts are in decline and so is confidence in them.[60] Should the Second Circuit resort to summary disposition in a third or a half of its cases, confidence in its decisions would not be as high as it is today.

Only rarely do per curiam opinions give the reasons for the result.[61] Counsel is unable to learn why the court ruled the way it did when it says, "Affirmed in open court."[62] A related objection, advanced by Jerome Frank and supported by Learned Hand, is that court of appeals judges "should use great caution in affirming on opinions of the district courts; for those opinions often contain strong dicta which we would not ourselves have uttered but which are later cited to us as if we had uttered them."[63]

When summary decisions are appealed, the Supreme Court in exercising its discretionary jurisdiction is deprived of the reasoning of the lower appellate court.[64] Proof that some appeals decided summarily raised important questions is the fact that it is not rare that the

[60] Llewellyn, *The Common Law Tradition* (Boston: Little, Brown & Company, 1960).

[61] As when they cite a previous decision that is regarded as controlling.

[62] The above arguments were attributed by Judge Clark to Learned Hand, who felt "that counsel is entitled to an opinion explaining the results in practically every case except one so clear as to make the appeal practically frivolous or one where the lower court decision may be completely accepted. He refers to the sound objections made by New York lawyers to the continual affirmances by the Court of Appeals without opinion" (letter of CEC to Arthur T. Vanderbilt, August 4, 1948).

[63] JNF to Colleagues, May 29, 1944. Judges Clark and Frank disagreed on almost anything that had to do with procedure, including this question: "I have puzzled a great deal over your suggestion. . . . For my experience is that members of our court exercise great care in scrutinizing all the statements of an opinion of a district judge before adopting it. . . . the practice . . . is an excellent one, which I have often thought we did not practice nearly as much as we could. It has indirect benefits of showing proper and adequate recognition to really outstanding jobs done by district judges and, I hope, gives them some incentive; but its main value, of course, is that it affords an expeditious way of settling a case without cluttering up both the records and the law reports with merely duplicating opinions where we should do no better than, and perhaps not as well as, the district judge has done" (CEC to JNF, May 31, 1944).

[64] This is the view of Judge Hays, cited in "The Second Circuit: Federal Judicial Administration in Microcosm," *Columbia Law Review*, 63 (1963), 897.

Supreme Court grants certiorari in cases that lower courts considered worthy of no more than a brief per curiam opinion.[65]

In the large number of cases not disposed of summarily, the judges of the Second Circuit follow a practice "hallowed by tradition"[66] and "believed to be unique" among American appellate courts.[67] The judges do not confer until about a week or so (usually the Wednesday or Thursday) after argument. In the interim, each judge working independently prepares a memorandum—actually a tentative opinion—on every case not yet decided, in which he gives his views and vote. It is understood that what is said in a memorandum does not preclude changes of mind later.

The significance of the memorandum system to the operations of the Second Circuit cannot be easily appreciated because the court's output (in opinions) is quite similar to that of the other courts of appeals. The impact is largely internal—on the mood and temper of the court, and on relations among the judges and the way they go about their work. For the judges of the Learned Hand court, many of the cases were routine and mundane, as were the memoranda prepared for them. But a goodly number of the tentative opinions contained what the judges could not or would not say in their published opinions. Attitudes toward the Supreme Court and its members, comments on current affairs and personalities, bits of philosophy, and just about anything that came to the mind of the writer were included in the memoranda of 1941–51, particularly those of Learned Hand,

[65] For example, for the Second Circuit, 1941–51, McGrath v. Chase National Bank, 182 F.2d 349 (2d Cir. 1950), reversed, Zittman v. McGrath, 341 U.S. 446 (1951), Commissioner of Internal Revenue v. Schroeder, 172 F.2d 864 (2d Cir. 1949), reversed summarily in Estate of Schroeder v. Commissioner of Internal Revenue 338 U.S. 801 (1949); United States ex rel. Lee Wo Shing v. Watkins, 175 F.2d 194 (2d Cir. 1949), reversed at 339 U.S. 906 (1950).

The foregoing discussion of summary disposition pertains only to where the appellate court affirms the court below. Reversals are a different matter. Except in extraordinary cases, reversal without an explanatory opinion is not justified. In fact, between 1941 and 1951 there were very few per curiam reversals and these either were cases in which the court had recently ruled on the very same question so that there was no need for another discussion, or instances where the appellate judges apparently wanted to rebuke the district court.

[66] CEC to Judge Henry Edgerton, May 9, 1941.

[67] Karlen, "Court of Appeals for the Second Circuit, p. 507. Once, Judge Clark indicated that the Eighth Circuit also used memoranda ("Role of the United States Courts of Appeals," p. 94). But a study by the Institute of Judicial Administration of Operating Procedures of American Appellate Courts did not show that to be the practice of that circuit.

Frank, and Clark. The latter two judges took great pains in preparing their memoranda, which, at times, were longer than most opinions. To Learned Hand, memorandum writing must have been a labor of love, so delightful were they. His memoranda would (should) make a book.[68]

The Second Circuit is so wedded to the memorandum system that one can safely predict that the practice will long remain part of its decisional process. The present judges, in any case, favor the system, although new judges will likely react as Judge Medina did when he was first introduced to it: "Well, I could hardly believe we were required to prepare these memoranda. Why, I said to myself, all this extra work?" But Judge Medina, too, came to believe that "this memorandum system is a wonderful thing."[69]

Whether today's judges take memo-writing as seriously as did their predecessors is a different matter. A few years ago Judge Medina stated emphatically that they did because "you can't just sit there and say, 'There is nothing in this case, I vote to affirm.' You send out a couple of memoranda like that and the other judges would not say anything, but they would have a lot of ideas running through their heads."[70] Other judges in interviews indicated that many memoranda are superficial and that often little more than lip service is paid to this hallowed practice. A number of memoranda to and by Judge Clark written in the 1950's after Learned Hand's retirement were studied and these were not as spirited or as irreverent (and irrelevant) as those of the earlier period.[71]

There is no set length for the memoranda; when a judge becomes enthusiastic he may write a memorandum which is tantamount to an exhaustive opinion. The memoranda of Judges Swan, Augustus Hand, and Chase usually were brief because exuberant, lengthy writing was not their style, not because they did not believe in the efficacy of the system.

An important question is the effect the practice has on the performance of the court. Obviously, it places an additional responsibility on judges who are said to be overburdened by their ordinary judicial work. It also draws out the decision-making process and may

[68] I have decided not to include excerpts from memoranda at this point, because I have relied on their contents throughout this study.

[69] Medina, "Some Reflections on the Judicial Function," p. 150.

[70] Medina, "Decisional Process," p. 17.

[71] A few weeks before his own death, on October 17, 1963, Judge Clark wrote to Learned Hand's widow: "Perhaps needless to say, I regret the fine old days which are now past, when I had the priceless privilege of close association with both Learned and Gus. Judicial work no longer affords the zest of those days."

add to the time that it takes to arrive at a final decision.[72] Another criticism, along different lines, is that

> with us one does form opinions which tend to be already firm before one talks with his colleagues. Perhaps that is the most questionable feature of the practice, even if we do not admit it. We always say we freely change our minds, and we refer to such-and-such a case where there has been a shift. In fact, there is a considerable shift of views as the conference develops, but I suspect a strong-minded judge, having put his thoughts on paper, does find it more difficult to change his mind. Because of this possibility I have at times had qualms as to our practice, but on the whole I am quite clear that it is too valuable in general to give up because of an occasional case where it may not have worked so well.[73]

More than offsetting possible disadvantages are several clearcut benefits inherent in the system.

1. It is the best method yet devised to prevent the practice reputed to be prevalent in a number of American appellate courts of "one-man opinions," under which each appeal is assigned in advance to a single judge who carefully reads the briefs and prepares the opinion for the entire court while the other judges concentrate on the cases assigned to them. In the Second Circuit, each panel member is familiar with and works on every appeal he hears.

2. Novel ideas, which may be overlooked in a conference held immediately after argument, are brought into the open during the extended examination of the cases by the judges and their law clerks. Yet, under the memorandum system it is unlikely that any of the principal points raised in the briefs and arguments will receive insufficient attention.[74]

3. Rather than make the subsequent conference superfluous, the preparation of memoranda leads to a more efficiently organized conference. The judges have seen each other's memoranda and are aware of the tentative votes. The major issues are pinpointed. The system is

---

[72] However, it is noteworthy that in the 1940's the Second Circuit was the fastest working court of appeals.

[73] Judge Clark, "Role of the United States Courts of Appeals," p. 95. In general, Judge Clark's criticism does not seem valid. The memoranda bring out numerous instances where judges did switch their vote. Indeed, it was not uncommon for the vote at the end of the memorandum to be specifically designated as "tentative." However, the impression is gotten from a study of the 1941–51 period that Judge Clark was the least likely member of the Second Circuit to change his mind.

[74] "It's amazing how often one of us sees an aspect of the case (re facts or legal rules) which the others overlooked" (Judge Frank, quoted in Wiener, *Effective Appellate Advocacy*, p. 22).

believed to be responsible for the relatively short conferences (usually two to three hours) held in the Second Circuit.[75]

4. In Judge Clark's words, memo-writing

is quite an invaluable thing when it comes to writing the opinions. I expect that probably we write our opinions more for our colleagues than for anyone else. One has to shoot at some audience; I suspect that ordinarily the appellate judge is aiming at the trial judge, or if not at him, perhaps at the abler counsel before him. But under our method we do this vicariously by writing to convince our colleagues. And that is a real help. When we get through we have felt it incumbent upon ourselves to answer all the arguments that have been brought out in this interchange of ideas not only with our colleagues but also with their bright law clerks.[76]

During the memorandum stage, law clerks play a fairly important role, checking the briefs and appendices, looking into authorities and precedents, and offering advice to their judges. Each judge, though, follows his own procedure in getting out his memoranda. Judge Friendly described his method:

Each afternoon, I will sit down with my law clerk and discuss rather briefly the cases that were argued that morning. These fall into three groups: The first is a group where I have practically arrived at a decision, subject, possibly, to verifying one or two small matters of fact or looking up a reference which can be expeditiously done; the second group involves cases where I have not yet made up my mind but where it is apparent that the field requiring investigation is fairly limited; and the third group consists of the cases where it is apparent that a fair amount of added research will be needed before I can come to any conclusion. I reserve my law clerk almost entirely for this third group. I endeavor to get rid of the first group currently and then use whatever time remains during the week of argument to make as much progress as I can on the second. The result is that out of a clutch of, say, 18 appeals, I will probably produce memoranda on 6 or 8 before the week is out.

By the end of the week or the beginning of the next, I should be getting memos or oral reports from my law clerk on the more difficult cases which have been assigned to him for study. Working in this manner, I can just about manage to get out all my memos in time for a conference toward the end of the second week.[77]

At the conference each case not disposed of earlier is discussed separately and a vote is taken. Because of the small number of partici-

[75] Karlen, "Court of Appeals for the Second Circuit," p. 508.
[76] Clark, "Role of the United States Courts of Appeals," p. 95.
[77] Friendly, "How a Judge . . . Works," p. 1.

pants, the conference is informal, with the presiding judge acting as a lenient chairman.

On appellate courts, the conference is the midpoint of the decisional process, the stage at which the total responsibility for the course of the appeal shifts to the judges. It is also the key point for formal interaction among the judges, the moment at which they bargain and reach results which, albeit tentative, usually are final.

Because of the focal nature of the conference, any disruptive factor weakens the entire performance of the court. Sharp personal clashes or the inability of the chief judge to control the conference, as was true of the Supreme Court under Stone, make difficult its proper operation. On the other hand, social cohesion and proper utilization of the conference contribute to a better-functioning court.

As was pointed out earlier in this chapter, from the social standpoint, the Learned Hand court was not a cohesive group. Physical dispersal affected post-conference bargaining, particularly when Judges Frank and Clark were on the same panel. As to the conference, the evidence suggests that it usually ran smoothly with few disruptions of any kind. However, this may have been less the result of issue solidarity than of the unwillingness of Judge Clark—the court's leading dissenter—to use the conference as the major forum for conveying his views to the other judges. In a letter to Augustus Hand he conceded, "My sad attempts at oral argument do trouble me and are, I suppose, at the root of my general feeling that conferences get little, if anywhere, and are more or less a waste of time. I imagine I do better in written presentation but, of course, I can be wrong there, too."[78]

Clark thus had little confidence in the conference, an appellate court's most direct medium of judicial interaction. Coupled with the geographical dispersal, which in turn fed Judge Clark's proclivity for letter writing, this meant that much of his meaningful relations with colleagues were conducted long distance—not the most efficacious method for successful bargaining.

After the votes are taken, the presiding judge assigns the writing of opinions, taking into consideration a fair division of labor and the wishes of his colleagues. "The assignment is very informal: if one of us asks to be assigned, his request will ordinarily be granted."[79]

Judge Medina gave an interesting glimpse into how opinions are sometimes assigned in the Second Circuit:

> The three judges, of whom I was one, were arguing in conference. One was for reversal, the second for affirmance, and the

[78] CEC to ANH, April 18, 1951. In a December 15, 1947, memorandum (McComb v. Utica Knitting Co.) Clark referred to "the comparatively little utility of our conference method."

[79] Judge Frank, quoted in Wiener, *Effective Appellate Advocacy*, p. 22.

third just could not as yet make up his mind. So, to my amazement, the presiding judge assigned the writing of the opinion to the judge who could not yet make up his mind which way to vote. But this makes sense doesn't it? That is the traditional way of handling such situations in the Second Circuit.[80]

The memoranda also play a role in the selection of opinion writers; it often happens that the judge who showed the greatest interest in his memorandum is given the assignment. Sometimes an assignment is made because a judge is recognized as an expert in a particular field. Assertions such as this one are not easy to document because judges do not like to admit that this is so; but it is inevitable, as Judge Parker once wrote, that this would be the occasional practice: "It is not desirable that there be specialization on the part of judges with respect to the branches of the law that they discuss, but men differ in learning and abilities and it is in the interest of an orderly development of jurisprudence that opinions be written by men who have familiarity with the legal subjects with which they deal."[81]

Several members of the Second Circuit said in interviews that there is some tendency to assign cases to experts, but other judges disagreed. Review of 1941–51 cases reveals several assignment patterns: patent cases went to Learned Hand or, in his absence, to Judge Chase; Judge Swan wrote often in immigration and naturalization appeals; Judge Augustus Hand specialized somewhat in selective service appeals; where Connecticut law was involved, Judge Clark would get the call, while most of the few Vermont cases went to Judge Chase.[82]

[80] Medina, "Some Reflections on the Judicial Function," p. 153.

[81] Parker, "Improving Appellate Methods," p. 12. Cf. Judge Medina: "We don't have specialists in our court. At the same time we must recognize the fact that every one of the judges has a more or less specialized background, and this plays some part in the assignment of the opinions ("Decisional Process," p. 39).

[82] It should be obvious that in view of the large volume of appeals, each judge gets cases which he had hoped would be assigned to a colleague. Judge Medina tells of the anxieties of judges when assignments are made:

"Some cases are as dull as dishwater. The facts are complicated, the opinions below either non-existent or not helpful, the briefs a mass of confusion. To make matters worse, these cases do not involve legal principles of general interest; they do involve a monumental amount of labor, and they do not mean a thing, except to the parties and to the cause of justice in general.

"By the way of contrast, other cases involve issues of immediate, sometimes critical importance to the public at large. It is not strange that a particular judge should like to get one of these every now and then, especially if he has been writing dissents on the very subject and now the court is at last coming around to his point of view. Footnote: is the head of the court supposed to write the opinions in all landmark cases?

"Then there are cases in which for one reason or another a particular judge does not want to write. If Judge A has the reputation of being an out-

The conference vote and assignment are not always the final disposition of an appeal by the court. While the post-conference procedure usually is routine and uncomplicated, primarily involving the drafting of opinions and their circulation for colleagues' comments, at times there is intense reassessment and bargaining and the conference vote will be changed.[83] When this occurs, the assigned judge continues to prepare his opinion. Should he now be in the minority, his opinion is a dissent, but unlike the usual dissenting opinion it summarizes the facts and crucial questions, gives the view of the majority judges, and may be the only opinion filed in the case.[84]

The memoranda can be transformed into majority, concurring, or dissenting opinions and consequently they make the job of preparing opinions easier. There is, of course, additional study and research to be done and the other members will have to be consulted. Because most appeals are one-sided—90 per cent are decided without dissent—bargaining, as such, occurs in a limited number of cases and usually involves nothing more than change of language. However, as is true of the Supreme Court, bargaining can result in the withdrawal of draft concurring and dissenting opinions. When this happens, the published opinions hardly convey the inner dynamics of the court's decisional process.

The panel system employed in almost all cases today (and exclusively during 1941–51) creates a number of problems in judicial relations. One of these is whether panel members should seek the advice of their non-sitting colleagues. As a rule, consultation makes no sense until after the conference has been held. In most cases the result is so obvious that there is no reason to seek the help of colleagues, but there are several situations where consultation with non-sitting judges occurs. One of these is when different panels are, at about the same

---

standing liberal, it is unlikely he will relish writing an opinion affirming the conviction of a wayward member of a union or sustaining the ban of the censor on an allegedly obscene book or motion picture, even if he thinks the judgment below should be affirmed" ("Some Reflections on the Judicial Function," p. 151).

[83] For example, *In Re* Meiselman, 105 F.2d 995 (2d Cir. 1939) in which the court in an opinion by Clark (joined by Swan, and with Chase concurring separately) reversed a district court affirmance of a turn-over order by a referee in bankruptcy. At the conference the vote was 3–0 to affirm.

[84] In Monarch Theatres v. Helvering, 137 F.2d (2d Cir. 1943) both Learned Hand and Augustus Hand dissented in part. But as the former explained: "The following opinion was written under the assumption that it would represent the opinion of all three of the judges. It turns out that . . . I am in the minority, for Judge Chase concurs in the opinion of Judge Augustus N. Hand. It has seemed to us best, however, to allow the opinion to stand" (p. 589).

time, deciding appeals that raise similar questions. Consultation is desirable because it might help to avoid intracircuit conflict.

More informal is the solicitation of the opinion of a colleague who is regarded as an expert in the branch of law in which the case falls. Informal consultation will also occur between judges who are good friends,[85] and when the judges lunch together.

Now that the Second Circuit hears some cases en banc, the need for these consultations may be reduced somewhat. For the Learned Hand court, judicial interaction of the sort just described often contributed to broader agreement on the issues before it; but it also led to some difficult moments.[86]

[85] "I learned soon after I came on the court, that Learned and Gus and Tom often go to one another for advice in cases in which one of them is sitting and the other two are not. I have found it exceedingly helpful to have such talks" (JNF to CEC, June 30, 1942).

[86] In mid-1942 Judges Clark and Frank became embroiled in two sharp disputes over the latter's discussions with non-sitting colleagues. A month-long exchange of very detailed memoranda did not resolve the issue, nor did it lead to full agreement as to what transpired. In the first case, Hoffman v. Palmer, 129 F.2d 976 (2d Cir. 1942), the conference vote showed a panel division of Swan and Frank on one side, with Clark in dissent. The majority opinion was assigned to Frank; what happened next, according to a letter from Frank to Clark: "When I was first writing my opinion, before I set pencil to paper, I discussed the question with Learned and Gus. Both of them disagreed with me. I, therefore, suggested that I ascertain how Harrie felt; I said to Learned and Gus that, if four of the six of us agreed with you, I felt it unwise that Tom and I should decide the question. Learned said No.

"2. Then you came to town, and you and I discussed the matter with Learned and Gus.

"3. Up to this time, no one but Tom had seen my opinion. Then Gus and Learned told me that you had sent them copies of your dissenting opinion. Do you think it was improper for me, in the circumstances, to show Gus mine? His reaction was, roughly, this: He had previously felt the evidence admissible; my opinion made him less sure.

"4. I chatted about the case with Harrie quite briefly, trying to state fairly both sides. I told Harrie that I wouldn't bore him with my draft opinion, then undergoing revision, but that he could read both views in print. From what he heard, his inclination was toward my views of the question.

"5. I don't understand the statement in your note of June 20 that 'it is quite improper to base any arguments upon views of our colleagues not sitting upon the court, obtained as a result of ex parte and wholly informal discussions.' I haven't done so here. I confess that I often discuss—usually in a casual manner—points with colleagues not sitting; and frequently thus obtain advice and citations. Is that wrong?" (JNF to CEC, June 22, 1942).

Clark replied the next day:

"Of course, there can be no objection to informal and casual discussion of cases with our colleagues not sitting. But if certain important conclusions to be used as having a persuasive effect, either upon the result or upon the views of sitting judges, are to be drawn therefrom, I think it is not fair to rely on such informal and necessarily one-sided discussions as a basis for those conclusions. It seemed to me that your last letter was making the suggestion that these informal discussions should have such effect. That, I felt, was not fair under the circumstances.

"As a matter of history I might state that because I feared such chances of misinterpretation, I refrained as much as I had felt I could from discussing this case with non-sitting colleagues. I did not raise the matter in first instance and should not have done so, and the first I heard was when you reported the views of Learned and Gus. Your suggestion that you and I discussed the matter with Learned and Gus, I think it not quite historically accurate except in this way, that at lunch you brought up the question and, it being thus open, I participated in the conversation. I certainly understood you to say that Learned and Gus had seen your opinion. I am sorry that I must have got this wrong, because this supposed knowledge led to my next step, which I considered with some care. It seemed to me then that, instead of attempting to argue the case, the only proper thing for me to do was to let them see what I had said in print, and therefore without any comment I sent copies of my dissent to them, which they returned. Since it did not appear when I was down that you had discussed the matter with Harrie, I carefully refrained from even mentioning it to him.

"Under the circumstances, therefore, I do not believe it is proper to say that Gus has shifted ground or that Harrie has passed upon the matter. All that it is possible to say is that the court is seriously divided on the question, and it is one which certainly ought to have gone before the full court.

"Please understand that when I think conclusions based on informal discussion with our colleagues are not to be considered binding, I have no intention whatever of attributing anything unfair to you in your presentation of the case. But we all know the effect of exuberance and the force of personality in securing accord from personal contact about matters concerning which one has not previously felt deeply. There is a question how far concurrence usually goes; I suppose President Roosevelt had gotten into a great deal of trouble because people have thought he was agreeing with them when he only thought he was being nice."

The second dispute, Corning Glass Works v. National Labor Relations Board, 129 F.2d 967 (2d Cir. 1942), was far more involved. The letters and memoranda settled nothing, and, in fact, reopened the Hoffman v. Palmer battle. In Corning Glass, the majority consisted of Chase and Frank, with the court's junior member once more the opinion writer and Clark dissenting. Among the highlights of the Corning Glass exchange were: (1) Learned Hand's objection to the inclusion in Frank's draft of the fact that non-sitting judges had been consulted (JNF to CEC, June 27, 1942); (2) Frank's reference to the difficulty of resolving disputes via U.S. mail: "And I wish that we had an opportunity, sometime soon, to chat together for I would like, once and for all, to obliterate from your mind any notion that I have the slightest desire to procure advance commitments from anybody" (JNF to CEC, June 30, 1942); (3) Frank's promise not to "show any opinion I have written to any judge not sitting in the case until your views are available and can be simultaneously expressed to that judge. I shall make that a rule, not because I think it wise, but simply to avoid any future misunderstandings" (JNF to CEC, June 30, 1942); (4) "I think a part of the

As we shall see, Judge Clark much preferred en banc proceedings as a means of resolving intracourt conflict. Of the 1941–51 judges, he was the only one to feel strongly that certain cases should be decided by the full bench, while Learned Hand steadfastly adhered to the panel system. Clark wanted to depart from three-judge courts, because the panel system denied him a direct opportunity to express his views on many important matters decided by the Second Circuit, and thus throughout the federal judiciary he would be identified with views that he actually opposed. His concern was primarily over procedural questions, where he felt that the court occasionally disregarded the plain intent of the Federal Rules and the Advisory Committee, which he served as Reporter. To compensate for the panel system, Clark would offer his views on appeals that were not argued before him. On one occasion, in the midst of a Second Circuit battle over interlocutory appeals, he sent a long memorandum to the other judges in order "to avoid foreclosure of my views . . . in case I may not be sitting in the other approaching cases." He went on to say:

> While I do not care to stress it at this time, my position in these procedural cases tends to become difficult and unhappy. Either because I have not been sitting at the time or because discussion was temporarily unnecessary and might provoke dispute, I have not been able to express my views before a later contrary decision is asserted to bind us all. . . . Since I am so publicly committed to advocacy of procedural rules both simple and uniform, it is distressing to me, as well as confusing to others who read, to have to announce and follow procedural views I oppose and which I feel are really the expression of only a court minority—often, opposed, too, to the views of other circuits. There are, of course, two remedies: one that of sitting in banc . . . and the other a little less formal obeisance to views with which we are

---

problem is that your mind works with such lightninglike speed that you are ahead of us in point of time" (CEC to JNF, July 1, 1942); (5) After a couple thousand words, "If you have any lingering doubts after reading the foregoing please tell me. I'm not an oblique or devious person and I hate being thought so, especially by a person whom I admire and for whom I have affection as I have for you. . . . In Hoffman, I tried my best to avoid having a minority write an opinion which would seem to be the views of all but one judge. In Corning, I tried to avoid having three judges criticize their three other colleagues. . . . If that's unfair or devious, I'm a wall-eyed parrot" (JNF to CEC, July 12, 1942). (6) "I certainly do not think you are devious. In fact, the adjective seems rather absurd as applied to you. I do think you are open and exuberant and quick. Because of these qualities I do not think you have realized that when you carry things before you this is more a matter of personality than of finally convincing your auditors; and hence the impressions you get from your contacts and reports are not the ones which we all would get if we had completely two-sided discussions" (CEC to JNF, July 14, 1942).

known to disagree which appear as the views of our court by virtue of the chance to which I have adverted. Since these are presently lacking, I resort to the only method I can think of, namely, this memo., which I hope you will read.[87]

Chief Judge Lumbard once proposed circulating all draft opinions to the entire court, a procedure followed in some appellate courts that employ the panel system; but a majority of the judges were opposed and the idea was dropped. A related proposal, to circulate draft opinions in cases which the panel members thought might be decided en banc, was tried for a brief period. The practice is no longer followed.

As is true of the preparation of memoranda prior to the conference, there is no uniform procedure for writing opinions. Judge Friendly, for instance, treats opinions in much the same way as he does memoranda, as described earlier. All of the judges make use of their law clerks in this phase of the decision-making process,[88] but they do so in different ways. Judge Medina does not allow his law clerks to handle facts because "I do not believe [that] is the kind of thing you can turn over to a law clerk who has not had experience appraising facts."[89] Judge Frank's law clerks were able to influence their boss. One of them recalled that

> the law clerk, barely out of law school, was encouraged by Frank to say why and where Judge Learned Hand, the dean of the federal judiciary, had erred. It was Frank who had been appointed to the Court by the President with the advice and consent of the Senate and so it was he who had the last word. But short of that point egalitarianism prevailed. Once, after I had prepared a draft of an opinion according to the dictates of the Court, I reported to the judge that the other law clerks and I disagreed with the position which the Court was about to take. Thereupon Frank raised the matter again with his colleagues. I should like to be able to report that the judgment of the "puisne judges," as Judge Hand calls the law clerks, prevailed, but that was not so.[90]

[87] Memorandum of CEC, January 23, 1951.

[88] For a general discussion of the role of law clerks, see Norman Dorsen, "Law Clerks in the Appellate Courts in the United States," mimeographed (New York: Institute of Judicial Administration, 1962). Court of appeals judges select their law clerks from the top rank of law school graduates. Because service as law clerk to a circuit judge is regarded by some Supreme Court members as a prerequisite to Supreme Court service, the positions are especially coveted.

[89] Medina, "Decisional Process," p. 30.

[90] Philip Kurland, "Jerome N. Frank: Some Reflections and Recollections of a Law Clerk," *University of Chicago Law Review*, 24 (1957), 662. Another of Frank's law clerks, Sidney Davis, remembers other responsibilities: "Every day I would cover three or four . . . [libraries]. . . . Sometimes he

Law clerks and their judges disagree as to the role the former play. As Judge Medina stated: "They say, 'See that opinion of mine that came down yesterday.' Why, to listen to that going around the courts you wouldn't think the judges had anything to do with an opinion except maybe to take a quick glance and say, 'Okay boy. Good work. Good work.' "[91]

Law clerks probably exaggerate their influence because most of them do in fact draft some opinions;[92] they fail to recognize that this is not the same as deciding the outcome of appeals. But it does seem that law clerks in the courts of appeals play a more important role than their counterparts on the Supreme Court.[93] This is because cases accepted for review by the Supreme Court are usually policy oriented, with philosophical or normative overtones. Since the justices are able to think out their own policy positions, the influence of the law clerks is severely circumscribed. In the courts of appeals, on the other hand, many appeals raise technical questions which do not involve judicial predilections. The range of law clerk influence is thus expanded. Furthermore, there are certain fields where judges who have spent many years of specialized practice prior to appointment are just not as well informed as their bright young assistants who are familiar with the most recent writings and ideas. Finally, unlike the Supreme Court, where most appeals present a single question or a cluster of closely related questions, thus limiting the choices available to the justices, quite a few appeals to the intermediate courts are multidimen-

---

would tell me what books he wanted. Sometimes he would just say he wanted books. It got so I would pick up an armful of just about everything except cookbooks." Quoted by Richard Rovere in "Jerome N. Frank," An Address at a Special Memorial Meeting of the New York County Lawyers' Association and the Association of the Bar of the City of New York, May 23, 1957, p. 25.

[91] Medina, "Decisional Process," p. 27.

[92] Learned Hand, however, "wouldn't even let a law clerk write a sentence, not one sentence. He would let the law clerk criticize. He would hand what he had written to the law clerk and let him make all the suggestions he wanted to make. But not one word of that opinion was anybody else's but Learned Hand's" (Medina, "Decisional Process," p. 26).

[93] In the middle of one of the longest and most confusing Clark-Frank battles, Clark's law clerk wrote to the law clerk of Judge Chase: "This letter is in connection with the Alaska Pacific Salmon case, which Judge Frank is writing and in which your boss and mine sit with him. This case worries me very much. . . . If you have not been following the correspondence and the opinion in its changing forms I suggest that you do so, and if you then agree with me perhaps you could put in a plug for right and justice with your boss . . ." (letter from Allen Gallen, July 23, 1947). Ten days later, Frank wrote to Clark: "Perhaps it's your law clerk who deems me a subtle Machiavellian . . ." (August 2, 1947).

sional and include minor questions of fact or law that can be overlooked by a busy judge. This, coupled with the fact that court of appeals decisions—particularly in bankruptcy and admiralty appeals—often modify rather than reverse the decision below, means that a perceptive law clerk can bring out points that lead to modification of the result originally decided upon by the judges.

The completed draft opinion is sent to the other panel members for comments. An opinion may be rewritten several times until all or a majority of the judges are satisfied. The length of opinions in the Second Circuit and the ten other courts of appeals varies greatly, depending upon the complexity of the case and the desires of the opinion writer. Typically, they range from two to about ten pages; when Jerome Frank was on the Second Circuit some of his opinions were twenty pages and longer. In 1961 the average Second Circuit opinion was six and one-half pages; in 1962 the average increased to seven and one-half pages.[94]

A majority of appeals, about 85 per cent according to a recent writer,[95] are decided by a unanimous court, without concurring or dissenting opinions. This is not surprising in view of the size of the panels and the large number of frivolous appeals. In the remaining cases, dissenting or concurring opinions are filed or, once in a while, dissent or concurrence is noted without opinion. The latter practice is open to serious criticism since it deprives both the Supreme Court and counsel of the reasons for the disagreement with the majority.[96]

[94] "Second Circuit," p. 897.

[95] Karlen, "Court of Appeals for the Second Circuit," p. 509.

[96] Since it is obvious that dissenting and concurring judges disagree with the majority opinion, the most plausible explanation for the occasional dissents and concurrences without opinion is that the minority judge is unable or unwilling to spend time on a minority opinion. In United States v. Epstein, 154 F.2d 806 (2d Cir. 1946), Judge Frank simply noted concurrence in the result. Judge Clark, the author of the court's opinion, wrote: "I am surprised that you concurred only in the result, indicating something wrong with the opinion. I should have been glad to modify the opinion if I knew what was wrong" (CEC to JNF, March 21, 1946). In reply, Frank outlined his disagreement with the majority and then said: "I had one of three choices: to suggest rather sweeping revision of your opinion; to write a concurring opinion, pointing out where I differed from your generalizations; or to concur in the result. As you had Learned with you, so yours became the opinion of the court, I could see no harm in selecting the last choice" (JNF to CEC, March 22, 1946). But the explanation is weak, particularly in view of Frank's behavior in so many other cases. Why didn't he even attempt to convince Learned Hand?

Where an appeal is decided by a 2–1 vote, concurrence without opinion is quite unjustified. In Carrier Corporation v. National Labor Relations Board, 311 F.2d 135 (2d Cir. 1962), Decided 2–1, Judge Swan concurred "in

The decision of whether to file a separate opinion is left to each judge, although subtle pressures are at times exerted to maintain the appearance of unity. There was a favorable attitude on the Second Circuit toward dissent which was quite distinct during the chief judgeship of Learned Hand and for several years thereafter. Judge Clark, for many years the court's most frequent dissenter, wrote to a new colleague in the 1950's: "I suppose perhaps we have too much of a tradition of slugging it out, since this is now our life and our world."[97] In a 1957 survey of operating procedures of appellate courts, the Second Circuit was the only court of appeals to indicate that dissent was "encouraged."[98] The general feeling on the court is not to "get too excited about the differences of opinion or the dissents. They are a sign of health and vigor."[99]

But generalizations about encouragement of disagreement convey only a partly accurate picture of the tension and dynamics of a court faced with an almost unceasing torrent of opinions to prepare. An appellate judge must decide, if he has failed to convince his colleagues, whether to go along quietly or to file a separate opinion. There are situations in which the reaction of fellow judges has to be calculated before a decision is made. In such instances, the reactions of judges on the same court may vary a great deal, irrespective of the court's mood or style regarding dissent.

It is not surprising that the judges of the Learned Hand court disagreed as to when they should disagree. Judges Augustus Hand, Swan, and Chase were more likely than their volatile brethren to abstain from dissent when a reconciliation of views was not possible. After preparing a dissenting opinion, Swan complained, "In the manner of disagreement, this court is getting regrettably like its

---

the result of Judge Waterman's [majority] opinion." The losing party then petitioned for a rehearing because "there is no opinion of the Court to guide the Board, the parties in this case, or the unions or employers who will inevitably find themselves in similar situations in the future." Judge Swan then amplified; he "concurred in the result not because I disagree with anything stated therein (I do not) but because Judge Waterman's opinion failed to include certain additional grounds for affirmance which I thought relevant" (p. 155).

[97] CEC to Judge John M. Harlan, May 4, 1954.

[98] "Appellate Courts—Internal Operating Procedures, Preliminary Report," mimeographed (New York: Institute of Judicial Administration, 1957), p. 112, col. 14.

[99] Medina, "Some Reflections on the Judicial Function," p. 150. In part, the relative frequency of dissent may be attributable to the memorandum system. These preliminary opinions can be turned into dissents with less labor than would be required if a judge had to begin from scratch.

superior in Washington."[100] Augustus Hand, in particular, sought to discourage dissent in panels over which he presided. The Learned Hand court was faced with no more bitter dispute than that which erupted between Judges Frank and Clark in *United States v. Sacher*,[101] which concerned the contempt of court convictions of the defense lawyers in the trial of the leaders of the Communist Party. The majority (Augustus Hand and Frank) upheld the convictions; Clark dissented. Shortly before the opinions were filed, after ten weeks of bitter memoranda, Hand made another attempt to get Clark to go along. Clark refused:

> I have pondered long—indeed to the extent to which I am capable—over your parting admonition or suggestion. Because of my respect and regard for you, I cannot take it lightly. Indeed, I have examined the possibility of going along, since I know your persuasive opinion will persuade all but inconsiderable doubters. And I see no immediate and perhaps no future results from a dissent. But if I get to relying on such considerations I really will have nothing to tie to during what may still prove to be a long course of future judging.[102]

Second Circuit judges, along with most appellate judges, believe that by and large it is best to suppress disagreement in "unimportant" cases. This was the view of five of the six 1941–51 judges, including Learned Hand and Frank, who would make a point also of foregoing public disagreement if the issue raised on appeal had been previously decided contrary to their opinion by a Second Circuit panel.

There is no test of what is "important" in a case, although procedural issues usually are put in the unimportant category. However Judge Clark steadfastly refused to accept any notion that procedural questions are not of major import, and some of his strongest dissents were in protest against Second Circuit handling of the Federal Rules of Civil Procedure. Perhaps irrespective of his activities on behalf of procedural reform, he would have dissented frequently. His philosophy, as expressed in one dissent, was that "in the lonely task of judicial adjudication, each of us must finally act as his own faculties

[100] TWS to CEC, November 29, 1946. Clark's reply was: "I do not feel badly about the number of dissents, but think we are now only hitting our stride. Indeed, when on the first week's cases we all concurred in everything, I was distressed for fear we had gone soft" (CEC to TWS, November 30, 1946).

[101] 182 F.2d 416 (2d Cir. 1950).

[102] CEC to ANH, March 30, 1950.

demand."[103] Yet the evidence suggests that it was on procedural matters that he most strongly felt a need to voice his disagreements with colleagues. He could not permit what he regarded as Second Circuit tampering with procedural rules to go unchallenged;[104] indeed, "the very brilliance of our court" contributed to Clark's uneasiness, "for the greater the judges, the less patience they will have with procedural matters."[105] This attitude was fed by the recognition that "the Supreme Court has not much interest in procedural reform . . . ,"[106] so that it was incumbent upon him to protect the rules.

In addition to disagreeing as to when to dissent, judges differ on the effect of dissenting opinions. It was the view of Judge Parker "that most dissents do much more harm than good. They foster resentment on the part of the losing party, they encourage groundless appeals and they introduce an element of uncertainty where certainty should if possible prevail. . . . Sometimes a dissent is an appeal to the 'brooding spirit of the law.' More often it is nothing more than an expression of individual pride of opinion."[107] Few, if any, of the Second Circuit judges of the past quarter of a century would go along with such harsh

[103] Commissioner of Department of Public Utilities v. New York, New Haven and Hartford Railroad Co., 178 F.2d 559, 570 (2d Cir. 1949). In *In Re* Realty Associates Security Corporation, 163 F.2d 387 (2d Cir. 1947), Clark dissented, though he conceded "that I had half a mind to let the thing go until I talked with Professor J. W. Moore" (CEC to TWS, July 22, 1947).

[104] In Zalkind v. Scheinman, 139 F.2d 895 (2d Cir. 1943), Clark dissented, though in his first memorandum (November 4, 1943) he admitted that "perhaps I ought to keep still." The case dealt with the question of whether a district court order was subject to appeal and brought on another heated Clark-Frank argument.

[105] CEC to LH, August 4, 1947.

[106] CEC to Judge Henry W. Edgerton, February 4, 1943. On another occasion, Clark argued: "As we know, members of the [Supreme] Court have not background or interest in this field and react as, unfortunately, courts and lawyers have done from, I suppose, the beginning of time, that, while they despise procedural rules as mere machinery, unworthy of the thought of intellectual persons, yet it can be made use of as an excuse for reaching a result which justice seems to require in a particular case" (letter to Judge Frank, on Queensboro v. Wickard, July 14, 1943). In the same letter Clark suggested that "as to procedure we can have perhaps some more hesitation than in other cases as to just what" the Supreme Court required. In Zalkind v. Scheinman (pp. 906–7), Clark advanced the argument that Supreme Court refusal to review cases raising procedural questions was not very meaningful.

[107] Parker, "Improving Appellate Methods," p. 13.

condemnation, certainly not Judge Clark[108] or Judge Frank, who spent so much of his life debunking the idea of certainty in the law.

In defense of dissents it should be pointed out that their frequency did not prevent the Learned Hand court from functioning smoothly; and that when judges disagree, to abstain from dissent in the name of preserving a mythical "certainty" is to disregard the judge's paramount responsibility, which is to decide each case as he believes it ought to be decided. Dissenting opinions in the courts of appeals also serve as cues to Supreme Court justices when they examine petitions for certiorari. A study of Supreme Court certiorari jurisdiction established that there is a significantly better chance of review being granted when there is dissent in the court below.[109] The dissenting intermediate appellate judge appeals not merely to the "brooding spirit of the law," but, more practically, to nine justices on the Supreme Court.[110]

The draft dissenting and concurring opinions are sent to the other panel members, who then do one of the following: (1) refuse to change their position; (2) accept the views of the dissatisfied judge; (3) revise the majority opinion to meet the objections, removing the incentive for a separate opinion; (4) revise the majority opinion to include material answering the dissent or concurrences.

[108] But in a letter to Professor Bernhard Knollenberg (May 31, 1944), Clark lamented, "I suppose that of the useless things which afflict mankind nothing is more useless than a dissenting opinion of an 'inferior' federal court where the Supreme Court refuses review." Many years later, Clark was gratified when the Supreme Court, in Watkins v. United States 354 U.S. 178 (1957), reversed the contempt conviction of one who refused to answer questions before the House Un-American Activities Committee, thereby accepting Clark's notable dissent in United States v. Josephson, 165 F.2d 82, 93 (2d Cir. 1948). John Frank wrote to Clark (June 21, 1957): "The parallelism between the two opinions is so strikingly close that it is obvious that in one of the most important works of your life you have been entirely vindicated. By being the first prophet to enter this field of thorns, you performed one of your life's public services; . . . this must indeed be, and should be, one of your proudest days."

[109] J. Tanenhaus, M. Schick, M. Muraskin, and D. Rosen, "The Supreme Court's Certiorari Jurisdiction: Cue Theory," in Glendon A. Schubert (ed.), *Judicial Decision-Making* (Glencoe, Ill.: Free Press, 1963), pp. 123–24.

[110] Actually, in another connection, we will see that overt appeals to the Supreme Court for reversal of court of appeals rulings, even by the majority, are not uncommon. One might argue that dissent is more justified, the lower a court is in the judicial hierarchy. Certainly there is less of a practical side to many Supreme Court dissents than there is to those of inferior judges. Something Jerome Frank once wrote comes to mind: " 'What,' someone once asked, 'has posterity done for me, that I should think of posterity?' " (Anon Y. Mous [Jerome N. Frank], "The Speech of Judges: A Dissenting Opinion," *Virginia Law Review*, 29 [1943], 640, n. 10).

There is no formal pattern for issuing opinions; "Opinions will be delivered at any time whether the court is in session or not, and are delivered by handing them to the clerk to be by him recorded."[111] They are then printed as slip opinions and distributed to the parties concerned, all judges (including district) within the circuit, all courts of appeals judges in the other circuits, Supreme Court justices,[112] and selected libraries and law schools.

On the average, seven to eight weeks pass from oral argument until the final opinion is issued.[113] This is about the same as the average for all circuits but significantly longer than the time record of the Learned Hand court.

Within fourteen days after entry of a decision, the losing party can submit a petition for rehearing. The Appellate Rules require that the petition briefly state the ground upon which the request is made. Rehearing is asked in about 50 per cent of the appeals, according to one estimate;[114] records of these petitions are not kept. It is believed that the percentage is higher in some of the other circuits;[115] in any event, the feeling in the Second Circuit is that too many are filed.[116] A Supreme Court justice who paid close attention to the operations of the courts of appeals cautioned that

> rehearings are not a healthy step in the judicial process; surely they ought not to be deemed a normal procedure. Yet one who has paged the Federal Reporter for nearly fifty years is struck with what appears to be a growth in the tendency to file petitions for rehearing in the courts of appeals. I have not made a quantitative study of the facts, but one gains the impression that in some circuits these petitions are filed almost as a matter of course. This is an abuse of judicial energy. It results in needless delay. It arouses false hopes in defeated litigants and wastes their money. If petitions for rehearing were justified, except in rare instances it

[111] Second Circuit Rule 24 (a).

[112] Justice Frankfurter read the slip opinions of the Second Circuit regularly.

[113] In determining the relative efficiency of appellate courts, this is, perhaps, the most meaningful statistic. The average for the Second Circuit—and the other courts of appeals—would be higher were it not for the summary decisions.

[114] "Second Circuit," p. 899.

[115] Ibid.

[116] "Such motions are getting to be as persistent in this court as in the Court of Civil Appeals of Texas" (Judge Augustus Hand, United States v. Cipullo, November 12 1948. After repeated petitions for rehearing, in a single case, Judge Lumbard lamented: "What about due process for the judges to protect them against harassment?" (Memorandum to CEC, Kleinman v. Kobler, December 4, 1957).

would bespeak serious defects in the work of the courts of appeals, an assumption which must be rejected.[117]

This criticism is not wholly justified. While most petitions for rehearing are summarily denied, a small number do lead to changes in the original decision "to eliminate an ambiguity or correct a misstatement."[118] This appears to be particularly true of bankruptcy appeals; the explanation is that in these cases the papers are often so voluminous and the facts so tangled that the judges, busy with other work, overlook relevant points or make errors in rendering the facts. Rehearings in the courts of appeals also have a much better prospect of leading to a reversal of the original result than do those in the Supreme Court. From 1941 to 1951 at least five petitions succeeded[119] and in several cases votes were switched although the results were unchanged.

When a petition for rehearing is granted, reargument is not permitted, except rarely, but the court will occasionally request a reply brief from the other party. Rehearings are closely related to the question of en banc proceedings in the courts of appeals, a matter of contention on the Second Circuit for almost a quarter of a century. The argument in favor of full bench hearing of certain appeals grows out of the defects of the panel system. Courts of appeals sitting in panels, particularly those with six or more judges, are open to the danger of court policy being determined by a minority of the active judges.

On the Second Circuit, for example, the tradition is to adhere to previous panel decisions, especially those that are recent. There have been innumerable instances where judges have declined to dissent because "the law of the Circuit has apparently been determined to the contrary, and so I shall join in my brothers' disposition."[120] Learned Hand, after sending out a memorandum urging the court to adhere to an old decision, added the following note to Judge Clark:

Charlie, I know what you have been thinking, if you have read the foregoing. "Why does the old fool flub around so much to

[117] Justice Frankfurter concurring in Western Pacific R.R. Corp. v. Western Pacific R.R. Co., 345 U.S. 247, 270 (1953).

[118] "Second Circuit," p. 898.

[119] Rockmore v. Lehman, 129 F.2d 892 (2d Cir. 1942); United States v. Liss, 137 F.2d 995 (2d Cir. 1943), conviction of one defendant reversed upon rehearing; United States v. Bollenbach, 147 F.2d 199 (2d Cir. 1945); Phillips v. Star Overall Dry Cleaning Laundry Co., 149 F.2d 416 (2d Cir. 1945); United States v. Allen, 159 F.2d 594 (2d Cir. 1947).

[120] Belk v. Allied Aviation Service Co. of New Jersey, 315 F.2d 513, 518 (2d Cir. 1963) (Judge Clark concurring). The example of Clark is noteworthy because more than any of the other members of the court he was ready to persist in advocating ideas that had been previously rejected.

save the face of a decision that was written over forty years ago by three lobsters long since 'turned to clay' who may be 'stopping a hole to keep the wind away?' " That is a secret, Charles, a secret which only the wisdom that comes from extreme old age can unravel; some day you will learn it, but never from me, never from me, never from me!!! [121]

In one case decided in 1949 a panel consisting of Judges Learned Hand, Swan, and Frank rendered a ruling "against the unanimous conviction of the court as constituted but in deference to a precedent established by a differently constituted court of the same Circuit."[122] The earlier decision was by a 2–1 vote; Learned Hand rationalized the acceptance of a minority position:

> It appears to all three of us in the present court most undesirable to repudiate a precedent so established. In a final court of varying composition it might be asking too much that the first decision should become an authoritative precedent against the convictions of the other members, but we are not in that predicament. . . . [The losing party] may be able to secure review by certiorari in the Supreme Court; and, if they fail, it is either because that court believes that the first decision was right, or because a solution of the issue is not of enough importance to demand its intervention. In either event we ought to be content, as we are, to sink our differences, and yield to the precedent, whatever our confidence in our conclusion.[123]

Judge Hand's placid acceptance of minority decision-making was not justified in view of the existence of a simple method for insuring that a majority determine circuit policy.

In 1941, in *Textile Mills Security Corp. v. Commissioner*,[124] the Supreme Court held that the courts of appeals were authorized to sit en banc. Seven years later, in a new section (46[c]) of the Judicial Code, Congress specifically provided that in the courts of appeals "cases and controversies shall be heard and determined by a court or division of not more than three judges, unless a hearing or rehearing before the court in banc is ordered by a majority of the circuit judges of the circuit who are in active service. A court in banc shall consist of all active judges of the circuit."

Most of the courts of appeals quickly set up procedures to comply with the congressional and Supreme Court mandates. But the Second

---

[121] Strom v. Peikes, October 27, 1941.

[122] Dickinson v. Petroleum Conversion Corp., 338 U.S. 507, 508 (1950).

[123] Dickinson v. Mulligan, 173 F.2d 738, 741 (2d Cir. 1949). The Supreme Court granted certiorari and reversed, saying, "we agree with the convictions of the court below and reverse its judgment" (at 338 U.S. 508).

[124] 314 U.S. 326.

Circuit rigidly maintained the panel system. Learned Hand would have nothing of en banc proceedings.

As early as 1940 Judge Clark urged his colleagues to consider full court hearings to avoid minority decisions.[125] The proposal ran smack into Learned Hand's opposition, which was enough to kill it for more than a decade. Clark persisted, although he received no support from the other second Circuit judges, with the possible exception of Judge Frank,[126] and the idea irked Learned Hand. In response to one of Clark's communications on the subject, Hand wrote:

> I have yours of the 20th once more suggesting that when we over-rule our own decisions we should sit all six together. For myself I have always felt a strong compulsion to follow our decisions, at least when they are recent, though not when they are fifteen or twenty years old. However, occasions do of course arise when all, or perhaps two, of the three who are sitting feel so strongly that they cannot accept an earlier decision that they will avowedly refuse to follow it. I have always believed—as I have often said before—that the Supreme Court is instituted as much to settle such conflicts as conflicts between circuits; the issue, so far as I can see, is just the same. Biggs' invention has never seemed to me to have any advantages; it certainly does not secure uniformity, and I should not think that it would be much more likely to prevent certiorari than if the difference of opinion manifested itself in two decisions. At any rate I am content to leave to the Supreme Court those cases where they believe they should inter-vene. It would be rash to say that there could never be a situation in which I should vote for a court of six . . . ; but I can only repeat that for myself I cannot at the moment think of any. It doesn't follow that the rest will continue to agree with me. I am sorry not to be more amenable.[127]

However appealing Judge Hand's arguments—toward the end of his life they were accepted somewhat by Judge Clark—the position

[125] Memorandum of CEC in United States v. Fallon, May 6, 1940: "I wonder if we ought not to give those of our non-participating colleagues who wish to do so an opportunity to express their opinions, particularly if there is something in the view that a minority of our court may bind all the rest of us—a view, I must confess, which has quite disturbing connotations for me."

[126] In the course of the 1942 battles over consultation with non-sitting judges, discussed previously, on several occasions Frank indicated support for full court hearing of appeals; e.g., "It was I who suggested to them [Learned and Augustus Hand], at that time, that we have a six-judge court decide the case" (JNF to CEC, June 30, 1942). However, there is no other evidence of Frank support and in some cases, notably P. Beirsdorf & Co., Inc. v. McGohey, 187 F.2d 14 (2d Cir. 1951), he implicitly rejected Clark's plea for an en banc hearing.

[127] LH to CEC, May 27, 1944.

they supported was weak. For while Hand was characteristically on the side of restraint in his willingness to accept prior panel decisions with which he disagreed, he was also acting counter to the wishes of the Supreme Court. Moreover, he and Frank often coupled their acceptance of panel precedents with pleas for Supreme Court reversal; for example, "I must be content with hoping that the Supreme Court, recognizing an 'intra-Circuit conflict,' will grant review and reverse this decision."[128] Taken seriously, such suggestions amount to disruption of the Supreme Court's certiorari jurisdiction, which, among other purposes, is designed to free the High Court from deciding issues that could easily be settled elsewhere. Unlike intercircuit conflict, where there obviously is no way to resolve the disagreement short of one circuit surrendering or Supreme Court review, intracircuit conflicts are within the domain of a single court. Many of the conflicts on the Second Circuit were over procedural questions; it truly would have burdened the Supreme Court if it had to intervene in all such situations in the lower appellate courts.

At first, Supreme Court annoyance with Second Circuit policy was limited to Justice Frankfurter. In a case dealing with bankruptcy turnover orders, a problem that had sharply divided the Second Circuit, largely because of its refusal to reject long-standing precedents, Justice Frankfurter dissented from Supreme Court action and lambasted the Second Circuit:

> Presumably, this avowed inability of the Circuit Court of Appeals for the Second Circuit to free itself from its own prior decision in this situation is not the reflection of a principle similar to that which binds the House of Lords to its past precedents. It must be attributable to the fact that the Second Circuit has six circuit judges who never sit en banc and that presumably they deem it undesirable for the majority of one panel to have a different view from that of a majority of another panel.[129]

In *Western Pacific R.R. Corp v. Western Pacific R.R. Co.*, decided in 1953, the Supreme Court "with at least an implication of criticism of our practice of never sitting en banc,"[130] stated that while "each Court of Appeals is vested with a wide latitude of discretion to decide for itself just how the power shall be exercised,"[131] "the

---

[128] Judge Frank in P. Beirsdorf & Co., Inc. v. McGohey, p. 15.

[129] Maggio v. Zeitz, 333 U.S. 56 (1948), p. 82, n. 5.

[130] *In re* Sacher, 206 F.2d 358, 362 (2d Cir., 1953) (Judge Clark dissenting).

[131] Western Pacific R.R. Corp. v. Western Pacific R.R. Co., 345 U.S. 247, 259 (1953). The vote was 8–1, with Chief Justice Vinson writing the majority opinion. The lone dissenter, Justice Jackson, conceded the utility of en banc hearings where there was an intracircuit conflict.

en banc power . . . is . . . a necessary and useful power—indeed too useful that we should ever permit a court to ignore the possibilities of its use in cases where its use might be appropriate."[132] The Supreme Court then elaborated "certain fundamental requirements"[133] that the courts of appeals should incorporate into their en banc procedures.[134]

Following the retirement of Learned Hand, Judge Clark renewed his efforts, which were further encouraged by the *Western Pacific* ruling. However, the Second Circuit's next two chief judges stood by the "Learned Hand precedent." When Clark became chief judge in late 1954, he took advantage of the opportunity to implement his views and in 1956 the court for the first time heard an appeal en banc.[135] From 1956 through May 1963 the Second Circuit heard thirty cases in that fashion.[136]

En banc proceedings raise two fundamental questions: (1) What procedures are to be followed in determining which cases should be dealt with by the full bench? (2) What types of cases should be handled in this manner?

In general, the Second Circuit has followed the requirements outlined by the Supreme Court in *Western Pacific*. Appeals have been heard en banc in these situations:

1. As an original hearing, when a majority of the active judges, at the suggestion of one of the judges, agree that the particular case merits the attention of the full court. At least six of the first thirty cases were original hearings.

---

[132] *Ibid.,* p. 260.

[133] *Ibid.;* see also pp. 260–62.

[134] These requirements have been summarized as: "(1) The courts of appeals should make clear to litigants the method by which the court en banc is convened; (2) the decision to sit en banc may be made by the full court, or it may be delegated initially to the hearing panel, although the full court retains the authority to revise the en banc procedure and to withdraw the delegated power; indeed, the courts must constantly consider whether their rules promote the purpose of the en banc statute; (3) litigants should be able to suggest that a particular case is appropriate for en banc determination, but these suggestions should not be treated like motions and should not require formal action by the court; (4) the courts may initiate en banc proceedings sua sponte; (5) whether to rehear a case before the panel or the court en banc are two separate questions which should be considered independently" ("En Banc Procedure in the Federal Courts of Appeals," *University of Pennsylvania Law Review,* 111 [1962], 220, 221).

[135] Matter of Lake Tankers Corp., 235 F.2d 383 (2d Cir. 1956).

[136] For a listing of these cases, see Walters v. Moore-McCormack Lines, Inc., 312 F.2d 893, 895–96 (2d Cir. 1963), and "Second Circuit," pp. 904–5. Because the cases decided en banc are important and almost always contentious, they present unique opportunities for studying voting relationships on the courts of appeals.

2. After a panel has heard a case, but before a final decision is reached, at the suggestion of one or more on the panel, the case is transferred to the full court.

3. Rehearing after the panel decision at the suggestion of one of the judges on the panel or one of the active judges.

4. Rehearing after the panel decision on the petition of one of the parties.

In all instances, en banc is ordered only if it has the support of a majority of the active judges.[137]

Ordinarily, a rehearing en banc is on the original briefs and without argument. Sometimes the court requests supplementary briefs and, in a few cases, there has been reargument.

The clearest statement of the criteria for invoking the en banc power was made by Justice Frankfurter in *Western Pacific:*

> Rehearings en banc by these courts, which sit in panels, are to some extent necessary, in order to resolve conflicts between panels. This is the dominant concern. . . . Hence, insofar as possible, determinations en banc are indicated whenever it seems likely that a majority of all the active judges would reach a different result than the panel assigned to hear a case or which has heard it. Hearings en banc may be a resort also in cases ex-

[137] For the mechanics of en banc procedure in the Second Circuit, see, "En Banc Procedure," p. 222. Rule 35 of the Appellate Rules of Procedure provides:

"(a) A majority of the circuit judges who are in regular active service may order that an appeal or other proceeding be heard or reheard by the court of appeals in banc. Such a hearing or rehearing is not favored and ordinarily will not be ordered except (1) when consideration by the full court is necessary to secure or maintain uniformity of its decisions, or (2) when the proceeding involves a question of exceptional importance.

"(b) A party may suggest the appropriateness of a hearing or rehearing in banc. . . . but a vote will not be taken to determine whether the cause shall be heard or reheard in banc unless a judge in regular active service or a judge who was a member of the panel that rendered a decision sought to be reheard requests a vote on such a suggestion made by a party."

The statutory requirement that the en banc procedure is in the hands of the "active" circuit judges, excludes the senior judges who continue to hear cases (United States v. American-Foreign S.G. Corp., 365 U.S. 685 [1960]). This means that senior judges sitting on panels can be overruled by their colleagues without their having anything to say about it and that the senior judges may be effectively excluded from deciding many of the important cases decided by the courts of appeals. Judge Clark called this exclusion "the accident of a poorly worded statute" (Foti v. Immigration and Naturalization Service, 308 F.2d 779, 789 [2d Cir. 1962]) (Clark, J., dissenting). The Judicial Conference of the United States proposed in 1959 that Section 46 (c) be amended to permit retired judges to sit en banc in the rehearing of a case when they were on the original panel.

traordinary in scale—either because the amount involved is stupendous or because the issues are intricate enough to invoke the pooled wisdom of the circuit.[138]

While Justice Frankfurter spoke for himself, his views have received general acceptance.[139] For the Second Circuit, Chief Justice Lumbard announced in 1963:

> The most important criterion for granting an in banc hearing is whether the case involves an issue likely to affect many other cases. Mere disagreement, or likelihood of disagreement, with the panel decision, has not generally been regarded as sufficient reason for a further hearing, although that is naturally one factor which is given some weight in our votes. In many cases the dissenting judge has opposed an in banc hearing because of the feeling that the question did not warrant the time of all the judges. Conversely, judges have voted to refer to the whole court their own majority opinions or those of other judges with which they agreed.

and, "As I understand the purpose of in banc review, the precise question which controls our decision whether or not to adopt this extraordinary procedure is whether a case presents an issue of sufficient concern to enough litigants who are or may become involved in similar situations so that the even-handed administration of justice will be benefited by a decision by the entire court."[140] The occasion for the chief judge's statement was the charge made in the same case by Judge Clark that the court was acting unfairly in selecting cases for en banc: "To generalize, it is clear that prosecutors and prison officials have traditionally had first call, and important property issues are given careful consideration. On the other hand, seamen's claims have practically no chance at all of *in banc* hearing, though these cases are now the most debated of all issues within the court."[141] The chief judge called this characterization "inaccurate and incomplete."[142]

At present, Chief Judge Lumbard's view seems to be representative of a majority of the active judges on the Second Circuit, but it is difficult to reconcile it completely with Justice Frankfurter's "dominant

[138] Pp. 270–71.

[139] Judge Albert B. Maris, "Hearing and Rehearing Cases in Banc; The Procedure of the United States Court of Appeals for the Third Circuit," 14 *Federal Rules Decisions* 91, 96.

[140] Walters v. Moore-McCormack Lines, Inc., 312 F.2d, 893, 894 (2d Cir. 1963).

[141] *Ibid.*, pp. 897–98 (dissenting opinion).

[142] *Ibid.*, p. 893.

concern": "to resolve conflicts between panels." Independent of Judge Clark's charge of prejudice, it does seem that the Second Circuit was lax in invoking the en banc power to resolve conflicts in seamen's cases. The majority was saying, in effect, that these cases are "unimportant" and thus do not merit full court hearing. Yet, the standard of "importance" that is given most frequently in cases heard by the full court[143] justifies the fears that en banc proceedings would make the courts of appeals miniature supreme courts.

This is not to say that in very important cases the entire bench should not be called on to decide the issues presented; only that the court should not downgrade the rationale for en banc hearings—intra-circuit conflict.[144]

Whether the Second Circuit would profit from adoption of Judge Clark's position is, again, another matter. Judge Clark did not really object to the "importance" test and the statement of Chief Judge Lumbard. His primary concern was what he considered the restrictive and prejudicial use of the en banc power. He wanted the full court to hear certain cases which previously had been left almost exclusively to panels. To Judge Clark a "powerful reason for full review—a reason which each one of my colleagues has found adequate justification from time to time for *in banc* in cases of special interest to him—is that the panel decision seems to me clearly in error."[145] The danger of this reasoning is that if the judges make it a habit to be solicitous of the views of one or two of their colleagues who do not like particular panel decisions, the en banc power, which should be reserved for a handful of extraordinary appeals each term, will hamper the court's ability to dispose expeditiously of its remaining business.

[143] "Second Circuit," p. 903. It is noteworthy that the use of "importance" in the selection of cases for en banc hearing parallels the development of criteria for the exercise by the Supreme Court of its certiorari jurisdiction. While Rule 19 of the Supreme Court's Rules places primary emphasis on various forms of intercourt conflict and on important questions not decided on previously by the Supreme Court as the reasons for granting certiorari, the Supreme Court most often agrees to review a case because of the "importance of issues" and in order "to decide the issue presented" (Tanenhaus, Schick, Muraskin, and Rosen, "Cue Theory," in Schubert, *Judicial Decision-Making,* pp. 113–16).

[144] The new rule on en banc proceedings, n. 137, above, encourages full court hearing only to resolve or avoid intracircuit conflict or when the case "involves a question of exceptional importance."

[145] Walters v. Moore-McCormack Lines, Inc., 312 F.2d 893, 899 (2d Cir. 1963). When Judge Clark argued for an en banc hearing on the ground that the panel decision was wrong, he was following what some observers believe to be the key to Supreme Court grant of certiorari: the feeling that the decision below is incorrect (Robert W. Gibbs, "Certiorari: Its Diagnosis and Cure," *Hastings Law Journal,* 6 [1955], 153).

The furor over en banc policy has subsided in the last several years. Still, a number of judges are of the opinion that it would be best to return to the inflexible panel system of the past, although they recognize that this is virtually impossible so long as the Supreme Court insists that courts of appeals sit en banc. Judge Medina (who as a senior judge is no longer directly involved in the question) once thought that Learned Hand's position was wrong, but he has since said, "Now I think he was right as usual."[146] Judge Clark, the judge who finally succeeded in getting the Second Circuit to utilize the en banc power, wrote less than a year before his death: "Because our *in banc* proceedings have actually settled so little, have emphasized division rather than allayed it, I could view with equanimity a decision, if legal, to return to our old course of hearing no cases *in banc*."[147]

[146] Medina, "Decisional Process," p. 39.

[147] Carrier Corporation v. National Labor Relations Board, 311 F.2d 135, 156 (2d Cir. 1962) (petition for rehearing en banc denied, Judge Clark dissenting).

4

Judicial Relations

THE UNITED STATES COURTS OF APPEALS ARE NOT ELEVEN ISOLATED LEGAL systems whose judges arrive at their decisions according to a set of internalized procedures shielded from external pressures; they are intermediate institutions, precisely located in a vast judicial system with ongoing relations with other courts and judges. They interact formally with the district courts below and the Supreme Court above, with courts on the same level, occasionally with state courts, and possibly also with nonjudicial forces.

The crucial relationships are with the Supreme Court in Washington and the district courts within the circuit. Because these relationships are hierarchical they involve more or less clearcut patterns of authority; the impact of personal factors is minimal. In the preceding chapter we saw how in the Second Circuit during Learned Hand's chief judgeship the absence of social cohesion affected the mode of decision-making. Personal factors can also be expected to be of relative importance in other relationships which are horizontal, non-authoritative, and informal. For instance, courts of appeals are free to accept or not to accept each other's decisions so long as the Supreme Court is silent; individual attitudes may well determine how one court of appeals deals with another's decisions. But where linkage is formal and vertical, such as between district courts and courts of appeals or between the intermediate courts and the Supreme Court, personal relations can only rarely affect judicial output.

Much of the dynamic quality of the Second Circuit, 1941–51, came from an unexpected quarter outside of the more formal boundaries of the judicial system, providing fuel for the Clark and Frank entanglements that enlivened the court. The two judges had close ties to the Yale Law School, which they maintained through teaching and personal contacts after ascending the bench. Thus they were provided with a forum for airing their differences and opportunities to solicit the views of Yale colleagues and friends on matters pending before the Second Circuit. Professors Arthur Corbin, Edwin Borchard, Fred Rodell, Vern Countryman, and, most important of all, Professor James W. Moore, were involved at one time or another in the business of the court of appeals, and Moore had a definite influence over the entire ten-year period.

Moore's importance was the result of the confluence of several factors. As the author of the many-volumed *Moore's Federal Practice* he was (and probably still is) the country's leading authority on judicial procedure and the Federal Rules; as we saw in the preceding chapter, Clark—as well as Frank—had strong views on procedural matters; both judges knew Moore quite well and saw and spoke to him at Yale, and Clark had the additional contact of serving with him on the Supreme Court's Standing Committee on Rules of Practice and Procedure. Inevitably, when disagreement arose over procedure, Moore would be drawn in, at times becoming the focal point of the dispute.

In his memoranda Judge Clark repeatedly referred to discussions with Moore, usually to buttress his contention that the Second Circuit had erred in procedural rulings or was subverting the Federal Rules. From the evidence available, his colleagues, with the exception of Jerome Frank, paid little heed to the invocation of expert authority. It was as if they could not care less what Moore thought, nor were they troubled by Clark's reliance on an outsider. But Frank reacted strongly and at times angrily. One illustration shows how Moore became a Clark-Frank issue.

In a case called *In Re P-R Holding Corporation*,[1] dealing with problems of corporate reorganization, Judge Frank's opinion for a unanimous court takes up seven paragraphs and makes no mention of Professor Moore. Yet, after Clark indicated that he had discussed the problems in the case with Moore, the issue of whether the court should rely on outside authorities came to the fore in an exchange between the two New Deal judges. The salient portions of the cor-

[1] 147 F.2d 895 (2d Cir. 1945).

respondence are set forth in the notes;[2] in their final letters on the subject Clark and Frank made their positions clear. First Judge Clark:

> I consider it such a privilege to be able to take up some matters with Moore, Corbin, and others, that I certainly want to be as fair as I can, and will say that I try to be and that by no means do we always agree. . . . Maybe I am wrong, but I think Moore and

[2] JNF to CEC, March 9, 1945:
"You know me well enough to know that I don't mind criticism, but on the whole rather enjoy it, if I'm allowed to reply. It does, however, irk me a little to have Professor Moore held up as one who, because of his greater wisdom and vaster experience, is more sensitive than I to the needs of practicality in reorganizations. True, I'm a pretty dumb egg; but, after all, I did work a good deal in the reorganization field in private practice; and, while I was on the SEC, I assisted in procuring the enactment of the Chandler Act and subsequently supervised the setting up of the Reorganization Division in a way which has led to its workability. I consider Professor Moore an exceedingly able man and doubtless there are many subjects on which he knows a great deal more than I. But I don't think a suggestion I make with respect to reorganization matters should be disregarded primarily because he is 'horrified' by it—especially when he apparently didn't bother to study it with care."

CEC to JNF, March 10, 1945:
"About Professor Moore, I am sorry I did not make explicit what I certainly had in my mind with reference to him, namely, that he and his assistant, Mr. Oglebay, were the leading academic authorities. I was not intending to put them up as anything more than the ultimate court of appeal many of us tend to make the professors. Please do not think I intended anything more, because I feel myself that Moore is too good a man to push out unduly on the realms of practical experience, where, of course, he has not gone far. But he and his assistant together do keep up with every decided case and put a great deal of care and thought on the matter, and I did discuss this P-R matter with both of them with some care."

JNF to CEC, March 12, 1945:
"I am answering your letter of March 10, although the subject is now academic, because it bears on the question of how far Professor Moore's views should be taken by you as having more cogency than those of your colleagues. Don't misunderstand me: I certainly think it desirable to know what he thinks on subjects concerning which he is an expert, and I envy you the possibility of frequently consulting him. But it is disadvantageous that, when you do consult him and reflect his views, your colleagues do not have the opportunity subsequently to talk the matter out with him.

The P-R case I think is illustrative. I think he there misunderstood my proposal, and your letters indicate that the concurring opinion you prepared and your subsequent correspondence (including your letter of March 10) reflect his views. For that reason, I shall now try to show that he, and therefore you, misunderstood my suggestion, as I think would not have been the case if I could have talked the matter out with you or him. . . . Perhaps my draftsmanship could have been improved, and perhaps Professor Moore could have improved it. But, as I didn't talk with him, I think he misunderstood my proposal and consequently advanced reasons for rejecting it, seemingly adopted by you, which I think were fallacious."

I by a little insistence are pushing people . . . to a sounder and more practical result than might have been reached had we been meeker.[3]

Judge Frank, in reply:

I think no such cooperative effort [in preparing the opinion] was possible because (1) Moore . . . started out unsympathetically and (2) you and I merely exchanged written notes while Moore was at your side. That situation, of course, puts me at a marked disadvantage: you couldn't hear what I said since Moore's voice drowned me out, and you regarded his voice as that of a superior expert. When Moore serves in that way, he is like a fourth member of the court with whom only one of the other three confers. In such circumstances, our conference technique cannot work at its best.[4]

Curiously, Frank's complaint about his colleague's ex parte discussions with Moore brings to mind Clark's argument in 1942 against Frank's consultations with non-sitting judges which was discussed in the last chapter.

There were some on the Yale faculty with whom Frank had a closer relationship than he had with Moore; he would justify his refusal to accept their views when cited by Clark on the ground that "I must, as a judge, ultimately rely on my own reasoning, no matter how able are those who disagree with me."[5]

The bitterest battle between the two judges over expert advice arose in 1946, and surprisingly the outsider was Professor Luther Noss, who happened to be the Yale University organist and a good friend of Clark. In the early 1940's a songwriter named Ira B. Arnstein brought suit in Southern District Court against Cole Porter, charging that some of Porter's songs—including "Begin the Beguine," "My Heart Belongs to Daddy," "Don't Fence Me In," and "Night and Day"— were plagiarisms of tunes composed by Arnstein. Previously, Arnstein had brought other suits of this nature without any success. Seemingly, the new litigation was destined for quick failure, and when Porter's lawyers moved for summary dismissal the trial judge tossed out the suit. Arnstein appealed to the Second Circuit and the case was heard by a panel consisting of Learned Hand, Clark, and Frank.

As we have seen, most appeals are so one-sided that the make-up of the panel has no bearing on the outcome; presumably Arnstein's appeal was such a case. But the action of the trial judge had added a

---

[3] CEC to JNF, March 12, 1945.

[4] JNF to CEC, March 13, 1945.

[5] JNF to CEC, February 6, 1952. Another illustration of the same: "I greatly respect Borchard. But, after all, his views do not bind us, while those of the Supreme Court do. I'm for good old Yale, but devotion to a law school ought not lead Circuit judges to attempted concealment of Supreme Court rulings" (JNF to CEC, July 13, 1943).

nice procedural question which already had stirred the Second Circuit: was summary judgment proper or should the district court have permitted the issue to come to trial before a jury? About a year earlier, Frank had sharply criticized the use of the summary judgment power[6] and the other panel members (Chase and Learned Hand) went along, although the latter wrote a partial dissent on another question. Thus even before Arnstein argued his case pro se, the luck of the draw had given him two judges who had serious qualms about summary judgments.

Judge Clark, on the other hand, consistent with his general approach to procedure, viewed the summary judgment rule as a valuable device for the expeditious handling of patently frivolous or vexatious suits. Also, no matter what reservations they might have, all judges would concede that there is litigation where a trial is not necessary. Perhaps *Arnstein v. Porter* was such a suit; after all, the idea that one of America's illustrious songwriters had plagiarized an unknown man's work seemed ludicrous.

In his first memorandum Judge Frank reported: "I have listened to them. I am relatively unversed in this field. But I think that (1) Porter's Begin the Beguine has some marked resemblances to (2) Arnstein's Duet from his Song of David, his Lord is my Shepherd, and his A Mother's Prayer. Ditto as to (1) Porter's I Love You and (2) Arnstein's La Priere. So too does my secretary who improvises music."[7]

Clark's method was somewhat similar: "I first went over the sheet music, studying plaintiff's dissection-analysis of alleged similarities, and listened to the records, reaching the conclusion that under no possibility of proof now available would there be anything actionable or anything even remotely suggesting access. This conclusion, I may add, was concurred in by my secretary and my law clerk, both of whom have studied music somewhat as I have." Then, "In order to be quite sure, and because plaintiff's charges against the court and the judges are so usual, I spent Sunday afternoon with my friend Professor Luther Noss . . . who is not above playing and understanding popular music. He did not use the records, but played and sang all the pieces. . . . His over all conclusion was that the claim of access and of copying was fantastic."[8]

[6] Doehler Metal Furnishing Co. Inc. v. United States, 149 F.2d 130, 135 (2d Cir. 1945).

[7] JNF Memorandum, January 11, 1946.

[8] CEC Memorandum, January 14, 1946. Clark suggested that his colleagues "do the same thing with a really good musician." The memorandum also cited Professor Moore's support of Clark's position on summary judgments, but this was later discounted by Frank, who pointed to the contrary position taken by one of Moore's top assistants. JNF Supplemental Memorandum, January 15, 1946.

Judge Frank's response to the involvement of Professor Noss was sharp: "Although in the old civilian practice the witnesses were heard in secret, at least each party knew who the witnesses were and was allowed to address interrogations to them."[9] Learned Hand supported Frank on the question of summary judgment, so by a 2–1 vote the case was returned to the district court for a jury trial, irrespective of the advice of Professor Noss.

Clearly unprepared for the majority's dual rejection of an important procedural reform and the expert testimony on music, Judge Clark reacted with a dissenting opinion as angry as any he or another Second Circuit judge authored during the ten-year period. "Music is a matter of the intellect as well as the emotions; that is why eminent music scholars insist upon the employment of the intellectual faculties for a just appreciation of music. Consequently I do not think we should abolish the use of the intellect here even if we could."[10]

The memoranda between Frank and Clark continued for several months after the opinions were filed, with Clark insisting that there was not the slightest justification for what the majority did. Quickly, Arnstein's suit came to trial and the inevitable result was in favor of the defendant. Once more an appeal was taken to the Second Circuit and before 1946 was over the court, in a very brief per curiam opinion, unanimously affimed.[11] Learned Hand and Frank, together with Chase, heard the second appeal.

But while the decision virtually ended Arnstein's prospects for victory—subsequently the Supreme Court denied certiorari—this was not the end of the case for the Second Circuit. It was a recurring feature of their relationship that Judges Clark and Frank could not liquidate their past battles and concentrate on the business at hand. Disagreements accumulated, remaining below the surface during periods of amiability, to re-emerge and open up as old wounds do in the midst of new disputes.

Seven years after the flare-up over Professor Noss, the issue of reliance on outside expertise arose again, although this time "the shoe was on the other foot," for it was Frank who was involved in ex cathedra discussions; it was Judge Clark who argued:

I do not believe our decision ought to be affected by somewhat uncertain quotations from experts consulted ex parte. It is hardly fair to the persons quoted. . . . In *Arnstein v. Porter* of blessed memory I was roundly criticized for obtaining (for my own

[9] JNF Memorandum, January 16, 1946.

[10] Arnstein v. Porter, 154 F.2d 464, 476–77 (2d Cir. 1946) (J. Clark dissenting).

[11] Arnstein v. Porter, 158 F.2d 795 (2d Cir. 1946).

personal benefit) the exact views of a musical scholar of distinction. While I did not think the criticism well taken, I have since tried to avoid even the appearance of transgression.[12]

To this, Judge Frank replied:

I never criticized (and don't now) Charlie's discussing the Arnstein case with a musical scholar. I didn't object when Tom, a few years ago, sought Corbin's advice. I don't see why it's wrong to get the views of Professor Moore about Rule questions. Of course, I shouldn't—and haven't purported to—report anything except his tentative reactions after he had talked with me alone. And I've suggested that all of us confer with him in such matters. In this case I referred to his tentative doubts in order to prove that my doubts were not frivolous.[13]

[12] CEC Memorandum, Malman v. United States, February 4, 1953.

[13] JNF Memorandum, Malman v. United States, February 7, 1953. The discussion continued after the decision came down. JNF to CEC, February 18, 1953: "I have never cited, to my colleagues, the views on a legal question of Professors Moore, Sturges, Shulman, etc., expressed informally and to me alone, as in any way authoritative. I have suggested that such views indicate that a full discussion by members of the court with one or the other of them might be helpful." JNF to CEC, February 24, 1953: "It would seem then that my remarks in 1946 about your discussion with a musician as to an issue of fact did not deter you in 1951 from consulting Moore as to a question of 'law' and reporting his views to your colleagues. Nor can I see any reason why you shouldn't have done so." CEC to JNF, March 9, 1953: "Far from objecting, I even urge that judges should seek for knowledge, not elsewhere easily available, from experts in whom they and the court as a whole may have confidence. This is, however, far from drawing in such experts as part of the argumentation against one's brethren when the court is divided in its view. What I did in the Arnstein case . . . was exactly in accord with what I am urging, I acted in Arnstein before I knew there was any division and of course went no further as soon as it developed. I have felt deeply, therefore, that the criticism you made of me in that matter was entirely unjust and uncalled for.

"In our recent cases you have relied upon opinions from elsewhere where we were at issue and as a means of beating down contentions, rather than of providing usable knowledge for the court. Further, it seems to me that you have not been fair either to the experts or to your colleagues, since you have gotten offhand and curbstone or stairway opinions."

In reference to another case (the appeal of summary convictions for contempt of court of the lawyers in the trial of the Communist Party leaders), in which Judge Clark dissented from the decision upholding Judge Medina, Clark wrote to Judge Augustus Hand: "Although I have not participated in a single discussion up here, I know that . . . [Frank] has been involved in some very vigorous discussions with members of the Yale Law faculty, of whose good opinion he is most avid, and has felt the need of self-justification, which I am quite sure is finding expression here" (CEC to ANH, May 13, 1950).

The Coolidge appointees apparently had little interest in these disputes. With the rare exception of Judge Swan—the only one of the four to come to the court from the academic world—they did not solicit the advice of experts or, if they did, they did not press on their colleagues views so obtained. In an overall sense, it cannot be said that the personal relationships between the two junior members and academics had any impact on the decisions of the court. Their effect was on the decisional process and the temper of the Second Circuit.

The work of the Second Circuit (and the other courts of appeals) goes on with little direct contact with the courts and judges of the states within the circuit. Prior to appointment to the federal bench, Judge Chase had served on the Supreme Court of Vermont and Judge Clark was long active in Connecticut judicial reform; both men had close ties with leaders of the legal profession of their respective states. Connecticut and Vermont, however, contribute little to the case load of the Second Circuit and, in any case, litigation in federal courts mostly involves federal laws. There are, of course, many diversity of citizenship suits, where, as a result of the Supreme Court's decision in 1938 in *Erie v. Tompkins*, federal judges must apply state laws as interpreted by state judges.[14] But diversity cases do not occasion any meaningful interaction between federal and state courts; federal judges are bound to accept state decisions they do not like.

There occurred in the spring of 1944 an unusual incident involving the Second Circuit and the chief judge of the Supreme Court of Errors of Connecticut. The previous winter, the Second Circuit had reversed (by a vote of 2–1) the federal district court and upheld the constitutionality of a Connecticut corporate franchise tax as applied to an interstate trucking business.[15] A threshold question raised was whether the federal courts had jurisdiction; the Second Circuit unanimously held that they did because there was no plain, efficient, and speedy remedy in the state courts. Judge Clark, who wrote the opinion for the court, said in his concluding paragraph: "Of course, this is a situation which the Connecticut Supreme Court of Errors could remedy deftly and simply by some clear-cut holding, such as that . . . the appeal provisions of the statute are available to attack the validity of the act. But we cannot put words into the mouths of state judges."

---

[14] 304 U.S. 64. The Supreme Court decision was quite unpopular with certain of the 1941–51 judges. Not long after Erie v. Tompkins, Learned Hand characterized the new role of the federal judiciary in diversity cases, as "we merely play the well-known aria from the opera, *Le Fin de Brandeis,* entitled *Erie R. R. v. Tompkins*" (Memorandum in New England Mutual Life v. Spence, March 27, 1939).

[15] Spector Motor Service v. Walsh, 139 F. 2d 809 (2d Cir. 1944).

The slip opinion was printed and distributed, including a copy to the West Publishing Company for the *Federal Reporter*. Almost three months later, without warning, Judge Clark received an angry letter from the chief justice of the Connecticut court, William M. Maltbie, asking "what sanction there is for your court to advise the Supreme Court of Errors of the State of Connecticut as to what it should or should not do. Does it not strike you as presumptuous in the extreme? It does me. I make bold to suggest its deletion before the opinion finds its way into the formal reports of the court."[16]

Clark thought little of Maltbie's protest but recognized that it was wise "to give him the soft answer."[17] Writing to the chief justice in a conciliatory tone of his distress at the interpretation given to the final paragraph, he wanted Maltbie to "please believe me that I never dreamed what I said to be in any way objectionable to you or to your court, or, indeed, had the slightest thought or intent to suggest to your court what it should do."[18] He then drafted a substitute paragraph, which was printed in the *Federal Reporter*.

The Second Circuit decision was reversed by the United States Supreme Court, which sent the case back to the state courts. In 1948 the litigation was before the Supreme Court of Errors of Connecticut; Chief Justice Maltbie wrote the court's opinion. He pointedly took issue with the Second Circuit ruling regarding the availability of an effective remedy in Connecticut courts and, while ostensibly refraining from doing so, he snidely commented on "the long delay which must ensue" due to the "invocation of the jurisdiction of the federal courts."[19] Two years later an appeal was taken once more to the Second Circuit; again there was a split vote, with Judge Clark writing for the majority. Although he did not have a high regard for the Connecticut jurist, in Clark's opinion, Maltbie was described as the "distinguished Chief Justice of Connecticut."[20] That seems to have ended what may have been the only "confrontation" between the Second Circuit and a state court while Learned Hand was chief judge.

Decisions of the intermediate appellate courts have no precedential value outside the circuit in which they are made. Ten courts of appeals may rule one way on a particular issue, the eleventh is free to accept or reject what they have done. The large number of intercircuit conflicts brought to the attention of the Supreme Court (and there are conflicts which are not appealed to the High Court) attest to this freedom.

[16] Letter to CEC, March 14, 1944.
[17] CEC to LH and JNF, March 15, 1944.
[18] CEC to Justice Maltbie, March 15, 1944.
[19] Spector Motor Service v. Walsh, 61 A.2d 89, 92 (1948).
[20] Spector Motor Service v. O'Connor, 181 F.2d 150, 152 (2d Cir. 1950).

This does not mean that in intercircuit relations, court of appeals decisions are without relevance or function. Intermediate judges pay some attention to the business of other courts; certainly their law clerks look at many of the slip opinions coming in from throughout the country. Briefs cite cases from other circuits, while among lawyers as well as judges in this country there is readily available an amazing array of "legal aid" material which permits them to learn in a matter of minutes what the case law is on any legal question. In short, judges often go about deciding appeals with a host of relevant decisions from different courts before them.

Intermediate status fairly conclusively determines attitude toward rulings of the Supreme Court and district courts. But what are the factors influencing utilization of cases from other circuits? Neither the published opinions nor the memoranda of Second Circuit judges are of much help in trying to answer this question. While it is commonplace to cite the law of another circuit, there is no evidence that what other circuits do contributes significantly to the result in the Second Circuit. The major function of intercircuit citation is to marshal support for a decision reached independent of such authority. Indeed, in most cases, where the result is reached without difficulty, it is mere routine to list supportive decisions from other circuits. In close cases, particularly where the judges are divided, there is an even greater tendency to stress cases which reach the same result, but invariably this is more a process of rationalization than reliance on the views of the courts that are cited. There is not much hesitation on the part of the appellate judge to reject decisions of courts of the same level.

Confirmation and not influence is the ordinary function of decisions from other circuits. To be sure there are exceptions, one of which will be mentioned shortly. Furthermore, where the ruling of another court of appeals is cited in support of a ruling, the reasoning of that court may suggest arguments that might not have occurred to the judges of the latter court. But the strong conclusion is that a court of appeals is not much swayed by what is done in the other circuits.

The single exception that comes to mind—and it is mostly speculative—is when a court of appeals is faced with a novel issue on which its judges do not have any set ideas. Then, the *authority* of a recent holding of a different court of appeals might be decisive.

Reliance on other circuits would probably be greater than it is if there were more personal contacts between judges of the different courts of appeals. Some circuit judges, notably the chief judges, participate in the work of the Judicial Conference of the United States, but this activity is mostly formal and does not lead to exchanges of views on the legal questions before their respective courts. By and large, the men who serve on the courts of appeals were active in legal or political affairs in their home states prior to appointment; upon ascending to the bench, earlier relationships continue to be important. Each court of appeals forms its own social unit with little contact with the ten other courts.

In all hierarchical policy-making systems, decision makers deal on a regular basis with persons above and below them in the chain of authority. Relationships of this sort are systematic and usually form clear patterns; because they are hierarchical there are laws or rules which govern the course of interaction, although idiosyncratic and personal factors always play a role in human relations. These observations are, of course, valid for any judicial system.

The basic function of the courts of appeals is to review the actions of other decision makers. In the case of an appeal from an administrative agency, the interaction between the two levels of policy makers is formal and impersonal. For one thing, the scope of appellate review of administrative agencies is somewhat narrower than that of trial courts because, in theory, these agencies possess special competence over the subjects that come before them. For another, only rarely do the reviewing judges know the members of the administrative board. Finally, most agencies deal with each of the courts of appeals so that special relationships do not normally develop between an intermediate court and an agency.

The situation is much different in respect to relations with district courts, the main source of business in the courts of appeals. Here the appellate function places a heavy judicial and personal burden on upper court judges, especially when review involves the work of judges with whom regular personal contact is maintained. In addition to appeals, the circuit judges are expected to supervise the performance of the district judges through the circuit's judicial council.

Although all federal judges are aware of the delicate questions inherent in their relations with inferiors and superiors in the judicial hierarchy, except for an occasional guarded expression in an opinion, little has been said by them on the subject. One informative speech by Judge Calvert Magruder, longtime chief judge of the Court of Appeals for the First Circuit, appropriately called "The Trials and Tribulations of An Intermediate Appellate Court," sheds some light on this relationship:

> In an intermediate appellate court, such as mine, the maintenance of this institutional prestige of the courts imposes upon us a certain judicial etiquette in our dealing with judges lower in the federal system, whose acts we are called on to review on appeal....

As to the trial judges, we must always bear in mind that they may be as good lawyers as we are, or better. They are under the disadvantage of often having to make rulings off the cuff, so to speak, in the press and urgency of a trial proceeding, and the main reason we on appeal may have a better chance of being right is that we have more time for reflection and study. Hence, we should approach our task of judicial review with a certain genuine humility. We should never unnecessarily try to make a monkey of the judge in the court below, or to trespass on his feelings or dignity and self-respect. Sometimes we may have contributed to an erroneous ruling below by an incautious statement made by us in an earlier opinion, in which case we should take care to point out that this is so, and that we may have been to blame for misleading the district court, which was only trying to follow us. Sometimes we may have occasion to reverse a judge of the district court on a ground not presented to it, or considered below. If so, we should be at pains to point that out. And if the district court has written a careful and full opinion, with which we agree, and which we feel unable to improve upon, we should affirm on the opinion of the court below.[21]

Another aspect of this respectful attitude is that courts of appeals should not summarily reverse the district court. In fact, such reversals do occur, but they are rare.[22]

The guidelines enunciated by Judge Magruder are probably adhered to by most appellate courts, yet every court is faced with special situations that are not covered by general principles of behavior. In the dynamics of judicial relations, for example, personal likes and dislikes develop and these may affect the handling of appeals.

The judges of the Second Circuit work in close proximity to most of the district judges of the circuit, especially those of the Southern District who have their chambers in the same courthouse at Foley Square. Direct contacts are frequent—in elevators, during lunch, at meetings, and on numerous other occasions. The reviewing judges form opinions of the ability and work of the trial judges through these contacts, as well as through the reading of records on appeal. At times previous service together on the district court shapes the attitude of intermediate judges toward former colleagues.[23]

[21] Magruder, "The Trials and Tribulations of an Intermediate Appellate Court," *Cornell Law Quarterly,* 44 (1958), 3–4. The respected chief judge of the District Court of Massachusetts briefly touched on some of these questions more than fifteen years ago. Charles E. Wyzanski, Jr., "A Trial Judge's Freedom and Responsibility," *Atlantic Monthly,* 190 (1952), 55.

[22] For example, Century Indemnity Co. v. Arnold, 145 F.2d 164 (2d Cir. 1944).

[23] Lewis Mayer writes: "A large part of the judges of the eleven federal courts of appeals served their judicial apprenticeship as federal district judges. In recent years, however, the practice of filling these judgeships from

Members of the Learned Hand court had definite views about some of the judges whose work they reviewed. The chief judge was known to have held in low regard a number of trial judges within the circuit.[24] But there were also several district judges who were greatly respected by their superiors; Judges Simon Rifkind and Robert Patterson of the Southern District Court were in this category. About the former, Jerome Frank wrote, "Excepting Learned Hand, this country, I think, has no abler judge than . . . Judge Rifkind . . . and he is a trial judge."[25] Following Patterson's death, Learned Hand said:

> His conclusions at times of course collided with ours; and nothing was to me more engaging, or more endearing, than the vigor with which he tore to pieces the fragile fabric with which we had tried to obscure his light. I can think of more than one instance in which I was not sorry that I could not be called into the open lists to defend my difference from him, but could resort to the seclusion of my position in the hierarchy.[26]

Deprecatory comments about trial judges were ordinarily confined to the internal memoranda. Thus in *New York Cinders Delivery Co. v. Bush Terminal Co.* the memorandum of Judge Augustus Hand, usually a mild man, was sharply critical of the trial judge "in whom I have no confidence," yet the decision came down as a routine reversal, without any criticism.[27] On occasion, words of rebuke were included in draft opinions, only to be removed at the request of one of the panel members. But there were time when the circuit judges were so upset

---

the district bench has tended to decline. The appointment of an outstanding lawyer or legal scholar to one of these courts, while not intrinsically objectionable, should be exceptional if the morale of the district bench is to be preserved, and if the appeals bench as a whole is to have, in the cases which it reviews, that realistic appreciation of what has gone on in the trial court that come best from experience as a trial judge."

Mayer adds that as of December 31, 1947, of the forty-nine judges on the courts of appeals, twenty-five had been on lower federal courts. He then cites a 1948 recommendation adopted by the Judicial Conference of the Ninth Circuit that "Congress enact legislation to the effect that in the United States Courts of Appeals there shall be appointed . . . judges from the districts of the circuit until at least a majority of the judges of each of the Courts of Appeals is composed of such judges" (*The American Legal System* [New York: Harper and Brothers, 1955], p. 387).

[24] Judge Clark once wrote to Justice Frankfurter of Hand's "distrust of the judgment and dependability of certain trial judges" (September 25, 1951).

[25] Jerome N. Frank, "Words and Music: Some Remarks on Statutory Interpretation," *Columbia Law Review*, 47 (1947), 1278, n. 8.

[26] L. Hand, "Robert P. Patterson," in Irving Dilliard (ed.), *The Spirit of Liberty* (New York: Vintage Press, 1959), p. 202.

[27] 178 F.2d 748 (2d Cir. 1950).

over the conduct of the trial that they were deliberately harsh on the judge who presided over it. In *United States v. Marzano* the Second Circuit unanimously reversed the conviction of an accused narcotics seller on the ground that Judge Grover Moscowitz, who presided, had acted improperly during the trial. The opinion was written by Learned Hand, who concluded with the following rebuke:

> the judge was exhibiting a prosecutor's zeal, inconsistent with that detachment and aloofness which courts have again and again demanded, particularly in criminal trials. Despite every allowance he must not take on the role of a partisan; he must not enter the lists; he must not by his ardor induce the jury to join in a hue and cry against the accused. Prosecution and judgment are two quite separate functions in the administration of justice; they must not merge.[28]

After the opinion was filed, Hand "had a rather painful interview" with Moscowitz, who felt "bitterly about what we said of him."[29] At Moscowitz' request the chief judge asked the West Publishing Company to hold up publication, drafted substitute language for the offending words, and consulted with the other panel members. One of these, Judge Augustus Hand, reluctantly assented to revision; the second, Judge Clark, maintained:

> The judicial process ought to be practical; and distasteful as it is, I think that, where the criticized judge has raised the point of further discussion, then we might well say that we want a further discussion before we modify criticism. Hence my own thought would be that at least the three of us, perhaps more, including Jerry, might well sit down with him and say that "if you want the criticism eliminated, you ought to do your part in avoiding these problems in the future and specifically should avoid situations

---

[28] 149 F.2d 923, 926 (2d Cir. 1945). It is of some note that these harsh words came from Learned Hand. He did not think much of many district judges, but he had served as a trial judge for fifteen years and knew that it was almost inevitable that errors would be committed in the course of a trial. He would caution against reversing convictions "because of minor excesses in the exercise of the judge's authority . . . ; separate passages cut from their context and from the trial as a whole, often have an apparent importance which in fact they do not deserve" (United States v. Warren, 120 F.2d 211, 212 [2d Cir. 1941]). In a per curiam opinion certainly authored by Learned Hand, the court said: "We do not forget the admonition that we must not lightly disregard errors in a charge; but it would be a perversion to read this as meaning that every syllable which emerges from a judge's mouth is as momentous as the utterances of the Delphic Oracle" (United States v. Rooth, 159 F.2d 659, 660 [2d Cir. 1947]).

[29] LH to CEC, June 16, 1945.

such as occurred in Cases *X, Y, Z,* and *Q,*" giving him page and number.[30]

No meeting with Moscowitz took place and the criticism was retained intact.

One of Judge Moscowitz' colleagues on the Eastern District court was Judge Matthew T. Abruzzo. While Learned Hand was chief judge none of the several dozen district judges within the Second Circuit was as lowly regarded or criticized so often in print by the appellate court as was Abruzzo. The memoranda crackle with the anger of the reviewing judges over his improper conduct; several examples: "If he would only keep his hands off until it comes time for him to act, our task would, as usual, be simpler"; "even as the trial opened, he displayed discourtesy and prejudice";[31] Judge Clark, referring to an earlier brush with the Eastern District judge, recalled, "We found that Abruzzo could not read";[32] "that Abruzzo wears a robe and is appointed for life does not seem to me to entitle him to ignore plain legal requirements upon which we would insist if he were a robe-less administrator appointed for a shorter term";[33] "should we not beat up Abruzzo, J. for sending us such a record?"[34]

Until a year or so after Learned Hand's retirement, the Second Circuit did not include the names of trial judges in its opinions, a practice that shall be discussed shortly. Thus any published criticism of district judges was veiled, although in the case of Judge Abruzzo many of bench and bar eventually got the idea that his work was not respected by the higher court. An example of the court's comments on the conduct of Abruzzo is from a 1944 criminal appeal:

> whether or not the outbursts of petulant irritation, which repeatedly marred the serenity of the court-room in the case at bar, prejudiced the accused, they were an indignity to counsel which we should not pass in silence, and in which we should have supported them, had they shown less forbearance than in fact they did. In . . . [an earlier case] we commented upon the same sort of conduct, and we regret to observe that what we then said does not appear to have had the result which we hoped it might. Con-

[30] CEC to LH, June 18, 1945.

[31] Memorandum of HBC in United States v. Hauck, January 22, 1946. In this case, the unanimous opinion reversing the convictions of five men was written by Judge Swan and contains one paragraph sharply critical of Abruzzo (155 F.2d 141, 143 [2d Cir. 1946]).

[32] Memorandum in United States *ex rel.* Levy v. Cain, April 28, 1945.

[33] JNF Memorandum in Matton Oil Transfer Corp. v. Tug Dynamic, November 10, 1941.

[34] LH Memorandum in Matton Oil, November 10, 1941.

tinuance in such habits must in the end tell heavily in the estimate of judicial service.[35]

Apart from public rebuke and, no doubt, also, a greater willingness to reverse judges who offend often, such as Abruzzo,[36] the Second Circuit has not taken any direct action against trial judges who preside in a prejudicial fashion. Except for the uncertain potential of the circuit's Judicial Council there is not much that it could do should it be disposed to act. In all probability the Council's supervisory powers will continue to be restricted to normal administrative matters. In the administrative sphere the Second Circuit, or more correctly its chief judge, has on at least two occasions taken steps to "remove" judges who were not doing their share of work. In early 1941 Chief Judge Hand wrote to Judge Frank Cooper of the Northern District of New York suggesting Cooper's retirement. Judge Cooper demurred, writing that "you may be sure when I feel that I cannot do the court work justice, I shall be the first suggesting retirement."[37] Within the year Judge Cooper stepped down.

Fifteen years later, after consulting with his colleagues, Chief Judge Clark attempted to get Judge Robert Inch to retire as chief judge of the Eastern District Court. Pressure for the move had come from bar associations and from the Administrative Office of United States Courts. Apparently, relations among the judges of the Eastern District made Judge Inch reluctant to accede to the request.[38] Finally, after he was "assured" of the right successor, he retired at the end of 1957.

Indirectly, the district judges were the cause of a drawn-out disagreement between Judge Clark and Learned Hand and, to a lesser extent, Judge Augustus Hand. The usual practice of appellate courts in this country is to include in the headnote to the opinion the name of the trial judge. The Second Circuit and the Court of Appeals for the District of Columbia did not do so, mostly out of an unwillingness to embarrass judges whose rulings were reversed by the higher court. In 1941, at the request of Judge Clark, it seems, Learned Hand sent a letter to the district judges of the circuit inquiring as to their feelings on the matter. A majority preferred retention of the existing practice

[35] United States v. Andolschek, 142 F.2d 503, 507 (2d Cir. 1944).

[36] This was confirmed in interviews with a number of the judges now on the court; as one of them put it: "The court knows who the good ones and bad ones are."

[37] Letter to LH, January 22, 1941.

[38] Letter from Judge Harold Kennedy of the Eastern District to C. C. Burlingham, April 18, 1956. A copy of this letter was sent to Judge Clark.

and Hand, who sympathized with them, decided that no change was in order. Clark was not pleased, but did not press the issue.[39]

A year later Clark had the question brought before the annual Second Circuit Conference. He "waited until a lull came in conference discussion before broaching the matter, but discussion was ended when I was told that I was making 'a mountain out of a molehill.' "[40] Clark was stung by the rebuke, probably uttered by the chief judge who chaired the conference,[41] and he referred to it frequently; but Clark remained undaunted in his effort to do away with the practice. In 1943, "with hesitation and deference and somewhat taking my life in my hands,"[42] he urged that the subject be reconsidered. Nothing happened. Another year went by and Judge Clark brought it up during lunch one day, to the chagrin of the Hands. He followed this with a letter to Learned and Augustus Hand in which, risking their displeasure, he again explained his position.[43]

That was the last the Learned Hand court heard of the issue. The other judges—Swan, Chase, and Frank—stayed out of the dispute, and the opposition of the Hands, the two members of the Second Circuit to have served as district judges, was too formidable for Judge Clark.

The issue was kept alive in Judge Clark's mind, and not long after Learned Hand's retirement he wrote to the new chief judge:

> Our course . . . has been a matter of confusion and annoyance to teachers, courts, the Administrative Office, and, I believe, to ourselves, as it certainly has been to me. . . . So I write to inquire if you see anything undesirable in a decision of this matter individually. If you do not, I shall take steps to prepare my opinions as I think they should be, understanding, of course, that my colleagues will also be making their own decisions. If you do, then I request that this matter . . . be brought before a council meeting.[44]

Subsequently, the question was considered at a conference of the district and circuit judges, where, buttressed by support from law

---

[39] CEC to LH, July 1, 1941.

[40] CEC to LH and ANH, March 21, 1944.

[41] Years later, responding to Justice Frankfurter's criticism for alleged rudeness toward the Hands, Judge Clark referred to Learned Hand as "a past master in the prime art of rudeness" and recalled that he "sat me down at Circuit conferences as making mountains out of molehills" (letter of September 29, 1954). Earlier, though, in a letter to Judge William Denman of the Ninth Circuit, Clark described the words as having come from "one of the gentler of my colleagues" (July 21, 1947). Since Augustus Hand sided with his cousin and he was by far the more gentle of the two, it is conceivable that it was he who uttered the criticism.

[42] Letter of CEC to his colleagues, May 22, 1943.

[43] Letter of March 21, 1944.

[44] CEC to TWS, October 31, 1951.

school professors and others, Judge Clark's proposal was finally adopted. There was little opposition at the meeting from district judges, but Judge Clarence Galston of the Eastern District, who did not attend, later wrote to Judge Clark that on the basis of his own experience he preferred the old practice because "not infrequently the opinion of the reviewing court was written in a tone that assumed that not only was the District Court an inferior court, but so also was the mind of the judge." He added, "I'd be willing to go along . . . if the Court of Appeals would forego the sort of spanking that a teacher administers to an erring pupil."[45]

After the Second Circuit altered its practice, the District of Columbia Court of Appeals decided to follow the procedure prevalent in all of the intermediate courts. It is noteworthy that the two appellate courts that for so long did not include the names of the district judges are the ones where the circuit judges have regular personal contact with the trial judges. This factor most likely contributed to their greater sensitivity for the feelings of the judges whose work they reviewed.

The close proximity of trial and appellate judges in the Second Circuit does not encourage the latter to discuss pending cases with the judges whose decisions they are reviewing. This was a policy insisted on by Learned Hand. Judge Medina remarks:

> You know, I learned a lot from old Learned Hand. I had not been long on the court of appeals when we had a question where there was an ambiguity, and I wondered if I ought to go downstairs to see the district judge and ask him about it.
> He said, "Now, Harold, principle number one. Never forget it. Never talk to the trial judge about anything having any bearing on any of the cases you have before you."[46]

[45] Letter to CEC, June 29, 1952. Judge Galston was on the Eastern District court, whose judges had been "spanked" quite often by their superiors.

[46] "The Decisional Process in the United States Court of Appeals, Second Circuit—How the Wheels Go Around Inside—with Commentary," Address at the New York County Lawyers' Association Forum Evening, April 26, 1952 (typewritten), p. 41.

The question apparently also came up early in Judge Clark's judicial career. In a letter to Judge Vincent Leibell of the Southern District Court (July 17, 1942), he wrote: "But I think you ought to know . . . that, however much I may concur in the ultimate conclusion, I cannot accept the specific ground raised by Learned. The thought that a trial judge would (a) want to, and (b) believe he could affect an appellate court's review of his cases by patronage seems to me so fantastic that I for one would certainly run the more than remote chance that somebody might think so."

But while direct discussions are not permissible, it is evident that in going about their business the judges of the courts of appeals interact in various ways with the trial judges and that, at times, this factor has an important bearing on what the reviewing judges do.

In turning to relations between circuit judges and the Supreme Court it is well to note at the outset that much of what has already been described is relevant to the interactions between the two levels of appellate courts. This should not be surprising, for not only are all these relationships judicial, so that some of the same rules will inevitably apply, but also the Supreme Court is directly above the courts of appeals in much the same way that the latter courts are above the trial courts in the judicial hierarchy.

The Supreme Court's position in the judicial system has importance beyond the obvious fact that it is the top and most authoritative decision maker in the system. There is a mystique and an aura of legitimacy surrounding the High Court that give it an influence and authority superior to that of other top policy-making organs. To be sure, there are limitations on Supreme Court power; these are mostly from sources outside of the judicial system or are self-imposed. To the extent that there are checks within the judicial system, usually they are confined to the state courts. The lower federal courts, if not always meekly acquiescent, do not bargain with the Supreme Court.

To some extent personal factors are relevant in relations between the Supreme Court and lower courts, although these are not as important as they are elsewhere; there are more or less formal rules requiring lower judges to accept the legal supremacy of the higher court. The Second Circuit of 1941–51 was closer—and not merely physically—to the Supreme Court than the other courts of appeals. With the exception of Judge Chase, each of its members was on friendly terms with one or more Supreme Court justices. Personal contact was not infrequent, especially between Justice Douglas and Jerome Frank and Justice Frankfurter and Learned Hand.

Yet the attitude of the Learned Hand court toward the Supreme Court was not one of respect. This is not surprising when we recall that during the decade when some considered the Second Circuit the outstanding appellate court in the nation, the Supreme Court was being severely criticized—first, for its internal disarray when Stone was Chief Justice, and, later, for the lethargy and supposed incompetence of the Vinson court. In their memoranda the intermediate judges were often scornful of their "betters in Washington." Admittedly, everything said in these internal documents should not be read literally, for one of the functions of the memoranda is to permit the judges to play private games and jokes; mischief ought not to be mistaken for malice. Still, patterns form, and at some point it becomes certain that scorn was intended; more than humor was conveyed by Learned Hand in his outlandish names for the Supreme Court, some of which were: The Blessed Saints, Cherubim and Seraphim, The Jolly Boys, The Nine Blameless Ethiopians, The Nine Tin Jesuses, and The Nine Blessed Chalices of the Sacred Effluvium. There is a serious ring to many of the deprecatory comments, mostly in the criminal law area, where the Second Circuit was not in sympathy with the Supreme Court's greater acceptance of claims of the accused.

Be this as it may, these attitudes did not contribute to any willingness to evade the mandate of the Supreme Court. Throughout, the Second Circuit judges were well aware of the obligations inherent in inferior status and they followed even where they were not convinced.

It is another matter whether the prestige of the Learned Hand court fostered deference to its rulings by the Supreme Court. We will see in a later chapter that the Second Circuit fared quite well in the Supreme Court from 1941 to 1951; this may have been the result of lower court fidelity to the dictates of the Supreme Court or the product of a greater reluctance to reverse the Second Circuit than the other courts of appeals. There is a strong implication of the latter in a tribute to Learned Hand from Justice Frankfurter: "Speaking for myself, the only gain possibly to be had from his retirement from the Court of Appeals is that hereafter I shall feel freer to act on my belief that a decision of the Circuit Court of the Second Circuit might give occasion for review by the Supreme Court, and I might even perchance at times feel that an opinion which he wrote might be wrong."[47] Such statements must not be taken too seriously; while they suggest that the Supreme Court was especially solicitous of the views of Learned Hand, an examination of the 1941–51 record does not bear this out. For example, Jerome Frank fared far better in the High Court than his more esteemed colleague. Likely, the success of the Second Circuit was, more than anything else, the result of its obedience to superior authority.

Another personal factor that may enter into these relations is the flow of direct and indirect communications between members of the two courts. One form of communication is gossip; in all social and political systems there is constant talk about what other participants or decision makers are doing, and there is usually more gossip about the

---

[47] Frankfurter, "A Great Judge Retires: American Law Institute Honors Learned Hand," *American Bar Association Journal*, 37 (1951), 503. See also Justice Harlan's remarks at "Proceedings of a Special Session," published as a special section in 264 F.2d (p. 23).

superior members of the system.[48] The judiciary is no exception. Because of the way the Supreme Court operates it is virtually impossible for any outsider to get reliable information about what it is doing until after its action has been made public. This curtain of secrecy tends to encourage gossiping, although it also means that much that is reported as reliable proves to be inaccurate. In any event, the Second Circuit had better channels of communication with the Supreme Court than had other lower courts. The friendships already mentioned, law clerks who graduated to the Supreme Court from the intermediate court, and other contacts in Washington, all provided the Second Circuit with information on what the higher court was doing in areas of interest to it. The judges were told of the attitudes of the justices toward its rulings and there was much guessing as to what would happen upon review.

In 1946 the matter of relations with Supreme Court came to the fore in the midst of a particularly sharp dispute between Clark and Frank over the "harmless error" rule. This rule provides that errors made in the course of a trial are not grounds for reversal unless it can be reasonably inferred from the total trial context that they may have affected the result. Frank was alone on the Second Circuit in pressing for a restricted use of the rule in criminal cases; he believed that it was virtually impossible for the reviewing court to learn what factors influenced the jury. Seemingly minor errors might actually be harmful. Learned Hand and Clark were adamantly opposed to this view; but although Judge Frank invariably was outvoted, powerful dissents by him led to several Supreme Court reversals of Second Circuit decisions involving the "harmless error" rule.

After the Second Circuit affirmed a conviction because the errors were harmless (Learned Hand and Clark in the majority, Frank dissenting),[49] Frank wrote to Clark protesting the latter's suggestion, made several times, "once in the conference with Learned on the Antonelli case . . . that I had improperly engaged in propaganda activities with the Supreme Court law clerks."[50] The letter also rebutted rumored criticism by Clark of Frank's intention to devote a session to the subject in his course on the judicial process at the Yale Law School.

---

[48] Richard Neustadt demonstrates the importance of the fact that the "Washington Community" is "a most incestuous community," in which "inside dope" may determine relations with the President, in *Presidential Power* (New York: New American Library, 1964), pp. 64–69.

[49] United States v. Antonelli Fireworks Co., Inc., 155 F.2d 631 (2d Cir. 1946).

[50] JNF to CEC, May 15, 1946.

Clark immediately returned the letter, saying he knew "nothing about the facts to which reference is made."[51] But, he continued, "it is my understanding that you have sent copies of your Antonelli opinion to various persons in or about the Supreme Court, and that this was done in previous cases. This does seem to me inappropriate. I think volunteered suggestions or pressure, direct or indirect, from us to our superiors in our cases which they are called upon to review is undesirable."

The ensuing correspondence lasted for about four months, touching upon numerous points of conflict and opening up old and new wounds. The issue of Supreme Court lobbying was submerged. Judge Frank conceded: "Since I've been on the bench, I've frequently sent copies of my opinions on divers subjects . . . to Douglas, Black and Frankfurter, each of whom is an old friend. They receive all our opinions in any event, so that my sending copies of particular opinions merely calls attention to them. No one of these Justices has ever thought the practice improper. . . . Surely you don't think I was putting 'pressure' on Black, whose views on harmless error are directly opposed to mine."[52]

If Supreme Court members do not object to lower court judges sending them their opinions, there is little reason for anyone else to enter a complaint; nevertheless it must be understood that where the court has yet to decide whether to grant certiorari, it is undeniable that, in the case of dissenting opinions, the lower judge is calling special attention to his views and increases the prospects for review. This may or may not be pressure, but it is not a totally ineffective exercise.

On the formal side of relations with the Supreme Court, Judge Magruder remarks: "Here too, we have to play the game according to certain well-accepted rules, and it makes no difference what our private opinion might be as to whether certain justices of the Supreme Court know more, or less, than we do about the law. We should always express a respectful deference to controlling decisions of the

[51] Clark's reply is quite puzzling. Six months earlier he had written to Learned Hand: "I am informed from Washington that Jerry has been down lobbying with the Supreme Court law clerks against what he likes to term the dreadful 'Second Circuit Rule' of harmless error, and that the law clerks are all emotionally upset—so much so that it is confidentially believed the Supreme Court only awaits an appropriate vehicle for Felix to write a scathing condemnation of us for our brutality" (November 21, 1945). Hand ignored the charge regarding Frank, simply replying, "What you say about the 'Second Circuit Rule' of harmless error, disturbs me. I am quite aware that Felix is 'hot and bothered' about the way we deal with criminal appeals, and it may be he will be able to get a majority with him; but from what I heard so far, he was not able to do so" (November 23, 1945).

[52] May 16, 1946.

Supreme Court, and do our best to follow them. We should leave it to the Supreme Court to overrule its own cases." On the subject of Supreme Court reversals of courts of appeals, he confides:

> Now, I don't enjoy getting reversed any more than any other judge, and when that happens, my first reaction is to repair to the nearest tavern and "cuss out" the Supreme Court. Sometimes, after we have given long study to a case and written a careful opinion, we find ourselves reversed by the Supreme Court in an opinion that strikes us as superficial and hastily prepared. We eventually cool off, when we come to realize that the opinion may indeed be superficial and hastily drawn from the very necessities and pressures under which the Supreme Court has to do its work. Another thing that tends to cool us off is the realization that, were our positions reversed, and were we required to perform our work in the environment and under the pressures prevailing in the Supreme Court, we probably could not do so good a job as they do.
>
> I do say without hesitation that where a court of appeals has written a full opinion which evidences a careful and painstaking study of the case, the Supreme Court of the United States owes it an institutional obligation not to reverse us except upon filing a reasoned opinion undertaking to show that our conclusion was mistaken. The only exceptions to this proposition that I can think of at the moment are two: (1) where the Supreme Court can cite, and rely upon, a supervening decision of its own in another case, which obviously covers our case and which serves well enough to indicate why it thinks we went wrong; (2) where the court of appeals has lost the confidence of the Supreme Court, which wishes curtly to manifest that lack of confidence to the world.[53]

Whether or not the Supreme Court follows the rules set down by Judge Magruder, most lower court judges are unhappy when they are reversed and their reaction is not likely to be as generous as his was. Learned Hand would often refer sarcastically to reversals by the Supreme Court. One of the Second Circuit's present judges, who claims he "doesn't give a damn" if he is reversed, admits that he keeps a scoresheet of how his opinions fare in Washington.[54] Whatever their reactions, there is little they can do, short of defiance, although, as Judge Magruder says, "we are not obliged, as part of our institutional obligation to the Supreme Court, to express agreement with everything the Supreme Court may choose to do."[55]

[53] Magruder, "Trials and Tribulations," pp. 4, 7–8.
[54] From an interview.
[55] Magruder, "Trials and Tribulations," pp. 10–11. Cf. Judge Hutcheson of the Fifth Circuit dissenting in Hercules Gasolene Co. v. Commissioner of Internal Revenue, 147 F.2d, 972, 974 (1945): "I recognize, of course, that the rule of stare decisis binds us to follow . . . [the Supreme Court] in respect of things decided by it. I know of no rule of stare 'dictis' which binds us to follow it in respect of things merely said by it." On certiorari, the majority was upheld by the Supreme Court (326 U.S. 425 [1945]).

In the vast majority of cases, lower federal judges faithfully follow and apply Supreme Court decisions. However, there are opportunities for evasion, a fact corroborated by the actions of certain federal judges in school segregation cases.[56] As Professor Walter F. Murphy notes, "The Supreme Court typically formulates general policy. Lower courts apply that policy, and working in its interstices, inferior judges may materially modify the High Court's determinations."[57] While most of the blatant examples cited by Murphy are from state courts, he demonstrates that lower federal courts too are capable of forgetting the supremacy of the Supreme Court.

The Learned Hand court usually was rigorously obedient to the Supreme Court (although, ritualistically, dissenting judges accused the majority of ignoring the High Court), so examples of defiance by it are difficult to find. In two cases, decided with the participation of visiting judges, the Second Circuit upset positions taken by federal administrative agencies, despite Supreme Court decisions restricting review of administrative rulings.[58] Judge Hutcheson of the Fifth Circuit sat in both of these appeals; in a letter to Judge Clark, who dissented in one of the cases, he made it clear that while "[it] may well be that the 'nine new men' will agree with you, . . . they have never changed my mind for me when I really thought I was right, and they won't change it now by issuing a decree that in the future anyone appointed by the New Deal to do anything can do everything."[59] Both decisions were reversed by the Supreme Court.

A third case provoked a different sort of defiance or evasion by the Second Circuit. In the late 1930's and early 1940's the Supreme Court substantially expanded the rights of accused persons and sanctioned habeas corpus proceedings in federal courts as a means of reviewing convictions that had been upheld in state courts. Taken as a whole, the Second Circuit did not like the new trend in criminal law and derogatory comments were included in many of the memoranda in criminal appeals.[60] In *United States ex rel Adams v. McCann*[61] the

[56] See Jack W. Peltason, *Fifty-Eight Lonely Men* (New York: Harcourt, Brace, and Co., 1961).

[57] Walter F. Murphy, "Lower Court Checks on Supreme Court Power," *American Political Science Review,* 53 (1959), 1018.

[58] Securities and Exchange Commission v. Long Island Lighting Co., 148 F.2d 252 (2d Cir. 1945), and Duquesne Warehouse Co. v. Railroad Retirement Board, 148 F.2d 473 (2d Cir. 1945).

[59] February 12, 1945.

[60] For example, by Judge Augustus Hand: "If we sanction writs like this we might as well give up, and inaugurate a school to correspond with jail birds and employ a staff of Murphys and Rutledges with proper psychiatrists to attend to all their wants" (Memorandum in United States *ex rel.* Steele v. Jackson, November 3, 1948).

[61] 126 F.2d 774 (2d Cir. 1942).

Second Circuit, with Judge Chase dissenting, granted a writ of habeas corpus and discharged from custody one who had without counsel waived his right to a jury trial. The waiver apparently had been made intelligently, yet Learned Hand for the majority granted the writ, ostensibly relying on several Supreme Court decisions. In fact, Hand's intention was to apply the higher court ruling in an extreme fashion in the hope that it would back down from its very liberal approach. This is what happened, for the Supreme Court reversed[62] "with a yell and a laugh at us . . . for supposing they intended such an inference."[63]

Ultimately, evasion (and certainly outright defiance) of Supreme Court mandates must fail. Professor Murphy, after describing how lower courts check the Supreme Court, concludes:

> The lower courts can and do check the Supreme Court, but the Supreme Court can act to counter lower court power. While it cannot fire and hire personnel as the President can sometimes do, the Court can review and reverse inferior judges. This is important beyond any effect on a particular case. Judges, no more than other men, enjoy the prospect of public correction and reprimand. The Supreme Court can put added bite to this psychological whip by sarcasm and scathing criticism of its own.[64]

A less overt instance of disregard of the Supreme Court's mandate, and consequently one that is less likely to meet direct rebuke by the High Court, occurs when lower judges, because of individual predilections, either do not apply or wrongly apply a prior decision of the Supreme Court. Indeed, often the Supreme Court contributes to this practice when it hands down decisions that are plainly compromises of competing doctrines advanced by the justices constituting the majority or which are quite ambiguous. A reading of all Second Circuit opinions of 1941–51 reveals that opposing judges frequently believe that their brethren have ignored the command of the Supreme Court. Charges of this sort are common in all circuits and flow naturally from the intermediate status of the courts of appeals. But it is important to recognize that in a large proportion of the cases in which there is disagreement over a Supreme Court ruling, the root of the argument is the clashing views of the inferior judges and not unsettled interpretations of what the Supreme Court did or did not decide, in which case Supreme Court rulings conveniently serve those who seek to justify their own positions.

[62] 320 U.S. 220 (1943).

[63] Memorandum of ANH in United States v. Grote, November 22, 1943. Learned Hand was surprised that he got Justices Black, Douglas, and Murphy to go along with him.

[64] Murphy, "Lower Court Checks," p. 1030.

A different situation exists when the judges agree that no Supreme Court decision controls the case before them, although previous rulings indicate the probable outcome in the Supreme Court. According to Judge Magruder there are two approaches available to the intermediate judge:

> (1) The first method is perhaps the more modest one. Since we are only a half-way house of judicial review, it might be said that we should focus on previous cases in the Supreme Court to see what consequences would flow from them as a matter of logic, and examine the dicta in that court, all with the purpose of concluding, if possible, how the Supreme Court would probably deal with the problem. . . .
>
> (2) The second method is to assume that the Supreme Court, in a matter on which it has not specifically ruled, is entitled to the benefit of whatever illumination the court of appeals may be able to throw upon the question of what ought to be the law, untrammeled by dicta or logic chopping from previous opinions of the Supreme Court which might point to the opposite conclusion.[65]

When this problem arises, the choice of method may well be influenced by the personal opinion of the judge and his (perhaps subconscious) evaluation of which method will most likely bring about the desired result.

Another question is what should be done when there is a Supreme Court decision more or less in accord with the case at hand, but there are signs that when the Supreme Court faces the issue anew it will reverse its previous holding. Should the lower courts adhere to the old ruling or should they anticipate the Supreme Court?

This problem arose several times during the first years of the Roosevelt court as a result of the fundamental policy changes wrought by it. Probably the outstanding example is the action of a three-judge district court headed by Chief Judge Parker of the Fourth Circuit in the celebrated West Virginia flag salute case. After the Supreme Court's ruling in *Minnersville School District v. Gobitis*[66] upholding the compulsory flag salute against charges of infringement of religious liberty, the public recantations of Justice Black, Douglas, and Murphy, plus changes in Supreme Court membership, raised the prospect of a new decision by the High Court. Writing for the district court, Chief Judge Parker pointedly refused to adhere to precedent:

> Ordinarily we would feel constrained to follow an unreversed decision of the Supreme Court of the United States, whether we agreed with it or not. It is true that decisions are but evidences of

[65] Magruder, "Trials and Tribulations," p. 5.
[66] 310 U.S. 586 (1940).

the law and not the law itself; but the decisions of the Supreme Court must be accepted by the lower courts as binding upon them if any orderly administration of justice is to be attained. The developments with respect to the Gobitis case, however, are such that we do not feel that it is incumbent upon us to accept it as binding authority. Of the seven justices now members of the Supreme Court who participated in that decision, four have given public expression to the view that it is unsound. . . . Under such circumstances and believing, as we do, that the flag salute here required is violative of religious liberty . . . we feel that we would be recreant to our duty as judges, if through a blind following of a decision which the Supreme Court itself has thus impaired as an authority, we should deny protection to rights which we regard as among the most sacred of those protected by the constitutional guaranties.[67]

Judge Parker and his colleagues were candid in stating that their view that the compulsory flag salute was unconstitutional was a strong factor in determining their attitude toward the *Gobitis* ruling. As things turned out they guessed right, for by a vote of 6–3 the Supreme Court overruled *Gobitis* and sustained the district court.[68] The outcome did not impress Judge Magruder, who maintained the view that the lower court "did an unseemly thing in counting noses."[69] However, siding with Judge Parker were Judge Clark, who praised his "rare prescience,"[70] and Judge Peter Woodbury, a colleague of Magruder on the First Circuit.[71]

[67] Barnette v. West Virginia State Board of Education, 47 F.S. 251, 252–53 (S.D. West Virginia, 1942).

[68] West Virginia State Board of Education v. Barnette, 319 U.S. 624 (1943).

[69] Magruder, "Trials and Tribulations," p. 4.

[70] Spector Motor Service Co. Inc. v. Walsh, 139 F.2d 809, 814 (2d Cir. 1944).

[71] United States v. Girouard, 149 F.2d 760 (1st Cir. 1945). The question in this case was whether a conscientious objector who was willing to serve as a noncombatant in the armed forces but was unwilling to take the oath to bear arms may be admitted to citizenship. The majority, relying on previous congressional and Supreme Court actions, answered in the negative; Woodbury dissented, although he conceded that "the indications of reversal [by the Supreme Court] are not as strong here as they were in the second flag salute case" (p. 767). He maintained, "Like all appellate courts I conceive it to be our judicial duty to decide cases as we think they should be decided, but as an intermediate appellate court one of the factors, and a highly important one, for us to take into consideration in concluding how we should decide a case is the view which we think the Supreme Court would take on the question at issue before us. Nothing is to be gained by our deciding a question contrary to the way we think the Supreme Court would decide it. And to determine how the Supreme Court would decide a question we ordinarily would follow and apply unreversed decisions of that court in point. . . . nevertheless on rare occasions . . . situations arise when in the exercise to the best

Examples of lower court refusal to follow a Supreme Court precedent because it believes that the High Court would no longer adhere to it are rare; nose-counting is not. The following is taken from a memorandum by Learned Hand:

> It is to be observed that the three dissenters . . . two—Hughes and McReynolds—have now left the court; and that all the four who made up the majority—Stone, Black, Frankfurter and Douglas—are still there. Of the four now there who took no part— Reed, Murphy, Jackson and Rutledge—it is much better than an even break that Murphy will go with Black and Douglas, and out of the covey of the other three—"sight unseen"—I will venture to guess that a shot will bring down at least one. (I dislike to speak so of my superiors, but, as you know, I am first of all a realist; and my job, as Holmes used to say, is primarily that of a psychologist, a prophet or a diviner; I must try to guess what a majority of these Jolly Boys are going to say at that particular moment of the cruise when this meal is dished up to them.) [72]

An interesting question that confronted the Learned Hand court was whether it is proper to anticipate new doctrinal trends before they are specifically announced by the Supreme Court. In the course of a wandering essay-opinion Judge Frank declared: "We would stultify ourselves and unnecessarily burden the Supreme Court if . . . we stubbornly and literally followed decisions which have been, but not too ostentatiously, modified. . . . when a lower court perceives a pronounced new doctrinal trend in Supreme Court decisions, it is its duty, cautiously to be sure, to follow not to resist it." [73]

---

of our ability of the duty to prophesy thrust upon us by our position in the federal judicial system we must conclude that dissenting opinions of the past express the law of today. When this situation arises and we do not agree with decisions of the Supreme Court I think it our duty to decline to follow such decisions and instead to follow reasoning with which we agree" p. 765). Like Judge Parker, Judge Woodbury correctly predicted the outcome in the Supreme Court. Girouard v. United States, 328 U.S. 61 (1946).

[72] Federal Deposit v. Tremaine, January 12, 1943.

[73] Perkins v. Endicott Johnson Corp., 128 F.2d 208, 217–18 (2d Cir. 1942). In a footnote Frank added: "No more than when courts generally are interpreting a statute should lower courts in interpreting Supreme Court decisions insist on excessive explicitness, saying, 'we see what you are driving at, but you have not said it, and therefore we shall go on as before.' " Frank's approach to "a pronounced new doctrinal trend" was cited approvingly by Learned Hand in Picard v. United Aircraft Corp., 128 F.2d 632, 636 (2nd Cir. 1942). In an article written while he was on the court, Frank reiterated his position: "A court like that on which I sit, an intermediate appellate court, is vis-a-vis the Supreme Court, 'merely a reflector, serving as a judicial moon.' Judges on such a court usually must, as best they can, cautiously follow new 'doctrinal trends' in the court above them. As their duty is usually to learn 'not the Congressional intent, but the Supreme Court's intent,' their originality is often inadvertent" ("Words and Music," p. 1271).

In a case dealing with the validity of a Connecticut business tax (discussed earlier in this chapter in another connection) Judges Clark and Frank—after some nose-counting—saw a new Supreme Court attitude toward state taxing power and voted to sustain the tax. As Clark said in his majority opinion, "the trends noted above have gone further in several specific cases fundamentally close to this and in divisions in the [Supreme] Court itself, which are certainly not without significance in forecasting the future course of the law. And our function cannot be limited to a mere blind adherence to precedent."[74]

Learned Hand dissented, but while some have viewed his position as against anticipation of changes by the Supreme Court, it is quite plain that he was not far from the view pressed by Frank and Clark:

> It is always embarrassing for a lower court to say whether the time has come to disregard decisions of a higher court, not yet explicitly overruled, because they parallel others in which the higher court has expressed a contrary view. I agree that one should not wait for formal retraction in the face of changes plainly foreshadowed; the higher court may not entertain an appeal in the case before the lower court, or the parties may not choose to appeal. In either event the actual decision will be one which the judges do not believe to be that which the higher court would make. But nothing has yet appeared which satisfies me that the case at bar is of that kind. . . . Nor is it desirable for a lower court to embrace the exhilarating opportunity of antici- pating a doctrine which may be in the womb of time, but whose birth is distant; on the contrary I conceive that the measure of its duty is to divine, as best it can, what would be the event of an appeal in the case before it.[75]

What Judge Hand argued, of course, is that only when the new trend can clearly be applied to the instant case can higher court precedent be disregarded; it is not enough to believe that ultimately the higher court will come around to a new position.

The Supreme Court reversed the Second Circuit on procedural grounds to permit Connecticut courts to rule on the application of the tax to the interstate business that challenged it. After some years, the litigation was back before the Second Circuit, and once more the tax was upheld in an opinion by Clark, who was joined by Frank. This time the majority was somewhat more cautious:

> it seems to have been thought in some quarters that our previous attempt to study doctrinal trends as to the fate of state taxation in interstate commerce was only an endeavor to guess the votes

[74] Spector Motor Service Inc. v. Walsh, 139 F.2d 809, 814 (2d Cir. 1944).
[75] Ibid., p. 823.

of Supreme Court justices. We certainly have no desire either to psychoanalyze or to Gallup-poll the Court and its newer members. . . . It is our duty to discover if there exists a fairly debatable issue where the bonds of stare decisis are wearing thin, and, if we do, then to resolve it on reason and persuasion, not by any supposed count of noses. When this case was before us earlier, we thought we did discover such an issue. Events in the meantime tend to confirm us more strongly in that view.[76]

Judge Swan, the third member of the panel, dissented, relying on the position taken by Learned Hand in the first appeal. Again certiorari was granted by the Supreme Court and the Second Circuit was reversed, this time on the merits. The state tax was declared unconstitutional as applied.[77] So after nearly a decade of litigation, it was clear that there was no new doctrinal trend, not even one that safely could be said to be "in the womb of time."

A second case raising a similar question of relations with the Supreme Court grew out of the effort by a number of baseball players to challenge the legality of the reserve clause that appears in all players' contracts and ties the ballplayers to the teams with which they contract. In 1922 the Supreme Court ruled that baseball was exempt from the provisions of the federal antitrust laws. By 1949 the business aspect of the sport had grown tremendously, so there was some feeling that if faced with the issue again the Supreme Court certainly would not adhere to its precedent. But the High Court had never suggested that it was ready to re-examine the question of the applicability of the antitrust laws to sports; there was nothing more to go on than the growth of baseball and the antimonopoly attitude manifested by the court since the advent of the New Deal. Still, a lower court might be expected to go by the only previous decision on the issue. This was the view of Judge Chase:

> In dealing with such a unique aggregate as organized baseball and with a decision in respect to it which seems to be directly in point on the facts, we should not be astute in seeking to anticipate that the court which has the power to do so will change that decision. To do so would not only be an unwarranted attempt to usurp the authority of that court but would make its task in general much more difficult. . . . until, and unless, we are advised by competent authority that it is no longer the law we should continue to abide by it.[78]

But Judge Chase was writing in dissent. Learned Hand felt that as a result of the widespread interstate broadcast of games there was an

[76] Spector Motor Service, Inc. v. O'Connor, 181 F.2d 150, 153 (2d Cir. 1950).

[77] Spector Motor Service, Inc. v. O'Connor, 340 U.S. 602 (1951).

[78] Gardella v. Chandler, 172 F.2d 402, 405 (2d Cir. 1949).

issue under the antitrust laws not previously decided by the Supreme Court. The other judge in the majority, Jerome Frank, went further: "No one can treat as frivolous the argument that the Supreme Court's recent decisions have completely destroyed the vitality of Federal Baseball Club v. National League . . . decided twenty-seven years ago, and have left that case but an impotent zombi."[79]

The case decided by the Second Circuit did not reach the Supreme Court; four years later the issue was conclusively decided by the Supreme Court when by a vote of 7-2 it reaffirmed, in a brief per curiam opinion, the "impotent zombi" of 1922.[80]

The situations discussed in this section suggest that personal views are a factor in lower court determinations of how the Supreme Court would decide particular questions. Still, the existence of other factors must be recognized. There are issues about which circuit and district judges do not have settled opinions; in addition to these instances, there are other occasions, including some when lower judges have their preferences, where the main effort is to determine how the Supreme Court would rule. The degree to which personal attitude is decisive seems to depend on the nature of the issue and also on the individual judge.

[79] *Ibid.*, pp. 408–9. Frank, however, based his argument on the claim that the two cases were distinguishable.

[80] Toolson v. New York Yankees, Inc., 346 U.S. 356 (1953).

5

The Obedient Judge

IN THE COURSE OF A JUDICIAL CAREER EXCEEDING FIFTY YEARS LEARNED Hand authored approximately three thousand opinions. The prevailing opinion about this tremendous output seems to be that Hand had an important impact on American courts and law, although the sheer number of opinions helps to explain why there has been very little meaningful analysis of the judge's true influence.[1] In any event, only a small number of his opinions are today of interest to legal practitioners, and this number will decrease with each passing year.[2]

[1] There has been no full-length study of Learned Hand, although since his death his family has been keenly interested in having one done. The nearest thing we have to a review of Hand's opinions is the series of articles published in 1947 in the *Harvard Law Review* in commemoration of his seventy-fifth birthday. Some of Hand's major opinions have been collected in Hershel Shanks (ed.), *The Art and Craft of Judging; The Decisions of Judge Learned Hand* (New York: Macmillan Co., 1968).

[2] "In time, hundreds of his specific rulings will cease to have interest for the most avid legal archaeologist" (Felix Frankfurter, "Judge Learned Hand," *Harvard Law Review*, 60 [1947], 326). Four years later, Justice Frankfurter went even further in predicting that Hand's "actual decisions will be all deader than the Dodo before long, as indeed at least many of them are already" ("A Great Judge Retires: American Law Institute Honors Learned Hand," *American Bar Association Journal*, 37 [1951], 503).

It is very difficult in the space of one chapter to attempt a definitive assessment of Learned Hand's career or to conclusively answer specific questions regarding his influence on the Supreme Court, other courts, and on particular areas of the law. When scholars get around to evaluating Hand's contributions to law and jurisprudence, they probably will conclude that his impact was less than his reputation would lead us to expect.

This may seem an unfair judgment, particularly because there is little doubt that Hand contributed mightily to the development of American law in such specialized fields as admiralty law, patent and trademark law, and conflict of laws, to mention just several areas. Yet, on the basis of available evidence, there are good reasons for predicting that the ultimate evaluation of Hand's influence will be lower than what it has been over the past quarter of a century.

Judge Hand's position in the judicial hierarchy sharply narrowed his influence. Particularly in a discipline such as law is formal authority a factor in determining influence; there can be no gainsaying that the intrinsic ascendancy of Hand's decisions could not overcome (except rarely) the fact that they were made by a judge of inferior rank. Furthermore, because of changes in the nature of American law since the turn of the century and even before, during Learned Hand's career the role of the lower federal judge had become somewhat diluted from what it had been previously.

The Second Circuit is not an important public law court, and certainly not in those areas where the Supreme Court has been most active since 1938. Only occasionally has the intermediate court had to decide the questions—First Amendment freedoms, equal protection of the laws, legislative apportionment, and the rights of criminal defendants— that have involved the Supreme Court in controversy for so long. When the two courts have dealt with the same problem, there is very little to suggest that either Learned Hand or his court measurably affected the action taken by the higher court. Noteworthy, too, in any study of Hand's influence, is the fact that implicit in the trend of Supreme Court decisions over the past generation is the rejection of the restraintist philosophy so fervently espoused by Hand. In view of the criticism he directed against the Supreme Court in his Holmes Lectures, it is simply impossible to argue that that court had been much swayed by his pleas for judicial modesty.[3]

[3] This writer has studied all cases from the Learned Hand court reviewed and decided with full opinion by the Supreme Court. As we shall see in Chapter 10, the data gathered clearly show that between 1941 and 1951 Jerome Frank was far more successful and probably more influential in the Supreme Court than Judge Hand. If we go beyond the 1940's to the activist Warren court, the latter's influence has certainly been greater than Hand's.

There was, of course, much more to the judicial career of Learned Hand than his rulings. Apart from his actions on the Southern District and Second Circuit, he eloquently expressed a philosophy of judicial power in various speeches and in some of his opinions, a philosophy that was timely when he preached it and yet was imbued with a sure timelessness, transcending in importance even his most significant decisions.

It might be expected that this body of thought accounted for the great reputation enjoyed by Learned Hand, and in a way it did. Yet strangely, however deserved, this acclaim was not (and to a great extent still is not) informed, for it is not based on an analysis or understanding of what Hand said and believed. For most people who regard him as a great judge, Hand's often expressed ideas about law and justice were not responsible for the lofty evaluation. To be sure, in a limited circle there has been considerable comment about Hand's philosophy, much of it unfavorable and provoked by the Holmes Lectures in 1958.[4] But even the criticism stirred by those lectures demonstrates the failure to look critically at Hand's full judicial record. The lectures on the Bill of Rights were his "last hurrah" grounded on a half-century of advocacy of judicial restraint; the views expressed by the old judge should not have come as a surprise to anyone familiar with his decisions and extrajudicial writings. Nor, might it be added, have the new critics seriously questioned Hand's place in the judicial hall of fame.[5]

In sum, opinion about Learned Hand may be nearly reduced to the proposition that he was great because he was reputed to be great. Once it was said that he belonged "to the race of the giants—Holmes, Brandeis, and Cardozo,"[6] it became unnecessary to make new evaluations of his thought and legacy.

[4] L. Hand, *The Bill of Rights* (Cambridge: Harvard University Press, 1958).

[5] Hand's standing as a liberal has not been seriously challenged, though Professor Kurland has written that, as a result of the lectures, Hand was "forever precluded from admission to the Liberal Pantheon." But Kurland's test to determine when critics of libertarian activist tendencies in the Supreme Court are still regarded as liberals—whether responses to the critics take the form of "attempts at reasoned answers to the charges made"—suggests that Hand remains in favor with liberals. See Kurland, Book Review, *University of Chicago Law Review*, 34 (1967), 704. Evidence that Hand is admired by libertarian activists, perhaps for the wrong reasons, is not hard to come by. One illustration is the Learned Hand Human Relations Award given by the liberal American Jewish Committee each year to the member of the legal profession whose career exemplifies the principle enunciated by Judge Hand that "right knows no boundaries and justice no frontiers." Does this principle faithfully convey Hand's ideas on liberty and freedom?

[6] Charles E. Wyzanski, Jr., "Judge Learned Hand's Contribution to Public Law," *Harvard Law Review*, 60 (1947), 349.

This neglect of the record—perhaps unnecessarily, the point should be made once more that Hand's eminence might well be deserved—was discerned as long ago as 1947 by Justice Frankfurter when he lamented that "Learned Hand is heading straight for the glory and the dangers of a legend. The glory needs no gilding. The dangers may be lessened by exposure. Legends too readily enlist laziness of thought and weaken the influence that comes from critical appreciation. It is important for American law and letters that Judge Hand remains a mentor and not a memory."[7] The key to what Justice Frankfurter had in mind is "exposure," for only through an intelligent understanding of Learned Hand's ideas could the seductive dangers of the legend be weakened and perhaps the legend itself be destroyed; only by examining his words and actions could Hand's admirers appreciate his philosophy of judicial restraint; only then could they see how close in attitude and approach were Frankfurter and Hand.

As is well known, Justice Frankfurter, in the course of a quarter of a century on the Supreme Court, strenuously argued that judicial review was not wholly compatible with a belief in democratic government and majority rule. In his view, courts were not the best agencies for determining governmental policies or for the protection of civil liberties. The remedy for inequities in legislation was wiser legislation by the appropriate representatives of the people, and not judicial fiat. These views were quite similar to those advanced by Justice Holmes and Judge Hand, the twentieth century's other major practicing exponents of judicial restraint. Yet Frankfurter was by far the most criticized of the three judges as a traitor to liberal causes and justice. This is not as surprising or unfair as it may seem, for Frankfurter's utterances on judicial review were not made, and could not be made, in decisional contexts that permitted him to emerge as a defender of liberty. Brief attention to Justices Holmes and Frankfurter sheds important light on the position of Learned Hand.

Justice Holmes was fortunate in that during his tenure, judicial restraint, by and large, meant a denial of the power of courts to invalidate on due process grounds federal and state social and economic legislation simply because judges did not like these laws. Skeptical as he was of the benefits of social legislation, Holmes would not say that legislative bodies were without authority to pass laws that regulated the working conditions of bakers[8] or penalized employers of child labor.[9] His vote in these and other cases in the economic field was in

---

[7] Frankfurter, "Judge Learned Hand," p. 325. Justice Frankfurter repeated his concern over the growing legend of Learned Hand at a 1951 ceremony honoring Hand upon his formal retirement and in 1959 when Hand had completed fifty years as a federal judge.

[8] Lochner v. New York, 198 U.S. 45 (1905).

[9] Hammer v. Dagenhart, 247 U.S. 251 (1918).

accord with the prevailing attitude of liberals who (unlike Holmes) actively supported remedial legislation. At the same time, his expressions in civil liberties cases were either far more acceptable to liberals than those of his conservative colleagues or have been overlooked or misrepresented by those who are wedded to the notion of Oliver Wendell Holmes, Jr., the great civil libertarian. Be this as it may, how far Holmes would go to sustain "reasonable" legislative action and his extreme unwillingness to use judicial power were demonstrated by his opinions in *Buck v. Bell*,[10] upholding a state law providing for the forcible sterilization of mental defectives, and in *Meyer v. Nebraska*,[11] in which he dissented from a ruling that a state could not prohibit the teaching of a foreign language in elementary schools.[12]

How differently did the wheel of fortune treat Justice Frankfurter! Of the three apostles of restraint he was the most sensitive to the plight of the unpopular and unfortunate and was the most likely to depart, on occasion, from the principles of judicial modesty.[13] He least represented the attitude of the mythical "Society of Jobbists," the first "presidents" of which were Justice Holmes and Judge Hand, and whose members "were free to be egoists or altruists on the usual Saturday half-holiday provided they were neither while on the job. Their job is their contribution to the general welfare, and when a man is on that, he will do it better the less he thinks either of himself or his neighbors, and the more he puts all his energy into the

---

[10] 247 U.S. 200 (1927).

[11] 262 U.S. 390 (1923). Mention also ought to be made of Holmes's dissent in Bailey v. Alabama, 219 U.S. 219 (1911), in which the Supreme Court struck down Alabama's peonage statute. This case "should be required reading," writes Holmes's admirer, Max Lerner, "for those who still cling to a lingering belief that Holmes was a humanitarian liberal in his impulses" (quoted in Samuel J. Konefsky, *The Legacy of Holmes and Brandeis* [New York: Macmillan Co., 1956], p. 258). But Frankfurter was "a humanitarian liberal in his impulses."

[12] In 1941 Professor Walton Hamilton wrote of Holmes, "If he served a liberalism, glorious in his day, but already on the way out, it was by adventitious circumstances" (quoted by Edward J. Bander, "Oliver Wendell Holmes, Justice in the Balance," *Arts and Sciences* [Winter 1966], p. 24). Mr. Bander assembles much of the criticism directed against Holmes and rather unsuccessfully attempts to provide a defense.

[13] This point can be documented by reference to two areas. In the school segregation cases he (1) consistently voted to strike down state segregation statutes and (2) appeared to relax in his insistence that procedural requirements be met before the Supreme Court would issue a decision. In the church-state area, Frankfurter was quite ready to use judicial power to invalidate state laws contrary to the no-establishment clause of the First Amendment.

problem he has to solve."[14] Yet while Frankfurter could not belong to a group that so completely rejected natural law principles,[15] he was regularly criticized by judicial activists, and far more harshly than either Holmes or Hand.

Frankfurter's misfortune arose from the fact that just about beginning with his service on the Supreme Court, judicial restraint came to mean the rejection of policies and decisions ardently espoused by civil libertarians. In Frankfurter's day, it was no longer possible to maintain a philosophy of judicial limitations and at the same time arrive at results pleasing to the liberal community.[16] The votes that

[14] From a letter by Justice Holmes to John Wu, March 26, 1925, quoted in Charles P. Curtis, *Law as Large as Life* (New York: Simon and Schuster, 1959), p. 178. Curtis also gives Hand's account of the Society (from a 1930 tribute to Justice Holmes) and then quotes from a letter to him by a Society "member," Judge Charles E. Wyzanski, who wrote what appears to be some of the strongest criticism of the Holmes-Hand attitude to the job of a judge: "Man has a chance to make a *moral* pattern—not merely something he likes, or something that has the beauty of the dance, or the virility of an ascent of Everest. If he restricts himself to what he likes and the way his taste runs, of course we may get a Learned Hand or a Paul Valery, but we may get Al Capone or Hitler. And to tell the young to make a pattern without at the same time telling them it is to be a moral pattern is to run the risk of which direction they arbitrarily will select. To advise them to make a *moral* choice is not to tell them *what* choice they must make. It is only to stress that in your way through your life you must try to build some coherent structure drawn from the experience of the race, from your background, from your personal insight, a structure that, of course, will last hardly longer than does the theme of a sonata in the mind of the listener."

In a letter to this writer (October 2, 1967), Judge Wyzanski states that his criticism was directed against "Curtis's literal reading of Holmes's frequently stated creed." Yet the conclusion is unavoidable that the criticism deserves to be leveled directly against Holmes and Hand. Indeed, in his reply to Wyzanski, Curtis showed that he was not guilty of literalism: "Morals are not wholly matters of feeling. There is a rational rectitude, even about loving your neighbor as yourself. A member of the Society of Jobbists is not confined to what he likes or to the way his taste runs. He may very well—indeed, I think he will be expected to—admit reason to its part in a moral choice. Capone or Hitler could no more be elected to the society than Martin Luther or Savonarola. Robin Hood would be rejected on both counts."

[15] See Frankfurter's opinions in Adamson v. California, 332 U.S. 46 (1947) and Rochin v. California, 342 U.S. 165 (1952).

[16] "It has been said of Holmes that he survived into his own generation. It may yet be written of Frankfurter that he was appointed as his was passing into history. He came to the Court beautifully equipped to carry on the Holmes-Brandeis opposition to judicial activism in the economic field. In twenty-three years on the bench, he had occasion to write just one such opinion" (J. A. C. Green, "Felix Frankfurter: A Dissenting Opinion," *UCLA Law Review*, 12 [1965], 1013, 1042).

flowed from principles of restraint often were diametrically opposed to those that would have emerged out of a concern for personal liberties, and Frankfurter had to choose. His task was even more painful because he fervently believed both in restraint and justice; his position was in some respects similar to that of Chief Justice Stone, whose difficulty was described by Learned Hand:

> Even before Justice Stone became Chief Justice it began to seem as though, when "personal rights" were in issue, something strangely akin to the discredited attitude towards the Bill of Rights of the old apostles of the institution of property, was regaining recognition. Just why property itself was not a "personal right" nobody took the time to explain; and perhaps the inquiry would have been regarded as captious and invidious anyway; but the fact remained that in the name of the Bill of Rights the courts were upsetting statutes which were plainly compromises between conflicting interests, each of which had more than a merely plausible support in reason. That looked a great deal as though more specific directions could be found in the lapidary counsels of the Amendments than the successful school had been able to discover, so long as the dispute turned on property.[17]

[17] Hand continued: "If needed little acquaintance with the robust and loyal character of the Chief Justice to foretell that he would not be content with what to him was an opportunistic reversion at the expense of his convictions as to the powers of a court. He could not understand how the principle which he had all along supported, could mean that, when concerned with interests other than property, the courts should have a wider latitude for enforcing their own predilections than when they were concerned with property itself. There might be logical defects in his canon, but it deserved a consistent application or it deserved none at all; at any rate it was not to be made into an excuse for having one's way in any given case. Most of all was its even-handed application important to the judges themselves, since only by not intervening could they hope to preserve that independence which was the condition of any successful discharge of their duties" ("Chief Justice Stone's Concept of the Judicial Function," in Irving Dilliard (ed.), *The Spirit of Liberty* [New York: Vintage Press, 1959], pp. 155–56).

Much of what Learned Hand said of Stone seems to be a restatement of his own position on judicial review and thus it has been said: "Judge Hand revealed his own attitude perhaps better than that of the Chief Justice" (Wyzanski, "Hand's Contribution to Public Law," p. 356). This is also the view of Alpheus T. Mason (Stone's biographer) and Professor Paul Freund. Admittedly, Hand did ignore some of Stone's activist statements on the Supreme Court's function in personal liberties cases, such as the celebrated footnote in the Carolene Products case and the dissent in Minnersville School District v. Gobitis. Yet Hand had maintained a correspondence with the Chief Justice over a long period and did have reason to believe that Stone's attitude was close to his own. In a letter to John Frank (February 23, 1949) Judge Clark wrote: "Judge Hand states that both Cardozo and Stone asserted to him privately very serious doubts of the Court's program." Also,

Justice Frankfurter was never able to resolve this conflict with the certainty of a Holmes or a Hand. Fairly often he joined with the libertarian activists on the Supreme Court. When he found that his attachment to the Holmesian view of the judicial function required him to sustain governmental action curbing individual liberty, he also felt compelled to demonstrate his personal liberalism by including in his opinions protestations that he regarded the actions he was sustaining unwise and unjust, albeit constitutional. This admixture of an affirmation of governmental action and an affirmation of a personal liberalism, so unlike the style of Justice Holmes and Judge Hand,[18] angered the activists, who believed that the outcome of each appeal is more important than considerations of judicial philosophy. So, although his eloquent dissent in *West Virginia v. Barnette*[19] was perfectly consistent with Holmes's dissent in *Meyer v. Nebraska*, Frankfurter was roundly attacked as an enemy of liberalism and also as a traitor to Holmes.

Learned Hand was a more consistent proponent of judicial restraint than Frankfurter. While the Holmes Lectures were not the

---

the Chief Justice was not the civil libertarian and judicial activist that some writers who like to divide the justices into two clear-cut groups of activists or restraintists have made him out to be. These writers do not understand the footnote and the different meanings to different judges of the "preferred position" doctrine. The fact is that Stone was closer to Frankfurter's position than to Black's; and Learned Hand is quite correct in stating that Chief Justice Stone could not accept the activist distinction between property rights and personal rights. The important question for Justice Stone was the relationship between legislation and the political process. Where the channels of political action were open to those who were directly affected by the legislation so that they could strive to remedy any injustices created by the legislation, Stone would not invoke judicial review; where these channels were unavailable (such as to disenfranchised minorities or to individuals who did not live in the state that enacted legislation affecting them), the Chief Justice was far less reluctant to invalidate legislation. Stone's comprehensive scheme of constitutional law provided for similar criteria of constitutionality in civil liberties, intergovernmental immunities, state tax, and interstate commerce cases.

Thus, at the end of the Carolene Products footnote, Stone says: "Compare *McCulloch* v. *Maryland* . . .; *South Carolina* v. *Barnwell Bros.* and cases cited." All of the previously cited cases dealt with the Bill of Rights; but McCulloch, of course, was concerned with state taxing power while Barnwell involved state regulation of interstate commerce.

[18] What Holmes wrote to Frankfurter about Brandeis is most applicable to Frankfurter: "It seems as if the gift of passionate enthusiasm were racial. It is a great one." And, on another occasion: "It seems as if an exquisite moral sensibility were the gift of many Jews." From Alexander M. Bickel, *The Unpublished Opinions of Mr. Justice Brandeis* (Cambridge: Harvard University Press, Belknap Press, 1957), p. 222.

[19] 319 U.S. 624 (1943).

most eloquent exposition of his views, they received far more attention than any of his earlier expressions on the proper limitations on judicial power. In them he argued that "there was nothing in the United States Constitution that gave courts any authority to review the decisions of Congress; and it was a plausible—indeed to my mind an unanswerable—argument that it invaded that 'Separation of Powers' which, as so many then believed, was the condition of all free government."[20] Yet, Hand continued, as an act of "statutory interpretation," there was justification for judicial review:

> For centuries it has been an accepted canon in interpretation of documents to interpolate into the text such provisions, though not expressed, as are essential to prevent the defeat of the venture at hand; and this applies with special force to the interpretation of constitutions, which, since they are designed to cover a great multitude of necessarily unforseen occasions, must be cast in general language, unless they are constantly amended. If so, it was altogether in keeping with established practice for the Supreme Court to assume an authority to keep the states, Congress, and the President within their prescribed powers. Otherwise the government could not proceed as planned; and indeed would certainly have foundered, as in fact it almost did over that very issue.
>
> However, since this power is not a logical deduction from the structure of the Constitution but only a practical condition upon its successful operation, it need not be exercised whenever a court sees, or thinks that it sees, an invasion of the Constitution. It is always a preliminary question how importantly the occasion demands an answer. It may be better to leave the issue to be worked out without authoritative solution; or perhaps the only solution available is one that the court has no adequate means to enforce.[21]

[20] L. Hand, *Bill of Rights*, pp. 10–11.

[21] *Ibid.*, pp. 14–15. This approach to judicial review represents an admirable synthesis of two of the cornerstones of Hand's attitude toward the judicial function. It is also an almost ingenious resolution of a problem that confronts the proponents of judicial restraint. The problem can be stated very simply: if judicial review is not granted to the courts by the constitution, what justification is there for even a limited or occasional review by the courts? To answer by referring to the standard usually employed by restraintists—the "reasonable man" test—and to say that judges are empowered to act only when legislatures pass unreasonable laws, is to beg the question, even if we were to suppose that a reasonableness test makes much sense. Moreover, to Judge Hand, the question might be more difficult, for he consistently denied that the Bill of Rights was anything more than an expression of mood. If so, what basis was there for an extreme exponent of judicial limitations to accept an even limited judicial review? Hand resolved this dilemma by resorting to the one area where he most boldly advanced

And, toward the conclusion of the lectures: "In the end all that can be asked on review by a court is that the appraisals and the choice shall be impartial. The statute may be far from the best solution of the conflict with which it deals; but if it is the result of an honest effort to embody that compromise or adjustment that will secure the widest acceptance and most avoid resentment it is 'Due Process of Law' and conforms to the First Amendment."[22]

Hand failed to clarify when courts might properly employ judicial review. He did not point to a single case and say, "here the legislature was impartial and the statute does not embody a compromise. Accordingly it was proper for the judges to declare it unconstitutional." To the contrary, the cases discussed are instances of judicial usurpation; as applied by him to the Bill of Rights, Hand's interpretation embodies the fullest limitation on judicial power and a rejection of virtually all of the policy-making by the Supreme Court since 1938. Perhaps it was the discussion of concrete cases and not Hand's conception of the role of courts, which by itself was a repetition of many past utterances, that aroused the dormant activists and provoked the great debate that developed after Hand spoke.

Hand's actions as a judge were no more of a guide to when he would sanction judicial review than were the cases cited in *The Bill of Rights*. Only rarely was he called upon to rule in cases presenting constitutional questions or to decide contentious civil liberties issues. On the bench, his philosophy of judicial limitation was confined to contexts of judicial power far narrower than situations of judicial review, to such questions as the scope of review of administrative agencies and the role of the judge in immigration and naturalization

---

notions of judicial competence, statutory interpretation. True, to Hand the Constitution was merely a sort of statute, but to him the process of statutory interpretation was a welcome opportunity "to reconstruct the past solution imaginatively in its setting and project the purposes which inspired it upon the concrete occasions which arise for their decision" ("The Contribution of an Independent Judiciary to Civilization," in Dilliard, *Spirit of Liberty,* p. 120). And, in one of his opinions he wrote: "There is no surer way to misread any document than to read it literally. . . . As nearly as we can, we must put ourselves in the place of those who uttered the words, and try to divine how they would have dealt with the unforeseen situation; and, although their words are by far the most decisive evidence of what they would have done, they are by no means final" (Guiseppi v. Walling, 144 F.2d 608, 624 [2d Cir. 1944]). In order to save the Constitution, to make it workable, it was necessary to read into it a limited judicial review, whatever the intention of the framers had been.

[22] *Ibid.,* pp. 66–67.

cases. It is believed that in all his years as a federal judge he held only one statute to be invalid.[23]

Looking at the emphasis that Hand frequently placed, in his formulation of judicial review, on the impartiality of legislation, we find an interesting parallel with the thought of Chief Justice Stone. In the second paragraph of his historic footnote in *United States v. Carolene Products,* Stone raised the question "whether legislation which restricts those political processes which can ordinarily be expected to bring about repeal of undesirable legislation, is to be subjected to more exacting judicial scrutiny."[24] Thus, where for example, the right to vote or freedom of press is restricted, the law-making process and subsequent legislation are not impartial for those whose rights have been infringed. This was Stone's view. Might not Learned Hand also accept an activist political process doctrine allowing for judicial review of legislation which denies fair access to the legislative process?

This question suggests that Hand, consistent with his general philosophy of restraint, might have permitted a broader judicial role in First Amendment cases. Yet, the parallel with Stone—who also was a restraintist—should not be overdrawn; it is certain that of the two men Hand was the far more unwilling to use judicial power to correct alleged legislative abuses. To be sure, both judges were concerned with compromise and accommodation, but the situations where they would strike down legislation were quite different. For Stone, the fact that a law deprived someone of a First Amendment right or another basic freedom was reason enough to make it suspect, even if the legislation

[23] Professor Paul Freund points out, as others have, that "one cannot recall his ever holding an act of Congress unconstitutional, though opportunities were not wanting in his more than fifty years of judging. He did, to be sure, rule in the *Schechter* case that the labor provisions of the N.R.A. were invalid, but the noteworthy aspect of that decision was that he did not pronounce a doom on the Act as a whole and in fact he sustained the trade-practice regulations that were later overturned by the Supreme Court" ("Learned Hand: A Tribute," *Harvard Law Record,* 33 [September 21, 1961], 11–12). It should not be thought, however, that the other Second Circuit judges invalidated much legislation. From 1941 to 1951 not a single federal statute was struck down by the court. In fact, in one case, McComb v. Frank Scerbo & Sons. 177 F.2d 137 (2d Cir. 1949), in a concurring opinion Learned Hand suggested that a section of the Fair Labor Standards Act might be unconstitutional. This brought about another concurring opinion by Judge Frank, who said, "I am unwilling to go along with Judge Hand's intimations about unconstitutionality. I think it always unwise for a court to cross hypothetical constitutional bridges; crossing actual ones is dangerous enough" (at p. 141).

[24] 304 U.S. 144, 152 n. 4 (1938).

was a compromise of other alternatives presented to the legislature. This was because it denied to those who were adversely affected by it the usual political means for reversing the legislative decision. In the *Carolene* footnote Stone favorably cites more than a dozen cases where the Supreme Court made clear its special concern for those who were denied fundamental constitutional rights. But to Judge Hand, "Practically, it *is very seldom* possible to say that a legislature has abdicated by surrendering to one faction; the relevant factors are too many and too incomparable."[25] Hand was unconcerned that some legislative accommodations of different interests might deprive individuals at some later date of the means through which they might participate in political actions affecting their rights and interests. Hand narrowed the type of issue that a reviewing court could raise when dealing with challenged legislation, thereby following a concept of the political process so restrictive as to effectively emasculate the entire function of judicial review. Yet Learned Hand was not naïve about politics and he knew well that laws are not the product of philosophical musings but the end of a process involving the marshaling of resources by opposing interests. Almost forty years before he lectured at Harvard he wrote to Justice Brandeis: "It is of course true that any kind of judicial legislation is objectionable on the score of the limited interests which a Court can represent, yet there are wrongs which in fact legislatures cannot be brought to take an interest in, at least not until the Courts have acted."[26] In view of this perception it is hard to understand why Judge Hand's formulation of judicial power did not cover situations where exclusion from political activity precludes meaningful legislative bargaining and adjustment, and where, consequently, without judicial activity the legislature cannot be brought to right the wrong.

Two plausible explanations of this seeming inconsistency, not exclusive of one another, readily come to mind. The first is that since judicial review, according to Hand, is no more than a condition for the successful operation of the Constitution, only legislation that might reasonably be thought to do damage to the constitutional system properly occasions its use. Impartial laws (and many that are not), even unconstitutional laws, should be allowed to stand so long as they do not threaten the preservation of our system of government. "It is always a preliminary question how importantly the occasion

[25] L. Hand, "Contribution of an Independent Judiciary," in Dilliard, *Spirit of Liberty*, p. 124. Emphasis supplied.

[26] Letter of January 22, 1919, quoted in Alpheus T. Mason, *Brandeis: A Free Man's Life* (New York: Viking Press, 1946), p. 579.

demands an answer,"[27] Hand cautioned in the opening lecture at Harvard.

The second explanation is that Learned Hand became so wedded to the canon of judicial limitations that he could no longer consider the practical results of legislation. Once Congress sets a policy, since it is a representative assembly, it no longer is proper or necessary for courts to investigate how it arrived at its decision. "I trust I shall always be docile to what Congress may command,"[28] he proclaimed in his seventy-eighth year while decrying a statute that fell far short of impartiality. In a way, Hand was trapped by his own rhetoric and theory of restraint, which in the final analysis left open not a single clear avenue for the exercise of judicial review. It is a measure of the gap between Hand's approach and the attitude of the moderates on the question of judicial power that one of the latter, Professor Herbert Wechsler, was severely attacked by libertarian activists after he advocated principles of neutrality as an alternative to Hand's extreme passivity.[29]

In area after area, Learned Hand as a judge applied his notions of judicial restraint, even where no constitutional issues were raised. He repeatedly subordinated his own views to those of Congress or the Supreme Court or administrative agencies or to the will of the community. Patent law, a field where he perhaps had no peer, was no exception. There, too, he came to accept what he regarded as superior authority. At the outset of his career, Hand tellingly questioned whether judges could properly determine patent disputes:

> I cannot stop without calling attention to the extraordinary condition of the law which makes it possible for a man without any knowledge of even the rudiments of chemistry to pass upon such questions as these. The inordinate expense of time is the least of the resulting evils, for only a trained chemist is really capable of passing upon such facts. . . . How long we shall continue to blunder along without the aid of unpartisan and authoritative scientific assistance in the administration of justice, no one knows: but all fair persons not conventionalized by provincial legal habits of mind ought, I should think, unite to effect some such change.[30]

[27] L. Hand, *Bill of Rights*, p. 15.

[28] Concurring in McComb v. Frank Scerbo & Sons, 177 F.2d 137, 141 (2d Cir. 1949).

[29] Herbert Wechsler, "Toward Neutral Principles of Constitutional Law," *Harvard Law Review*, 73 (1959), 1.

[30] Parke, Davis & Co. v. H. K. Mulford Co., 189 F.95, 115 (S.D.N.Y., 1911).

Yet, he became bolder in this area as the years went by. In one of his first patent rulings, after his appointment to the appellate court, he wrote:

> Objective tests may be of value vaguely to give us a sense of direction, but the final destination can be only loosely indicated. An invention is a new display of ingenuity beyond the compass of the routineer, and in the end that is all that can be said about it. Courts cannot avoid the duty of divining as best they can what the day to day capacity of the ordinary artisan will produce. . . . when all is said, there will remain cases when we can only fall back upon such good sense as we may have, and in these we cannot help exposing the inventor to the hazard inherent in hypostatizing such modifications in the existing arts as are within the limited imagination of the journeyman. There comes a point where the question must be resolved by a subjective opinion as to what seems an easy step and what does not. We must try to correct our standard by such objective references as we can, but in the end the judgment will appear, and no doubt be, to a large sense personal, and in that sense arbitrary.[31]

In many subsequent cases Judge Hand, relying on his admittedly subjective opinion, held that challenged patents were valid. But by the 1940's the Supreme Court had clearly manifested a more stringent approach toward patent claims, making them more difficult to sustain. Obedient as ever, Learned Hand reflected this new attitude and voted to invalidate patents that in an earlier time he would have sustained. As he explained in a memorandum in a patent case decided only weeks before his retirement: "I have always felt that it was the duty of an inferior court to suppress its own opinions, and, in the words of O. W. H[olmes], to try to prophesy what the appellate court would do. *God knows, I have often been wrong in that too; but I have at least been obedient, which is as I conceive it a judge's prime duty.*"[32]

The suppression of personal views was clearly demonstrated by his rulings in some appeals dealing with New Deal legislation and administrative agencies. Hand was never much of an admirer of the New Deal, although he was especially contemptuous of the defenders of the old order. In a letter to Chief Justice Stone he admitted that "personally, the Fillii Aurorae make me actively sick at my stomach; they are so conceited, so insensitive, so arrogant. But on the whole the Old Tories are intellectually so moribund, that as a mere matter of my own personal conceit, I can't flock with them. They seem to me as persons more fit associates for a gentleman. . . . but they are so stupid

[31] Kirsch Manufacturing Co. v. Gould Mersereau Co. Inc., 6 F.2d 793, 794 (2d Cir. 1925).

[32] Youngs Rubber Corp. v. Allied Latex, March 26, 1951. Emphasis supplied.

and emit such dreary, hollow sounds."[33] His memoranda show, as Judge Wyzanski wrote, that Hand "felt that the courts, if they had not been so narrow in their sympathies, might have done the work of deciding economic and social controversies better than have the executive agencies."[34]

But in cases coming from administrative bodies Hand invariably spoke of the special competence and great expertise of the members of these agencies. Because they had a much narrower compass of questions to deal with and concentrated exclusively on the problems that came before them, administrators could attain a degree of competence that could not be matched by judges. Hand's rule was that "such tribunals possess competence in their special field which forbids us to disturb the measure of relief which they think necessary."[35] He elaborated in a labor case:

> Conceivably labor disputes might have been considered as demanding no such specialized knowledge for their solution. On

[33] February 6, 1934, quoted in Alpheus T. Mason, *Harlan Fiske Stone: Pillar of the Law* (New York: Viking Press, 1956), p. 384. In a memorandum, Hand once lampooned New Deal legislative draftsmanship: "Translated into New Dealese, this could have been more impressively and pretentiously stated as follows: 'The semantic categorization of the factual congeries of circumstances presented by this nexus of jurally operative occurrences is inevitably determined in favor of inclusion rather than exclusion. Coincidentally therewith, and projected more realistically and less legalistically, and therefore more coercively in respect of authoritative finality, it demonstrably appears that the indisputable functional consequences, inherent in, and deductible from, the employment of the terms and locutions selected, make inevitably and pragmatically compulsive the inference and conclusion that the aforesaid semantic categorization can be brought into juristic accord with the schematic objectives in contemplation' " (Tito Neri v. United States, April 15, 1953).

[34] Wyzanski, "Hand's Contribution to Public Law," p. 362. Later in the same article Wyzanski added that, despite his doubts, Learned Hand received the commissions' work "with an exemplary hospitality that belied any internal misgivings he may have had" (p. 365). This assertion may be an exaggeration, for in some cases Hand was either sarcastic or doubtful in explaining why the court could not disturb the administrative ruling: "We do not forget that from time immemorial this duty has been entrusted to courts, but that is irrelevant. Congress having now created an organ endowed with the skill which comes of long experience and penetrating study, its conclusions inevitably supercede those of courts which are not similarly endowed" (Herzfeld v. Federal Trade Commission, 140 F.2d 207, 209 [2d Cir. 1944]). In setting aside an order of the N.L.R.B.: "It would be fantastic, we think, to say that only those versed in labor relations are competent to determine the meaning of such language as that we have quoted" (National Labor Relations Board v. Dadourian Export Corporation, 138 F.2d 891, 892 [2d Cir. 1943]).

[35] Herzfeld v. Federal Trade Commission, 140 F.2d 207, 209 (2d Cir. 1944).

the other hand they may have been made the occasion of wide study, and a very large literature has arisen with which these only are familiar who have become adepts. Like any other group of phenomena, when isolated and intensively examined, those relations appear to fall into more or less uniform models or patterns, which put those well skilled in the subject at an advantage which no bench of judges can hope to rival.[36]

Similar language abounds in opinions in appeals from the Tax Court, which too was given limited immunity from judicial review by Congress and the Supreme Court.[37]

Interestingly, it was Learned Hand's strong insistence on a very limited power of review of administrative agencies which led to reversal and criticism of the Second Circuit by the Supreme Court in an opinion by Justice Frankfurter. After the Taft-Hartley Act was passed, the question arose whether the scope of review given to the courts of appeals in labor relations cases had been enlarged by Congress. The new law provided that findings of the N.L.R.B. "shall be conclusive . . . if supported by substantial evidence on the record considered as a whole." Formerly, N.L.R.B. findings were conclusive "if supported by evidence." When the issue came before the Second Circuit, the judges were divided, with Judge Hand concluding "that no more was done than to make definite what was already implied."[38]

[36] National Labor Relations Board v. Standard Oil Co., 138 F.2d 885, 887–88 (2d Cir. 1943).

[37] Hand was generally more willing than his colleagues to forego review of Tax Court decisions, perhaps because he did not relish the task of interpreting the Internal Revenue Code. "We can think of no legal question as to which we ought more readily yield than that at bar; in that thicket of verbiage, through which we have been forced to cut a way, it must surely be an advantage to have been familiar with other tangles of the same general sort; and, while it is the pleasure of Congress to express itself so apocalyptically, we may well be grateful that we are permitted to put our hand into those of accredited pathfinders" (American Coast Line v. Commissioner of Internal Revenue, 159 F.2d 665, 669 [2d Cir. 1947]). In a tax appeal decided a few months earlier, Learned Hand, over the vigorous dissent of Augustus Hand, went further than in any other case in narrowing review of the Tax Court. He concluded his opinion by asking whether there remained any basis for review of this agency. "That finality depends . . . upon the added competency which inevitably follows from concentration in a special field. Why, if this be so, we—or indeed even the Supreme Court itself—should be competent to fix the measure of the Tax Court's competence, and why we should ever declare that it is wrong, is indeed an interesting inquiry, which happily it is not necessary for us to pursue" (Brooklyn National Corp. v. Commissioner of Internal Revenue, 157 F.24 450, 452, 453 [2d Cir. 1946]).

[38] National Labor Relations Board v. Universal Camera Corp., 179 F.2d 749, 752 (2d Cir. 1950). Judge Frank supported Hand while Judge Swan dissented.

In unanimously overruling the Second Circuit, the Supreme Court left no doubt that the lower court had too modestly conceived its function:

> Courts must now assume more responsibility for the reasonableness and fairness of Labor Board decisions than some courts have shown in the past. Reviewing courts must be influenced by a feeling that they are not to abdicate the conventional judicial function. Congress has imposed on them responsibility for assuring that the Board keeps within reasonable grounds. . . . The Board's findings are entitled to respect; but they must nonetheless be set aside when the record before a court of appeals clearly precludes the Board's decision from being justified by a fair estimate of the worth of the testimony of witnesses or its informed judgment on matters within its special competence or both.[39]

Another instance where the Second Circuit was reversed because it had too modestly construed its power came about in a case in which Learned Hand made one of his greatest contributions to public law. As is well known, "an extremely rare, if not unique, situation in the history of the [Supreme] Court,"[40] arose in the antitrust suit brought by the federal government against the Aluminum Company of America. Because of disqualifications, the Supreme Court lacked a quorum to hear the appeal from the district court's ruling in favor of

[39] Universal Camera Corp. v. National Labor Relations Board, 340 U.S. 474, 490 (1951). Subsequently, Hand became bolder in reviewing N.L.R.B. orders. As he put it, "A burnt child dreads the fire and Felix singed my fanny" (Memorandum in N.L.R.B. v. Radio Officers Union, February 14, 1952). Ironically, after the Second Circuit rendered its first decision in Universal Camera, but before it was reversed by the Supreme Court, Hand justified his modest approach to review of the Labor Board by pointing to an earlier reversal of a Second Circuit ruling by the High Court "After the Phelps-Dodge case (313 U.S. 177 [1941]) where Felix shook his august finger and said that slops like us couldn't possibly have the 'experience of these halcyon harbingers of a Better World,' I am cowed" (Memorandum in N.L.R.B. v. Quest-Shon Mark, October 9, 1950).

The Universal Camera case was returned to the Second Circuit, which then reversed the N.L.R.B. (National Labor Relations Board v. Universal Camera Corp., 190 F.2d 429 [2d Cir. 1951]). Learned Hand again wrote the court's opinion; Jerome Frank concurred, however, his opinion was actually a partial dissent: "Recognizing, as only a singularly stupid man would not, Judge Hand's superior wisdom, intelligence and learning, I seldom disagree with him, and then with serious misgivings. In this instance, I have overcome my misgivings because I think that his modesty has moved him to interpret too sweepingly the Supreme Court's criticism of our earlier opinion written by him" (p. 431).

[40] United States v. District Court, 334 U.S. 258, 265 (1948) (J. Frankfurter concurring).

the company. Congress then provided by special statute for review by a panel of the Second Circuit consisting of the three judges senior in service on the court. In a monumental opinion by Learned Hand the trial court was reversed. Hand established standards for determining monopolistic practices, and these standards had a direct and great influence on the development of antitrust law in the Supreme Court.[41] After the district court entered a judgment pursuant to the mandate of the court of appeals, the government petitioned the appellate court for a writ of mandamus directing the trial judge to vacate part of his judgment. But Learned Hand (joined by Swan and Augustus Hand) held that the Second Circuit had no more jurisdiction over the litigation because its special powers were limited to deciding the original appeal. As the chief judge put it, "If the intent had been that we should retain jurisdiction over the action to the end, Congress would not have limited us to a decision of 'the appeal'; it would have transferred all appellate jurisdiction."[42] Without a dissenting vote (7–0), the Supreme Court reversed the Second Circuit's most distinguished panel. In a concurring opinion, Justice Frankfurter was a bit caustic: "For reasons that seem to me too obvious to need spelling out, that [Congressional] Act should be interpreted as transferring to the Circuit Court of Appeals *the case* and not merely a stage in its disposition."[43]

As was to be expected, Hand's attitude toward the use of judicial power extended to areas where he had little sympathy for the policy enacted by Congress. This was most clearly seen in immigration and naturalization appeals.

A long-standing section of the Nationality Act provides that in order for an alien to attain citizenship he must have been of "good moral character" for the five years preceding his petition for naturalization. Congress, however, has not defined what constitutes "good moral character" or what conduct demonstrates immoral character, so when a question arises whether a petitioner is eligible for citizenship, the courts often must determine whether the statutory requirement has been met. One problem facing judges in these cases is whose standard of morality to apply.

According to Professor Edmond Cahn, "For the first twenty years following his appointment to the bench, Judge Hand's opinions in

[41] United States v. Aluminum Company of America, 148 F.2d 416 (2d Cir. 1945). Judge Hand's decision was, in effect, affirmed by the Supreme Court in American Tobacco Co. v. United States, 328 U.S. 781, 811–14 (1946).

[42] United States v. Caffey, 164 F.2d 159, 161 (2d Cir. 1947).

[43] United States v. District Court, 334 U.S. 258, 265 (1948).

cases involving deportation, exclusion, or naturalization of aliens, were direct, forthright expressions of his intelligence and sympathy for humanity."[44] Then, in 1929, in a case involving the "moral turpitude" of one who was convicted of several minor violations of the prohibition law, Learned Hand held that the standard of what constitutes "moral turpitude" was not what the judges themselves might set, but the "commonly accepted mores," that is, the moral conventions accepted at the time by the community.[45] In the same year he made a notable address before the American Law Institute in which he argued that law existed independently of a common will. "The truth appears to be that what we mean by a common will is no more than that there shall be an available peaceful means by which law may be changed when it becomes irksome to enough powerful people who can make their will effective. We may say if we like that meanwhile everybody has consented to what exists, but this is a fiction. They have not; they are merely too inert or too weak to do anything about it."[46]

Although there were some who thought that there are "rather weighty disparities" between the judge's duty in deportation cases and his responsibilities in naturalization appeals,[47] Judge Hand ruled that a community standard must be followed in the latter cases in determining "good moral character." In several situations where the community test was employed, liberal results were reached. Thus, an applicant, one Francioso, was admitted to citizenship although he had lived incestuously with his niece and had four children by her—and the Second Circuit decision was the occasion for a celebrated opinion by its chief judge:

> Cato himself could not have demanded that he should turn all five adrift. True, he might have left the home and supported them out of his earnings; but to do so would deprive his children of the protection, guidance and solace of a father. We can think of no course open to him which would not have been regarded as more immoral than that which he followed, unless it be that he should live at home, but as a celibate. There may be purists who would insist that this alone was consistent with "good moral conduct"; but we do not believe that the conscience of the ordinary man demands that degree of ascesis; and we have for warrant the fact that the [Catholic] Church—least of all complaisant with sexual lapses—saw fit to sanction the continuance of this union.[48]

[44] Cahn, "Authority and Responsibility," *Columbia Law Review*, 51 (1951), 842.

[45] United States *ex rel.* Iorio v. Day, 34 F.2d 920, 921 (2d Cir. 1929).

[46] L. Hand, "Is There a Common Will?," in Dilliard, *Spirit of Liberty*, p. 41.

[47] Cahn, "Authority and Responsibility," p. 846.

[48] United States v. Francioso, 164 F.2d 163, 164 (2d Cir. 1947).

Likewise, an unmarried man who admitted to occasional sexual intercourse with unmarried women was found to be of good moral character "so far as we can divine anything so tenebrous and impalpable as the common conscience."[49]

However, Learned Hand was satisfied that an individual who had deserted his lawful wife, failed to make court-ordered payments to her, and lived with another woman, did not meet the standard judged by the prevailing common conscience.[50] The same result was reached in a case that must have been most difficult for Hand to decide. A little short of five years prior to applying for citizenship, Louis Repouille deliberately put to death his thirteen-year-old son. As Judge Hand's majority opinion put it, the reason for this act was that the child had "suffered from birth from a brain injury which destined him to be an idiot and a physical monstrosity malformed in all four limbs. The child was blind, mute, and deformed. He had to be fed; the movements of his bladder and bowels were involuntary and his entire life was spent in a small crib."[51] Repouille had been an exemplary father in all respects to his four other children. Following the "mercy killing," he was convicted of second degree manslaughter; the jury recommended "utmost clemency" and he was placed on probation.

Learned Hand presented the facts in a way most sympathetic to the poor father, yet his opinion upheld the denial of the application. "We can say no more than that, quite independently of what may be the current moral feeling as to legally administered euthanasia, we feel reasonably secure in holding that only a minority of virtuous persons would deem the practice morally justifiable, while it remains in private hands, even when the provocation is as overwhelming as it was in this instance."[52]

[49] Schmidt v. United States, 177 F.2d 450, 452 (2d Cir. 1949). Professor Cahn pointed out that while he applied the community test, Judge Hand demonstrated "its worthlessness," when he conceded that there was no practicable way "to conduct an inquiry as to what is the common conscience on the point. Even though we could take a poll, it would not be enough merely to count heads, without any approval of the voters. A majority of the votes of those in prisons and brothels for instance ought scarcely to outweigh the votes of accredited churchgoers. Nor can we see any reason to suppose that the opinion of clergymen would be a more reliable estimate than our own" ("Authority and Responsibility," p. 848; the quote is from Schmidt, at p. 451).

[50] Johnson v. United States, 186 F.2d 588 (2d Cir. 1951).

[51] Repouille v. United States, 165 F.2d 152 (2d Cir. 1947).

[52] Ibid., p. 153. In a curiously mild dissenting opinion, Judge Frank argued that "judicial impotence has its limits" and proposed that the determination of whether Repouille was of "good moral character" should be based on the views of "our ethical leaders" (p. 154).

In the Repouille case Learned Hand's private beliefs were presumably on the side of the petitioner. Because he deferred to the community conscience he was severely criticized by Professor Cahn:

> By subordinating his own moral principles to those of the marketplace, Judge Hand seriously distorted the function of the court as pedagogue and moral mentor in a democratic society. He distorted the court's function because instead of exercising such influence as he could to raise the level of the marketplace to a level approaching his own, he expressed an attitude of resignation in the face of fraud. Although he did not condone the fraud, his opinion lends aid and comfort to those who would palliate the practice of evil. Resignation can be twisted by the guilty into acquiescence if not condonation.[53]

Cahn recognized that Learned Hand was one of the great judges, but

> it is the best and finest judges who afflict themselves with the whips of doubt while their inferior colleagues remain in a state of complacency. What the community needs most is the moral leadership of such a man as Learned Hand and the full benefit of his mature and chastened wisdom. The community is perhaps not at fault when it calls upon him and those like him to taste and determine the good moral character of aliens who wish to join its ranks.[54]

In deportation cases, as well, Learned Hand rigorously adhered to his philosophy of judicial limitations and did not permit his own notions to determine the outcome. In *United States ex rel. Kaloudis v. Shaughnessy* he made it clear that "the interest which an alien has in continued residence in this country is protected only so far as Congress may choose to protect it."[55] No matter what hardship might be caused to the alien's wife and child, the court would not review the Attorney General's refusal to suspend the deportation order:

> Nor has the relator any constitutional right to demand that we should. As we have said, any "legally protected interest" he ever had has been forfeited by "due process of law"; forfeited as completely as a conviction of crime forfeits the liberty of the accused, be he citizen or alien. The power of the Attorney General to suspend deportation is a dispensing power, like a judge's power to suspend the execution of a sentence, or the President's to pardon a convict. It is a matter of grace, over which courts have no review, unless—as we are assuming—it affirmatively appears that the denial has been actuated by considerations that Congress could not have intended to make relevant. It is by no

[53] Cahn, "Authority and Responsibility," p. 844.
[54] *Ibid.*, p. 851.
[55] 180 F.2d 489, 490 (2d Cir. 1950).

means true that "due process of law" inevitably involves an eventual resort to courts, no matter what may be the interest at stake; not every governmental action is subject to review by judges.[56]

Another case involved the exclusion of an alien by an order of the Attorney General. Ignatz Mezei had come to the United States and lived for twenty-five years in Buffalo, New York. He was married to a native-born American and his children were born in this country. In 1948 he left the United States to visit his dying mother in Rumania. Refused permission to enter that country, he remained in Hungary, where he encountered difficulty in obtaining an exit permit. Finally, he was permitted to sail to the United States, but when he reached New York City he was temporarily excluded by immigration authorities. After three months he was ordered permanently excluded by the Attorney General as a bad scurity risk. The Attorney General refused to give Mezei a hearing and the precise basis for the order remained "an undisclosed secret known only to the Attorney General's staff."[57]

Because other nations refused to accept him, Mezei was confined at Ellis Island for twenty-one months. Then he was ordered released on bond by a district court judge after a habeas corpus proceeding. The government appealed to the Second Circuit, which was faced with two questions: Was the Attorney General's order subject to judicial review? Was the indefinite confinement at Ellis Island constitutional? The court's majority—Judges Swan and Clark—held that the exclusion order could be challenged in court and that the detention was illegal. Learned Hand dissented; he did not like the statute authorizing exclusion, but he wrote, "think what one may of a statute based upon such fears [of aliens] when passed by a society which professes to put its faith in the free interchange of ideas, a court has no warrant for refusing to enforce it. If that society chooses to flinch, when its principles are put to the test, courts are not set up to give it derring-do."[58]

---

[56] *Ibid.*, pp. 490–91. Judge Hand's opinion in this case is hard to reconcile with his going along, ten days later, with an opinion by Judge Frank reversing the Attorney General's refusal to suspend deportation and grant a hearing to an alien (Mastrapasqua v. Shaughnessy, 180 F.2d 999 [2d Cir. 1950]). In dissenting, Judge Chase cited Learned Hand's opinion in the Kaloudis case in support of the view that the court should not reverse the Attorney General (p. 1010).

[57] United States *ex rel.* Mezei v. Shaughnessy, 195 F.2d 964, 967 (2d Cir. 1952).

[58] *Ibid.*, p. 971. In his memorandum, Hand said that the detention of Mezei was "monstrous," and then added, "But that bridge has been crossed for Congress has said he may be excluded without giving any reason" (February 12, 1952). In a memorandum in the same case two months later, in which he voted to deny the government's motion to stay the Second Circuit's

This obedient attitude in large measure also accounted for Judge Hand's famous opinion in the appeal of the first-string Communist Party leaders from their conviction under the Smith Act.

> [Hand] did not believe in the attempts to meet the threat of Communism embodied in the Smith Act of 1940. . . . That was not the way to handle the matter. But Congress thought otherwise, and he sustained the constitutionality of the Act, disappointing many of his liberal admirers. If the United States determined that her protection involved trying to stop this kind of business by a criminal statute, why should a judge stand in the way, no matter how dearly he held to the freedoms, not only as an end, but as a good way of life.[59]

Before examining the *Dennis* opinion, some attention must be paid to a much earlier decision by Learned Hand, which stands as perhaps his most notable judicial pronouncement about freedom of speech. In 1917 the Postmaster of New York, acting under the Espionage Act of the same year, sought to ban from the mails an issue of the *Masses*, a left-wing antiwar journal, because it contained material that allegedly encouraged this country's enemies and hampered the government in its conduct of the war. By present-day standards much of the offensive material seems quite tame; but the year 1917, and several years thereafter, are not noted for permissive attitude on the part of government toward its critics.

The crucial question facing District Judge Hand involved the meaning of the Espionage Act; his ruling turned on whether Congress intended to bar from the mails materials such as that published in the *Masses*. In view of his at least later reluctance to invalidate statutes, it is noteworthy that Hand was not presented with a constitutional issue.[60]

---

mandate, he wrote: "I have no sympathy with this frenetic panic about a man, anonymously charged as a 'subversive.' Let the Attorney General apply for a stay to our Betters in Washington" (April 9, 1952).

The Supreme Court granted certiorari and by a 5–4 vote upheld Mezei's exclusion (Shaughnessy v. United States *ex rel.* Mezei, 345 U.S. 206 [1953]). Justice Jackson wrote an impassioned dissent, concluding: "It is inconceivable to me that this measure of simple justice and fair dealing [a hearing and notice of the charges] would menace the security of this country. No one can make me believe that we are that far gone" (p. 228). Justice Frankfurter joined in this dissent, one more indication that in certain areas he was more willing than Hand to utilize judicial power to prevent results that were contrary to justice and fair play.

[59] Francis Biddle, *In Brief Authority* (Garden City, N.Y.: Doubleday Co., 1962), p. 93.

[60] The significance of this fact is that, apart from any other considerations, it might have accounted for the difference between Hand's opinion in the two cases. At the beginning of his decision in the Masses he explained:

In his decision Hand conceded that the publication would "enervate public feeling at home . . . and encourage the success of the enemies . . . abroad."[61] Still, the Postmaster's action "in so far as it involves the suppression of the free utterance of abuse and criticism of the existing law, or of the policies of the war, is not, in my judgment, supported by the language of the statute."[62] Hand specifically rejected a "bad tendency" test for speech: "The tradition of English-speaking freedom has depended in no small part upon the merely procedural requirement that the state point with exactness to just that conduct which violates the law. It is difficult and often impossible to meet the charge that one's general ethos is treasonable; such a latitude for construction implies a personal latitude in administration which contradicts the normal assumption that law shall be embodied in general propositions capable of some measure of definition."[63]

To Hand, the proper test of illegal speech is one that simply depends on the nature of the words used:

One may not counsel or advise others to violate the law as it stands. Words are not only the keys of persuasion, but the triggers of action, and those which have no purport but to counsel the violation of law cannot by any latitude of interpretation be a part of that public opinion which is the final source of government in a democratic state. . . . To counsel or advise a man to act is to urge upon him either that it is in his interest or his duty to do it. While, of course, this may be accomplished as well by indirection as expressly, since words carry the meaning that they impart, the definition is exhaustive, I think, and I shall use it. Political agitation, by the passions it arouses or the convictions it engenders, may in fact stimulate men to the violation of law. Detestation of existing policies is easily transformed into forcible resistance of the authority which puts them in execution, and it would be folly to disregard the causal relation between the two. Yet to assimilate agitation, legitimate as such, with direct incitement to violent resistance, is to disregard the tolerance of all methods of political agitation which in normal times is a safeguard of free government.

"It must be remembered . . . and the distinction is of critical consequence throughout, that no question arises touching the war powers of Congress. It may be that Congress may forbid the mails to any matter which tends to discourage the successful prosecution of the war. It may be that the fundamental personal rights of the individual must stand in abeyance, even including the right of freedom of the press, though that is not here in question. . . . It may be that the peril of war, which goes to the very existence of the state, justifies any measure of compulsion, any measure of suppression, which Congress deems necessary to its safety, the liberties of each being in subjection to the liberties of all" (Masses Publishing Co. v. Patten, 244 F 535, 538 [S.D.N.Y., 1917]).

61 *Ibid.*, p. 539.
62 *Ibid.*, p. 540.
63 *Ibid.*, p. 543.

The distinction is not a scholastic subterfuge, but a hard-bought acquisition in the fight for freedom, and the purpose to disregard it must be evident when the power exists. If one stops short of urging upon others that it is their duty or their interest to resist the law, it seems to me one should not be held to have attempted to cause its violation.[64]

Applying this standard, the district court ordered the ban on the *Masses* lifted.

Hand's intrinsic test—judging the words by what they say—is at least as promotive of a tolerant attitude toward speech as Holmes's "clear and present danger" test and certainly a good deal easier to apply. For, unlike "clear and present danger," which makes the speaker responsible not only for his own words but also for the context in which they are uttered, Hand's formula is limited to a consideration of what was said. Yet, in application, the two tests might produce the same result.[65]

Whatever its relative place on a liberalism scale, the *Masses* opinion went quite far in protecting speech against suppression by government. In 1920 Professor Zechariah Chafee of Harvard dedicated his famous study, *Freedom of Speech,* to Learned Hand, "who during the turmoil of war courageously maintained the tradition of English-speaking freedom and gave it new clearness and strength for the wiser years to come." Chafee and other civil libertarians were no doubt disappointed—and perhaps surprised, as well—by Hand's opinion in the *Dennis* case.[66]

---

[64] *Ibid.,* p. 540.

[65] Thus reliance upon the words used may have been sufficient to sustain the conviction of Schenck for distribution of antidraft circulars during the First World War. On the other hand, Schenck did not directly counsel violation of the Conscription Act. His conviction was, of course, upheld by a unanimous Supreme Court in an opinion by Holmes in which the "clear and present danger" test made its first appearance (Schenck v. United States, 249 U.S. 47 [1919]).

Professor Zechariah Chafee preferred the "objective standard" of Hand over Holmes's approach (*Freedom of Speech* [New York: Harcourt, Brace & Co., 1920], p. 63). But he suggested that the two approaches might be indistinguishable, such as when he traced both to Holmes's opinion in the Massachusetts case of Commonwealth v. Peaslee (pp. 53, 89). Chafee's description of the Masses opinion as putting beyond the pale of protection, speech which has "the strong danger that it will cause injurious acts" (p. 48), is suggestive of the "clear and present danger" test.

[66] But at least Judge Wyzanski correctly anticipated Dennis. In 1947 he wrote about Hand's views on civil liberties: "Some who know only his [Masses] opinion . . . may suppose that if such an issue comes before Learned Hand he will march with a flaming torch at the head of the "children of light." But I suspect that the crusaders will have to discover their promised land without him in their zealous band" ("Hand's Contribution to Public Law," p. 354).

As was previously pointed out, a major difference between the suppression of the *Masses* and the conviction of the Communist Party leaders is that the latter alone raised a question of the constitutionality of a federal statute. For a judge like Learned Hand, with strong disinclinations toward judicial review, this distinction was of significance. A second difference between the two cases is that in 1917, although a trial judge, Hand was writing on a clean slate, with virtually no Supreme Court precedent to guide him. But beginning with Holmes's opinion in *Schenck v. United States*[67] in 1919, the Supreme Court handed down many decisions in the free speech area, so that by 1950 lower federal judges were bound to follow and apply previous High Court rulings. In short, in the *Dennis* case Hand was a good deal less free to interject his own views than he was in the *Masses* decision.

Indeed, even before *Schenck* was decided, Hand had to back away from his objective words test when his reversal of the Postmaster of New York was in turn overruled, only four months later, by the Circuit Court of Appeals for the Second Circuit.[68] Ever obedient, Hand never returned to the standard that he announced and defended in the *Masses*,[69] not even a year later when he sustained the indictment against Scott Nearing and Max Eastman for violation of the Espionage Act.[70]

When the appeal of the Communist Party leaders came before the Second Circuit in 1950, it was after a decade of more or less regular use by the Supreme Court of the "clear and present danger" test in a host of appeals raising First Amendment questions. As a lower judge, Hand had to apply that standard, even though the precedents were not altogether clear as to what it actually required. His leeway was further limited by the Supreme Court's ruling in *American Communication Association v. Douds*,[71] sustaining the constitutionality of the "non-Communist affidavit" section of the Taft-Hartley Act against an allegation of infringement of First Amendment freedoms. *Douds* was decided six weeks before the Second Circuit began to hear argument in *Dennis;* it clearly presaged what the Supreme Court would do if it heard the appeal of the Communist leaders.

[67] 249 U.S. 47 (1919).

[68] Masses Publishing Co. v. Patten, 246 F.24 (2d Cir. 1917). In his opinion for the appellate court, Judge Rogers explicity rejected Hand's approach: "If the natural and reasonable effect of what is said is to encourage resistance to a law, and the words are used in an endeavor to persuade to resistance, it is immaterial that the duty to resist is not mentioned, or the interest of the persons addressed in resistance is not suggested" (p. 38).

[69] See Chafee, *Freedom of Speech*, p. 55, n. 32.

[70] United States v. Nearing, 252 F.223 (S.D.N.Y. 1918) and United States v. Eastman, 252 F.232 (S.D.N.Y. 1918).

[71] 339 U.S. 382 (1950).

Familiarity, then, with Learned Hand's philosophy of obedience and limitations on judicial power should have removed much of the guessing as to how Dennis and his co-defendants would fare in the court of appeals. The only real surprise in Hand's *Dennis* opinion is his treatment of the "clear and present danger" test, not his affirmation of the verdict.

Hand was faced with a dilemma: the Supreme Court had (1) made "clear and present danger" the standard whereby speech was to be judged under the First Amendment, and (2) in *Douds* made it apparent what the decision would be in *Dennis* in the event of an appeal. But (3) a literal application of the words "clear and present danger" could easily support a decision that the advocacy of the Communist Party leaders was protected speech. To be sure, the danger posed by the Party's advocacy of the overthrow of the government was both grave and clear; what was uncertain was the proximity of the evil. To resolve this problem, Learned Hand recast the words of the test: "in each case," courts must ask, "whether the gravity of the 'evil,' discounted by its improbability, justifies such invasion of free speech as is necessary to avoid the danger."[72]

It cannot be gainsaid that this reinterpretation of "clear and present danger" served to enlarge the scope of permissible governmental restriction of speech; still, it is wrong to believe, as some do, that Hand's formula was nothing more than a fancier version of the "bad tendency" test that prevailed in the Supreme Court during the 1920's.[73]

[72] United States v. Dennis, 183 F.2d 201, 212 (2d Cir. 1950). The dilemma of the Second Circuit was alluded to by Justice Frankfurter in his concurring opinion in Dennis: "In all fairness, the argument [that the "clear and present danger" test requires a situation of imminent peril] cannot be met by reinterpreting the [Supreme] Court's frequent use of 'clear' and 'present' to mean an entertainable 'probability.' In giving this meaning to the phrase 'clear and present danger,' the Court of Appeals was fastidiously confining the rhetoric of opinions to the exact scope of what was decided by them. We have greater responsibility for having given constitutional support, over repeated protests, to uncritical libertarian generalities" 341 U.S. 494, 527 (1951).

[73] For example, Professor Martin Shapiro: Hand's test "is simply the remote bad tendency test dressed up in modern style. The test is even more extreme than bad tendency for it considers the gravity of the evil discounted by its improbability—not the improbability that the speech in question will bring the evil about, but that it will occur from any cause. The majority in *Gitlow*, from whom Holmes dissented, would have had no difficulty in concurring in *Dennis*" (Shapiro, *Freedom of Speech* [Englewood Cliffs, N.J.: Prentice-Hall, 1966]), p. 65.

The key contribution of Hand was his substitution of the concept of probability for that of proximity of remoteness in the Holmes formulation. According to Hand, probability of danger includes the question of its remoteness, but that question is only one of several factors relevant to determine how improbable the danger is. The decisive factor is the judge's examination of the situation that existed at the time that the challenged speech was uttered. As Hand explained:

> We have purposely substituted "improbability" for "remoteness" because that must be the right interpretation. Given the same probability, it would be wholly irrational to condone future evils which we should prevent if they were immediate; that could be reconciled only by an indifference to those who come after us. It is only because a substantial intervening period between the utterance and its realization may check its effect and change its importance, that its immediacy is important.[74]

Hand then examined Communist Party activity in light of this "clear and probably danger" test and, relying on the international situation prevailing between 1945 and 1948, found that there existed a "danger of the utmost gravity and of enough probability to justify" the suppression of the Party[75]—this conclusion after he admonished that "our democracy, like any other, must meet that [Communist] faith and that creed on the merits, or it will perish, and we must not flinch at the challenge."[76]

In the Supreme Court the conviction of the leading communists was again affirmed; for the majority, Chief Justice Vinson adopted Learned Hand's interpretation of "clear and present danger."[77] While Hand's formulation made it easier for the Supreme Court to avoid explicit rejection of the Holmes standard, it is patent that the opinion of the lower court judge did not significantly influence the decision of the High Court.

The prosecution of the communist leaders provided one of the few major instances of Learned Hand subordinating personal liber-

---

Shapiro's error is clearly revealed by the fact that in the Second Circuit's disposal of Dennis, Judge Chase concurred separately, principally because he thought that the Hand opinion had by-passed Gitlow and the bad tendency test, and he wanted to affirm the conviction on the basis of Gitlow. See Dennis v. United States, 183 F.2d 234–37 (2d Cir. 1950).

[74] *Ibid.*, p. 212.
[75] *Ibid.*, p. 213.
[76] *Ibid.*, p. 212.
[77] Dennis v. United States, 341 U.S. 494, 510 (1951).

tarian beliefs during his tenure as chief judge.[78] In the face of so
many early ex cathedra and judicial pronouncements cautioning judicial restraint, an activist opinion in *Dennis* would have been reason for
astonishment. Yet, despite (or perhaps because of) the remarkable
consistency over so long a period between the philosophy of judicial
power expressed in the speeches and the decisions handed down from

[78] Learned Hand's opinions in criminal law appeals are not discussed
in this chapter principally because cases in this area only rarely raise the
questions of judicial authority that have been discussed in the preceding
pages. Brief attention, however, ought to be given to Hand's attitude in
these cases.

Hand's decisions in criminal law appeals were less the product of a
broad attitude toward the role of the appellate judge than of certain pragmatic considerations which were derived from his experience as a trial
judge. This factor accounted for his attitude toward the harmless error rule,
which provides that errors committed during a trial are not grounds for
reversal unless there is reason to believe that they contributed to the verdict.
See Orrin G. Judd, "Judge Learned Hand and the Criminal Law," *Harvard
Law Review,* 60 (1947), 405, esp. pp. 408–11. As Judge Hand said in refusing
to reverse a conviction although the trial judge had made some wrong
rulings: "No judge in so extended a trial can avoid on occasion rulings that
on reflection he will see to have been wrong; but, unless they cut off some
really substantial aspect of the truth, or let in too distracting issues, they are
not important" (United States v. White, 124 F.2d 181, 186 [2d Cir. 1941]).
Judge Hand believed that "nothing conduces less" to insurance by an
appellate court of an impartial trial "than an over jealous scrutiny of every
word that may fall from the judge's mouth" (United States v. Warren, 120
F.2d 211, 212 [2d Cir. 1941]).

As part of this pragmatic outlook, Hand believed that appellate courts
should not "upset the conviction of a plainly guilty man" (United States v.
Lotsch, 102 F.2d 35, 37 [2d Cir. 1939]). Because of this he, at times, employed
strong language in rejecting the contentions of criminal appellants. Several
illustrations follow: "The accused had a fair trial; their guilt was manifest;
their offense struck at the nation's protection in its hour of peril; if punishment is ever justified, the sentences they received were just. Their sordid
contribution toward breaking down the collective effort to conserve our
national resources, was morally removed only a step from giving aid and
comfort to the enemies of their country" (United States v. Center Veal &
Beef Co., 162 F.2d 766, 772 [2d Cir. 1947]). "We are satisfied that the
accused had an impartial trial, and that no honest jury could have failed to
convict them. The crime [blackmail] struck at the heart of civilized society;
its very possibility is a stain upon our jurisprudence" (United States v.
Compagna, 146 F.2d 524, 529 [2d Cir. 1945]). "It is a strange conception of
justice that, if one only tangles one's crimes enough, one gets an immunity
because the result is beyond the powers of a jury to unravel" (United States
v. Cohen, 145 F.2d 82, 88 [2d Cir. 1944]). Finally, the conclusion of an
opinion by Hand upholding a conviction for fraudulent business activity
during the Second World War: "An appeal . . . has been made to us . . .
based upon the severity of the sentences . . . in the face of the jury's
recommendation of 'utmost clemency.' We have of course no control over

the bench, there were, in a real sense, two Learned Hands. There was the Learned Hand of liberal impulse, rather widely known to the public, who fervently declared:

> Risk for risk, for myself I had rather take my chance that some traitors will escape detection than spread abroad a spirit of general suspicion and distrust, which accepts rumor and gossip in place of undismayed and unintimidated inquiry. I believe that that community is already in process of dissolution where each man begins to eye his neighbor as a possible enemy, where non-conformity with the accepted creed, political as well as religious, is a mark of disaffection; where denunciation, without specification or backing, takes the place of evidence; where orthodoxy chokes freedom of dissent; where faith in the eventual supremacy of reason has become so timid that we dare not enter our convictions in the open lists, to win or lose.[79]

These words were spoken in 1952 when the spirit of McCarthyism silenced so many persons of liberal persuasion. And, in 1955, Learned Hand said, "It is still in the lap of the gods whether a society can succeed which is based on 'civil liberties and human rights' conceived as I have tried to describe them; but of one thing at least we may be

---

the sentences. . . . That, however, makes it not improper to say that we can see nothing to justify the jury's recommendation, and especially not the mawkish and sentimental impertinence which one of the jurors addressed to the judge. While the Nation was at grips with its most deadly enemy, and in peril of its very existence, these men combined to frustrate it. . . . That was in effect, though of course not in law, aid and comfort to the enemy; and if severity is ever proper, we cannot imagine a better occasion for its exercise than upon those whose creed led them to such scurvy disloyalty" (United States v. Gottfried, 165 F.2d 360, 368 [2d Cir. 1948]).

The sharp words in these cases, however, do not mean that Learned Hand was a "hanging judge." His rulings in a number of search and seizure cases and in other criminal appeals manifested a deep concern for the safeguarding of the basic procedural rights afforded to accused persons. In reversing a conviction because the arrest and accompanying search were illegal, he strenuously declared: "If the prosecution of crime is to be conducted with so little regard for that protection which centuries of English law have given to the individual, we are indeed at the dawn of a new era; and much that we have deemed vital to our liberties, is a delusion" (United States v. Di Re, 159 F.2d 818, 820 [2d Cir. 1947]).

The impact of Hand's decisions on criminal law was not great, though this writer has been told that, particularly in regard to search and seizure, Hand was influential. There is little evidence to support this view. Certainly Orrin Judd's 1947 survey, cited earlier in this note, does not lead to any conclusion that Hand's rulings were very influential with respect to the major criminal law issues that have confronted the courts. By and large, this is an area where the Supreme Court usually determines judicial policy.

[79] L. Hand, "A Plea for the Open Mind and Free Discussion," in Dilliard, *Spirit of Liberty*, p. 216.

sure; the alternatives that have so far appeared have been immeasurably worse; and so, whatever the outcome, I submit to you that we must press along."[80]

These humane and libertarian impulses were, of course, sincere and stimulated Learned Hand's personal response to many social and political questions. But all along there was another Learned Hand who at least as early as 1916 was saying in criticism of the conservative activist trend of the day:

> There is a hierarchy of power in which the judge stands low; he has no right to divinations of public opinion which run counter to its last formal expressions. Nevertheless, the judge has, by custom, his own proper representative character as a complementary organ of the social will, and in so far as conservative sentiment, in the excess of caution that he shall be obedient, frustrates his free power by interpretation to manifest the half-framed purpose of his time, it misconceives the historical significance of his position and will in the end render him incompetent to perform the very duties upon which it lays so much emphasis. The profession of the law of which he is a part is charged with the articulation and final incidence of the successive efforts toward justice; it must feel the circulation of the communal blood or it will wither and drop off, a useless member.[81]

If in the public's mind the image of a libertarian Learned Hand was dominant, the philosophy of restraint dominated Hand's career. To the public, the full conception of the "spirit of liberty" lay in principles of freedom and justice, indeed, in a program of judicial action designed to promote justice and due process of law. In fact, in his great address on "The Spirit of Liberty," Hand had stressed restraintist ideas: "I often wonder whether we do not rest our hopes too much upon constitutions, upon laws and upon courts. These are false hopes; believe me, these are false hopes. Liberty lies in the hearts of men and women; when it dies there, no constitution, no law, no court can save it; no constitution, no law, no court can even do much to help it. While it lies there it needs no constitution, no law, no court to save it."[82]

[80] "A Fanfare for Prometheus," *ibid.*, pp. 224–25.
[81] "The Speech of Justice," *ibid.*, pp. 11–12.
[82] "The Spirit of Liberty," *ibid.*, p. 144. Fourteen years earlier, in 1930, he said much the same thing; liberty "is the product not of institutions, but of a temper, of an attitude towards life; of that mood that looks before and after and pines for what is not. It is idle to look to laws, or courts, or principalities, or powers, to secure it. You may write into your constitutions not ten, but fifty, amendments, and it shall not help a farthing, for casuistry will undermine it as casuistry should, if it have no stay but law" ("Sources of Tolerance," *ibid.*, p. 59).

This theme, which appeared so often in Hand's speeches, at times with special attention directed to the feebleness of the Bill of Rights, was based on a misconception of the libertarian activist position and also on a somewhat erroneous understanding of the contribution of courts to the maintenance of democratic institutions. The activists, of course, know that in a society where the underpinnings of democracy have eroded, courts will not save democracy. But in this respect courts are no different from other governmental institutions; their role is the resolution of the conflicts brought before them, the handling of which will probably have little to do with the functioning of democracy on a grand scale. As Judge Jerome Frank put it in a speech (in which he also said "I am unabashed in my admiration" of Learned Hand and "no man do I esteem more highly") :

> Judge Hand thinks it folly to believe that the courts can save democracy. Of course, they cannot. But it seems to me that here, most uncharacteristically, Judge Hand indulges in a judgment far too sweeping, one which rests on a too-sharp, either-or, all-or-nothing dichotomy. . . . Obviously the courts cannot do the whole job. But, just as obviously, they can sometimes help to arrest evil popular trends in their inception. Not only are the Supreme Court's opinions educational in a general way; they have also had discernible practical effects in stopping undemocratic tendencies.[83]

We must believe that Learned Hand recognized that the activist demands on courts were not as broad as he made them out to be and that he deliberately posed the question of judicial power so sweepingly because his intention was to educate the public that it was in their hands and not in the hands of judges to safeguard liberty. Hand feared that reliance on the judicial branch to redress grievances and to abort injustice would eventually erode confidence in the ability of the people to rule through elected representatives and this, in turn, would undermine democracy. Therefore, it was not the job of the judge "to arrest evil popular trends" or to stop undemocratic tendencies, roles assigned to the judiciary by Frank. Hand insisted that

> the judge must always remember that he should go no further than he is sure the government would have gone, had it been faced with the case before him. If he is in doubt, he must stop, for he cannot tell that the conflicting interests in the society for which he speaks would have come to a just result, even though he is sure that he knows what the just result should be. He is not to substitute even his juster will for theirs; otherwise it would not

[83] Jerome N. Frank, "Some Reflections on Judge Learned Hand," *University of Chicago Law Review,* 24 (1957), 697.

be the common will which prevails, and to that extent the people would not govern.[84]

Finally, underlying Hand's philosophy was the attitude that when judges get involved in policy-making and insuring justice, they inevitably lose their independence and authority. In a much-quoted address on "the contribution of an independent judiciary to civilization," he declared:

> And so, to sum up, I believe that for by far the greater part of their work it is a condition upon the success of our system that the judges should be independent; and I do not believe that their independence should be impaired because of their constitutional function. But the price of this immunity, I insist, is that they should not have the last word in those basic conflicts of "right and wrong—between whose endless jar justice resides."[85]

In the final analysis, the debate between the activists and restraintists over judicial power can be reduced to the question whether a policy of judicial intervention imposes the risks and costs that Learned Hand thought it did. But to pose the question is not to bring the debate to any quick or early resolution, for, assuming that we can reckon the costs, certain philosophical and even semantic difficulties remain. What is the common will? Do judges truly retain their integrity and independence when, out of fear of reprisals, they limit their own authority? Are courts democratic institutions? And so on. These are primarily normative questions, and thus, no matter how the issue between activists and restraintists is phrased, we may be certain that there is no scientific answer to it.

But those who reject Learned Hand's strictures on judicial power cannot comfortably, as much of the attentive public did for so many years, accept his philosophy as if it had no implications for the decisions that a judge may make. Hand, no less than a number of his critics, believed in libertarian ideals; yet, when faced with the question of power while on the bench, he plainly subordinated his liberal self. His choice may have been wrong, but surely he was right in teaching that democracy and liberty are often conflicting principles and programs of action.

[84] L. Hand, "How Far Is a Judge Free in Rendering a Decision?," in Dilliard, *Spirit of Liberty*, p. 84.

[85] L. Hand, "Contribution of an Independent Judiciary," *ibid.*, p. 125. Earlier in the same speech he delineated the role of a judge as "to compose inconsistencies, to unravel confusions, to announce unrecognized implications, to make in Holmes' hackneyed phrase, 'interstitial' advances; these are the measure of what . . . [judges] may properly do" (p. 121).

However, only in the later years of Hand's career were these tensions discerned. For the most part, his innate liberalism, the encouragement he gave in his principal speeches to the promotion of justice and liberty, and his fortune in not having to decide very many civil liberties cases, all served to immunize him against sustained criticism from the libertarian camp. When reaction to Hand's views is compared to that accorded to similar expressions by Justice Frankfurter, we can grasp the full meaning of Frankfurter's claim that Hand was "lucky" in not being appointed to the Supreme Court. It was this good fortune that permitted the legend of Learned Hand to grow. Paradoxically, the strength of the legend also means that Learned Hand failed to communicate successfully his principles to the American people.

How legal philosophers and historians will regard Learned Hand ten, twenty, or fifty years hence can only be guessed. His legend—the divorce from reality—may prove more durable than that of Justice Holmes, in many ways a legendary figure, who was the subject of some nasty attacks only a few years after his death.[86] Moreover, it is quite apparent, as Justice Frankfurter recognized long ago, that Hand's "actual decisions will be all deader than the Dodo before long, as indeed at least many of them are already."[87] Hence, evaluations of Learned Hand will continue to rely heavily on his extra-judicial writings.

Should the time come when scholars disregard the Learned Hand legend and seek to examine anew his career and philosophy, their efforts will most likely reinforce the favorable view of him and he will be regarded as a remarkable and great judge. His position as one of the United States' greatest judges is secure for a number of reasons.

Perhaps foremost among these is his impact on the development of many areas of American law. To be sure, as was suggested earlier, Hand played a small role in the determination of the major constitutional law issues that receive the greatest public attention and are ordinarily within the province of Supreme Court action. Yet, in many commercial law areas, Hand's contributions were very significant, equal at least to those of any other twentieth-century judge. Karl Llewellyn rated him as one of the nine greatest of all English-speaking

---

[86] Nastiest, perhaps, if we are to judge by titles, was Ben W. Palmer, "Hobbes, Holmes, and Hitler," *American Bar Association Journal*, 31 (1945), 569. Much of the reaction against Holmes was inspired by the wartime emphasis on moral principles, though Catholic and other natural philosophers never had much use for Holmes's positivism.

[87] Frankfurter, "A Great Judge Retires," p. 503.

commercial judges.[88] An English authority, not wholly uncritical in his evaluation of Learned Hand, wrote shortly after the famous American judge died: "His legacy to American law was that during the years, and particularly in maritime law and unfair competition, whole fields of law were developed and directed by his opinions. In fact he was often considered to be the greatest admiralty judge in his time in the United States."[89] Judge Wyzanski was of the opinion that Hand "more than any other lower court judge . . . was the architect of our present structure of antitrust law."[90] While a leader of the patent bar spoke of his "natural affinity with inventors and authors,"[91] a quality that made him great in patent and copyright cases, the same writer emphasized that Learned Hand was not a mere specialist in a few areas of the law: "To say that Judge Learned Hand is a great patent, copyright or common-law judge is simple tautology—his abilities do not vary with the kind of case before him."[92] The catholic nature of his interests and influence was attested to in the memorial resolution of the Judicial Conference of the Second Circuit: "The range of subject-matter of his opinions was as broad as American federal jurisprudence. He never thought of himself as a specialist in any particular field. Nor do we. The structure of the law covering every controversy with which he dealt, he explored to its foundations. He was a master in every subdivision of the field."[93]

Hand's reputation is sure to be enhanced, in any future assessment, by his performance on the bench. By all accounts, he was an outstanding trial and appellate judge, yet it was while he was chief judge that he and his court achieved enduring fame. The Second Circuit, although burdened with the heaviest case load of any of the courts of appeals, was consistently the most efficient of these courts.[94] Professor

[88] Llewellyn, *The Common Law Tradition* (Boston: Little, Brown and Co., 1960). The book is dedicated "to the undying succession of the Great Commercial Judges whose work across the centuries has given living body, toughness and inspiration to the Grand Tradition of the Common Law."

[89] D. W. M. Waters, "Judge Learned Hand," *Solicitor Quarterly*, 1 (1962), p. 32. From John Frank we learned that in difficult collision cases, Learned Hand often arrived at a decision after moving models of vessels across his desk ("The Top U.S. Commercial Court," *Fortune* [January 1951], p. 96).

[90] Wyzanski, "Learned Hand," *Atlantic Monthly*, 208 (December 1961), 55.

[91] Stephen H. Philbin, "Judge Learned Hand and the Law of Patents and Copyrights," *Harvard Law Review*, 60 (1947), 394.

[92] *Ibid.*

[93] "Learned Hand Memorial Issue," *New York State Bar Journal*, 33 (1961), 413.

[94] When he retired as chief judge, the Judicial Conference of the United States resolved: "As Chief Judge of one of the most important and busiest circuits of the nation, he kept his court abreast of the docket and furnished to all of us a brilliant example of how an appellate court should be run" (*Report of the Judicial Conference of the United States, 1951, p. 2*).

Freund was right in 1961 when he wrote, "Learned Hand was born to be a judge . . . [he was] a judge's judge, a lawyer's judge, a student's judge."[95] He was a master craftsman and a brilliant writer whose opinions surely rank with those of Holmes and Cardozo as the best American legal prose of the century.[96] His ability to write beautifully did not lead him to the quick production of glossy opinions that did not explore the full complexities of a case. To the contrary, he usually worked hard and long until he was satisfied with what he had written. It was not enough to base a decision on outdated formulas and on legal clichés; throughout his career he sought to adapt the law to the rapid changes in society and industry.

Illustrative of Hand's craftmanship was his approach to the interpretation of statutes. While "to many on the bench and at the bar the whole process of statutory interpretation is mechanical drudgery quite unworthy of their fine minds,"[97] Learned Hand viewed the process as a welcome challenge "to reconstruct the past solution

[95] Freund, "Learned Hand," p. 11.

[96] To Judge Wyzanski, "a Learned Hand opinion is comparable to a sonnet" ("Learned Hand," p. 57). Judge Frank, who had little good to say of Cardozo, held that Hand's opinions were superior to those of Holmes. The latter, according to Frank, too often struck only at the jugular, ignoring the more hard to get at issues in a case ("Some Reflections," p. 670).

The writer is in accord with Judge Frank. But it must be conceded that, oddly, Hand's superb style makes an assessment of his opinions and qualities as a judge more difficult. One is so impressed with Learned Hand's lucidity and grace, with his natural ability to turn a sharp or beautiful phrase, with the way in which his decisions sparked with philosophy and poetry, that it is easy—actually tempting—to ignore the meaning of what Learned Hand wrote. Learned Hand was intoxicated with words and this feeling is transmitted to his readers, also. Learned Hand, of course, was always concerned with substance, but it is far from certain that this is true of his admirers who read what he produced. Thus the mythology of Learned Hand becomes more difficult to overcome.

The problem can be illustrated by reference to patent law, a field in which Learned Hand is commonly believed to have had few peers. Judge Harrie Chase of the Second Circuit was also an outstanding patent judge. Yet, a reading of the opinions of Hand and Chase in this area is likely to leave the impression that not only was Hand the better writer, but also that he knew more about science and machinery and had a better idea of what was involved in the inventions that were subject to litigation.

On balance, though, Hand's writing style must be regarded as strongly supporting the conclusion that he was a great judge. This is so because writing is a quality by which judges (among others) are properly judged; in virtually all fields a felicitous and graceful style is usually evidence of clarity of thought and superior grasp of the subject matter. Particularly in law, though, style is important as a factor in determining influence. Learned Hand's impact on other courts and judges was great; because he was able to put forth his ideas and formulas so clearly, courts and judges readily relied on what he had written.

[97] Wyzanski, "Hand's Contribution to Public Law," p. 360.

imaginatively in its setting and project the purposes which inspired it upon the concrete occasions which arise for their decision."[98]

Learned Hand's qualities as a judge were summed up by his colleagues on the Second Circuit:

> His reputation as perhaps the greatest judge ever to grace the Second Circuit Bench—indeed as one among the greatest of all American jurists—derived not from the accident that by inheritance he had acquired merely a splendid mind. This was only the foundation of his equipment. For he also had an intellectual curiosity which led his mind, nurtured in literature and the liberal arts, into the sciences and the far reaches of the history and the nature of men and of nations. And his mental equipment was coupled with a sturdy physique which gave him the strength for incredible labor and research. The fusion of these characteristics produced an incomparable power of analysis which rested not solely on his own acute personal observations but also on the

[98] L. Hand, "Contribution of an Independent Judiciary," in Dilliard, *Spirit of Liberty*, p. 120.

Elsewhere, in his warm tribute to Judge Swan, Learned Hand brilliantly elaborated on this function of judges:

"What then are the qualities, mental and moral, which best serve a judge to discharge this perilous but inescapable duty? First he must be aware of the difficulty and the hazard. He must hesitate long before imputing more to the 'enactment' than he finds in the words, remembering that the 'policy' of any law may inhere as much in its limits as in its extent. He must hesitate long before cutting down their literal effect, remembering that the authors presumably said no more than they wanted. He must have the historical capacity to reconstruct the whole setting which evoked the law; the contentions which it resolved; the objects which it sought; the events which led up to it. But all this is only the beginning, for he must possess the far more exceptional power of divination which can peer into the purpose beyond its expression, and bring to fruition that which lay only in flower. Of the moral qualities necessary to this, before and beyond all he must purge his mind and will of those personal presuppositions and prejudices which almost inevitably invade all human judgments; he must approach his problems with as little preconception of what should be the outcome as it is given to men to have; in short, the prime condition of his success will be his capacity for detachment. There are those who insist that detachment is an illusion; that our conclusions, when their bases are sifted, always reveal a passional foundation. Even so; though they be throughout the creatures of past emotional experience, it does not follow that that experience can never predispose us to impartiality. A bias against bias may be as likely a result of some buried crisis, as any other bias. Be that as it may, we know that men do differ widely in this capacity; and the incredulity which seeks to discredit that knowledge is a part of the crusade against reason from which we have already so bitterly suffered. We may deny—and, if we are competent observers, we will deny—that no one can be aware of the danger and in large measure provide against it" ("Thomas Walter Swan," in Dilliard, *Spirit of Liberty*, pp. 164–65).

impact of the sweep of history upon the whole contemporary scene.[99]

Consistent excellence in a judicial career that exceeded fifty years assures Learned Hand's place among the English-speaking world's very great judges.

Finally, future scholars will rank Learned Hand as one of the country's most important judicial philosophers. His ideas will remain important not because they were unique and correct—few people will agree with all that he advocated—but because they were expressed in the face of a libertarian activist trend which, in the absence of renewed iteration of the restraintist position, threatened to educate future Americans that the preservation of democracy is assured so long as the courts are functioning. During the 1940's and 1950's we needed Learned Hand's reminder that courts and judges alone cannot do the job. We needed, in Professor Wallace Mendelson's words, Learned Hand's patient democracy: "And surely today we can greatly rejoice that men may say of us in aftertimes 'He lived in the time of Learned Hand and followed his teaching.' "[100]

[99] "Learned Hand Memorial Issue," *New York State Bar Journal*, p. 412.
[100] *Proceedings of a Special Session of the United States Court of Appeals for the Second Circuit to Commemorate Fifty Years of Federal Judicial Service, by the Honorable Learned Hand,* April 10, 1959, 264 F.2d.

6

Three Quiet and Sometimes
Conservative Judges

IT IS COMMONPLACE TO LABEL JUDGES, ESPECIALLY THOSE WHO SIT ON
the Supreme Court, as either "conservative" or "liberal." This practice
has been severely criticized as an inadequate, simplistic substitute for
a deeper analysis of judicial decisions and reasoning and as a barrier to
an intelligent understanding of what the judicial process is about.
Certainly there is much merit to this criticism: Justice Black is
described as a liberal, with some exception being made for his recent
opinions concerning racial demonstrations. But what of his attitude in
search and seizure cases? Or his votes in many criminal appeals during
the Second World War, not merely his much-studied and attacked
majority opinion in the *Korematsu* case? Or Justice Frankfurter, the
supposed leader of a conservative bloc, who was most liberal on search
and seizure and certainly so on separation of church and state?

Yet, while abuse of these terms is to be decried, benefit can be
derived from the careful application of the labels, particularly when
they are employed to describe relative tendencies and not absolute
positions. After all, if it is acceptable to refer to legislative actions in
such areas as civil rights, free speech, social security, and apportion-

ment as achieving liberal or conservative results, why is it wrong to characterize judicial action in the same areas in a similar fashion?

Accordingly, while it may make little sense to describe Justice Frankfurter as a conservative and leave it at that, it is both accurate and useful to say that in certain areas he was more conservative than various colleagus. Likewise, it is meaningful to call the Roosevelt court more liberal than the pre-1937 Supreme Court or Judge Clark generally more liberal than colleague Harrie Chase.

Actually, it is more difficult to use the terms in the context of the votes and decisions of intermediate appellate judges than it is with reference to the Supreme Court. The discretionary jurisdiction of the nation's highest court allows it to select for review the most important and contentious cases, those in which public policy questions usually are clearly defined and highlighted. Criminal appeals, for instance, have virtually no chance of getting beyond the preliminary certiorari stage, unless an important procedural or constitutional issue affecting the outcome is raised. In a significantly large percentage of cases where review is granted, counsel and the justices emphasize the aspects of the case that encourage voting and analysis along liberal-conservative lines. This tendency is obvious in civil liberties cases and criminal appeals, but it also is found in various economic fields, such as antitrust and patent appeals and Federal Employers' Liability Act cases, where it is relatively easy to discover an economic underdog.

The lower appellate courts, on the other hand, do not enjoy a discretionary jurisdiction; they must hear all criminal appeals, including many that are patently frivolous. What statistical or philosophical significance is there in the votes of the Second Circuit judges in hundreds of criminal cases, 80 per cent of which are decided without any difficulty? How are we to choose the handful that develop liberal and conservative attitudes?

In another way the votes of intermediate judges indicate less about their views than do the votes of Supreme Court justices, for while the latter are almost always free to rule according to their policy predilections, the lower judges are restricted by what the High Court has previously decided. A judge following Supreme Court precedent may vote to reverse a conviction although his personal feeling is that it should be upheld. There are of course many other illustrations.

Finally, the panel system that is in effect in the vast majority of cases in all but one of the circuits[1] complicates analysis by permitting only a fraction of a court's judges to participate in deciding any one case. Judges Frank and Clark did not hear the appeal in the *Dennis*

---

[1] The exception is the First Circuit, which has but three judges.

case; there has been speculation as to how they would have voted had they been given the opportunity to do so, and their opinions in that case would have added considerably to our knowledge of their views about free speech. Yet, the fact is that because they did not sit on *Dennis* there is no way of knowing how they would have voted in the most important civil liberties case decided by the Learned Hand court.

After these significant qualifications are noted, the belief remains that there is considerable justification for the use of the conservative and liberal labels to refer to particular trends and tendencies on a court such as the Second Circuit.

On balance, during the 1940's the Second Circuit was probably as liberal as any of the other courts of appeals, and certainly a good deal more so than most. It generally upheld the rulings of the National Labor Relations Board and other New Deal agencies; within bounds set by Congress and the Supreme Court it clearly was sympathetic to aliens in deportation and naturalization cases; the Second Circuit was forward looking in Selective Service appeals; it broadly applied the Fair Labor Standards Act to employees on the periphery of interstate commerce; the court was usually antimonopolistic in its key antitrust rulings; and it evinced a fairly lenient attitude to seamen and other employees in negligence cases. To be sure, there was a much more conservative side to the court, such as in its niggardly attitude toward the rights of criminal defendants. Also, while the Second Circuit was infrequently asked to decide First Amendment questions, its few rulings in that area tended toward illiberal results.

In fact, the rulings of the Learned Hand court were liberal only in relation to the decisions being made in other circuits; if this comparative frame of reference is removed, an evaluation of the court would likely as not show that it had distinctly conservative tendencies. The explanations for this is that three of its judges—Swan, Augustus Hand, and Chase—were of conservative bent, albeit in different ways.[2] As we will see in Chapter 9, these judges formed the only voting bloc on the Second Circuit; when they comprised the panel, conservative decisions were to be expected,[3] which is not surprising in view of their appointment by Coolidge and their conservative, rural backgrounds.

[2] In interviews with the author, Judges Swan and Chase agreed that the conservative label accurately applied to them.

[3] Cf. with the following, written by John Frank in 1951: "In social outlook the majority of C.A. 2 are, by modern standards, personally conservative. But they make an awfully strong effort to enforce the laws, as nearly as they can, in the spirit in which they were written and in which the Supreme Court has interpreted them. . . . In general outlook, Chase and

The views of these judges will be discussed in this chapter. It would be an error to regard Swan, Chase, and Augustus Hand as being of one mind and one orientation. Of the three, Judge Chase was surely the most consistently conservative, while Judge Hand was the least so. Some may question Hand's designation as a conservative; and although this seems to have been his own appraisal of his position, it may be more accurate to label him a moderate. Like Learned Hand he had little faith in rebels and reformers; he put his faith in the democratic processes and in the spirit of moderation. He once said of liberals and conservatives:

> The talk of the average conservative about the movements of the day is distressingly ignorant and can hardly be exceeded in intolerance or stupidity by that of the liberal who advocates everything that involves change and has the imprimatur of the "children of the dawn."
> Learned Hand, whose offspring, like mine, are all girls, once said to me that he was reconciled to having no boys for he feared that any son he might have had would have been a "cheer leader." The great trouble in times like these is that the warring camps are composed of dogged resisters to change on the one hand and "cheer leaders" on the other.[4]

This spirit of moderation pervaded his attitude toward review of administrative bodies. He said of the New Deal agencies:

> Some of the others of more recent date deal with new and highly controversial subjects, have evoked deep seated passions and have sometimes been administered by such ardent crusaders that their decisions have been subject to criticisms. Whether a more ample review should be afforded to litigants or these tribunals should be allowed further time to build up a satisfactory procedure is not for me to discuss here. I will only say that I feel sure that nothing will be gained by an assumption by the Courts of supervisory jurisdiction

---

Swan are strongly conservative, the Hands moderates, Clark and Frank New Dealers still. Where pure policy must take over judgment, highly conservative results are likely, particularly if neither Clark nor Frank is on a particular panel" ("The Top U.S. Commercial Court," *Fortune* [January 1951], p. 108). The alignment of Jerome Frank with Judge Clark is valid insofar as economic questions are concerned; in other areas nominally subject to liberal-conservative classifications, Judge Clark often was less liberal than his fellow New Dealers. Learned Hand, by the same token, was more liberal than his cousin.

[4] A. Hand, "Lawyers in a Revolutionary Age," *Pennsylvania Bar Association Quarterly*, 18 (1946), 46. This passage is remarkably similar in tone to Learned Hand's letter to Justice Stone in 1934 (see pp. 167–68, above).

Later in the same address Judge Hand said, "We are paying the price for many follies in this country of ours—for holding back needed changes too long and then carrying them out too swiftly and with too much emotion" p. 56).

that is not fairly granted by the terms of the constituent acts. For the present parties must be left to "fry in their own fat" until the legislative branch sees fit to change the procedure or the administrative tribunals themselves become more circumspect.[5]

Although he was in no sense a judicial activist, Augustus Hand was, at least before he was elevated to the appellate bench, less adamant on the subject of judicial review than was his cousin. Unlike the view expressed in "The Bill of Rights," Augustus Hand believed in 1922 that judicial review "was not logically inevitable" but "the course Marshall took had ample justification in the ideas expressed in the Constitution, in the clause making the Constitution the Supreme Law of the Land and indeed in the whole history of the colonies and the states prior to the adoption of the Federal Constitution." He also said of judicial review: "The power seems to me desirable because I believe the courts to be the places where in the long run the most impartial hearing is likely to be afforded, and where through the customary processes familiar to them in administering the common law the safest check upon arbitrary legislation is likely to be obtained."[6] This confidence in courts was far from Learned Hand's view on the same subject.

Perhaps because of these views Judge Wyzanski avoided the conservative tag and called Hand "a nineteenth-century liberal."[7] In view of his close alignment with Judges Swan and Chase, his votes in criminal appeals and other areas, and the general opinion of various Second Circuit judges, the designation of Judge Hand as a conservative has merit. Interestingly, Hand and Chase had the highest rate of agreement for any pair of Second Circuit judges over the ten years. Judge Hand was also the most infrequent dissenter on the court, averaging only about one dissent per year. The explanation for his high rate of agreement with Chase, and of much of his conduct on the appellate bench, is that he strenuously worked to avoid dissent and to accommodate his views to those of his colleagues.

Their style, perhaps even more than their votes, marked Judges Swan, Chase, and Augustus Hand as conservatives. They were much less given to fancy rhetoric or to displays of anger in their opinions than were the other three judges; nor were they prone to include in

---

[5] A. Hand, "Lawyers in a Revolutionary Age," pp. 54–55. This exact language was used by Hand six years earlier in a little-known speech before the Vermont Bar Association on "The Practice of Law—Then and Now," *Proceedings of the Vermont Bar Association*, 34 (1940), 76–77.

[6] A. Hand, "A Sketch of Constitutional Law in America," reprinted in *Lectures on Legal Topics*, vol. 3 (New York: Macmillan Co., 1926), p. 367.

[7] Wyzanski, "Augustus Noble Hand," *Harvard Law Review*, 61 (1948). 587. Wyzanski pointed out that Hand "kept a level head during the espionage prosecutions after World War I."

their opinions dicta or formulas going beyond the issue at hand. They did not try to establish general rules for deciding other appeals in the same area. This was much less true of Learned Hand, Frank, and Clark; for instance, the Chief Judge's opinions in such diverse areas as taxation, patents, review of administrative agencies, and criminal appeals, apart from deciding particular cases, often contained language and criteria laying the foundation for determining future cases.

The more conservative judges, by being more restrained stylistically, were thereby also less quotable; in fact they were less quoted and relied on by other courts and judges, and also less quoted than their colleagues in their own circuit. Accordingly, while internally the influence of the conservatives on Second Circuit decisions was relatively large, outside the Circuit it was not. To be sure, as we shall contend in the concluding chapter, the entire legal influence of the Second Circuit was limited, a result solely of its inferior position in the judicial hierarchy and not the product of intrinsic deficiencies. Still, the influence of the stylistic activists was relatively greater than that of their brethren. Their opinions were more often discussed in the law reviews and cited by other courts. Judges and professors may disagree whether by "clear and present danger" Justice Holmes meant to propose a standard for determining the right of government to punish or limit speech that went beyond the needs of the *Schenck* case. Whatever Holmes's intent, undoubtedly his felicity of style gave to his opinion in that case an importance far transcending its application to the questions decided there. Quotability is an element in the making of legal influence. This point might well be illustrated by reference to the work of Learned Hand and Harrie Chase in patent cases. Chase was greatly esteemed by his colleagues for his competence in patent appeals. His technical grasp of the issues in these cases equaled and perhaps exceeded that of Learned Hand. Yet, one has to look hard and long for a Second Circuit decision in the patent area in which Chase's language from another case was employed to explain or justify what the Court was now holding. Not so with Learned Hand; in fact, he was not infrequently cited by other circuits in their patent decisions, and in the *Harvard Law Review's* 1947 tribute to him there is an article devoted to his contributions to patent law.

It is fair to describe the typical Second Circuit opinion authored by any of the conservatives as dull; there were few exceptions.[8] It is

---

[8] Their memoranda were invariably briefer than those of Learned Hand and the New Dealers, and those of Swan and Chase were especially dull. But Augustus Hand was, as Judge Clark noted in tribute, capable of "glories of expression." Some of his memoranda bore a close resemblance to those of his cousin. Here is one example: "If I were to seek by and large over this Home of the Brave and Land of the Free for the minimal, miniscular and

almost as if they instinctively shied away from anything spectacular, not only in their opinions but in their total demeanor as judges. They were quiet men. The headlines and speeches and law review pieces were for their colleagues, judges who contributed importantly to the temper and tone of the legal profession. The conservatives were content to go about their business quietly, with a bare minimum of notice and clamor. Their style complimented their philosophy, yet one was not derived from the other. Their style had little in common with that of other conservative judges such as Justice James C. McReynolds or Judge Hutcheson of the Fifth Circuit. Restrained in attitude and approach, and lacking any desire to engage in battle, they not surprisingly wrote short opinions and occounted for fewer than 30 per cent of the dissenting opinions of the 1941–51 Court.

Augustus Hand exemplified this restraint to a degree probably unparalleled at a time when dissenting opinions were commonplace. He wrote only 11 dissenting opinions in the ten years—and on a court that encouraged separate opinions. His influence is measured much less by his opinions and the precedents they established for the Second Circuit and other courts than by the impact he had on what his colleagues did, by the role he often had in determining what they put in and left out of their opinions. Judge Wyzanski, who served as one of his law clerks, has accurately pointed out Judge Hand's "ability to swing the court to an unforeseen result," at times "even after memoranda have been distributed, a conference has been held, a tentative vote has been taken and a preliminary opinion written."[9] In close cases his role often was that of a mediator, offering suggestions to the two colleagues on the panel as to what revisions might be made in prospective opinions and doing his best to reconcile opposing views. Here is an illustration from a letter to Judge Clark:

> Jerry Frank has just sent in a comment on your opinion and a suggestion of a substitution. . . . His substitution seems to me to be advantageous (1) because it eliminates an additional opinion. . . . I am in the position of an innocent third party. . . . He has now in substance conceded your construction of the complaint. Your opinion with the suggested modification of Jerry would meet

---

vestigial chemical 'trace' of cerebral activity, I should unhesitatingly choose FTC to bear the Moronic Standard. Here is a new device which probably is cheaper and indistinguishable from 'conventional' engravings which stinking snobs prefer only because it costs more and is old; and these drivellers insist on putting the company out of business—for it probably will—because it won't tell competitors how to do it. How such a controversy is in 'the public interest' not even Solon could discover" (Memorandum in Benton Announcements v. FTC, June 10, 1942).

[9] Wyzanski, "Augustus Noble Hand," p. 583.

the views of all of us and contain nothing that anyone could object to.[10]

The decision came down shortly thereafter with Clark speaking for the entire court.[11]

In another case, where the panel was made up of the two Hands and Clark, the judges were divided after the conference, with Learned Hand in the minority. Augustus Hand was quite a bit persuaded by the draft dissent of his cousin and suggested to Clark that "we ought to talk over the . . . case further. . . . Perhaps by talking the thing over we can improve matters."[12] When the decision came down, the opinion of the court was by Clark; Learned Hand concurred in an opinion joined by Augustus Hand.[13]

Where he could not completely avert conflict, Judge Hand did his best to reduce it. In an appeal from the dismissal of a writ of habeas corpus sought by an alien who was being detained without bail, Hand was faced with a difficult situation brought by the panel's stalemate. His colleagues were Judges Chase and Clark and they usually took strongly opposing positions in cases involving the rights of aliens. Writing for the court, Augustus Hand reversed the dismissal of the writ and remanded the cause to the district court. His concluding paragraph plainly stated that the Attorney General had broad discretion over detention of aliens and that courts would be satisfied so long as the alien received a fair hearing. Clark objected to this limitation on the judicial role and prepared a concurring opinion; before the decision came down he asked Hand to revise the final paragraph. Hand's reply was, "I am inclined to think I have gone as far as is prudent under all circumstances. . . . Chase has signed a tab concurring with my opinion. I had feared an outright dissent."[14] He then suggested that Clark forego a separate opinion. Clark refused,[15] but what is significant is that Hand's handling of the issue had averted a dissent by either of his colleagues.[16]

[10] March 2, 1949. The case discussed was Market v. Swift & Co.

[11] 173 F.2d 517 (2d Cir. 1949).

[12] ANH to CEC, March 24, 1941.

[13] Sexton v. Sword S.S. Line, Inc., 118 F.2d 708 (2d Cir. 1941).

[14] ANH to CEC, July 28, 1948. The case was U.S. *ex rel.* Potash v. District Director.

[15] Although, he wrote: "Your letter has given me the greatest concern because I know both how far you have come to approach my views and how rarely you make suggestions about the other fellow's opinions. Indeed I have pondered the matter all weekend" (CEC to ANH, August 2, 1948).

[16] United States *ex rel.* Potash v. District Director of Immigration and Naturalization, 169 F.2d 747 (2d Cir. 1948).

Obviously, Hand's technique did not always succeed in eliminating or toning down dissent. In the *Sacher* case,[17] (the appeal by the lawyers in the *Dennis* case from their convictions for contempt of court), he was caught in the middle of a bitter exchange between Judges Clark and Frank. After weeks of sharp correspondence between these two over Frank's decisive vote to sustain the convictions, Hand asked Clark to go along with the majority. As was to be expected, Clark said no; what is surprising is that the request was made at all in the face of what had already occurred. Only Augustus Hand could have made such a request; as Clark himself wrote:

> I have pondered long—indeed to the extent which I am capable—over your parting admonition or suggestion. Because of my respect and regard for you, I cannot take it lightly. Indeed, I have examined the possibility of going along, since I know your persuasive opinion will persuade all but inconsiderable doubters and I see no immediate and perhaps no future results from a dissent. But . . . I have . . . come to the conclusion that I should stick to my own reactions, however poor they may be. At least I have attempted to state them as mildly as I can.[18]

Economic issues, more than any other, divided the conservatives from the rest of the court. By and large, they distrusted New Deal regulatory agencies and labor unions and narrowly applied legislation favorable to employees. However, their published opinions are not the best index of their attitudes on these matters, for what they could write or how they could vote was circumscribed by decisions of the Supreme Court and in their own court by the generally wide latitude given to administrative agencies. Moreover, as in other areas, many administrative appeals were one-sided and there was no special meaning in the way the judges voted. Accordingly, the voting record of the conservatives in economic cases, except for occasional dissents, was not much different from that of their brethren. In one important decision Swan, Augustus Hand, and Chase comprised the panel and broadly upheld the authority of the Securities and Exchange Commission under the Public Utilities Holding Act of 1935.[19]

Once in a while, in their memoranda the conservatives were able to give vent to their views. The following examples, representative of others, are from memoranda in which the writer concluded by at least tentatively affirming the rulings of administrative agencies. Swan: "However, it is the [National Labor Relations] Board's province to interpret the words in the light of the 'background' and I don't believe

[17] 182 F.2d 416 (2d Cir. 1950).
[18] CEC to ANH, March 30, 1950.
[19] North American Co. v. Securities & Exchange Commission, 133 F.2d 148 (2d Cir. 1943).

the Holy Nine . . . would let a mere court overrule the inferences which the 'experts' put upon the words."[20] Chase: "As so often happens the [National Labor Relations] Board resolved everything it possibly could in favor of the Union and against the respondent but that sort of thing can't be corrected during the present state of affairs."[21] Augustus Hand: "If I were to seek by and large over this Home of the Brave and Land of the Free for the minimal, minicular and vestigial chemical 'trace' of cerebral activity, I should unhesitatingly choose F.T.C. to bear the Moronic Standard. . . . But we can't do a thing about it."[22]

In a few cases the basic disagreements over the actions of administrative agencies came to the fore in decisions. This was especially true of Judge Swan, who wrote some of his more notable dissents against decisions upholding the N.L.R.B.[23] Once, voting to reverse an N.L.R.B. cease and desist order against an employer who had formulated a rule forbidding union solicitation, Swan questioned the idea that courts could not disturb administrative rulings unless it could be shown that such rulings had no support in the evidence: "My colleagues think this is within the Board's exclusive province. I cannot agree, for I am unable to see why the Board is supposed to have more competence than the courts to pass upon the reasonableness of the [employer's] rule in the absence of evidence tending to show that it unduly interferes with the employee's right to form, join or assist labor organizations."[24]

But usually the economic conservatism of the three judges was expressed more as a mood than in terms of hard votes. This was sensed by the Second Circuit judges and by others close to the court's work, surfacing only rarely when opportunity presented itself in the rulings the court had to make.

[20] N.L.R.B. v. American Laundry Machine Co., November 6, 1945. Chase and Clark were also on the panel; the unanimous decision upholding the Board was written by Swan (152 F.2d 400 [2d Cir. 1945]).

[21] N.L.R.B. v. Dadourian Export Corp., October 11, 1943. But the other judges, Learned Hand and Clark—two liberals—thought otherwise, and the decision came down as a unanimous reversal of the Board's order, illustrating once more how opinions are changed after the memoranda are written (National Labor Relations Board v. Dadourian Export Corp., 138 F.2d 891 [2d Cir. 1943]).

[22] Benton Announcements v. FTC, June 10, 1942.

[23] For instance, Republic Aviation Corporation v. National Labor Relations Board, 142 F.2d 193 (2d Cir. 1944); Independent Employees Association v. National Labor Relations Board, 158 F.2d 448 (2d Cir. 1946); National Labor Relations Board v. Universal Camera Corp., 179 F.2d 749 (2d Cir. 1950).

[24] Republic Aviation Corporation v. National Labor Relations Board, 142 F.2d 193, 197 (2d Cir. 1944).

The spirit of economic conservatism appeared in several other areas. The Second Circuit generally took a very liberal approach in interpreting the scope of the Fair Labor Standards Act of 1938 with its provisions concerning minimum wages and maximum hours for employees engaged in interstate commerce. One of the most difficult questions in this area facing the federal courts in the 1940's dealt with workers who performed ancillary services for employers involved in interstate commerce. In 1941, in *Fleming v. Arsenal Building Corporation*, a panel composed of Learned Hand, Clark, and Frank held that the Wages and Hours Act applied to maintenance employees in a building whose tenants were principally engaged in the production of goods sold throughout the country.[25] The Supreme Court granted certiorari and affirmed, with only Justice Owen J. Roberts dissenting.[26] Later, in *Borella v. Borden Co.*[27] and *Callus v. 10 East Fortieth Street Building*,[28] the Second Circuit extended F.L.S.A. benefits to building employees such as elevator operators. In the second case less than half of the area of the building was rented by firms producing goods for interstate commerce. The Supreme Court reviewed both cases, affirming in *Borden*[29] but reversing the Second Circuit in *Callus*.[30] In *Borden*, Swan dissented, holding that "porters, elevator operators, and night watchmen of the defendant's office building are too remotely related to 'the production' of goods for commerce to be within the coverage of the Act,"[31] even though there was no question of the employer's direct involvement in interstate commerce.

In Federal Employers' Liability Act cases, Judges Swan and Chase at times disagreed with their colleagues' sympathetic application of the statute's provision to injured railroad employees whose injury may have been the result of their own negligence. Once when Learned and Augustus Hand joined to reverse the trial judge's dismissal of a suit brought by the estate of a deceased railroad worker, the majority held that the question whether the employee had suffered a heart attack as a result of exertion while trying to throw a defective railroad switch should have been left to the jury to decide. Chase dissented, arguing that there was no evidence of negligence on the railroad's part: "So what was the defendant's negligence? It is said to

[25] 125 F.2d 278 (2d Cir. 1941).
[26] A. B. Kirschbaum Co. v. Walling, 316 U.S. 517 (1942).
[27] 145 F.2d 63 (2d Cir. 1944), panel composed of Learned Hand, Swan, and Clark.
[28] 146 F.2d 438 (2d Cir. 1944), panel composed of the two Hands and Frank.
[29] Borden Co. v. Borella, 329 U.S. 679 (1945).
[30] 10 East 40th Street Building v. Callus, 325 U.S. 578 (1945).
[31] 145 F.2d 63, 65 (2d Cir. 1944).

have been in permitting a new switch, which the deceased was hired to throw in the course of his work, to operate so hard he could not take hold of the handle and throw it as such switches ordinarily are thrown. It should not be forgotten that he was not required to pull any harder than he saw fit and that after he had tried and failed he was at liberty simply to report that fact. . . . The work of a railroad brakeman is, of course, strenuous and men who follow it must at times exert themselves harder than at others." He went on:

> It may be a good policy to enact laws which will make the industry bear the pecuniary loss of such accidents as this, but until then and while tort liability alone is relied on, I cannot believe that juries ought to be allowed to decide how easy a new railroad switch should turn. That will certainly create differing standards; perhaps as many as there may be judges to decide; and such standards on the same railroad will vary from jury to jury. It will supplant the judgment of railroad engineers based upon training and experience in actual railroad operation with that of the collective notion untrained and inexperienced jurors may get from the evidence weighed in the light of their own ideas on the subject. . . .[32]

In another dissent from a decision in favor of a railroad worker, Chase complained that "if my brothers [Clark and Frank] are right, it would seem . . . that recovery may now be had under the Federal Employers' Liability Act as though it were a sort of Workmen's Compensation Act providing, upon proof of injury, simply for the assessment of damages by a jury. . . ."[33]

Judge Swan's attitude in FELA cases was exemplified by his dissenting opinion in *Mostyn v. Delaware, Lackawanna & Western R.* The question was whether an employee of a railroad which provided shelter and food for its workers was in its employ when his foot was cut off while he was sleeping near the railroad tracks. Learned Hand, supported by Clark, upheld the jury decision in favor of the worker. But Swan thought differently: "During the night hours normally

[32] Stewart v. Baltimore & Ohio R., 137 F.2d 527, 530 (2d Cir. 1943). Two weeks later, Judge Chase joined Judges Clark and Swan in upholding a jury verdict in a Jones Act case that a seaman had been injured as a result of his employer's negligence. It is a bit difficult to understand Chase's vote, particularly since the court conceded that "we view the plaintiff's story as somewhat incredible," still, "we cannot say that there was not in all this conflicting testimony sufficient evidence to take his case to the jury" (Herring v. Luckenbach S.S. Co., 137 F.2d 598, 599 [2d Cir. 1943]). The court then cited the decision in Stewart.

[33] Korte v. New York, New Haven & Hartford R., 191 F.2d 86, 91 (2d Cir. 1951). Another F.E.L.A. dissent by Chase came in Morris v. Pennsylvania R., 187 F.2d 837 (2d Cir. 1951).

devoted to sleep the employee owes no duties to his employer. . . . Therefore the question whether he was employed in interstate commerce during the night is no different than it would be had he been sleeping at a boarding house in the village or at his own home and suffered injury through the negligence of the railroad. . . ."[34] A lack of sympathy for the worker similarly accounted for Swan's dissent from a holding that a release signed by an injured railroad worker did not preclude his bringing suit against the railroad.[35]

In conclusion, while in the large majority of appeals involving economic issues the conservative attitudes of the three judges did not affect their votes, either because the cases were one-sided or because the Second Circuit was bound by previous decisions, in those cases where there was division on the court, the conservatism of at least Judges Swan and Chase comes through.

It is even more difficult to generalize about civil liberties decisions of the Learned Hand court. Very few cases that came to the court raised the types of issues that have occupied much of the Supreme Court's attention over the past generation. Most of the criminal appeals were routine; the Second Circuit got fewer First Amendment cases than some of the other courts of appeals, notably the one for the District of Columbia; and the court was hardly concerned at all with racial discrimination. Yet, in the handful of cases in these areas decided by the Second Circuit, definite attitudes could be discerned. Moreover, in two areas, Selective Service and aliens' rights, the Learned Hand court made some important rulings.

The appeal of the first-rank leaders of the Communist Party from their Smith Act convictions was the single most significant civil liberties case to come before the Second Circuit in the decade. Much attention has been paid to Learned Hand's opinion for the court and none to the votes of his colleagues on the panel. The other judges were Swan and Chase. The former went along with the Chief Judge, while Chase concurred separately in an opinion which Learned Hand described as arguing that the majority had too much "enlarged" the zone of protected speech.[36] Chase's opinion was far less tolerant of speech than his colleagues' or, for that matter, the majority who decided the *Dennis* appeal in the Supreme Court. Indeed, while Learned Hand and Chief Justice Fred Vinson deliberately avoided the "bad tendency" test of the 1920's and *Gitlow v. New York,* and at least tried to salvage the "clear and present danger" doctrine, Chase based his affirmance of the convictions on *Gitlow.* This is amazing in view of

[34] 160 F.2d 15, 19 (2d Cir. 1947).
[35] Ricketts v. Pennsylvania R., 153 F.2d 757 (2d Cir. 1946).
[36] United States v. Dennis, 183 F.2d 201, 234 (2d Cir. 1950).

a number of Supreme Court decisions in the preceding decade in which the "clear and present danger" test was employed. Yet, according to Chase:

> The only answer to the rule of the Gitlow case is, I believe, that individuals have a constitutional right to revolt. Of this, the Constitution contains its own refutation. The Preamble; Art. I, Sec. 8; Art. III, Sec. 3; Art. IV, Sec. 4. History confirms this also. One need only refer to the so called "Whiskey Rebellion" and the secession of the Confederate States.
>
> That Gitlow v. People of State of New York was correctly decided and is controlling here seems, to me at least, abundantly clear. It has never been overruled. . . . It is true that language from the dissenting opinions in the Gitlow and Whitney cases has frequently been referred to, though sometimes with disapproval. This is as it should be, for that language has sometimes been helpful in cases where the challenged statute prohibits, not specific utterances, but results which the utterances may tend to bring about. The Gitlow and Whitney cases remain good law. They are applicable here, and binding upon us. The principle they stand for is sound. I believe that they should be followed directly, and not merely by-passed.[37]

In a 1940 speech before the New Hampshire Bar Association, Judge Chase took what may be fairly described as a very conservative position on the preservation of freedom of speech:

> In the right to freedom of speech which we cherish is found one of the most effective ways to spread the foreign doctrines and the false notions of security which may destroy us. As we deprive others of the right to advocate what they believe, or profess to believe, to that extent we deny one of the principles of our faith that what is false will fall of its own weight if allowed to try to find its support in public opinion. The answer to that problem, and to others like it is clear. The existence of a great emergency calls for such action as may be necessary to preserve our American people and our American government in such well-being and strength that when the dire days are gone we may return to the normal freedom of thought, speech, and action which otherwise will be forever lost. Though there is always danger that the innocent will suffer from the hysterial over-reaching of those both in power and out, that is no good reason for throwing away our liberty for lack of effort to save it by some temporary curtailment. Consistent vigilance will protect us only if those who look upon our determination to save our democratic ideals as one of our weaknesses which they can exploit are dealt with so firmly that they will respect and not despise us.[38]

[37] *Ibid.*, pp. 236–37.
[38] Proceedings of the Bar Association of the State of New Hampshire, 1940–41, p. 92.

Judge Chase wrote the majority opinion for the Second Circuit in *Sweeney v. Schenectady Union Publishing Co.*, in which the court reversed the dismissal of a libel suit against a newspaper brought by a congressman. Rejecting the argument that the suit was barred by the First Amendment, Chase said that "freedom of speech is, as it always has been, freedom to tell the truth and comment fairly upon facts and not a license to spread damaging falsehoods in the guise of news gathering and its dissemination."[39] He was supported by Learned Hand, while Judge Clark wrote a vigorous dissent. The Supreme Court affirmed by an equally divided court.[40] The Supreme Court ruling in *New York Times Co. v. Sullivan* that the First Amendment barred libel suits by public officials unless they could show malicious intent implicitly rejected the Second Circuit's *Sweeney* decision.[41]

An appeal in which the issue was the authority of the House Un-American Activities Committee to question persons about their political beliefs and associations was decided by Judges Swan and Chase, along with Judge Clark. Leon Josephson, a Communist, was convicted in 1947 after a jury trial in the Southern District of New York for refusing to be sworn and testify before a subcommittee of HUAC. He appealed to the Second Circuit, which upheld his conviction by a vote of 2–1, with Chase writing the majority opinion and Clark dissenting.

Because Josephson refused to be sworn, Chase rejected his contention "that the language of the authorizing statute is so vague that a witness before the Committee has no criteria to indicate in doubtful cases what questions asked would have the requisite pertinence."[42] Chase then disposed of the arguments that the committee's investigation was into the private affairs of private individuals and that it had as its principal goal exposure and notoriety and not legislation. "It is immaterial," he said, "that in the past this particular committee has proposed but little legislation."[43] Chase dealt next with the major point made by Josephson and the *amici* supporting him, that the First Amendment outlawed HUAC's investigation. "If this be true, the Constitution itself provides immunity from discovery and lawful restraint for those who would destroy it."[44] Chase continued:

> The appellant's argument necessarily, therefore, is reduced to the absurd proposition that because the facts resulting from the Committee's investigations conceivably may also be utilized as the

---

[39] 122 F.2d 288, 290 (2d Cir., 1941).

[40] Schenectady Union Publishing Co. v. Sweeney, 316 U.S. 642 (1942).

[41] 376 U.S. 254, 268 (1964).

[42] United States v. Josephson, 165 F.2d 82, 87 (2d Cir. 1947).

[43] *Ibid.*, p. 89.

[44] *Ibid.*, p. 90.

basis for legislation impairing freedom of expression, the statute authorizing such investigations must be held void. But clearly Congress can and should legislate to curtail this freedom at least where there is a "clear and present danger" that its exercise would, as by armed rebellion or external attack, imperil the country and its Constitutional system, including until amended, the peaceful process of amendment.[45]

The majority's view in *Josephson* was in tune with the temper of the times (Judge Clark's dissent will be considered in the next chapter). The Supreme Court refused certiorari, although three justices voted to grant it.[46] Several months after the Second Circuit decision the same result was reached by a panel of the Court of Appeals for the District of Columbia.[47] It was not until 1957, when the Cold War was much colder than it had been a decade earlier, that the Supreme Court willingly faced a test of the power of the House Un-American Activities Committee and reversed a contempt conviction sought by HUAC. The High Court then implicitly rejected the *Josephson* decision.[48]

The one significant appeal involving a civil liberties issue participated in by Judge Augustus Hand was that of the lawyers for the Communist parties from their summary convictions for contempt of court. Hand apparently persuaded Jerome Frank to vote for upholding the conviction and this precipitated an ugly battle between the latter and Judge Clark, who dissented. Hand's majority opinion was, for the most part, a dry recitation of what took place at the trial of the leaders; there is no language to engage the interest of those concerned with the civil liberties implications of the case. Hand rejected the defense that the "obstructive tactics and impudent charges" were provoked by the rulings and demeanor of trial judge Medina, an argument which later got a fair measure of support in the Supreme Court. For, "it must be borne in mind," countered Hand, "that when counsel differ as to the rulings of a judge, they acquire no privilege to charge him with bad faith and misconduct, and to obstruct the trial. Their only remedy is by an appeal."[49]

[45] *Ibid.*, pp. 90–91. Here Chase was more aware of the "clear and present danger" test than he was three years later in Dennis.

[46] Josephson v. United States, 333 U.S. 838 (1948). Justice Black apparently voted against review, and this is puzzling. Had he gone the other way, under the "rule of four" the appeal would have been heard.

[47] Barsky v. United States, 167 F.2d 241 (D.C. Cir. 1948); Justice Edgerton dissented.

[48] Watkins v. United States, 354 U.S. 178 (1957).

[49] United States v. Sacher, 182 U.S. 416, 430 (2d Cir. 1950). Frank's and Clark's opinions will be discussed in the next chapter. By a vote of 5–3 the Supreme Court affirmed the Second Circuit (Sacher v. United States, 343 U.S. 1 [1952]).

In an important appeal raising claims of racial discrimination in the Armed Forces, the Second Circuit's rejection of the claim was determined largely by the panel's composition. A Negro inductee challenged the Army's policy of issuing separate draft calls for whites and Negroes, a practice derived from the existence of segregated military units. There was no denial that there was a quota system based on race; at issue was whether the system was a discriminatory practice in violation of the Selective Service Act.[50] The majority, consisting of Judges Augustus Hand and Swan held that the statute did not outlaw the Army's practice while Judge Clark dissented in one more opinion giving evidence of his libertarian attitudes.

Hand's opinion took a rather unimaginative view of the Negro struggle for equality and fair treatment, even from the standpoint of the social attitudes of the 1940's. The Negro conscript's complaint that under the quota system he was not drafted in turn was put aside by Hand because

> if the appellant was called for induction later than his turn, his grievance seems to be that the military custody in which he now finds himslf should have begun at an earlier date. But how does the fact that the Army should have had him sooner make unlawful its having him now? . . . In failing to prove that the requisition under which he was called for induction resulted in calling him ahead of his turn in the draft, a majority of the court believes that the petition [for a writ of habeas corpus] was properly dismissed for failure of proof that he was aggrieved by the discrimination, if any there was.[51]

The section of the Selective Service Act that plainly banned racial discrimination in the selection and training of men was deemed not relevant. "Reading the Act as a whole and in the light of the Army's long established practice of segregating enlisted men into separate white and colored units, we believe that requisitions calling for a specified number of whites and a specified number of Negroes for induction . . . is a necessary and permissible procedure, and the regulations which sanction it are not violative of the Act."[52]

Judge Hand, it would seem, personally believed that military segregation was a good policy, a conclusion supported by his dictum that to hold otherwise "would frustrate, or at least impede, the development of an effective armed force."[53] And he concluded his opinion by re-

[50] There was no challenge on constitutional grounds.
[51] United States *ex rel.* Lynn v. Downer, 140 F.2d 397, 399 (2d Cir. 1944).
[52] *Ibid.*, p. 400.
[53] *Ibid.* In his memorandum of December 14, 1943, written shortly after the argument, Hand complained: "We live in a progressive age surrounded

ferring to Supreme Court decisions upholding the "separate but equal" doctrine, including *Plessy v. Ferguson*.[54]

In another case, in which the civil rights issue was subordinated to a technical question, Judges Frank and Clark joined to reverse the trial judge and held that a Negro who had been refused permission to use the dining car of a railroad could sue the railroad company. Judge Swan dissented.[55]

During the Second World War the Second Circuit reviewed a number of Selective Service cases; it was in this area that Augustus Hand wrote what is probably his most significant opinion of the decade, one that has been frequently cited by the Supreme Court and other federal courts. *United States v. Kauten*[56] was an appeal from a conviction for violation of the Selective Service Act. Mathias Kauten, claiming exemption from military service on the ground that he was a conscientious objector, refused to obey an induction notice after his claim was rejected. At his trial he attempted to show that he was wrongly denied exemption, but this defense was not allowed by the trial judge, who ruled that an alleged error in classification could not be used as a defense for failure to report for induction.

On appeal, the Second Circuit unanimously held (Judges Clark and Frank joining Judge Hand) that "the registrant was bound to obey the order to report for induction even if there had been error of law in his classification."[57] Judge Hand did not stop there, for he also ruled that no error had been made in the classification. Kauten's claim was based on philosophical and political considerations about war, but "the conviction that war is a futile means of righting wrongs or of protecting the state, that it is not worth the sacrifice, that it is waged for base ends, or is otherwise indefensible" is not a ground for exemption under the statute which requires that opposition to military service be based on "religious training and belief."[58]

After completely finding against Kauten, Hand, in the part of the opinion that has gained wide attention, went on to declare that the requirement of "religious training and belief" did not mean member-

---

by many who cherish the illusion that black is white and white is black. I think that it would be most difficult to organize an army without colored regiments and that it would be pretty absurd not to permit the army to have them."

[54] Certiorari was denied by the Supreme Court "on the ground that the case is moot, it appearing that petitioner no longer is in respondent's custody" (United States *ex rel.* Lynn v. Downer, 322 U.S. 756 [1944]).

[55] Barnett v. Texas & Pacific R., 145 F.2d 800 (2d Cir. 1944).

[56] 133 F.2d 703 (2d Cir. 1943).

[57] *Ibid.*, p. 707.

[58] *Ibid.*

ship in any church whose religious teachings were against war; "a compelling voice of conscience, which we should regard as a religious impulse" would be sufficient to obtain exemption. Such a conviction "may justly be regarded as a response of the individual to an inward mentor, call it conscience or God, that is for many persons at the present time the equivalent of what has always been thought a religious impulse."[59]

Hand conceded the difficulty of defining "religion" and yet, in a rare departure from the spare style characteristic of his opinions, he wrote:

> Religious belief arises from a sense of the inadequacy of reason as a means of relating the individual to his fellowmen and to his universe—a sense common to men in the most primitive and in the most highly civilized societies. It accepts the aid of logic but refuses to be limited by it. It is a belief finding expression in a conscience which categorically requires the believer to disregard elementary self-interest and to accept martyrdom in preference to transgressing its tenets. A religious obligation forbade Socrates, even in order to escape condemnation, to entreat his judges to acquit him, because he believed it was their sworn duty to decide questions without favor to anyone and only according to law. Such an obligation impelled Martin Luther to nail his theses on the door of the church at Wittenberg and, when he was summoned before Emperor Charles and the Diet at Worms, steadfastly to hold his ground and to utter the often quoted words: "I neither can nor will recant anything, since it is neither right nor safe to act against conscience. Here I stand. I cannot do other. God help me. Amen." Recognition of this obligation moved the Greek poet Menander to write almost twenty-four hundred years ago: "Conscience is a god to all mortals"; impelled Socrates to obey the voice of his "Daimon" and led Wordsworth to characterize "Duty" as the Stern Daughter of the Voice of God.[60]

This broad conception of religious belief did not help Kauten and it was rejected by several courts of appeals; it was applied in other cases decided by the Second Circuit and ultimately the Supreme Court came around to a similar definition.[61]

Not long after *Kauten* was decided, a panel of the Second Circuit by a vote of 2–1 relied on it to reverse a ruling denying conscientious objector status to a writer whose opposition to war was based on

[59] *Ibid.*, p. 708.
[60] *Ibid.*
[61] United States v. Seeger, 380 U.S. 163 (1965). The Seeger-Kauten rule was recently expanded by the Supreme Court in Welsh v. the United States. See *United States Law Week*, June 16, 1970, p. 4486.

humanitarian ideals.[62] Similarly, the court unanimously reversed the denial of exemption in another case because the hearing officer for Selective Service had determined that religious belief "necessarily connoted some concept of deity" and therefore ruled that a humanitarian position on war was insufficient to gain classification as a conscientious objector.[63] Because the appellate court was uncertain whether the Selective Service appeals board or the Director of Selective Service had actually relied on this narrow definition of religious belief, it remanded the case for further proceedings. When it returned to the Second Circuit, a somewhat differently constituted panel heard the appeal and once more the decision was favorable to the claimant and against Selective Service, although the second time around Judge Chase dissented.[64]

With the exception of Chase, the Second Circuit clearly accepted the *Kauten* doctrine. Chase's refusal to go along with the others probably was not the result of his holding different views on the meaning of religious belief, for he did not address himself to that question. Rather, he believed that Selective Service rulings should be regarded as administrative orders subject to only a limited review by courts. Only when these rulings were "clearly erroneous" could they be reversed by judges. The issue, said Chase in a dissenting opinion, "is whether the duly authorized classification agency conscientiously considered the evidence; found all the material facts proved; and lawfully classified him accordingly."[65] If the answers were "yes," then "whatever classification . . . should be given is the one his draft board arrived at after due consideration of the facts as reported by an able and impartial hearing officer."[66]

Chase felt strongly about draftees fulfilling their patriotic duty of military service. Any attempt to avoid 1-A status was regarded by him as a sort of draft evasion. In one appeal he dissented from a decision granting a writ of habeas corpus to an individual who had long tried to avoid military service and who was found upon induction, after examination by an Army doctor, to be suffering from a medical

[62] United States *ex rel.* Phillips v. Downer, 135 F.2d 521 (2d Cir. 1943). The majority opinion was written by Judge Clark, who was supported by Judge Augustus Hand; Judge Chase dissented. However, in a memorandum after the decision came down, Hand conceded that he "always doubted the decision although I reached my conclusion after unusual care and deliberation" (Phillips v. Downer, February 2, 1944).

[63] United States *ex rel.* Reel v. Badt, 141 F.2d 845 (2d Cir. 1944).

[64] United States *ex rel.* Reel v. Badt, 152 F.2d 627 (2d Cir. 1945).

[65] United States *ex rel.* Phillips v. Downer, 135 F.2d 521, 526 (2d Cir. 1943).

[66] *Ibid.,* pp. 526–27.

condition that required classification as 4-F. Incredibly, this man's local draft board refused to reclassify him. In dissenting from a ruling adverse to the draft board, Chase had nothing more to say of its action than that it was "an irregularity in the procedure under which he was inducted into the Army."[67]

However, Judge Chase aside, the Learned Hand Court achieved a liberal reputation in Selective Service matters[68] and, as was indicated before, its definition of religious belief was accepted unanimously by the Supreme Court.

The one civil liberties area in which the Second Circuit was active during the 1940's was the rights of aliens. Many different problems arose: detention of "enemy aliens," due process for aliens, deportation and exclusion of aliens, rights of persons applying for citizenship, and so on. There was no single pattern to the court's rulings, although the general tendency was distinctly libertarian. As we should expect, the Second Circuit was substantially limited in leeway by the Supreme Court and by the Nationality Act of 1940 and other legislation.

Judge Swan seems to have been the Second Circuit's leading spokesman in alien and naturalization cases and it was he who was largely responsible for the court's sympathetic attitude. "Bird O'Freedom Swan," was the way Augustus Hand referred to him in an alien case memorandum and Hand went on to say that Swan "has been harboring enemy aliens for years."[69]

In 1943 Swan wrote opinions in three cases that raised the question whether aliens who came from Austria were, by consequence of that country's annexation by Germany, German citizens and hence enemy aliens subject to arrest and detention under a presidential proclamation. In each case, the alien had been arrested and sought release through a writ of habeas corpus, which was denied by the

[67] United States *ex rel.* Beye v. Downer, 143 F.2d 125, 127 (2d Cir. 1944). One of Chase's angriest dissents came in United States v. Hoffman, 137 F.2d 416 (2d Cir. 1943), where the majority (Judges Clark and Swan) reversed a conviction for failing to report for induction because the trial judge had committed prejudicial error in excluding evidence favorable to the defendant. This, said Chase, "was relieving a stubbornly guilty man, at least temporarily, of the consequences of his guilt" (p. 422).

[68] Mention ought to be made of the 2–1 decision in United States *ex rel.* Hirshberg v. Malanaphy, 168 F.2d 503 (2d Cir. 1948). Judge Swan for the court, joined by Judge Clark, held that an individual could be court martialed for offenses that were committed during a prior enlistment from which he had already been discharged. The Supreme Court unanimously reversed on statutory grounds (United States *ex rel.* Hirshberg v. Cooke, 336 U.S. 210 [1949]).

[69] Memorandum in U.S. *ex rel.* Schirrmeister v. Watkins, December 16, 1948.

district court. In the first appeal, Swan was supported by Learned Hand and Frank in reversing the lower court ruling, although the appellate judges did not come to the question whether the alien was, according to American law, a "denizen" of Germany. The ground for reversal was that the trial judge wrongly held that the question whether the alien was "a native, citizen, denizen, or subject" was one of law, not of fact. The matter was remanded for determination by the district court.[70]

The second case was similar in nature in that once more the district judge had not allowed a hearing on the alien's status, but because there was no disagreement over the essential facts, the court of appeals decided to get to the merits. Paul Schwarzkopf, a Jew born in Prague, was a naturalized citizen of Austria when he came to the United States in 1936. Less than two years later he declared his intention to become an American citizen. A day after the United States declared war against Japan he was taken into custody as an enemy alien. The government contended that Schwarzkopf was a German citizen, a position that was both cruel and disingenious in view of a German government order of 1941 depriving overseas Jews of German citizenship, the obvious fact that the United States did not recognize as legal the Nazi annexation of Austria, and the extermination program being practiced against Jews. But it was argued that practical measures taken by the United States government prior to its entry into the Second World War amounted to de facto recognition of Germany's annexation.

In his opinion Swan dismissed the notion that Schwarzkopf was a German citizen, for, irrespective of American recognition of Germany's action, under international law Germany could not through annexation impose her citizenship on persons no longer residing in Austria. Nor did it make any difference that Austria had ceased to exist as a sovereign nation:

> On general principles of justice we think that civilized nations should not recognize the asserted distinction. If the invaded country has ceased to exist as an independent state there would seem to be all the more reason for allowing its former nationals, who have fled from the invader and established a residence abroad, the right of voluntarily electing a new nationality and remaining "stateless" until they can acquire it. In our view an invader cannot under international law impose its nationality upon non-residents of the subjugated country without their consent, express or tacit.[71]

[70] United States *ex rel.* Zdunic v. Uhl, 137 F.2d 858 (2d Cir. 1943).
[71] United States *ex rel.* Schwarzkopf v. Uhl, 137 F.2d 898, 902 (2d Cir. 1943).

Swan was supported by Chase and Clark. In a companion appeal, decided the same day as *Schwarzkopf,* with Frank replacing Chase on the panel, Swan was in dissent. The *D'Esquiva* case presented a somewhat different question. The alien, also a Jew, was born in Austria; while under the *Schwarzkopf* ruling he could not be regarded as a German citizen, the government contended that he was a "native" of Germany and an enemy alien by virtue of Germany's annexation of Austria.

Clark and Frank, in the majority,[72] held that one remains a native of the country of his birth even when he moves away and becomes a subject of another country. Accordingly, they reasoned, if the United States did in fact grant either de jure or de facto recognition to what Germany did in Austria, D'Esquiva was a German native. However, because the statements and acts of the executive branch left doubt regarding recognition of Austria as part of Germany, the majority reversed the district court and remanded the case for a hearing on the issue of American recognition.

Swan was unhappy with this resolution. He would have released the alien from custody without further proceedings. "In my opinion one who was born a native of Austria remains a native Austrian even though his country loses its identity as an independent state. . . . a native of the conquered country who has removed himself before the conquest has no reason whatever to favor the conqueror; on the contrary he has every reason for antipathy."[73]

Two interesting appeals in which Swan participated dealt with the detention of aliens who had been brought to the United States involuntarily. Jacob Bradley, a Norwegian who was a member of the Quisling Party, had been seized in Greenland by the Coast Guard in 1941 and taken to this country as a prisoner. He was inexplicably classified as a potential immigrant, denied admission as an immigrant, and held in custody for ultimate return to Norway. In ordering

[72] At the conference the vote was 2–1 in favor of Swan and the alien. Clark's draft dissent, however, "persuaded'" Frank and the vote was reversed (JNF to CEC, August 6, 1943).

[73] United States *ex rel.* D'Esquiva v. Uhl, 137 F.2d 903, 907 (2d Cir. 1943). Inexplicably, four years later in another enemy alien appeal, Judge Swan said in a footnote to his opinion for the court: "The writer of the present opinion dissented in the D'Esquiva case, but further reflection has caused me to doubt the validity of my dissent" (United States *ex rel.* Gregoire v. Watkins, 164 F.2d 137, 139, n. 3 [2d Cir. 1947]). Swan did not elaborate; to this writer, his earlier reasoning seems valid. In the Gregoire case the decision was in favor of the alien, who was born in Lorraine when it was part of France. Lorraine was restored to France by the Treaty of Versailles so that Gregoire was both a native and citizen of that country and hence no "enemy."

Bradley's release (to allow him to voluntarily leave the country), Swan used as sharply libertarian language as he did in any other opinion in the entire ten years:

> The theory that an alien can be seized on foreign soil by armed forces of the United States Navy, brought as a prisoner to our shores, turned over to the immigration authorities as being an "applicant for admission to the United States," held in custody by them for nearly six years, and then deported to the country of his nativity by virtue of the exclusion order savors of those very ideologies against which our nation has fought the greatest war of history.[74]

Learned Hand supported Swan, but the third member of the Second Circuit's senior panel, Augustus Hand, was of the opinion that under the statutory definition of "an alien departing from any place outside the United States destined for the United States" Bradley was an immigrant. Hand reasoned that Bradley "literally 'departed' from Greenland when he was transported from that country; likewise he was 'destined for the United States' when he left Greenland for America."[75] Swan's position prevailed on the Second Circuit as the *Bradley* ruling was reaffirmed in two cases, Swan writing the court's opinion in one of these.[76]

In a number of cases the Second Circuit had to determine the scope of judicial review of deportation orders of the Attorney General, such as the question whether aliens ordered deported were entitled to hearings. In *United States ex rel. Schlueter v. Watkins,*[77] the court (Frank, supported by Learned Hand and Chase) ruled that under the Alien Enemy Act enemy aliens were not entitled to hearings. This decision was accepted by another panel which heard a similar case. But, in the second case, Judge Augustus Hand, after admitting the "doubtful propriety for a court ever to express an opinion on a subject over which it has no power," suggested that "justice may per-

[74] United States *ex rel.* Bradley v. Watkins, 163 F.2d 328, 332 (2d Cir. 1947).

[75] *Ibid.*

[76] United States *ex rel.* Ludwig v. Watkins, 164 F.2d 456 (2d Cir. 1947). Judges Clark and Chase served on this panel, also. The other case, with the same judges, was United States *ex rel.* Paetau v. Watkins, 164 F.2d 457 (2d Cir. 1947), Clark writing the opinion.

However, in United States *ex rel.* Schirrmeister v. Watkins, 171 F.2d 858 (2d Cir. 1949), Swan dissented from a holding by Clark and Augustus Hand that an alien who had been forcibly brought to the United States could be deported as an illegal immigrant if he did not voluntarily leave the country within ninety days after being given the opportunity to do so.

[77] 158 F.2d 853 (2d Cir. 1946).

haps be better satisfied" if the plea of the alien would be reconsidered.[78]

In several appeals by alien Communist leaders ordered deported by the Attorney General, the Second Circuit was asked to permit bail while deportation was being challenged. The Second Circuit took the position that the Attorney General did not have unlimited discretion over admission of aliens to bail. In a leading case, the court, in an opinion by Augustus Hand, reversed the district court and ordered it to determine whether there had been an abuse of discretion in denying bail.[79] However, Hand made it plain that the Attorney General still had wide latitude in bail matters and that he "need go no further than necessary to meet any evidence of arbitrary action that is given."[80]

One alien case that received a good deal of attention in the press and in Congress in the late 1940's and early 1950's involved the attempt of a German war bride to win admission to the United States. Several different appeals involving this woman came before the Second Circuit, only one of which need be mentioned here. While the courts invariably ruled against her, Mrs. Ellen Knauff did finally win her battle, apparently because she had some friends in Congress. The reasons for her exclusion were never given by the Attorney General, as they were alleged to be based on confidential information, the disclosure of which would endanger American security. Mrs. Knauff challenged the exclusion order, arguing that she was entitled to a hearing; on this question she lost both in the Second Circuit[81] and the Supreme Court.[82] Judge Chase's opinion in the lower court expressed his view that nonresident aliens have virtually no rights, constitutional or statutory in deportation proceedings.[83]

[78] United States ex rel. Ludecke v. Watkins, 163 F.2d 143, 144 (2d Cir. 1947). The Supreme Court, after first denying certiorari, affirmed the lower court by a vote of 5–4 (Ludecke v. Watkins, 335 U.S. 160 [1948]). One of the dissenters, Justice Black, called attention to the plea of the Second Circuit (p. 183).

[79] United States ex rel. Potash v. District Director of Immigration and Naturalization, 169 F.2d 747 (2d Cir. 1948). Various companion appeals to this case are reported at 169 F.2d 753.

[80] Ibid., p. 752. Judge Clark strongly objected to placing the entire burden of proof on the alien and wrote a concurring opinion. In an exchange of letters, Clark tried to get Hand to amend his opinion, but the latter refused, writing that "the feeling about hysteria over Communists which you express in your letter is mine but after all we are not the A. G. and the case against him [the A.G.] must be very clear" (ANH to CEC, July 28, 1948).

[81] United States ex rel. Knauff v. Watkins, 173 F.2d 599 (2d Cir. 1949).

[82] United States ex rel. Knauff v. Shaughnessy, 338 U.S. 537 (1950). The vote was 4–3.

[83] Judges Augustus Hand and Frank were with Chase on the appeal. Frank's vote is a little surprising in view of the clear civil liberties issue and

Chase was probably more liberal in the alien area than elsewhere but still less so than his colleagues. In one appeal the court upheld the claim of an Italian alien who had been ordered deported without a hearing. The majority felt that the Attorney General had capriciously determined that while he would grant hearings to others, no hearings would be afforded to a particular class of Italians.[84] In a brief, sharp dissent, Chase complained that "judges should not offhandedly—without any showing that there are no administrative, or other, conditions which may make such a classification not only reasonable but, perhaps, practically necessary—hold it to be so capricious that its application amounts to a reviewable failure to exercise discretion at all."[85]

In cases in which Chase participated but did not write an opinion, at times his vote was in favor of the alien's claim and at times it was not, but over the years it was rare for Chase to write any opinion evincing deep concern for the rights and problems of aliens.[86]

All in all, the development of the law regarding aliens in the Second Circuit was in a significant way the responsibility of Judge Swan. It is likely that he was regarded as a specialist in the field and that opinion assignments were made with this in mind. With few exceptions Swan's opinions showed sincere sympathy for aliens and naturalized citizens, underdogs battling the government's attempts to deny or revoke citizenship or to deport or detain aliens. Interestingly, this attitude of Swan's did not appear in any other area where it might have been said (as Frank and Clark contended) that helpless persons were being deprived of their lawful rights by an all-powerful government. But when it came to aliens there was little doubt of where he stood. Typical was his comment in a case in which the Second Circuit reversed the dismissal of a writ of habeas corpus sought by one whose citizenship was taken away while he was in prison: "we

---

"underdog" overtones. Later, in another stage of the same proceedings, when all looked lost for Mrs. Knauff, Frank—supported somewhat weakly by Learned Hand in a concurring opinion, with Swan dissenting—ordered a stay of deportation because there was a bill pending in Congress to grant her admission, and while he refused to do it in her case, the usual practice of the Attorney General in such situations was to postpone deportation (United States *ex rel.* Knauff v. McGrath, 181 F.2d 839 [2d Cir. 1950]).

[84] Mastrapasqua v. Shaughnessy, 180 F.2d 999 (2d Cir. 1950). Frank and Augustus Hand made up the majority.

[85]*Ibid.*, p. 1010.

[86] Perhaps one pro-alien opinion of consequence by Chase was his majority opinion in United States v. Sotzek, 144 F.2d 576 (2d Cir. 1944), Clark dissenting in part, in which it was held that membership in the pro-Nazi German-American Bund prior to naturalization was insufficient to support a finding that citizenship had been fraudulently obtained when the applicant swore his support of the United States Constitution.

think that a court should not assume to cancel the priceless benefits of citizenship when its jurisdiction to do so rests on hearsay so unconvincing as that presented to the New Jersey court."[87]

For the quiet, conservative members of the Learned Hand court, Thomas Swan's activism and importance in asserting aliens' rights was exceptional. On other subjects, Swan, Augustus Hand, and Chase did not write the types of opinions that cause other courts and judges to take notice. True, their attitudes usually prevailed, but this was more a reflection of their ability to determine the outcome in particular cases than of an enduring impact on legal policy. Circumscribed in any case by their inferior status, their influence on law was further limited in time and scope by their conservative style.

The decisions summarized in this chapter point up also the limitations in labeling these judges as conservatives: Swan was a liberal in regard to aliens and Augustus Hand was in many respects a moderate, adhering to neither polar position. What was stressed earlier must be repeated once more, that the terms "liberal" and "conservative" have been used specifically to indicate relative positions on the court. As such, Swan and Chase were without doubt conservatives; in their decisions, with the important exception of Swan's on aliens, there was simply no area where they were more liberal than their colleagues, and in many they were decidedly less so.

[87] United States *ex rel.* Stabler v. Watkins, 168 F.2d 883, 885 (2d Cir. 1948).

7

The Battling New Dealers*

FROM NOT LONG AFTER JEROME FRANK TOOK HIS SEAT ON THE SECOND
Circuit until the retirement of Learned Hand a decade later, the outstanding feature of the court's work—except for the decisions handed
down—was the virtually uninterrupted friction between Judges Clark
and Frank, the court's junior members. After nine years of judicial
service with Clark, Frank expressed admiration for his colleague as a
judge and as a person, in one of his innumerable "Dear Charlie"
letters. "But," he went on, "somehow you seem to have obtained the
impression that I'm antagonistic to you. Through some fault of mine,
I got off on the wrong foot with you. I'd like to start again. I hope

* In writing about the relationship between Judges Clark and Frank, I
have been constantly faced with the problem of how to use the internal
memoranda of the court and the correspondence that have been made available to me. Some observers of the judicial scene are squeamish about publishing parts of letters and documents that reveal judicial conflict, some of it
of a personal nature; Professor Alpheus T. Mason was criticized (most
unfairly I believe) in certain quarters for some of the things he included in
his lively biography of Chief Justice Stone. On the one hand, nonjudicial
material often has a direct bearing on how and what decisions are made and
can shed light on a subject that is shrouded in the mystery and mythology of
law and courts. The relationship between Judge Clark and Judge Frank was
not merely a Second Circuit sideshow, irrelevant to the important business at
hand. It was an integral aspect of the Learned Hand court, going to the
innermost source of that institution's vitality. It is simply not possible to

that, during the next year, you'll let me try."[1] They did not have to wait another year to see whether their relations would improve; ten days later they were again shooting off letters, and charges and rebuttals were flying back and forth.

---

write about the period without placing a certain emphasis upon this relationship. Illustrations from letters and memoranda document the conflict and give it perspective in a way that would not be possible if only the existence of disagreement were reported without proof being supplied. On the other hand, in the midst of a battle a judge, like anybody else, can get carried away and write something gratuitous, which because of its bitterness or anger or sarcasm might seem especially quotable years later. I have tried not to include any such material, because I do not think it truly conveys the continuing relations on this remarkable court.

On balance, I suppose, I have included more than others would, a reflection of my judgment that what went on between the two New Deal judges was central to the operations of the court. In this I may be expressing the attitude of a political scientist, which would be different from that of a lawyer. If so, all the better, for presumably social scientists studying courts and judges should have their own approach to the subject.

[1] JNF to CEC, June 1, 1950. Frank's letter was part of the correspondence over the *Sacher* contempt case, which is discussed in the next chapter. Attempts at "reconciliation" were not unusual; after a year on the Second Circuit Frank wrote: "We seem not yet to have reached the end of our misunderstandings. I'm bent on clearing them up, if that's possible, so as to eliminate totally unjustified suspicions you still entertain about me in order that you and I can, as we should, work together without mental reservations concerning one another" (JNF to CEC, July 12, 1942). Again, from Frank to Clark on August 1, 1946: "From the point of view of the public interest or our own pleasure in our daily tasks, it would be calamitous if in our court there should develop anything remotely like the discord now rife in the Supreme Court. To prevent such a misfortune, I want to do everything I can."

All efforts—if this is what they can be called—to reduce disagreement failed, and perhaps it could not have been otherwise, given the real differences between them and the emotional and intellectual make-up of the two men. But the adverse effect on their relations of their mode of communication can hardly be exaggerated. They communicated very often, yet it seems that they hardly spoke to one another about their differences; letters may be a fine way to cement a friendship, particularly when physical separation leaves no alternative, but they are an awfully ineffective way of ending personal conflict. In general, as I have mentioned previously, judges (and others) are more likely to resolve conflict if they communicate directly and personally. Letters and memoranda tend to be guarded, at least when it comes to making concessions to the recipient; in the case of correspondents who disagree, they are strategic ploys; in the case of judges who disagree over matters before their court, they also are nit-picking exercises. Whatever the reasons for their continued use of a communications medium that exacerbated conflict—whether it was because they viewed their relations as a contest of wits or logic or because they felt less comfortable talking things over—they should have been aware of the appalling impact of their letter wars.

Selections from letters and memoranda included in Chapters 3 and 4 have already demonstrated that their incessant conflict contributed importantly to the life and style of the Learned Hand court.[2] Hardly anything relating to their activities during the 1940's was off limits to the combatants. Frank's course on fact-finding at the Yale Law School, Clark's work on the Supreme Court's Advisory Committee on the Federal Rules of Civil Procedure, relations with Supreme Court justices and with colleagues on the Second Circuit, the extrajudicial writings of both judges, their law clerks, and their writing styles—all these, and many other matters, figured at one time or another in their disagreements. If nothing else, the Second Circuit would have been a much duller bench without these New Dealers.

The fact that, at least as judges, Frank and Clark did not get along is surprising on two counts. In the first place, the scant literature on the Second Circuit gives no hint of the undercurrents of battle that constantly pervaded the court. John Frank, an astute observer of Supreme Court affairs, could write a journalistic article on America's "top commercial court" giving a picture of amity and serenity, both on the surface and below. This view has barely been disturbed by published recollections of several of Frank's law clerks and the handful of other writers on the court. Some of the lawyers and professors who paid attention to the Second Circuit were on friendly terms with one or the other protagonist and knew of their battles, and yet they have not revealed anything to indicate how things were between Clark and Frank. Actually, Judge Clark came about as close as anyone else to disclosing his relations with Frank when in his brief memorial for the *Yale Law Journal* he referred to "battles serious and absorbing" which "must loom large in retrospect."[3] Perhaps the explanation for avoiding a discussion of this sensitive subject in print is that lawyers believe such matters are unimportant or irrelevant in the context of a court's main responsibility of deciding cases. If this is the reason, there is something seriously lacking in the study of the judicial process.

The second surprising aspect of these disagreements is that they occurred so frequently and so intensely. Clark and Frank were New Dealers, certainly in the economic sense, and they were appointed by President Roosevelt to a bench consisting otherwise of Coolidge appointees, each of whom was to one degree or another skeptical

[2] I have not carefully studied the relations between Clark and Frank after 1951, until the latter's death in early 1957. It may be that they got along better over the last five or six years, particularly from the time that Clark became chief judge. However, the factors that made for conflict during their first decade together did not disappear in the 1950's and some of the cases and memoranda of this period that I have seen point to continued conflict.

[3] Clark, "Jerome N. Frank," *Yale Law Journal,* 66 (1957), 817.

about the New Deal. But there was something else in their intellectual make-up which made their combat unexpected. Each was a vigorous (and courageous) champion of the underdog and each had rejected the old mechanical jurisprudence, Frank in the 1930's as the author of *Law and the Modern Mind,* as the iconoclastic leader of the realist school, and as a member of the Yale faculty; Clark in the same period as Dean of the Yale Law School, a position that presumably gave him some say in Frank's appointment to the school.[4]

Yet, there is no paucity of explanations of their conduct on the bench; indeed, many of the factors that might have led to harmonious relations contributed to the intensification of conflict when they did disagree, as in a marriage gone wrong. For example, the fact that they were at Yale in the 1940's and shared associates and friends made things worse. Moreover, their styles and personalities, similar in many respects, widened the gap between them; each was combative, possessed it seems with inexhaustible energy for prolonging debate and with a comparable capacity and penchant for committing to writing whatever was believed in at a particular moment. Memoranda and letters flew back and forth; reading them now conjures up the picture of each man pacing in his chambers, holding the other's latest broadside in his hand, while rapidly dictating a new reply.[5] Clark, it is significant, felt insecure in verbal combat; his forte, as John Frank noted, was in "correspondence wars."[6] In Jerome Frank he found a formidable adversary.[7] Other factors that contributed to the character

[4] It is likely that Clark welcomed Frank's appointment to the Second Circuit. On August 7, 1940, Clark wrote to Attorney General Robert Jackson expressing the wish of the court that the vacancy on the bench not be filled so long as there remained a possibility that Judge Patterson would return. He added, "I know you will do your best to insure that we get a new member who is at once able and liberal in viewpoint," in the event Patterson stayed in Washington. Jerome Frank certainly fit the bill.

[5] It is evident that some of their letters were not mailed but were dispatched by messenger: letters sometimes bore the same date as the communications they were intended to answer.

[6] John P. Frank, "The Top U.S. Commercial Court," *Fortune* (January 1951), p. 108.

[7] The intellectual and physical energy invested in their correspondence is truly astounding; many of their letters were substantially longer than the average Second Circuit opinion. It must be kept in mind here that, at the same time, they were carrying their share of the court's work, writing an inordinate number of dissenting opinions, and also doing quite a bit of extrajudicial writing. Moreover, their correspondence was directly tied to the opinions they were writing. They were constantly criticizing each other's draft opinions and revising their own opinions to meet or to answer objections raised in the latest letter. Here is one illustration: first, Frank writing to Clark: "The third paragraph of your memo, as I understand it, comes to this: you've written an opinion stating that the plaintiff's letter . . . is not an

of their relations were their conflicting views about criminal justice, Clark's habit of bringing up old disputes, and Frank's rather irritating tendency to concentrate less on the broader issues than on minor points, dissecting them minutely, as if their arguments were exercises in logic or polemics.

But all of these matters served more to escalate conflict than to give birth to it. For the most part there was a single root cause, something which both men, and probably their colleagues, too, eventually recognized. On one subject which ordinarily would be of infrequent—and, at that, peripheral—importance in the business of a court of appeals, including the Second Circuit, Clark and Frank were in fundamental disagreement: they were far apart on questions of judicial procedure. Of course, each had secured much of his reputation for his work and writings on procedure, but this did not help at all. Nor did it serve as a cohesive factor that Clark and Frank had strongly challenged procedural assumptions and rules as they found them. Each critic had attacked a different status quo, Frank's more nebulous than his colleague's. Clark directed his criticism at the state of judicial procedure of the first third of this century—the separation of law and equity, the rules that encouraged piecemeal appeals, and the practices that contributed to delays in court. Substantively, his approach was largely unrelated to the jurisprudential ferment of the same period. For the defects he sought a procedural remedy and he found one, or so he believed, in the Federal Rules of Civil Procedure; this was a truly epic milestone in the struggle for judicial reform. Once the new

---

admission as to the contract price. But, if I dissent, then you'll change the opinion to state that that letter is an admission. I can't say that I admire such a decisional technique. Of course, if you employ it, I shan't mention your shift of position. But I wish it could be publicized as an illustration of the fact that when a court has a will it finds a way" (December 23, 1944). Clark replied the next day: "Truly I am surprised at your objection to what you call my 'decisional technique.' I had thought the real reason for a bench of several judges was the combined judgment of the many, and that there was a corresponding obligation for the members to try first to see if the differences of opinion could not be reconciled in various ways, including naturally some appropriate middle ground. Hence far from wishing to conceal my attempts at the result, I should be glad to have them made as public as possible. . . . Please add to the story anything you think pertinent. Fancy your going naive! Merry Christmas."

It is also clear that, as a result of their correspondence, separate opinions prepared after great effort were at times withdrawn. Another interesting thing to be noted is that, as argument quite often continued after the decision was handed down, revisions were made in their opinions after decision but prior to publication in the *Federal Reporter*. In view of all this it is truly remarkable that Clark and Frank and the entire court were able to handle the large volume of business with such great dispatch.

rules were adopted, the major battle for reform—at least at the federal level was won; what remained was the need to get the states to accept similar reforms in their judicial systems, and an effort to accomplish this end occupied Clark's attention throughout his judicial career. But it was also necessary to protect the new rules against attack by carping critics and the refusal of judges to properly abide by them. Once a heretic himself, Clark found no justification for the continued heresy of Judge Frank or for the other Second Circuit judges' lukewarm concern for the Federal Rules.[8]

Frank's approach to procedure was so much different. His incisive attacks against the old practices were founded not so much on their intrinsic inadequacy, although that was a factor, as on his unending belief that no set of rules should be permitted to dominate the judicial process, to the point that form would be more important than substance or that some procedural requirement would justify an injustice. He was the perennial heretic, equally the enemy of old and new rules, more so, however, when they were viewed as ends or in-flexible tools of judging. "I think reformers traduce their own basic ideals when they resist efforts to improve their improvements, so that a standpatter reformer is a paradox . . .,"[9] Frank wrote in answer to a complaint of Clark's that he had been hostile to one of the Second Circuit's rules.

In sum, the rule-skepticism of Frank clashed headlong with the Federal Rule-conservatism of Clark. True, the latter's attitude as expressed in one dissent was not far from that of Frank: "Procedure should be viewed simply as a means of doing justice, not as an end in itself or as something which requires vindication without respect to results; and the new rules were designed to afford not only speedy and efficient adjudication of actions on the merits, but also, wherever fair and possible, disposition of cases without the time and expense of trial."[10]

[8] In reply to Learned Hand's suggestion that he had been "too boister-ous" regarding a procedural issue, Clark wrote: "I suppose we procedure guys get too excited when our babies appear maimed" (CEC to LH, February 2, 1944).

[9] JNF to CEC, the date is unclear.

[10] MacDonald v. Du Maurier, 144 F.2d 696, 701 (2d Cir. 1944).

Justice Frankfurter, much noted of course for his own emphasis on procedural matters, distinguished his approach from that of Clark. While his concern with procedure was principally derived from a preoccupation with federal-state relations, Clark was "preoccupied with what I might call pro-cedure as such" (letter to CEC, February 19, 1952). There are those who would disagree with Frankfurter's characterization of his own position; in a letter to Clark (November 10, 1944), Thomas Reed Powell referred to "the legal objectivity of Felix, who never cares where he lands so long as the flight is free from mishaps."

But, for the most part, Judge Clark rigorously defended procedural rules irrespective of results. As Judge Frank taunted in
dissenting from a Clark opinion:

> Procedure, we have often heard, should be but the "handmaid"
> of justice. I think that here the servant has achieved mastery. My
> colleagues . . . overlook Rule I which says that the purpose of all
> the Rules is "to secure the just, speedy, and inexpensive determi-
> nation of every action." If interpreted constantly with that purpose
> in mind, the Rules will represent an admirable achievement.
> Otherwise they will become but one more of the procedural "re-
> forms" which have earned justified criticism of the courts.[11]

Their differences over procedure formed a pattern. As Clark put
it mildly in his memorial, "if we differed, he and I, it tended to be
here, where he felt that my aspirations for a uniform procedure,
impartial as to all, were likely to rest heavily on some poor person not
prepared therefor, and that such a person must be protected, whatever future inconsistencies might come back to trouble us."[12] In an
internal memorandum four years earlier he put it more directly: "we
are utterly unreal if we do not recognize differences in approach to
procedural rules. I have no reason to criticize Jerry's approach, for it
is part of his personal judicial activity, with which I have no right to
interfere. But he has made no secret—in books as elsewhere—of his
impatience with procedural uniformity; and certainly he does not feel
the compulsion which I as a Reporter to the Committee and as a
teacher in the field do to make the rules workable."[13] Apart from some

---

[11] Clark v. Taylor, 163 F.2d 940, 952–53 (2d Cir. 1947). Frank used
similar language in other opinions in deriding Clark's position on procedure.
The witticism about procedure being the handmaiden of justice is an
especially potent (and perhaps vicious) jab at Clark. In 1938 Clark had given a
lecture on procedure titled "The Handmaid of Justice," in which he expressed
ideas similar to those later articulated by Frank. Of course in 1938 Clark
was not yet a judge; and the new Federal Rules had not yet been "mis-
treated" by some federal judges. In the lecture Clark said: "A handmaid, no
matter how devoted, seems never averse to becoming mistress of a household
should opportunity offer. Just so do rules of procedure tend to assume a too
obtrusive place in the attentions of judges and lawyers—unless, indeed, they
are continually restricted to their proper and subordinate role." The lecture
is reprinted in a collection of Clark's essays put out two years after his death
by two of his law clerks (Charles Alan Wright and Harry M. Reasoner [eds.],
Procedure—The Handmaid of Justice [St. Paul, Minn.: West Publishing Co.,
1965]; the quotation may be found on p. 69).

[12] Clark, "Jerome N. Frank," p. 818.

[13] Memorandum in Malman v. U.S., February 4, 1953.

caustic remarks in his opinions,[14] in his writings Judge Frank was guarded in his criticism of Clark. Concluding a chapter in *Courts on Trial* denouncing "procedural reformers," he parenthetically exempted from his scathing criticism "some of these reformers, among them my colleague, Judge Charles E. Clark."[15]

Obviously Frank's criticism in *Courts on Trial* applied about as much to Clark as to any other procedural reformer. Since Frank had little fear of public combat and he regularly derided other writers in his books and articles, the likely explanations for the misleading exception of Clark are that he wanted to avoid increased friction between him and his colleague and also that he believed it improper to criticize the views of another judge outside of the opportunities provided in judicial opinions. In any case, Clark was not persuaded that he was not among those Frank had in mind; in a memorandum in a case in which he sat with Frank he commented on the "contempt expressed for all naive procedure reformers in Chapter Seven of the book."[16]

Perhaps because he wrote more directly on procedure, and in his textbooks on pleading and code pleading reported and commented on cases dealing with procedural issues, Clark was more openly critical of Second Circuit decisions in his outside writings than was Frank.

Clark believed that Frank used his course on fact-finding at Yale to ridicule his opinions and this subject came up several times during the 1940's. Thus in a memorandum in a case heard by Augustus Hand and the two "Yale" judges, he noted that the course was "designed to point up the deficiencies of the undersigned and other colleagues in treating facts in heretofore decided cases."[17] Frank quickly wrote back "to avoid the appearance of acquiescence in your thoroughly mistaken intimation (made, I hope, facetiously . . .) that my course at Yale is 'designed' (or used)," etc. But he did not attempt to rebut the charge specifically. The same issue also arose, as we shall see, in the course of their heated battle over the harmless error rule in criminal cases. Clark may have gotten the impression that Frank's teaching was critical of him from members of the Yale Law faculty or from some of his law clerks, all of whom came from Yale.

[14] For example, Judge Frank concurring in Rieser v. Baltimore & Ohio R., 224 F.2d 198, 206 (2d Cir. 1955): "I believe Judge Clark is seeing ghosts when he asserts that, should the Supreme Court agree with Judge Hand . . . many of the Rules would perish. Previous similar expressions of apprehension by Judge Clark about the death of most of the Rules, as a result of decisions which he deemed unfortunate, have proved unfounded."

[15] Jerome N. Frank, *Courts on Trial* (Princeton, N.J.: Princeton University Press, 1949), p. 107.

[16] Pabellon v. Grace, July 20, 1951.

[17] McComb v. Utica Knitting Co., December 15, 1947.

It would take a volume to detail the various quarrels these judges had over rules and procedure. They disagreed over the summary judgment rule, which permits the trial judge to give judgment for the defendant, without a trial, on the basis of the papers that have been submitted. Clark had advocated such a procedure long before he came to the bench as a means of avoiding patently baseless litigation and streamlining the judicial process. He also felt that where summary judgment was granted, appellate judges should not lightly reverse and order a trial. Frank was wary of allowing trial judges such a broad discretion and it was this issue that led to the remarkable dispute in 1946 in the case of *Arnstein v. Porter*,[18] which was discussed in Chapter 4.

The two judges were on opposite sides on special verdicts, though this procedural issue came up in only a few cases. Under the special verdict rule, the trial judge submits individual specific fact questions to the jury. On the basis of the answers given by the jury and the controlling legal principles, the judge then orders judgment. Frank firmly believed, as he had advocated in his nonjudicial writings, that special verdict—or "fact verdicts" as he chose to call them—were preferable to general verdicts in civil suits. Where a jury returns the latter, he contended, "it usually has the power utterly to ignore what the judge instructs it concerning the substantive legal rules."[19] Clark might have been expected to go along on this subject, since the device was specifically provided for in the Federal Rules and it does by and large serve to simplify procedure. But in one opinion he expressed reservations as to the practice, particularly "in a relatively simple factual situation . . . where the details asked for may not be the whole story."[20]

In a number of patent cases there was especially sharp argument over whether courts, under the Federal Declaratory Judgments Act, could decide on the issue of validity even though there was no dispute as to infringement. In *Cover v. Schwartz,* Judge Frank, supported by

[18] 154 F.2d 464 (2d Cir. 1946). In the 1952 edition of his casebook, *Cases on Modern Pleading,* Clark quotes from two opinions by Judge Frank dealing with summary judgment and cites two other cases critical of the rule, and then comments: "Those statements by appellate courts then become cliches of trial courts" (p. 523).

[19] Skidmore v. Baltimore & Ohio R., 167 F.2d 54, 57 (2d Cir. 1948). Frank's opinion for the court is a full explication of his views on the subject.

[20] Morris v. Pennsylvania R., 187 F.2d 837, 841 (2d Cir. 1951). In a concurring opinion Judge Frank disagreed with the tenor of Clark's "general remarks about the value and purpose of special verdicts" (p. 843). They apparently had disagreed much earlier on this issue, for in a letter (August 12, 1946) reviewing their differences over the rules, Frank, referring to special verdicts, asked, "in that respect, which of us is inimical to the Rules?"

Learned Hand, took the position that a federal court could not decide the validity question alone because under the Constitution it had jurisdiction to decide "cases and controversies" and thus it could not give advisory opinions. The statute, Frank conceded, "affords a new remedy of inestimable value. But that remedy must stay within the constitutional bounds of jurisdiction."[21] Clark had long championed use of declaratory judgments as a way of insuring that issues would be decided and not avoided: "The pain of decision should not be avoided by reliance on some procedural technicality,"[22] he contended in a sharp dissenting opinion.

> Clearly, in the light of the authorities and the federal rules of civil procedure, this is not a decision compelled by something outside the court; it represents a purely human choice, and must go back to some felt demand of policy. . . . I am clear that it is at best an unnecessary result; to copper-rivet it in terms of jurisdiction seems to me an undesirable argumentative technique, as well as peculiarly unfortunate in forcing the court into a juristic straitjacket.[23]

Despite repeated protests against the *Cover* ruling[24] and his involvement of Professor Borchard of the Yale Law School,[25] long the

[21] 133 F.2d 541, 544 (2d Cir. 1943).

[22] *Ibid.*, p. 550. The phrase "procedural technicality" sounds strange coming from Clark.

[23] *Ibid.*, p. 547.

[24] For example, concurring in McCurrach v. Cheney Bros., 152 F.2d 365 (2d Cir. 1945) and dissenting in Addressograph-Multigraph Corp. v. Cooper, 156 F.2d 483 (2d Cir. 1946). Judge Clark believed that the "*Cover* case has been carefully considered by both Learned and you, but . . . nothing shows any such consideration by any other members of the court" (CEC to JNF, March 1, 1945). He also felt that the Supreme Court did not go along with the ruling. Clark was in error as to the views of the other judges, as decisions of the Second Circuit demonstrate and he indirectly recognized in the same letter to Frank: "How far I should concur in what has seemed to me always the biggest defect of the Second Circuit, known and criticized for years in other connections than merely this one, namely, the avoidance of adjudication by narrow, confining, and unconvincing jurisdictional prohibitions, of course is a problem. It is perhaps more so for me than for others, since I have spent practically a lifetime of teaching and writing objecting to just this sort of unundertanding limitation on judicial action."
As to the Supreme Court, a footnote in Altvater v. Freeman, 319 U.S. 359, 363, n. 2 (1943) implied acceptance of Cover.

[25] The Cover decision provoked a round of correspondence among Borchard, Clark, and Frank; the letters between the two judges raised the question of reliance on outside authorities (Borchard), a subject which was discussed in Chapter 4. In a letter to Borchard (January 9, 1943) Clark referred to the Professor's exchange with Frank: "I really feel that I have relinquished the torch to someone who can do a better job on Jerry than I

most active proponent of declaratory judgments, Clark's position did not prevail.

The most intense, most publicized, most far-reaching and long-lasting of the Frank-Clark procedural battles involved the appealability of trial court orders. Significantly, this was a matter that concerned Clark from the moment that he came to the Second Circuit. In addition, Clark was as much in disagreement with Learned Hand in this area as he was with Frank. The subject of appealability, final judgments, and interlocutory appeals is complex and confusing, as numerous judicial decisions and the discussion of it in *Moore's Federal Practice* attest.[26] Understanding of the issue as it was debated on the Second Circuit is complicated by the fact that during the 1940's, as a result of the strong division on the court, the relevant Federal Rule 54(b) was amended. Subsequent to the revision, Judges Clark, Frank, and Learned Hand took positions substantially different from their earlier ones. Until 1948 or so, Clark was opposed to interlocutory appeals while the others were more tolerant of them; after 1948 the positions were largely reversed.

Generally, in the federal courts, except for a few statutory provisions permitting them, interlocutory orders are not permitted. To be appealed, trial court orders must be final. In relatively simple cases this requirement does not raise problems. Difficulties come up when a single action involves multiple claims. Then the issue is whether all of the claims must be disposed of before an appeal can be taken or whether individual claims be separated from the rest so that when they are decided they can be appealed even though judgment has not been rendered on the other claims. A major argument against separate or "piecemeal" appeals is that they would burden appellate courts with additional (but unnecessary) work and would also lead to delays in deciding cases. On the other hand, at times these appeals might be useful, as when a delay in appeal could ultimately mean that the entire lawsuit would have to be tried over if the appellate court upset a single order.

---

can myself." Earlier (January 4, 1943) Borchard wrote to Clark that he had answered Frank that all he could do about the argument was to "refer the case to the highest court of appeals, the nonbelligerent editors of the *Yale Law Journal*. There I presume it will be written up." There it was written up, in a student law note, with the "appeal" being decided in Clark's favor (52 [1943], 909). In the same volume of the *Journal* Borchard wrote a long article on declaratory judgments conceived, no doubt, before the Cover appeal arose. In a footnote he referred to Judge Clark's "strong dissenting opinion," which seems "sounder" than the majority opinion. Edwin Borchard, "Challenging 'Penal' Statutes by Declaratory Action" (*ibid.*, pp. 445, 449, n. 10).

[26] See 6 *Moore's Federal Practice*, 2d ed., pp. 162–292.

Prior to the adoption of the Federal Rules of Civil Procedure, each cause was regarded as a single judicial unit, irrespective of the number of claims, and thus an appeal could be taken only after the entire unit was adjudicated. Rule 54 (b) provided that, where multiple claims were presented, the trial court could separately enter a judgment disposing of a particular claim. When this was done, the trial court action respecting that claim was terminated and the parties could appeal.

Judge Clark and Professor Moore interpreted the new rules as permissive, giving the trial judge the discretion to render judgment, though he was not required to do so; the single unit approach had been modified by the new rule, but it was not abandoned. Moreover, even when the trial judge entered an order respecting a claim, a court of appeals did not have to allow an appeal when it regarded the order as not disposing of the entire claim or cause of action. This issue troubled Judge Clark almost from the moment he came to the bench[27] and it was a matter of great contention on the Second Circuit for almost a decade. The court rendered a number of contradictory decisions which caused a great deal of confusion in the circuit and elsewhere, as a result of which the original rule was amended.

Judges Frank and Clark clashed sharply in several early cases in which the issue of appealability was raised. In 1943, in *Audi Vision Inc. v. R.C.A. Manufacturing Co.,* Judge Clark, writing for the court, dismissed the appeal because the finality requirement had not been met and he made clear his broad opposition to interlocutory appeals.

Interlocutory appeals in cases other than those provided by statute at times seem appealing as affording opportunity for the quick correction of errors which may have occurred in the course of the proceedings below. And since any general rule is always subject to exceptions, undoubtedly there will be times when in the actual posture of a case a short-cut ruling may be helpful. But there seems no question that in the long run fragmentary disposal of what is essentially one matter is unfortunate not merely for the waste of time and expense caused the parties and the courts, but because of the mischance of differing dispositions of what is essentially a single controlling issue. Moreover, as experience under certain practices permitting such appeals shows, there is an unfortunate tendency under such a system to stress decisions on pure points of procedure in the hope that these may shorten

[27] See his reluctant concurring opinion in Collins v. Metro-Goldwyn Pictures Corp., 106 F.2d 83, 86 (2d Cir. 1939). He later withdrew his "somewhat qualified support" of the decision in Collins in favor of appealability in Musher Foundation, Inc. v. Alba Trading Co., 127 F.2d 9, 13 (2d Cir. 1942, dissenting opinion).

or evade a trial, but with the unfortunate consequence of shifting emphasis from merits to form.[28]

Judge Frank, who was far more tolerant of permitting appeals, concurred because there was no doubt that the appeal was interlocutory. But he accused Clark of discussing the merits of the case while denying that the appellate court had jurisdiction. And he used his opinion in an unusual way, as a forum for "recommending changes in the statutes so as to confer on the courts of appeals discretion to allow interlocutory appeals where necessary to prevent substantial injustice."[29] In defending his proposal, Frank denied that it would burden the courts of appeals. But, "if justice requires that we should be given such discretion, we should be glad to take on the additional labors, if any; should they prove to be too great, doubtless Congress would provide for the appointment of additional judges."[30]

Judge Frank pressed for legislation in other opinions, and while his proposal did not get wide support in the 1940's,[31] it may have led to the amendment of Rule 54 (b); when the new rule did not satisfy him, as we shall see, Frank revised and reintroduced his recommendation. Legislation incorporating much of his proposal was adopted by Congress in the 1950's.

The issue of finality divided Judges Clark and Frank in several cases in which there were complications because the litigation involved both federal and non-federal claims.[32] In *Zalkind v. Scheinman*[33] a majority consisting of Learned Hand and Frank held that two claims, a federal one for patent infringement and a nonfederal one for damages prior to the issuance of the patent, were sufficiently distinct to oust

[28] 136 F.2d 621, 624–25 (2d Cir. 1943).

[29] *Ibid.*, p. 625. Frank went on: "The making of recommendations in judicial opinions for statutory changes has distinguished precedent." But the illustrations given in a footnote do not directly support this contention, and while the judge's action may not have been improper, as Clark believed, it certainly was virtually unprecedented.

[30] *Ibid.*, p. 627.

[31] In a letter to Chase (August 9, 1951), Clark wrote: "Jerry's definite arguments presented some years ago to the House Judiciary Committee and to the Supreme Court and the Rules Committee really aroused no support whatsoever so far as I could see." Clark was discussing Frank's latest proposal for legislation.

[32] Apart from his strong views on finality, Judge Clark was equally insistent that when there was a viable federal claim, the federal courts had jurisdiction. His approach on this subject was directly related to his broad distrust of state courts and his belief that it was desirable to enlarge the jurisdiction of federal courts.

[33] 139 F.2d 895 (2d Cir. 1943).

federal jurisdiction over the latter. Accordingly, the trial judge's order striking out this claim was final and appealable. Frank's opinion was exceptionally sharp; as he had done in other cases, Frank charged Clark with going to the merits while holding that the court did not have jurisdiction. "Were we to follow the suggested course," he taunted, "we would create a new type of judge-made extra-statutory, appeals, i.e., we would invite appeals, to procure our advisory opinions, concerning matters not properly before us under the statute."[34]

Clark's dissent began with a concession: "Since my attempts to secure complete adjudication federalwise of all claims . . . have been found so unpersuasive by my colleagues . . . I have little excuse for writing more."[35] But he found reason to go on because "the leading academic authority has criticized our holdings quite unmercifully." He then went on to criticize Frank's proposal for legislation which had been urged once more, although in somewhat altered form in the majority opinion. To Clark, it was "doubtful as to whether a judicial opinion is a proper forum for the discussion of pros and cons of legislative reforms."[36]

In *Zalkind v. Scheinman,* Learned Hand strongly sided with Frank, apparently to the surprise of Clark. Actually, this was the pattern in other Clark-Frank procedural battles, as in their disagreement over summary judgment. During the early years, at least, Clark failed to grasp that Hand's attitude on matters procedural might have been arrived at independent of any "selling job" by Frank. While *Zalkind* was being decided he wrote to Hand, "I am still a little sorry that you did not give me an opportunity to argue the point somewhat with you before you accepted Jerry's views."[37] However, after the Chief Judge informed him that he had firm views of his own on interlocutory appeals, Clark conceded that his earlier appraisal was "not the case."[38] We shall return to the relationship between Learned Hand and Frank later in this chapter when the role played by the four Coolidge judges in the battles on the Second Circuit is examined.

The argument over finality continued for the next several years[39] while the Advisory Committee considered proposals to revise the rule. A new Rule 54(b) was adopted and it went into effect in 1948, but even

[34] *Ibid.,* p. 904.
[35] *Ibid.,* p. 905.
[36] *Ibid.,* p. 907.
[37] CEC to LH, November 17, 1943.
[38] CEC to LH, November 23, 1943.
[39] For example, Libbey-Owens-Ford Glass Co. v. Sylvania Industrial Corp., 154 F.2d 814 (2d Cir. 1946). Clark and Swan were in the majority, Frank dissented. The case was decided when the process of amending Rule 54(b) was almost concluded. Yet Clark ends his opinion for the court defending the old rule; he says that while there was "some initial confusion as to the

this did not serve to end the conflict over the original rule.[40] The amended rule provided that in the case of multiple claims the trial judge "may direct the entry of a final judgment upon one or more but less than all of the claims only upon an express determination that there is no just reason for delay and upon an express direction for the entry of judgment. In the absence of such determination . . . any order . . . which adjudicates less than all the claims shall not terminate the action as to any of the claims."

---

working of Federal Rule 54(b)," this "has now been settled by the precedents. . . . The law now carries out the historic federal policy . . . the policy is the fruit of experience and embodies a general judgment which is not to be cast aside for an occasional aberrant case. . . . And even if there be individual judicial doubts about the policy, it nevertheless seems both desirable and necessary that it be followed, for that is the essence of a procedure uniform throughout the country" (p. 817).

To Judge Frank, in dissent, the majority "brushed to one side at least seven recent decisions of the Supreme Court, together with a half-dozen or more of our own" (p. 817).

Clark v. Taylor, 163 F.2d 940 (2d Cir. 1947), decided before new Rule 54(b) went into effect, also had a majority opinion by Clark (joined by Chase), ruling against appealability, and a dissent by Frank. The latter was very bitter: "I think that a ruling, like that of my colleagues in this case . . . ought not to be made merely to afford satisfaction to those interested in maintaining the aesthetic proportions of a procedural theory. More important than delight in such verbal symmetry . . . is the avoidance of needless unfairness to litigants. A legal theory no matter how beautiful in outward form, cannot be a wise theory, if, in actual practice, it works substantial injustice" (p. 951).

[40] In Dickinson v. Mulligan, 173 F.2d 738 (2d Cir. 1949), a panel composed of Learned Hand, Swan, and Frank disagreed with the ruling in Clark v. Taylor (see the preceding note). But in an opinion by Learned Hand, the decision in Clark v. Taylor was accepted because "it appears to all three of us in the present court most undesirable to repudiate a precedent so established" (p. 741). The court then invited the Supreme Court to reverse its ruling and, by implication, Clark v. Taylor also. The Supreme Court accepted the invitation and reversed in Dickinson v. Petroleum Conversion Corp., 338 U.S. 507 (1950).

Clark v. Taylor and Dickinson v. Mulligan are quite troublesome. Why did Frank go along with the majority in Dickinson after years of adhering to different views on finality? Was it because in this case Judge Clark was not on the panel? Or because he got his colleagues to repudiate Clark v. Taylor and to suggest Supreme Court reversal? The repudiation of the earlier decision also raises questions. Frank and Chase heard both appeals; if two judges believe that a recent decision of a panel on which they sat was wrong, are they bound to accept it as a "precedent." Furthermore, how are we to understand the votes of Judge Chase, who was with the majority in both cases?

Perhaps Clark was right, as he complained many times, that Dickinson did not present the same issue as the earlier appeal. As we have noted, Frank and Learned Hand were close on procedural questions; they may have deliberately decided Dickinson as they did in order to undermine Clark's

To a layman, at least, the new rule was much clearer than its predecessor and could have been expected to eliminate the confusion and conflict on the Second Circuit. It generally left it up to the district court to set the status of its orders; those that were declared final would be appealable, all others would be interlocutory. In some instances this would mean a liberalization of the final judgment rule while in others its effect would be to restrict appeals. This was the view of Clark and Moore, but for reasons that are hard to grasp it was not the position of either Learned Hand or Jerome Frank. Actually, the new rule went a long way toward accepting the arguments of these two judges. "Now to a considerable extent," Clark wrote to Chase, "Moore and I have . . . accepted and applied the views of L.H. and J.W.F. to make some of these matters appealable."[41]

---

position. In any case, they did not have to handle this appeal in the manner they did.

The Second Circuit decisions in Clark v. Taylor and Dickinson v. Mulligan and the Supreme Court ruling in the appeal from the latter were made under the old rule. Presumably the 1948 amendment created a new situation not controlled by the old rulings. In Republic of China v. American Express, 190 F.2d 334 (2d Cir. 1951), Judge Frank, supported by Learned Hand and Chase, held that because the trial judge did not make a certificate, an order that would have been appealable under the former rule could not be appealed. Rather gratuitously, Frank noted the Supreme Court action in Dickinson, which he interpreted as a reversal of Clark v. Taylor also (p. 337). Clark, who already was bitter over the treatment accorded him by his colleagues in Dickinson, felt that Frank had needlessly reopened the old dispute. In a letter to Chase he complained that since the Supreme Court decision in Dickinson, "Jerry seems to have been thirsting to draw the apparently deep personal satisfaction he felt by asserting that the Supreme Court thus overruled our decision in Clark v. Taylor, although it was in definite accord with the statement we had made on the exact point at issue. The protests I have uttered headed him off from making such a statement in an opinion, notably in P. Beirsdorf & Co. v. McGohey. . . . He took out his statement there, but then inserted it in considerably expanded form in the Republic of China case, which did strike me as hitting below the belt, since I was not in that case to meet the issue directly. Moreover, as J. W. Moore has pointed out, it would seem to me that the amendment to Rule 54 was specifically for taking care of such rather useless debates as in Clark v. Taylor; and except as a matter of personal privilege and vindication there wasn't much use to rehash the matter over again" (CEC to HBC, August 9, 1951).

[41] CEC to HBC, August 9, 1951. Why were Clark and Moore willing to compromise? Clark definitely did not come around to Frank's views; in opinion after opinion he had specifically rejected them. The likely explanation is that Clark and Moore wanted to eliminate the pressure from Frank's campaign to get legislation. It is significant that the first draft proposal for an amended rule was prepared by the Advisory Committee on the Federal Rules, of which Clark was Reporter, in the spring of 1944, which was not long after Frank proposed congressional action.

But Hand and Frank would not accept any "olive branches"[42] and the fight blazed anew, more intense than ever. Three cases that were decided by the Second Circuit after Learned Hand stepped down as chief judge illustrate the new stage of the conflict. In each of these cases the question before the court was whether an order that was interlocutory under the old Rule 54 (b) was appealable under the amendment if the trial judge certified that it was final.

The first case was *Pabellon v. Grace Line, Inc.*,[43] where the question might have been avoided. The three sitting judges, Chase, Clark, and Frank, agreed that an order of the trial court was appealable under the old rule. In addition, to satisfy the new rule, the district judge had certified that his order was final. Since there was no real issue as to appealability, no party raised the issue on appeal. But in the conference after argument, the judges "discussed [it] among ourselves, since we must be sure of our own jurisdiction before we act."[44] In short, Frank and Clark could not control their impulses to disagree over finality, even where there was an easy way out.

In his opinion for the court, Clark called the amendment of Rule 54 (b) an "expansive clarification,"[45] by which he meant that its intention was to allow appeals from certain orders that previously were nonappealable. Judge Frank, in a concurring opinion, took issue with this "dictum." He insisted that

> this court has no jurisdiction of appeals . . . other than that created by Sec. 1291 [28 U.S.C.A.], which provides: "the courts of appeals shall have jurisdiction of appeals from all final decisions of the district courts . . ." Consequently, I do not agree with Judge Clark's dictum that amended Rule 54 (b) may be interpreted to authorize a trial judge, by making a "determination," to render final and appealable an order which, absent that Rule, would have been interlocutory and not appealable under Sec. 1291. For if that Rule were so interpreted, then I think it would be invalid, as beyond the statutory power of the Supreme Court.[46]

This position was echoed eight days later by Learned Hand in *Flegenheimer v. General Mills,* a case heard by him, Swan, and Augustus Hand. Clark's interpretation of the rule in *Pabellon* was obiter and hence the second panel did not "feel forced, in accordance with our usual practice, to yield to it, though we did not agree."[47] To

---

[42] *Ibid.*
[43] 191 F.2d 169 (2d Cir. 1951).
[44] *Ibid.,* p. 173.
[45] *Ibid.,* p. 174.
[46] *Ibid.,* p. 176.
[47] Flegenheimer v. General Mills, Inc., 191 F.2d 237, 241 (2d Cir. 1951).

accept Clark's view would result in a strange anomaly, for

> Although there are of course abundant instances where appellate courts are granted a discretion as to what they will review, so far as we know, this would be unique, if it conferred a power upon a lower court to determine the jurisdiction of a higher court. Had the Supreme Court intended so revolutionary an inversion of what had been the uniform custom theretofore, we believe that it would have expressed its intent less indirectly; and that conclusion is reinforced when we remember the self-denying ordinance which it imposed upon itself in Rule 82. No doubt the answer is not as clear as one might wish; else the courts would not be so at odds as they are. In the end the Supreme Court will no doubt have to pass upon it; meanwhile we can only follow what light we have.[48]

Hand's opinion was severely criticized by Professor Moore as a "tortured construction of the Rule";[49] Clark's reaction was open bitterness. Not only did he believe that his attempt to work out a fair approach to the subject was being subverted, he also felt that Hand's rejection of his opinion of a week earlier was a calculated insult. To Judge Chase he wrote: "Do you see what Learned Hand has been doing . . .? I don't know whether to laugh or cry over what seems to be almost a pursuit of your humble servant by our distinguished colleagues who seem ready with a sledge hammer to smash my poor feeble attempts—now continued over some years on the Rules Committee and elsewhere—to work out a rule of appeal that anybody, even lawyers, can understand."[50] A memorandum from Swan acclaiming an opinion he had written as "a magnificent job" which "does credit to the court and to you personally,"[51] was for Clark "a shot in the arm, for several developments were tending to get me down." The principal one was Hand's opinion, "about which I rather wanted to speak to you. It did seem to me rather strange medicine for a colleague's work—without notice or any consultation."[52]

It was certain that Clark would use the first opportunity presented to him to reply to Learned Hand; he found one before 1951 was out. Actually the case, *Lopinsky v. Hertz-Drive-Ur-Self System*,[53] was an easy one to decide and ordinarily would not have been a forum for exposition of opinion on interlocutory appeals. In a per curiam

---

[48] *Ibid.* Rule 82 provides: "These rules shall not be construed to extend or limit the jurisdiction of the United States District Courts or the venue of actions therein."

[49] 6 *Moore's Federal Practice,* 2d edition, 212.

[50] CEC to HBC, August 9, 1951.

[51] TWS to CEC; the probable date was August 18 or 19, 1951.

[52] CEC to TWS, August 21, 1951.

[53] 194 F.2d 422 (2d Cir. 1951).

opinion, Judges Swan and Augustus Hand held that the judgment of the district court was appealable. But "in view of developments in this Circuit," Clark found the ruling an excuse for writing a concurring opinion which turned out to be a strong rejection of Learned Hand's position.

Hand's opinion in *Pabellon* had "provided no documentation for its holding either in the past history of rule-making or in precedents" and it "necessarily put in jeopardy fully a third of the federal civil rules."[54] Clark therefore found it necessary to protect the rules because, while an attack against a federal statute automatically brought forth its defense by the Attorney General, there was no procedure for protecting the rules. Most of Clark's opinion described the development of the rules and showed that there was ample authority for the promulgation of rules relating to appeals. Hand's repudiation of Clark's opinion of the previous week was "confusing not only to the public, but also to colleagues who have no notice of the impending doom before it appears in print." To this was appended the footnote: "Nor is the blow softened by describing opprobriously a colleague's hard work as only 'dictum.' "[55] Most of the other courts of appeals sided with Judge Clark, yet the argument continued to rage on the Second Circuit[56] until 1956 when the Supreme Court resolved at least the immediate issue by accepting the Clark position.[57]

Before leaving this subject, which more than any other continually occupied the attention of Judges Clark and Frank for more than a decade, two sidelights to the dispute over finality warrant attention. As we have seen, from the early 1940's on, Jerome Frank used his opinions to advocate legislation granting the courts of appeals some discretionary jurisdiction to hear appeals from orders that otherwise would not be appealable. Except for the 1946 amendment of Rule 54 (b), this effort at first met with little direct success. When Frank found the revised rule not to his own liking and he and Clark resumed the old battle, he returned to his proposal for congressional reform. In *Pabellon* he detailed the bill that he wanted passed; it was closely patterned after the certiorari jurisdiction of the Supreme Court.

[54] *Ibid.*, pp. 424–25.
[55] *Ibid.*, p. 429 and n. 16.
[56] For example, Rieser v. Baltimore & Ohio R., 224 F.2d 198 (2d Cir. 1955). Clark's opinion for the court repeated his earlier views; Frank reluctantly concurred in the result. As he explained, "I do so because I feel constrained by decisions in very recent cases in this circuit. Had I been sitting in those cases, I would have dissented. For those decisions overruled the carefully thought-out decision in *Flegenheimer v. General Mills* . . . where the opinion was by our wisest and most experienced living judge, Learned Hand" (pp. 205–6).
[57] Sears Roebuck & Co. v. Mackey, 354 U.S. 527 (1956).

While the Second Circuit was embroiled in the *Pabellon-Flegen-heimer-Lopinsky* battles in the latter part of 1951, Judge Frank prevailed upon the court's new chief judge, Judge Swan, to submit his proposal to the Judicial Conference of the United States for consideration at its September meeting.[58] Clark's reaction was swift: he submitted a "substantial memorandum" to the conference "in opposition, both to the proposal itself and to the ouster of the Advisory Committee from a matter upon which it has worked for years with satisfactory outcome in the new amended Federal Rule 54 (b)."[59] Clark probably hoped that his opposition would ward off action, but his colleague enlisted powerful support from, among others, Learned Hand and, surprisingly, Professor Moore,[60] in addition to Justice Frankfurter and other members of the Supreme Court. Accordingly Clark backed down somewhat, disclaiming "any wish on my part to stop the Conference from considering the matter through some new committee of its own, if now with the information as to background before it, that course seems most feasible."[61]

The Judicial Conference, no doubt eschewing direct involvement in the controversy, set up a special committee under the chairmanship of Judge Parker of the Fourth Circuit to look into the matter. This committee got the views of federal judges from throughout the country and then reported that it was unanimously opposed to Frank's draft legislation. This recommendation was accepted by the Judicial Conference, which also continued the committee to examine other problems concerning interlocutory appeals. In 1953 it suggested that interlocutory appeals be permitted where both the trial judge and the court of appeals agree that an immediate appeal would materially advance the ultimate disposition of the litigation. This proposal was adopted by the Judicial Conference and after several more years the

[58] Swan sent Frank's recommendation to Henry Chandler, Director of the Administrative Office of United States Courts. The Chief Judge wrote: "You will note that Judge Clark wishes to file a memorandum in opposition to Judge Frank's proposal." He went on to say that "the proposal has not been considered by the judges of the Second Circuit in conference."

[59] CEC to Henry Chandler, September 12, 1951. It appears from subsequent correspondence between Clark and Justice Frankfurter (see n. 61) that Frank responded to Clark's memorandum and that, in turn, this elicited a second reply from Clark.

[60] Dissenting from a per curiam (Chase and Clark) dismissal of an appeal, Judge Frank wrote in 1949: "It is of interest that Professor Moore, who has played an important part in the drafting of the Rules, has joined in proposing a statutory amendment which would permit far more interlocutory appeals" (American Machine & Metals, Inc. v. De Bothezat Impeller Co., 173 F.2d 890, 892–93).

[61] CEC to Justice Frankfurter, September 26, 1951.

Interlocutory Appeals Act was passed by Congress in 1958, a year after Judge Frank died. [62]

While the evidence is not altogether clear, the internecine conflict in 1951 over interlocutory appeals probably led to a curious criticism of Judge Clark by Justice Frankfurter. In September of 1954, Frankfurter was in New Haven and visited at the Clarks'. In the midst of some light conversation, the host remarked that his wife occasionally chided him for rudeness; the Justice immediately interjected that Clark had been rude in some of his opinions toward the Judges Hand.

Whatever the source of Frankfurter's view of Clark's relations with Learned and Augustus Hand (it may be surmised that it came from conversation or correspondence with Learned Hand; however, it is known that Frankfurter read the Second Circuit opinions that were sent to him as a member of the Supreme Court and this could have been his own interpretation) his criticism stung the "inferior" judge. Frankfurter was way off base, for in the entire ten-year period there is not a single line in any Clark opinion which can be fairly read as rude to Augustus Hand. Clark deeply respected the court's oldest member, an attitude which came across in the internal memoranda. As for Learned Hand, there was a rather small number of sharp exchanges, but the printed record contains nothing that can be fairly interpreted as rudeness. Judged by Supreme Court standards of the 1940's they seem rather mild.[63]

[62] The new statute was much narrower than the one proposed by Frank in 1951 and it generally has been interpreted in a restricted manner by the courts of appeals. In 1955, in a footnote in Rieser v. Baltimore & Ohio R., 224 F.2d 198, 207, n. 6, Judge Frank wrote that he, Learned Hand, and Moore "would prefer a less restricted new statute," one which did not require action by the district judge as a prerequisite for exercise by the appellate court of its jurisdiction. "Nevertheless," he concluded, "we think the proposed statute would be an important step forward."

Judge Clark discussed the development of the statute in two opinions: Fleischer v. Phillips, 264 F.2d 515, 517 (2d Cir. 1959) and Gottesman v. General Motors Corp., 268 F.2d 194, 196 (2d Cir. 1959).

Professor Wright has ascribed the requirement that trial judges certify their approval of interlocutory appeals to Judge Clark (Charles Alan Wright, "The Interlocutory Appeals Act of 1958," 23 *Federal Rules Decisions* 202, n. 19).

[63] Comparison with the Supreme Court is surely gratuitous and yet it is impelled by the harshness of Frankfurter's unjust criticism. In reply to Clark's written "defense," Frankfurter repeated "Holmes' dictum about judicial disagreements during his days here: 'We ought not to behave as though we were two cocks fighting on a dunghill.' " Judicial battle on the Supreme Court has far more often violated Holmes's dictum than anything that occurred on the Second Circuit, and this includes Frankfurter's conduct (as seen through his opinions) as well as that of other justices.

Clark felt impelled to "rehabilitate" himself and so he wrote a long reply to the "devastating" comment. As to Augustus Hand, he maintained, "I know there is absolutely nothing on my part which shows anything but the deepest regard, and very real affection." Then, "as to Learned, too, I think there can be found surprisingly little in view of his well-known explosive characteristics." The former chief judge was also "a past master in the prime art of rudeness." Clark then recited the *Pabellon-Flegenheimer-Lopinsky* sequence of 1951, which he regarded as what Frankfurter had in mind. His own opinion in the last of the cases was defended as a necessary response to Hand's *Flegenheimer* opinion, which was "highhanded and outrageous, both intellectually and personally, as affecting his relations with his brethren." The letter concluded:

> I referred above to Learned's ability to give and also to receive blows. My impression is that in this case he appreciated my efforts; at any rate our personal relations, so far as I know, are cordial and happy. . . . And I fancy his opinion of me would have gone down had I retreated from the joust made necessary by his challenge. Indeed, I wonder if he would be too happy at your protective concern for him. I think we are and will remain good friends. But thanks for the friendly advice; I shall re-examine anew, just as often as I can, all tendencies towards vigor and (or) rudeness.[64]

Irrespective of the accuracy of Frankfurter's remark or the situation between Learned Hand and Clark in the mid-1950's or earlier, indisputably Hand, and by and large the other three judges, were considerably closer to Jerome Frank than they were to Charles Clark. Quite often the four Coolidge appointees were innocent and silent bystanders, permitting the disputes to go on without becoming involved themselves. This was most true of Augustus Hand, Swan, and Chase in the course of the extended debate over interlocutory appeals; indeed, in this area it is difficult to account for the votes of these judges.

[64] CEC to Justice Frankfurter, September 29, 1954. Justice Frankfurter wrote back immediately and this time he was even more unfair than he was at the Clarks'. He began, "You have more in common with Jerry than some people might think," because "just as would be true of Jerry, a critical remark of mine uttered in a spirit of great friendliness would fetch a full-dress rebuttal from you. Being a great believer in the catharsis of expressing feelings and getting rid of it, instead of having it turn to acidity within, I am very glad you wrote me. But while I am about the business of ruffling your feathers I might as well make a good job of it" (Justice Frankfurter to CEC, October 1, 1954). And "a good job of it" he made as he went on to compound the original injustice.

At times, usually after disagreement had delayed handing down a ruling, one notes a sense of exasperation in the comments of the non-combatants, such as in a letter of Learned Hand to Clark: "After you and Jerry get through amending your opinions, and stop shouting, for God's sake file the opinions."[65] Or, after an incredibly long battle via letters and memoranda, from Judge Chase: "As you both know, I had hoped that you would be able to resolve your differences concerning Jerry's opinion in the above case [*Alaska Pacific Salmon v. Reynolds Metal Co.*]. But in spite of the earnest effort which has been made it is now apparent that you cannot. So I suppose the time has come when I ought to say more than I have as yet."[66] The final illustration, again from Learned Hand, is truly delightful:

> I like to dance in the moonlight as well as any man, but my wind is not as good as it once was, and I cannot keep time with the antiphonal strophe and antistrophe of my youthful colleagues. "When, as, and if" between you—and supposing that happy time shall ever arrive—you come to the point of exhaustion, I shall play upon the harp and timbrel and lift up my voice in praise to God. BUT, while all this agitating cerebration remains in parturition, I shall merely sit on the side lines, contemplate my navel, and repeat the syllable, OM.[67]

Perhaps it would have been a good thing had Clark's and Frank's colleagues intervened more often, for when they did they were able to get the opinions out even if they could not resolve the disagreement.

It is not surprising that the two Hands, Swan, and Chase were more in harmony with Frank than with Clark. Judges who had served long before the adoption of the Federal Rules and who had played no significant role in judicial reform could not be expected to share Clark's passion and fervent devotion to the rules and the work of the Advisory Committee. No doubt they were much less interested in the entire subject of procedure than either of the New Dealers and it is true that they did not always accept Frank's free-wheeling approach, yet as between the rigidity of Clark and the over-flexibility of Frank they were far more likely to veer toward the latter. And on certain issues, for instance summary judgments and interlocutory appeals, Learned Hand on his own directly rejected Clark's position.

A second explanation for the tendency of the four judges to side with Frank has nothing to do with the business of the court, either

[65] LH to CEC, November 26, 1943.

[66] HBC to CEC and JNF, July 28, 1947.

[67] Memorandum on Petition for Rehearing in Cover v. Schwartz, January 6, 1943.

substantive or procedural. Frank was clearly far better equipped than Clark (and, one gathers, just about everyone else) to communicate with people orally and to get across, in a spirit of friendliness and enthusiasm, ideas which the listener was hostile to. Frank "was at his zenith," writes Professor Kurland, "as a conversationalist rather than as an author or lecturer."[68] Clark, on the other hand, avoided direct verbal contacts and stuck to communicating his ideas through memoranda and letters. On paper he was combative and often prickly as was Frank, but for him there were few informal exchanges to ease the stiffness provoked and conveyed by the written communications. His style largely consisted of a statement of disagreements followed by a defense of his own position; it was all work and no play. In his letters Frank was at least as harsh and combative, but when talking things over he was humorous, charitable, and flexible. Indeed Clark recognized Frank's advantage and his own communications gap and at times he would (in writing, of course) complain that his opponent had discussed a question in dispute with another colleague and had thereby unfairly created the impression that Clark was in the minority. "We all know the effect of exuberance and the force of personality in securing accord from personal contact about matters concerning which one has not felt deeply,"[69] Clark wrote in the midst of an early argument. And three weeks later, when the issue of Frank's consultations with nonsitting colleagues came up in another case, he wrote: "I do think you are open and exuberant and quick. Because of these qualities I do not think you have realized that when you carry things before you this is more a matter of personality than of finally convincing your auditors; and hence the impressions which you get from your contacts and reports are not the ones which we all would get if we had completely two-sided discussions."[70]

[68] Kurland, "Jerome N. Frank: Some Reflections and Recollections of a Law Clerk," *University of Chicago Law Review,* 24 (1957), 664.

[69] CEC to JNF, June 23, 1942.

[70] CEC to JNF, July 14, 1942. Since Clark and Frank disagreed over just about everything else, it is not surprising that they would also occasionally argue about what their colleagues thought of them. "I think you are in error as to the attitude of our colleagues towards me," wrote Frank after a protracted dispute over the harmless error rule. He went on: "According to you, they (like you) consider me intractable, uncooperative, unwilling to 'make real changes' in opinions which they suggest, but, as they are more tactful than you, they do not tell me how they feel.

"I do not agree. Were such their attitude, they would be consummate hypocrites—or worse. For they—especially Learned, Tom and Harrie (I've seen little of Gus this past Term)—have not remained silent. . . . They have gone out of their way, and within very recent weeks, *to say to me* that they find it easy to work with me, that I am cooperative, and that, in particular,

Frank's style of written argument—consisting usually of a description of his opponent's position followed by a point-by-point dissection and rejection of that position—often angered Clark, who would complain that Frank was deliberately submitting him to ridicule. In fact, that was exactly what Frank was doing; in books and articles and in judicial opinions directed at colleagues, Frank indisputably was a master at ridicule and also at shooting holes in straw men. Except occasionally, this feature of his psycho-intellectual make-up did not disturb the two Hands or Swan or Chase. These judges had the benefit of direct contact with Jerome Frank, the charming and brilliant conversationalist, and their few sharp disagreements with him did not escalate into correspondence wars.

Not so with Charles Clark. The sheer number of disputes, the incessant angry letters and memoranda, the dozens of sharp dissents—all of these joined to forge in his mind a clear picture of a colleague who was determinedly hostile. No sooner did Frank say that it was not his intention to be rude in one argument than they would become embroiled in something else. It mattered little to Clark that Frank could be brutal with others when the fact was that his adversary was almost always unfriendly toward him. He came to believe that ridicule was Frank's ordinary way of responding to him.

It is interesting that the four senior members of the court did not seriously bother to argue with Frank; if he wanted to rip apart their opinions, this was okay so long as he did not unduly delay the administrative process of the Second Circuit. Because these judges did not write sharply to him or because they did not fight back, Frank had little incentive to write sharply against them. Clark did fight back, and this gave Frank a psychic shot in the arm to try harder to demolish his opponent. It probably was true, as Clark apparently thought at times, that Frank's opinions against him were much sharper than those directed against the views of the other judges. Once, after charging that a draft dissent by Frank was a personal attack, Clark wrote: "In fact, you do not always do so, as shown by the two dignified

they like the fact that I'm always ready to alter opinions I've written for the court in order to meet their suggestions" (JNF to CEC, August 4, 1946).

Eight days later, from Frank to Clark: "It is important, in its bearing on your approach to me, to clear up the question whether (as you've suggested several times) your estimate of my recalcitrance, etc. is also Learned's. As you may perhaps believe that his recent remark to me, to which I referred in my last letter . . . was but a bit of urbane soft-soaking, I suggest that you ask Learned directly just what is his attitude towards my cooperativeness or lack of it."

Since most people want to avoid any stress or tension in personal relations, it is of course possible that both Clark and Frank were correct in their assessments.

dissents against Harrie's opinions appearing in the current number of the F 2d."[71] The record seems to support the charge.[72]

Be this as it may, style factors contributed in part to the greater success of Jerome Frank with the Coolidge judges. He had an interesting relationship with Learned Hand, which is difficult to describe or explain. Throughout his career, Frank had written so critically about others that, even accounting for his private warmth and friendship, it is difficult to imagine him as a hero-worshiper. Yet, that was his posture toward Learned Hand; here was the dialectic of his iconoclasm. In some opinions he was openly worshipful,[73] and *Courts on Trial* is dedicated "to Learned Hand Our Wisest Judge." "It is hard to find an analogue to the feelings of Judge Frank for Judge Hand," writes Professor Kurland in an introduction to Frank's tribute to Learned Hand, which was published shortly after the former's death in 1957.[74] In his "hymn of praise," Frank quoted from a letter he wrote to his hero:

> "No one else I've ever known has excited in me such admiration and affection. You are my model as a judge. More, you have influenced my attitude in incalculable ways towards all sorts of matters, intellectual and others. For your eminence lies not alone in the singular nature of your mind, but in the manner in which you infuse your ideas with emotions, both noble and humorous. You are, par excellence, the democratic aristocrat."

To this, Frank added, somewhat unnecessarily: "I am unabashed in my admiration."[75]

[71] CEC to JNF, August 15, 1947. The case was Clark v. Taylor. In reply the next day, Frank denied any personal attack but he ignored the charge about milder dissents against other judges. In 1952 Frank responded to a similar accusation: "Of course, as Fed. (2d) shows, I have no 'principle' of 'unwillingness to stand alone' with you 'whenever that could be avoided.' Consider, e.g., my going along with you twice, against Learned's dissent in the Spector Motor case, and the decision, against Harrie's dissent last term, adverse to the New Haven Rail Road. . . . If I took the time, I could cite many instances" (JNF to CEC, February 6, 1952). The reply is not very convincing; Hand's Spector dissent was in 1943.

[72] For instance, Frank's rather mild dissents in Repouille v. United States, 165 F.2d 152 (2d Cir. 1947) from a denial of citizenship to a man who, as an act of mercy, killed his child who was virtually a freak, and United States ex rel. Hirshberg v. Malanaphy, 168 F.2d 503 (2d Cir. 1948), from a decision extending court martial jurisdiction.

[73] "I have the highest respect for Judge Hand. To sit with him is an inestimable privilege, a constant source of education. Consequently, I usually suspect my own tentative opinions, when they vary from his" (Frank dissenting in United States v. Rubenstein, 151 F.2d 915, 920 [2d Cir. 1945]).

[74] Kurland, "Jerome N. Frank," p. 661.

[75] Jerome N. Frank, "Some Reflections on Learned Hand," *University of Chicago Law Review*, 24 (1957), 666.

Learned Hand did not openly respond to any of these warm expressions; while he no doubt at least partly reciprocated the feelings of his junior colleague in correspondence, it is not likely that his admiration for Frank matched that of Frank for him. It is certain, though, that except for a few areas the views of the two judges corresponded and that Hand liked the erratic New Dealer. Several months after Jerome Frank died, Learned Hand wrote to Mrs. Frank: "We had grown together in a way that is not common at my age; and that too in spite of differences in our professional outlook."[76] Frank's relations with his colleagues were best summed up by Judge Clark:

> Now I realize full well the wide support your ability, persuasiveness, and verve do give your views. Not only do I not deny this, but, indeed, I show clearly that I am disturbed by it so far as concerns the immediate matters we are discussing. I know you can put matters over faster and more completely than slowpokes like myself. . . . And there is no doubt of Learned's real affection for you; further I know that in certain matters procedural you are closer to him than I.[77]

But in the final analysis, procedural questions and not conflicting styles accounted for the Clark-Frank differences and also for the better reception Frank got from their colleagues. Significantly, on procedural issues the intermediate appellate judges have more freedom than they have when deciding substantive questions. The Federal Rules were still new in the 1940's and the judges who interpreted them did so largely unencumbered by earlier rulings. More importantly, in procedural disputes the likelihood of intervention and resolution by the Supreme Court is small. Lower judges may disagree among themselves over freedom of speech or tax law or administrative agencies, but

[76] LH to Mrs. Jerome N. Frank, June 5, 1957. A few days after Judge Frank died (January 20, 1957), Learned Hand wrote the following condolence letter to Mrs. Frank.

"It is just a week ago that I heard of Jerry's death, and it keeps coming over me with increasing unreality that I shall not see him again. I think it is not necessary for me to tell you how deeply we agreed about the real values of life, much as we often differed about the ways and means. This created a bond between us which I shall not succeed in making again in the court, and has left a memory which I shall never lose. His just and gentle nature, his irrepressible insistence upon giving all of himself to what he undertook, and the absence of any self-seeking in his work, made a cumulative effect in my friendship that it has been bitter indeed to part with.

"It is idle for me to try to find any words to say to you that will serve as consolation; I shall not try to. We can get from each experience nothing more than the hope that in dealing with them we may help to realize in ourselves one of those achievements that, when all is said, make up the best of our values."

[77] CEC to JNF, November 17, 1948.

at some point the Supreme Court will step in and lay down the law, thereby narrowing the range of disagreement in the lower judiciary. This is not true of procedural disputes, and Charles Clark and Jerome Frank were usually free to battle it out, as in fact they did.[78]

In a way, both men were hampered by the approaches to procedure which they took prior to becoming judges and by their outside activity while they were on the Second Circuit. Because he was more free-wheeling and flexible, this was less true of Frank; just the same, it was important that Frank's perception of procedural problems was framed outside of a judicial context, that his was an iconoclastic approach. Paradoxically, he was so enmeshed in a loose attitude toward procedure that he occasionally lost sight of or denigrated the substantive issues presented in appeals.

Clark's difficulty was far more pronounced, as he once admitted in a candid letter to Learned Hand:

> The truth of the matter is that I sometimes find difficulty in my two capacities of judge and of reporter for the rules. It is hard to know where to draw the lines. . . . Maybe the two jobs will become more and more fundamentally incompatible. The fact of the matter is that our circuit is giving and is likely to give more concern about the rules than any other. That, I suppose, is natural; since we have more cases than any other, the result is an indicated one. Moreover, the undue emphasis of New York lawyers and courts upon procedural details and the very brilliance of our Court point the same way; for the greater the judges, the less patience they will have with procedural matters. That has raised a problem for me before as a reporter for the Committee. Maybe I ought to resign from the Committee, though for the present I am still inclined to keep on trying to effect certain compromises and adjustments.[79]

[78] Clark held that, as to following "our masters of the Supreme Court in matters procedural," courts of appeals judges "can have perhaps some more hesitation than in other cases as to just what they are requiring of us" (CEC to JNF, July 14, 1943).

[79] CEC to LH, August 4, 1947.

8

Judges Frank and Clark and the Law of the Second Circuit

CHARLES CLARK AND JEROME FRANK WERE ON OPPOSITE SIDES IN FIFTY-eight appeals decided by the Second Circuit in the 1941–51 period. In a large number of these, their disagreement was over some procedural question, without which the appeal would have been decided with little difficulty or delay, either because the case was one-sided or because there was substantial agreement over the other questions. On substantive matters the Roosevelt appointees were not far apart, which is not surprising. In fact, except for strongly divergent views regarding criminal rights, it is hard to find any area of law where they consistently took opposing positions.

As a rule, both men gave liberal interpretations to New Deal legislation such as the Fair Labor Standards Act and they usually supported the rulings of federal administrative agencies. As a former chairman of the Securities and Exchange Commission, Frank, quite predictably, gave the agencies broad discretion to handle problems within their fields of competence. When he took issue with the administrative ruling, he took pains to declare that he was not making his decision out of any antipathy toward the agency. Thus, in dissenting from a decision favorable to the Interstate Commerce Commission, he wrote: "My reaction here must not be taken as an expression of any general hostility to administrative agencies (nor to the I.C.C. in particular). On the contrary, I have elsewhere stated in some detail, my objections to blanket denunciations of those agencies as engaged in 'administrative absolutism.' "[1] Clark's votes in this area were generally along the same lines as those of Frank, but with what was perhaps a significant difference in emphasis in cases from the National Labor Relations Board. In the 1940's he supported the Board more out of a strong personal conviction that its pro-labor, antibusiness rulings were right than out of a feeling that courts had only a limited review over the independent agencies. Actually, after Congress passed the Taft-Hartley Act, legislation which Clark was bitterly opposed to, and the Labor Board began to turn against unions, he became hostile to many of its holdings and probably had as strong an anti-Board attitude as any of his colleagues. When the Second Circuit, in an opinion by Frank, upheld a pro-union order of the N.L.R.B., but modified a provision requiring the reinstatement of one employee, Clark declared in a partial dissent:

> This perhaps is a small matter; but the smaller it is, the more I am troubled that my brethren can discover grounds, or feel impelled, to interfere with the remedial action found necessary by the Board. . . . Such a scrutiny of the decision of an expert agency for small flyspecks seems to me the wrong type of judicial review, yielding constructive advantage to no one, but promoting confusion and doubt in the factory and as to the administration of the statute.[2]

However, even prior to adoption of Taft-Hartley, when the N.L.R.B. decided against a labor union, Clark found new power for

[1] Old Colony Bondholders v. New York, New Haven & Hartford R. Co., 161 F.2d 413, 448 (2d Cir., 1947). Elsewhere in the same opinion Frank said: "To condone the Commission's conduct here is to give aid and comfort to the enemies of the administrative process, by sanctioning administrative irresponsibility; the friends of that process should be the first to denounce its abuses. If the courts declare themselves powerless to remedy those abuses, judicial review will become a sham" (p. 451).

[2] Colonie Fibre Co. v. National Labor Relations Board, 163 F.2d 65, 70 (2d Cir. 1947). Other noteworthy pro-labor opinions by Clark during this period were: National Labor Relations Board v. Arma Corp., 122 F.2d 153 (2d Cir. 1941), Clark dissenting in part; Corning Glass Works v. National Labor Relations Board, 129 F.2d 967 (2d Cir. 1942), Clark dissenting in part; National Labor Relations Board v. Remington Rand, Inc., 130 F.2d 919 (2d Cir. 1942), Clark concurring; and Allen Bradley Co. v. Local Union No. 3, 145 F.2d 215 (2d Cir. 1944). In the last named case, Clark wrote the opinion for the court, which held that a Supreme Court decision that labor unions were exempt from the antitrust laws also covered combinations in restraint of trade entered into by unions and business groups. Judge Swan dissented. The Supreme Court granted certiorari and reversed (Allen Bradley Co. v. Local Union No. 3, 325 U.S. 797 [1945]); the vote was 8–1.

the court to review agency orders.[3] After the Labor Management Act was amended in 1947, Clark's pro-labor attitude became more pronounced.[4] He saw "the weapons of propanganda open to one side and the poor labor unions . . . inept and open to every attack.[5]

Paralleling his views on unions was his firm distrust of big business. This came through in his opinions in N.L.R.B. appeals and in several cases not involving unions. In an appeal arising out of a suit for recovery of accidental death benefits, the majority supported the position of the insurance company. But Clark dissented: "Insurance contracts," he stated, "may easily amount to traps for the uninitiated."[6]

One of Clark's finest opinions was a dissent from a determination that the New York Stock Exchange was not responsible for its failure to take action against a member-broker who had embezzled clients.[7] While the Supreme Court refused to hear the case, Clark's pioneering opinion received great attention and it probably contributed to increased surveillance by stock exchanges of the activities of their members.

Clark also was quite sympathetic to small businessmen in financial difficulty, as was evidenced by two dissenting opinions he wrote in bankruptcy cases.[8]

Few men in American legal history came to the bench so set in their ideas about matters that would come before them as judges as did Clark and Frank. Politics and legal practice, the two interrelated areas which serve as the virtually exclusive recruiting grounds for prospective judges, rarely prepare lawyers for the types of questions

[3] See, e.g., his dissent in National Labor Relations Board v. National Broadcasting Company, 150 F.2d 895 (2d Cir. 1945).

[4] See, e.g., International Brotherhood of Electrical Workers v. National Labor Relations Board, 181 F.2d 34 (2d Cir. 1950), Clark dissenting. In Douds v. Local 1250, Retail, Wholesale Department Store Union, 170 F.2d 695 (2d Cir. 1948), Clark reluctantly concurred with the Second Circuit's affirmance of an injunction barring a strike. In his separate opinion he wrote that "it cannot be gainsaid that the [Taft-Hartley] Act does put the federal courts far into the task of terminating strikes" (p. 699). See, also, his dissent in the companion case involving the same parties, reported at 170 F.2d 700, 701.

[5] Letter to Philip J. Wickser, September 16, 1947.

[6] Bush v. Order of United Commercial Travellers, 124 F.2d 528, 531 (2d Cir. 1942). It is not very easy to locate the reasons for Clark's apparent hostility to large corporations. While of course he was not in any sense a poor man, it seems that he had less wealth than any of the other members of his court.

[7] Baird v. Franklin, 141 F.2d 238, 240 (2d Cir. 1944).

[8] In re Herzog, 121 F.2d 581, 582 (2d Cir. 1941) and Benjamin v. Jaspan, 144 F.2d 58, 59 (2d Cir. 1944).

that will face them after they don their robes. In the case of politics it is obvious that this is true; with respect to the practice of law, it must be remembered that lawyers usually work in rather narrow and specialized fields. The final two appointees to the Learned Hand court had devoted a good deal of time in the 1920's and 1930's writing and acting upon issues that later confronted them as judges. We have seen how their backgrounds on legal procedure significantly affected the operations of the Second Circuit. The same was true of other areas, such as Clark's approach to federalism and federal jurisdiction and Frank's attitudes toward criminal law, where their procedural biases proved to be relevant.

It is ironic that about the same time that Clark achieved his great goal with the adoption of the Federal Rules of Civil Procedure, a reform which he hoped and expected would serve as the standard for similar judicial improvements in the states, the Supreme Court, in effect, rejected the century-old concept of a federal common law applied by federal courts in diversity of citizenship cases arising in the states. In a real sense, as Clark quickly recognized, the decision of *Erie Railroad Co. v. Tompkins*[9] negated much of the impact of the Federal Rules.

Clark never liked the much-praised ruling in *Erie*,[10] and throughout his tenure as a judge, in opinions and essays, he unsuccessfully tried to undermine its philosophy and acceptance. His attitude toward this case and his concept of federal judicial abstention from deciding questions of state law was rooted partly in his rigidly held opinion that courts should not use technical devices as excuses for not deciding issues. In a notable essay he described *Erie* and its progeny as "an attempt to avoid the unavoidable—to ask judges not to judge, not to exercise their judicial capacity or the power of their minds, even though Congress and the Constitution have given them jurisdiction over the case."[11]

A second basis for his constant support of federal jurisdiction was his feeling that many of the states had not achieved the desired reforms in their rules of procedure and for this reason it would be better to allow the federal courts to handle litigation that also could be

[9] 304 U.S. 64 (1938).

[10] See his 1945 Benjamin N. Cardozo Lecture before the Association of the Bar of the City of New York, "State Law in the Federal Courts: The Brooding Omnipresence of Erie v. Tompkins," reprinted with a 1953 postscript in Charles Alan Wright, and Harry M. Reasoner (eds.), *Procedure—The Handmaid of Justice* (St. Paul, Minn.: West Publishing Co., 1965), p. 170. Also, see his much later essay, expressing similar views, "Federal Procedural Reform and States' Rights; To a More Perfect Union," *ibid.*, p. 99.

[11] *Ibid.*, p. 109. In the Cardozo Lecture he said: "Hence my plea is for freedom for the Federal judicial process to be judicial" (*ibid.*, p. 192).

decided by the states. But, in this connection, it is significant that at the end of his life, when a large number of states had adopted major reforms largely as a result of his effort and advocacy, he still did not weaken in his opposition to *Erie* and to the emasculation of the federal judicial role in diversity cases.

More fundamental, perhaps, than his procedural grounds for opposing the trend away from federal jurisdiction were his strong doubts about the value of federalism. The changes in American society and politics, the inexorable creation of a national economy and polity which was manifested by the New Deal, amounted to an erosion of the place of the states in the totality of American life. This meant to Clark that in all areas, specifically including judicial affairs, the national trend was irreversible. Supreme Court rulings enhancing state judicial power went against this trend and made no sense, a view he expressed in dissenting from a decision which curtailed federal jurisdiction:

> Because the immediate issue of curtailment of federal relief to a seemingly deserving suitor seems to me serious enough, I have refrained from discussing the wider social and governmental implications involved in this steady, if not now precipitous, contraction of federal jurisdiction. But the ironic overtones do seem to me apparent. While events national and international do steadily press our people into a closer union, the national courts alone make their possibly gallant, but surely eventually futile, attempts to restore states-rightism.[12]

A nationalistic theme runs through much of Clark's writings; he concluded a 1961 lecture on procedural reform and states rights with the prophecy that the judiciary, too, would accept the inescapable:

> I will say boldly that I do not believe these doctrines working against national unity can stand. I suggest as an article of faith that our definite direction is to make ourselves into a very great country, a country in which we all share as equals and in the building of which the federal courts have a large and important role to play. . . . I realize how foolish it is for an inferior judge to prophesy the course of Supreme Court decisions. But nevertheless I shall take the risk. I am going to venture the thought—and this you may check fifty-years hence—that what I am now saying will be even truer than I believe it to be at this moment.[13]

Clark did not live to see this prophecy fulfilled, and, in view of the current trend in the federal courts, it is unlikely that it will come true very soon. But we still have a long way to go until the fifty years are up.

[12] P. Beiersdorf & Co. v. McGohey, 187 F.2d 14, 17 (2d Cir. 1951).
[13] Clark, "Federal Procedural Reform," in Wright and Reasoner, *Procedure*, pp. 113–14.

The relevance of Jerome Frank's pre-Second Circuit experience to his performance as a judge is even easier to trace. There is remarkable continuity of thought in all of his writings on legal subjects, from *Law and the Modern Mind* in 1930, to the many law review articles written over the ensuing quarter of a century, to the judicial opinions in his sixteen years as a judge, to *Courts on Trial* in 1949, and finally to *Not Guilty*, published shortly after his death. Justice Douglas lists as the "common threads" in Frank's writings: "First, the treacherous nature of the fact-finding process in the law. . . . Second, the problem of changing the nature of legal education. . . . Third, the problem of reconciling the freedom from government. . . . Fourth, his concern that even-handed justice be done not only to those who are influential, but to the lowly, the indigent, and the despised."[14]

The first of these, Frank's "fact-skepticism," was, as Professor Edmond Cahn stressed, the unifying theme:

> For about twenty-five years Jerome Frank's corruscating and marvelously restless mind planned and built and developed the meaning of fact-skepticism. Fully aware that his approach was novel, he deliberately repeated and reiterated his doctrines, phrased them first this way and then that, and summoned analogies, from every corner of the cultural world to make his ideas clearer. . . . Gradually, beneath the surface of the repetitions, the essential doctrine cumulated and moved forward.[15]

Cahn defined fact-skepticism as a "single doctrine with three associated prongs. It criticizes our capacity to ascertain the transactions of the past; it distrusts our capacity to predict the concrete fact-findings and value judgments of the future; and finally, it discloses the importance of the personal element in all processes of choice and decision."[16]

[14] Douglas, "Jerome N. Frank," An Address at a Special Memorial Meeting of the New York County Lawyers' Association and the Association of the Bar of the City of New York, May 23, 1957 (printed), pp. 9–10.

[15] Cahn, "Judge Frank's Fact-Skepticism and Our Future," *Yale Law Journal,* 66 (1957), 824.

[16] *Ibid.,* p. 828. *Courts on Trial* was Frank's most detailed discussion and application of the concept to the judicial decision-making process, particularly at the trial court level. After this book appeared in 1949, he developed the idea further in several journal articles, notably, "A Conflict with Oblivion: Some Observations on the Founders of Legal Pragmatism," *Rutgers Law Review,* 9 (1954), 442, and " 'Short of Sickness and Death': A Study of Moral Responsibility in Legal Criticism," *New York University Law Review,* 26 (1951), 547.

It is impossible to discuss in a few pages all of Frank's judicial opinions in which the concept of fact-finding appeared. Julius Paul has prepared a list of Frank's opinions according to the major categories of thought in his extrajudicial writings, in *The Legal Realism of Jerome N. Frank* (The Hague, Netherlands: Martinus Nijhoff, 1959), pp. 154–56.

Frank's doubts as to the "capacity to ascertain the transactions of the past" put him in an interesting position with regard to the jury system. As is well known, both off and on the bench he steadfastly criticized our reliance upon untrained jurors as fact-finders and strongly advocated abolition of the jury in at least all civil suits. Yet, never abandoning this view, he recognized that appellate judges were even less able than jurors who hear testimony and see witnesses to get a true picture of what actually happened in a disputed situation which results in a lawsuit. For this reason, with the important exceptions of criminal cases and occasional appeals involving the lowly, he regularly voted to affirm jury verdicts. As he put it in one of his first dissents, "When, by constitution or otherwise, the jury is the established instrument of fact-finding, it is not, I think, for judges, whatever personal doubts they may have as to its efficacy, to fetter its historic function of passing on the credibility of witnesses."[17]

Where the evidence consisted largely of oral testimony, he was even more reluctant to upset the findings of trial courts:

> Determination of the facts of a lawsuit, when the witnesses disagree about them, always presents difficulties. As the facts necessarily occurred in the past, and not in the trial judge's presence, he must undertake an historical reconstruction; and the wiser historians tell us that any such reconstruction is inherently

---

While on the Second Circuit, Frank's pet course at the Yale Law School was on judicial fact-finding. According to Fred Rodell, he once tried a unique way of showing the students how courtroom testimony was unreliable in determining facts. Recalled Rodell:

"He had his law clerk go in first, explain that Judge Frank would be a little late, and quietly start to give out reading assignments. Suddenly Jerome burst through the door, complete with false moustache, monocle, stick, and British accent. Quivering, he surveyed the room, then stormed down the aisle toward a student (who was in on the gag), raging about some injustice done him, demanding his rights, and creating a mighty uproar. The student muttered a couple of planned apologetic sentences and fled through the door with Jerome in hot pursuit. (That one of those silly and costly little leaded panes of glass got smashed as they exited was not planned.)

"A couple of minutes later, Jerome reappeared—urbane, moustacheless, monocle-less—and asked the twittering class to describe, in writing and in detail, the incident they had witnessed barely an instant before. Perhaps it was because the divergence of the various accounts made so vivid the unreliability of eye-witnesses' testimony in court that Jerome never, to my knowledge, pulled that trick again. After all, he was supposed to spend a whole term teaching Fact-Finding" (Fred Rodell, "Jerome Frank: A Remembrance," *Yale Law Report*, 3 [1957], 5).

[17] Willis v. Pennsylvania R., 122 F.2d 248, 251 (2d Cir. 1941). He added in a footnote that "it happens that I have, elsewhere, expressed such doubts concerning the jury in noncriminal cases."

guessy. For the likelihood is small that any mere mortal can acquire absolutely certain knowledge of bygone events. The probability is less that such knowledge will be approximated by upper-court judges, reading but a printed record, than by a trial judge who sees and hears the witnesses testify. For that reason . . . we have repeatedly refused to retry the facts of a case when the evidence was oral.[18]

But it would be an error to conclude from this that, during his judicial career, Frank's skepticism was reserved for his outside writing and that while on the bench, with the exception of clearly erroneous decisions, he faithfully accepted the limitations of an upper-court judge. Frank, at least as much as any other man to hold high federal judicial office, used his position to help the unfortunate and society's rejects. Underdogs and losers—people who he urgently felt could not adequately protect themselves in litigation against the vast resources of big government and big business—received his sympathetic attention. Poor widows, injured seamen and railroad workers, small bankrupts, struggling businessmen, convicts, and Indians, all found in Frank a champion of their legal rights, often irrespective of procedural obstacles or judicial precedents.[19] He was their spokesman and his

---

[18] Erie Railroad Co. v. The Cornell No. 20, 164 F.2d 763, 765 (2d Cir. 1947). The same idea was explained somewhat differently in a strong dissent in a trademark case:

"There is no escape from the circumstance that the trial judges, because they conduct the fact-finding process, are the most important judicial officials. Fact-finding, when a judge sits without a jury and the record consists of oral testimony, is his responsibility, not that of the upper courts. Only when it is clear beyond doubt that he has closed his eyes to the evidence, may an upper court properly ignore his version of the facts. Since his 'finding' or 'facts,' responsive to the testimony, is inherently subjective (i.e., what he actually believes to be the facts is hidden from scrutiny by others), his concealed disregard of evidence is always a possibility. An upper court must accept that possibility, and must recognize, too, that such hidden misconduct by a trial judge lies beyond its control. Only, perhaps, by psycho-analyzing the trial judge could his secret mental operations be ascertained by us; and we are not skilled in that art, which, at the least, would require many hours of intensive personal interviews with the judge" (La Touraine Coffee Co. v. Lorraine Coffee Co., 157 F.2d 115, 123–24 [2d Cir. 1946]).

[19] Obviously, when there was a recent Supreme Court ruling clearly on the same point, Frank's inescapable obligation was to follow. Thus, because of a Supreme Court decision, Frank held against a taxpayer from whom the government had unlawfully collected taxes. But Frank added: "It shocks the conscience that the government of the United States may be able, on the basis of such a vestige or shadow of a once virile rule, to defeat the just claim of a citizen. . . . When . . . a sum has been collected unlawfully under the guise of a tax, and its repayment is concededly a

extraordinary powers of reasoning were employed on their behalf; their claims carried in his eyes a favorable presumption, and caveats against appellate court fact-finding were disregarded. Where underdogs were concerned, he could be a nit-picker par excellence.

This activist conception of judicial power was articulated by him in a bankruptcy appeal:

> But we think that courts, in civilized communities, should do more than decide cases one way or another, without regard to consideration of justice, merely to prevent private brawls and breaches of the peace. Government having, through its courts, established, in large areas, a monopoly of dispute-deciding, should try, as far as possible, to decide cases correctly—both by ascertaining the actual facts as near as may be, and then by applying correct legal rules in an effort to do justice to the parties affected by their decision. And not merely the parties, but the public as well, are interested that justice shall be done. . . . While the obligation to do justice does not mean, of course, that courts can ad lib, the fact that such tribunals are called "courts of justice" is surely not without any significance.[20]

The same attitude was evident in cases dealing with Indians. In rejecting the claim of an Indian that he was not a citizen and hence not subject to the draft, Frank made it plain that "because of the historic relation of the United States to the Indians, we reach that conclusion most reluctantly."[21] In a far more important case, involving an attempt by the Seneca Nation of Indians to cancel leases on reservation land, Frank took judicial notice of the "unhappy realization that the dealings of certain of our citizens with the Indians have often been far from praiseworthy";[22] with this in mind, he deliberately ignored or rejected centuries of common law precedent to arrive at a decision favorable to the Indian landlords. Moreover, to arrive at this result, the upper court, led by Frank, reversed the trial court and rejected its findings.[23]

---

matter of both justice and legal right, to block that repayment, merely because of a rule of law which once had substance but no longer has—merely because, in passing, the Supreme Court has reiterated language which no longer has any substantial meaning—is to provoke justified dissatisfaction with government" (Hammond-Knowlton v. United States, 121 F.2d 192, 198–99 [2d Cir. 1941]).

[20] In re Barnett, 124 F.2d 1005, 1010 (2d Cir. 1942).

[21] Ex parte Green, 123 F.2d 862, 863 (2d Cir. 1941).

[22] United States v. Forness, 125 F.2d 928, 941 (2d Cir. 1942).

[23] But it should be noted that the Second Circuit found that "the findings proposed by the defendants [the tenants] were mechanically adopted" by the trial judge (p. 942).

Frank showed special concern for protecting the rights of seamen. One notable essay-opinion dealt at length with the question whether seamen, because of their historically weak position in relations with employers, required special protective treatment from the courts. Frank argued that the modern "liberty of contract" notion that seamen are aware of their rights diverges significantly from the more reasonable and humane approach that developed in medieval times and was accepted well into the nineteenth century. He advocated a return to the old policy. "The liberty of the individual employee to bind himself firmly . . . in a contract with his employer, no matter how harsh or unusual its terms," he urged, "is not to be strictly applied to workers who go to sea. As to such provisions in their contracts, because they are 'wards of admiralty' a distinctive doctrine is applicable; a peculiar burden is cast on the employer."[24] Applying this principle to the case before him, Frank—supported by the other panel members—reversed a summary judgment against a seaman who without knowing that he was suffering from tuberculosis gave the company a release in return for a small payment.

The same humane attitude was applied to injured railroad workers, and, in a sense, to other employees who could not protect their own interests in dealings with their employers. "I believe," said Frank in one case, "that the courts should now say forthrightly that the judiciary regards the ordinary employee as one who needs and will receive the special protection of the courts when, for a small consideration, he has given a release after an injury."[25]

Writers were also the beneficiary of Frank's tendency to support those parties he regarded as inherently weak. In return for $1600, a poor, unknown song writer had transferred all his forthcoming royalties from sixty-nine songs—including "When Irish Eyes Are Smiling"— to a music publisher. Twenty-two years later, when the original copyrights were about to expire, the writer assigned the renewal rights to these songs to a second publisher. By a vote of 2–1 the Second Circuit (Clark and Augustus Hand in the majority) interpreted the Copyright Act as not forbidding advance assignment of copyright renewal rights; accordingly, it ruled that the original assignment was valid and effectively barred future re-assignments. Frank disagreed; after showing how the original arrangement was, from the financial standpoint, incredibly disadvantageous to the songwriter, he contended that the

[24] Hume v. Moore-McCormack Lines, 121 F.2d 336, 347 (2d Cir. 1941). Also on seamen, see Frank's dissenting opinions in Montoya v. Tide Water Associated Oil Co., 174 F.2d 607, 610 (2d Cir. 1949), and Daranowich v. Land, 186 F.2d 386, 388 (2d Cir. 1951).

[25] Concurring in Ricketts v. Pennsylvania R., 153 F.2d 757, 768 (2d Cir. 1946).

court "should take judicial notice of the economic capacities and business acumen of most authors. . . . We need only take judicial notice of that which every schoolboy knows—that, usually, with a few notable exceptions (such as W. Shakespeare and G. B. Shaw), authors are hopelessly inept in business transactions and that lyricists . . . often sell their songs 'for a song.' "[26] Frank labeled the majority view "stingy statutory interpretation,"[27] inconsistent with congressional intent. Even though Congress did not explicitly legislate against assignment of copyright renewal rights, the courts should "carry out what Congress meant to achieve for the protection of authors."[28]

In most areas, Frank's willingness to battle against venerable legal policies which he felt were unfair to underdogs did not meet with quick success. A major exception was bankruptcy law. Like Judge Clark, his sympathy was with the small businessman who was forced into bankruptcy.[29] When Frank became a judge, a long-standing rule in bankruptcy proceedings required officers of bankrupt corporations to turn over to bankruptcy trustees the assets they had withdrawn from the corporation, even in the absence of any evidence that these assets were still in their possession. The turnover rule, which was designed to discourage fraudulent practices, was based on the presumption that the withdrawn assets remained in the possession of the corporation's officers. If, in fact, the property was no longer in the hands of those who took it, a turnover order could not be issued. Common sense dictates that the property would not be retained; likely, a businessman who has abused his position to gain control of such assets would quickly get rid of them, in order to get much-needed money. Yet, the presumption in favor of continued possession was maintained.

---

[26] M. Witmark & Sons v. Fred Fisher Music Co., 125 F.2d 949, 955 (2d Cir. 1942). In a second case concerning a writer, Frank took "judicial notice of the fact that many authors retain no adequate duplicates of the writings they send to publishers" (Newman v. Clayton F. Summy Co., 133 F.2d 465, 466 [2d Cir. 1942]).

In the copyright renewal case, the Second Circuit's ruling was reviewed by the Supreme Court and affirmed in a 5–3 decision. Said Justice Frankfurter for the majority, in an obvious dig at Frank's anguish over poor, duped writers, "We cannot draw a principle of law from the familiar stories of garret-poverty of some men of literary genius" (Fred Fisher Music Co. v. M. Witmark & Sons, 318 U.S. 643, 657 [1943]). The dissenters in the High Court wrote no opinion of their own, as they expressly relied on Frank's lower court dissent.

[27] M. Witmark & Sons v. Fred Fisher Music Co., p. 968.

[28] *Ibid.*

[29] See, for instance, his dissenting opinion on behalf of a bankrupt who was "an ignorant person unaware of the way in which most businessmen conduct their business operations" *In re* Sandow, 151 F.2d 807, 810 (2d Cir. 1945).

Learned Hand was greatly troubled by these turnover proceedings, but he was not disposed to do anything about them, particularly in view of Augustus Hand's strong support of the practice.[30] Under the prodding of Frank, the Chief Judge, while continuing to follow the precedents, sharpened his criticism of the rule. "The whole proceeding," he said for himself and Frank, "is an abuse of the process of the bankruptcy court."[31] Frank's first opinion on the subject came in 1944 in a brief concurrence in which he expressed the hope "that the Supreme Court will soon grant certiorari in some such case as this and overrule precedents that fasten upon us what seems to . . . [Learned Hand] and me an irrational rule of presumption, obviously contrary to fact, which enables trustees in bankruptcy to employ civil actions as substitutes for criminal proceedings."[32]

Two years later he was considerably more forthright in his opposition to turnover proceedings, although he once more upheld the order. The case was *In re Luma Camera Service.* Maggio, the former president of the bankrupt corporation, had failed to comply with a turnover order, whereupon he was adjudged in contempt by the district court judge and was committed to jail until he turned over merchandise valued at $17,500 or that sum of money or until the court ordered him released. He appealed to the Second Circuit; Judge Frank wrote for the court:

> Here, were we free to do so, we would say that, since of course Maggio no longer had possession, the trustee did not seek to have Maggio surrender goods or money he possessed, but sought, with the aid of a transparent fiction, to have the court, after a trial without a jury punish him for a crime (i.e., that of concealing assets or of a false oath in a bankruptcy proceeding) with the hope that such punishment would induce Maggio's close relatives and friends to put up the money. . . . We would hold that a *turnover proceeding may not, via a fiction, be substituted for a criminal*

[30] In his opinion for the court (Swan and Frank were with him) in Seligson v. Goldsmith, 128 F.2d 977 (2d Cir. 1942), Learned Hand wrote that "were the matter now before us as res integra, we should reverse the order. . . . Nevertheless, we do not feel justified in overruling a body of authority so nearly uniform, to the building of which we have contributed so largely" (p. 979).

[31] Robbins v. Gottbetter, 134 F.2d 843, 844 (2d Cir. 1943). Augustus Hand concurred, since the result was to affirm the turnover order. But his separate opinion was unusually sharp, certainly for so passive a judge. After pointing out that "those exceptionally alert guardians of civil rights, Justices Holmes, Brandeis, and Stone" had gone along with a Supreme Court decision upholding such orders, he concluded: "Nor am I persuaded that the creditors of thieving bankrupts should be curtailed in employing the only practical means of obtaining restitution" (p. 845).

[32] Cohen v. Jeskowitz, 144 F.2d 39, 40–41 (2d Cir. 1944).

prosecution so as to deprive a man of a basic constitutional right, the right of trial by jury.[33]

Frank could have reversed the contempt conviction on the ground that the trial judge ignored Maggio's poor health, a factor that according to the statute had to be considered in a case of this kind. But he upheld it, and deliberately followed the logic behind the presumption of continued possession: Since Maggio, according to the presumption, still had the merchandise, he could easily have purged himself of contempt by complying with the order. What Frank wanted to do was to put the turnover-order presumption in the worst possible light, to show that "Maggio is worse off than if he had been criminally prosecuted."[34] In short, his intention was to put the maximum pressure on the Supreme Court that could be exerted by a lower-court judge to reverse the Second Circuit and to reject the long-standing judicial policy in favor of turnover orders.

This approach worked, for the High Court accepted the case and decided that "turnover orders should not be issued or affirmed on a presumption thought to arise from some isolated circumstance, such as one time possession, when the reviewing court finds from the whole record that the order is unrealistic and unjust."[35] Once more, Judge Frank had made an impact on American law.

While Frank's role in the patent law area was quite limited, here, too, his opinions were marked by a characteristic desire to protect consumers against monopolistic practices.[36] In an early opinion on the subject, in which he conceded his ignorance of patent matters, he argued that "the actual enjoyment of a patent monopoly—which of course, has its effect on the public—may, it seems, often depend on the fact that the patent is owned by a wealthy concern and that alleged infringers lack funds to defend themselves. But the exploitation of such a monopoly should not turn on such fortuitous circumstances. Judicial determination of validity should not be limited to those

[33] 157 F.2d 951, 953–54 (2d Cir. 1946).

[34] *Ibid.,* p. 956.

[35] Maggio v. Zeitz, 333 U.S. 56, 66 (1948). Justice Frankfurter was the sole dissenter, though he was less opposed to the substantive decision than to the manner in which it was reached. Frankfurter was openly scornful of Frank's opinion below (*ibid.,* pp. 85, 90).

[36] On the protection of consumers, generally, see, Frank's notable opinion for the court in Associated Industries v. Ickes, 134 F.2d 694 (2d Cir. 1943), in which it was held that coal users had a right to challenge the Department of Interior's raising coal prices. Another pro-consumer opinion was his dissent from a decision exempting a price-fixing arrangement that was valid under state law from the Sherman Anti-Trust Act (Adams-Mitchell Co. v. Cambridge Distributing Co., 189 F.2d 913, 917 [2d Cir. 1951]).

patents which happen to be the subject of patent litigation privately instituted."[37] Instead, he proposed, that "as the public interest is deeply involved, it would seem wise that representatives of the public should at least participate in decisions of any such matters."[38]

At the same time, he recognized that patents may protect small businessmen, encourage invention, and stimulate investment; hence, to denounce them "merely because they create monopolies is to indulge in superficial thinking."[39] On the whole, though, he did not view patents with very much favor, and because of this in patent litigation he was more concerned with the validity of the patent than with its alleged infringement. Once, when the court refused to reach the question of validity because it had already decided that a patent had not been infringed, Frank strenuously urged that it also be held invalid: "An invalid patent masquerading as a valid one is a public menace, and should be fair game."[40]

A similar antimonopoly attitude pervaded Frank's opinions in trademark cases.[41] When Augustus Hand and Clark ruled that the trademark "Seventeen," held by the magazine of the same name, was infringed by a manufacturer of girdles sold under the name, "Miss Seventeen," Judge Frank dissented.[42] He denied that prospective customers would associate the girdle with the magazine. This is how he put it:

> I think that we should not pioneer in amplifying the trade-name doctrine on the basis of the shaky kind of guess in which the trial judge indulged. Like the trial judge's, our surmise must here rest on "judicial notice." As neither the trial judge nor any member of this court is (or resembles) a teen-age girl or the mother or sister of such a girl, our judicial notice apparatus will not work well unless we feed it with information directly obtained from "teen-agers" or from their female relatives accustomed to shop for them. Competently to inform ourselves, we should have a staff of investigators like those supplied to administrative agencies. As we have no such staff, I have questioned some adolescent girls and their mothers and sisters, persons I have chosen at

[37] Concurring in Picard v. United Aircraft Corporation, 128 F.2d 632, 642 (2d Cir. 1942).

[38] Ibid., p. 645.

[39] Ibid., p. 643.

[40] Concurring in Acro Spark Plug Co. v. B. G. Corporation, 130 F.2d 290, 294 (2d Cir. 1942).

[41] See, for instance, his reluctant concurring opinion in Standard Brands v. Smidler, 151 F.2d 34, 37 (2d Cir. 1945); his dissenting opinion in La Touraine Coffee Co. v. Lorraine Coffee Co., 157 F.2d 115, 119 (2d Cir. 1946): and his dissenting opinion in General Time Instruments Corporation v. United States Time Corporation, 165 F.2d 853, 855 (2d Cir. 1948).

[42] Triangle Publications, Inc. v. Rohrlich, 167 F.2d 969 (2d Cir. 1948).

random. I have been told uniformly by my questionees that no one could reasonably believe that any relation existed between plaintiff's magazine and defendant's girdles.[43]

The opinion concluded with an explicit statement of his position on trade names: "Question has been raised as to whether the trade-name doctrine, by its creation of 'perpetual monopolies' has not injured consumers, a question of peculiarly serious import in these days when living-costs are notoriously oppressive. Since, however, the Supreme Court has approved the doctrine, an intermediate court (such as ours) must enforce it. But, in the absence of legislation so requiring, we should not expand it."[44]

Concern for the unfortunate and disadvantaged, combined with his usual doubts about judicial fact-finding formed Jerome Frank's approach to criminal cases. It was in this area that Frank had his sharpest disagreement with his colleagues on the Learned Hand court and another heated battle with Judge Clark. Ultimately, the Supreme Court was influenced by Frank's advocacy, although perhaps not to the extent that some people think.

Probably more than any other federal judge of the past generation—a period of great judicial expansion of First Amendment and defendants' rights—Frank felt a strong obligation to examine closely criminal appeals and to fashion the law so that the utmost be done to assure a fair trial for the accused. Frank, it must be understood, was much more than a judicial activist in the intellectual and legal sense; his interventionist attitude had strong emotional roots, which is why he was ever the polemicist. To him the crucial area of civil liberties was criminal law and he was not comfortable with conventional civil libertarianism, which concentrated so much on publicized freedom of expression litigation. This is what he told a group of lawyers in 1953, while the controversy over McCarthyism was raging:

Unforgivably I think, too few liberals interest themselves in the undramatic plight of obscure men in nonpolitical criminal cases. In all too many such trials, the prosecutors utilize unjust techniques to obtain convictions of men who may be innocent. Sometimes the unjust practices constitute more or less hidden deviations from the conventional procedures. More frequently, the conventional practices are themselves unjust, and badly need reform. To disregard courthouse injustices to the humble, obscure man is to disregard that which renders a democratic society distinctively

[43] *Ibid.,* p. 976. He then admitted "that my method of obtaining such data is not satisfactory. But it does serve better than anything in this record to illuminate the pivotal fact."

[44] *Ibid.,* pp. 980–81.

antitotalitarian: its devotion to the worth of each person as a unique, unduplicatable, individual.[45]

Perhaps this was largely self-justification, in view of his paltry record in the usual civil liberties areas. Yet, Frank correctly saw that for a lower federal judge in his position, the meaningful opportunities to promote personal rights were presented in criminal law appeals. Here he truly shone, as Learned Hand spoke from the bench two days after Frank's death, "I am sure you have all felt his passionate resentment on any occasion in which the defenseless or the weak were oppressed, especially if they were accused of crime; how tireless was his insistence upon the utmost protection and fairness with which the charges against them must be prosecuted."[46] This feeling was articulated in many opinions and was, indeed, known to many prison inmates. The following letter was sent by an inmate in a New York prison to a Yale Law School professor:

> I guess you know the bad news by now, I have read last week in Times Magazine. One of the Great Judge's of the Federal Judge's for the poor man and for a man's constitutional rights, Hon. Judge Jerome N. Frank has died. He was our friend and one of the Judges in the appeal that granted me the appeal. He died in Conn. State, 67 years old. He put out some big opinions in all cases. That is one Judge I can speak for best. The good always died, the old saying goes . . . Judge Frank has all my blessings, I cannot say no more. It really shock me when I read it. He will be greatly miss by all. He really knew law and was a Liberal Judge. Without him I would never had a chance.[47]

While many of Frank's contentions regarding criminal rights were not accepted by his brethren or, at the time, by the Supreme Court, this was because (from the perspective of what has happened since he died) he was ahead of his time. A number of his opinions have a jurisprudential kinship with decisions of the Warren court. In *United States v. Ebeling*[48] the majority (Clark and Swan) held that where the trial judge had examined the confidential F.B.I. report on the chief witness against a criminal defendant and had declared that he found nothing exculpatory of the defendant in it, counsel for the accused was

---

[45] Jerome Frank, "On Holding Abe Lincoln's Hat," reprinted in Barbara Frank Kristein (ed.), *A Man's Reach* (New York: Macmillan Co., 1965), p. 7.

[46] L. Hand, "Tribute from the Bench," *Yale Law Report*, 3 (1957), 9.

[47] *Ibid.*, p. 12. Judge Clark recalled "that alone among judges, I think, he always carefully considered and *answered* every communication from a prison inmate in our circuit—a real and ever increasing task" ("Jerome N. Frank," *Yale Law Journal*, 66 [1957], 818).

[48] 146 F.2d 254 (2d Cir. 1944).

not entitled to inspect it. In dissent, Frank argued that at least the appellate court should defer decision until it looked at the report to see whether it contained anything that could have affected the guilty verdict. "In such circumstances," he wrote, "nothing will be lost and much which is dear to the spirit of our democratic institutions may be gained by making haste slowly. I, for one, could not sleep well if I thought that, out of a desire for unnecessary expedition, I had helped to affirm the conviction of a man who may be innocent."[49] In *Jencks v. United States*[50] the Supreme Court decided that F.B.I. reports relevant to the evidence presented at the trial must be made available to the defense.

In view of the recent emphasis on the self-incrimination clause of the Fifth Amendment as the cornerstone of constitutional protections for accused persons, Frank's approach to the privilege is most revealing. At a time when the Fifth Amendment right was widely regarded as a secondary freedom, Frank expressed strong feelings for its proper maintenance. Rosario St. Pierre, testifying under subpoena before a federal grand jury, confessed that he had embezzled money entrusted to him. But, invoking the Fifth Amendment, he refused to name the person who had been embezzled; without this information

[49] *Ibid.*, p. 258. Frank, I am convinced, was possessed of a dread that as a judge concerned, in part, with criminal appeals, he might play a role in depriving an innocent person of his liberty. His final book, *Not Guilty*, co-authored with his daughter Barbara, dealt with persons who were convicted of crimes they did not commit. One of his last dissents was over whether one convicted after a trial was entitled to appeal *in forma pauperis* and to the assignment of a lawyer to handle the appeal if the trial judge certified that the appeal was frivolous and not taken in good faith. The majority (Hincks and Medina) said that under the statute a pauper's appeal was not to be allowed. Frank wrote an impassioned dissent. "Surely, even if but one out of a hundred attempted appeals by indigents has merit, justice compels the conclusion that that appeal shall be heard. It is no answer that so many appeals will result as to 'crowd the docket.' If so, more judges should be appointed. True, the cost of running the government will somewhat increase. But I, for one, cannot sleep well if I think that, due to any judicial decisions in which I join, innocent destitute men may be behind bars solely because it will cost the government something to have their appeals considered" (United States v. Johnson, 238 F.2d 565, 571–72 [2d Cir. 1956]). The same fear was expressed in other criminal appeals. Frank's view in United States v. Johnson bears some comparison with the Supreme Court decision the same year in Griffin v. Illinois, 351 U.S. 12, in which it was held that where a state allowed appeals, it was obliged to provide an indigent defendant with the transcript that he needed on appeal. The Supreme Court accepted Frank's position, unanimously reversing the Second Circuit in a per curiam decision (Johnson v. United States, 352 U.S. 565 [1957]).

[50] 353 U.S. 657 (1957).

the government had no case. The district court judge ordered St. Pierre to divulge the name; when he did not do so, he was convicted of contempt and sentenced to prison. Learned Hand, joined by Clark, upheld the conviction on the ground that St. Pierre, by testifying, had waived the privilege. As Hand put it, "After a witness has confessed all the elements of the crime, he may not withhold the details."[51] While the majority was following a considerable body of precedent, Frank disagreed; "Not the disgrace of admitting criminal conduct but the danger of punishment is at the heart of the privilege," he said.[52]

To Frank, the issue was more fundamental than whether St. Pierre had technically waived his right. The real question was the place of the Fifth Amendment in the American scheme of justice. "To avoid misunderstanding," Frank disclosed the "springs" of his dissent in remarks directed to the critics of the constitutional right:

> Those critics, regarding that privilege as pernicious, and knowing that it is difficult to procure the repeal of the constitutional provision which confers it, urge the courts to eliminate it by emasculating interpretations. Any judges who do not readily comply with that suggestion they call "reactionary."
>
> It is easy to caricature the privilege. . . . I have no quarrel with those who assert that the constitutional guaranty of freedom from unreasonable searches and seizures is, at least today, far more important for the preservation of democracy, and far more justifiable on rational grounds, than the constitutional privilege against self-incrimination. But it is not, I think, the business of judges, when deciding cases, to consider the desirability of constitutional provisions. . . .
>
> The privilege is still in our Constitution whether we like it or not, and whether or not we call it a foolish sentimental safeguard of criminals. I happen to think that there is more to be said for the reasonableness of the privilege than its harshest critics will admit . . . reasonable or unreasonable, it is part of the Constitution which we, as judges, took an oath to enforce.[53]

[51] United States v. St. Pierre, 132 F.2d 837, 840 (2d Cir. 1942).

[52] Ibid., p. 842.

[53] Ibid., p. 847. Frank concluded: "I am, then, not moved in this dissent by any sentimental desire to protect criminals or by a desire to prevent as full judicial scrutiny as is practicable of the facts of cases. I am moved by fear of consequences to democratic government in general, and to the courts in particular, of judicial disregard of specific unrepealed sections of the Constitution. Courts, when they conduct themselves in that manner, invite popular rejection of our established legal institutions by unlawful means" (p. 850).

The Supreme Court granted certiorari but then dismissed the appeal because St. Pierre had served his term, making the matter moot (319 U.S. 41 [1943]). The precise question raised in this case apparently has not been decided by the High Court, although before he died Frank doubted that the

In *In re Fried*[54] Frank went further than any other federal judge had gone in suppressing illegally obtained confessions. In this case, Frank and Learned Hand combined to hold that evidence unlawfully obtained in violation of constitutional rights should be suppressed, prior to indictment. In rejecting the government's contention that "an indictment founded upon such illicit evidence will do the appellant no harm, since such evidence will not be admitted at the trial," Frank wrote:

> That is an astonishingly callous argument which ignores the obvious. For a wrongful indictment is no laughing matter; often it works a grievous, irreparable injury to the person indicted. The stigma cannot be easily erased. In the public mind, the blot on a man's escutcheon, resulting from such a public accusation of wrongdoing, is seldom wiped out by a subsequent judgment of not guilty. Frequently, the public remembers the accusation, and still suspects guilt, even after an acquittal.[55]

Frank then launched into an angry denunciation of the persistent use of "third degree" methods in this country: "We have cause for shame as a nation that such foul exploits by government officials are designated 'the American method.' Until such miserable misbehavior is stamped out, it will remain an empty boast that we have, and that we respect, a Constitution which guarantees civil liberties, blocks representatives of government from lawless incursions on the rights of the individual."[56]

Because police and prosecutors continue to use illegal methods to secure evidence, Frank believed that, as a rule of federal judicial administration, all confessions or evidence illegally obtained, whether in violation of the Constitution or of a statute, should be suppressed in advance of indictment.[57] "The F.B.I. and the office of United States Attorney," he pointed out, "are but two different branches of the Department of Justice. I think it irrational that one branch of the

---

majority ruling still had validity (United States v. Courtney, 236 F.2d 921, 923 [2d Cir. 1956]).

Most of Frank's important opinions on self-incrimination were written after 1951. See, particularly, his concurring opinion in United States v. Scully, 225 F.2d 113, 116 (2d Cir. 1955) and his dissent in United States v. Grunewald, 233 F.2d 556, 571 (2d Cir. 1956).

[54] 161 F.2d 453 (2d Cir. 1947).

[55] *Ibid.*, p. 458–59.

[56] *Ibid.*, p. 459.

[57] As to suppression of evidence obtained in violation of a statute, Frank's opinion was a dissent. Learned Hand agreed only that suppression should apply where constitutional prohibitions were infringed. Augustus Hand was against all advance suppression.

Department should be allowed to bring about an indictment through evidence which has come into its possession through any illegal acts of another branch."[58] To the charge that adoption of his position would mean the "coddling of the criminal classes," he answered that it reflected "a failure to recognize that, in its criminal procedure, a democratic society perforce pursues conflicting aims—to convict the guilty without endangering the innocent."[59]

During the 1940's, Frank and Clark disagreed in a number of criminal appeals, but there was no serious clash.[60] Likely, the disagreements were temperate because the issues raised were substantive ones, while, as we have seen repeatedly, the greatest tension between them generally was related to procedural issues.

In fact, Clark's approach to criminal appeals was fundamentally different from that of his more liberal colleague. Applying the labels generally used in referring to Supreme Court justices' votes in this area, Clark certainly would be identified as a strong conservative. In his eyes, even the Supreme Court of the 1940's was guilty of encouraging "the flouting of the criminal law."[61] In one case, Clark wrote a dissenting opinion which brings to mind some recent criticism of Supreme Court decisions on procedural rights as being lax toward criminals. Learned Hand and Swan had reversed a conviction that was based on evidence seized in the course of an arrest made without a warrant. The Second Circuit's two senior judges decided that the police had no reasonable ground for making the arrest and thus the accompanying search was a violation of the Fourth Amendment. Clark could not have disagreed more:

> Of course, the test here is the normal and appropriate reactions of police officers, not the more sophisticated after-rationalizations of a judge in his chambers. True, a judge, particularly an intermediate judge, cannot be insensitive to a present strong trend toward special care and consideration in criminal prosecu-

[58] *In re* Fried, p. 460.

[59] *Ibid.*, p. 461. Certiorari was granted, but later dismissed at the request of the petitioner, the United States government (332 U.S. 807 [1947]).

[60] In United States v. Ebeling, discussed above, Clark wrote the court's opinion rejecting the contention that the defendant's lawyer was entitled to the F.B.I. reports, and in United States v. St. Pierre, Clark supported Learned Hand's view that by testifying he had committed a crime, St. Pierre forfeited later claim to the privilege against self-incrimination. In both cases, and in other criminal cases where they sat together and disagreed, there were few angry words.

[61] Memorandum in U.S. v. Samuel Dunkel & Co., February 17, 1949. In a 1940 memorandum he wrote that the "Supreme Court has gone too absurdly far in the wire tapping cases already" (U.S. v. Falcone, May 6, 1940).

tions, perhaps even more so where the guilt of the accused is clear. This is surely understandable in the case of many important crimes as a reasonable, even if quixotic, demonstration to a world calloused to brutality of the beneficent contrast afforded by the American spirit of fair play. But it has less desirable consequences in the enforcement of regulatory legislation, where our undisciplined individualism makes even so desirable a war measure as the conservation of gasoline resented and thwarted all too often. Here so gigantic was the task of enforcement, so few the number of federal enforcing authorities, that a breakdown of the law must inevitably have occurred unless the co-operation of local police officers was assured. Any one who has worked at law enforcement—particularly in smaller communities, where cause and effect are more quickly and surely traced—knows how a lack of support from the agencies higher up is accepted as a legitimate excuse for weariness or laxity of the officers on the street. That does not excuse illegality. It does suggest that a decision which must operate as a limiting direction to the police should carry conviction of its own accommodation to the realities of everyday life and the practical thinking of ordinary persons, lest it discourage honest effort at necessary policing. I venture to believe that, given a few restrictive and ununderstood decisions of this nature, the local police would be led to leave the federal men to their own more polite means of and attempts at law enforcement.[62]

The one criminal law issue which provoked a direct conflict between Clark and Frank involved both substantive and procedural questions. The Federal Rules of Civil Procedure[63] and the Federal Rules of Criminal Procedure[64] provide that errors made in the course of a judicial proceeding which do not affect substantial rights or justice shall be disregarded. The purpose of this "harmless error" doctrine is to eliminate setting verdicts aside simply because mistakes had been made in the course of a trial when these mistakes could not have affected the outcome. As Justice Rutledge put it in a key Supreme Court decision on the doctrine, the rule "comes down on its face to a very plain admonition: 'Do not be technical, where technicality does not really hurt the party whose rights in the trial and in its outcome the technicality affects.' "[65]

To Judge Clark, whose constant aim it was to avoid complicating procedure, the concept of "harmless error" made good sense, both in civil and criminal litigation. The rule simplified the judicial process

---

[62] United States v. Di Re, 159 F.2d 818, 821–22 (2d Cir. 1947). The Second Circuit ruling was affirmed in the Supreme Court by a 7–2 vote (United States v. Di Re, 332 U.S. 581 [1948]).

[63] Rule 61.

[64] Rule 52.

[65] Kotteakos v. United States, 328 U.S. 750, 760 (1946).

and, if properly interpreted, meant that counsel for the losing party could not gain a new trial whenever minor errors were committed. Jerome Frank, too, was an ardent proponent of the rule, at least in civil cases. In an early 1942 opinion for the court he wrote that "there has developed—the doctrine of 'harmless error,' which, to the chagrin of those devoted to a conception of litigation as a game of skill, has led to a marked reduction of reversals based upon procedural errors which do no real harm."[66] Significantly, the decision in this case was in favor of a bankrupt widow.

Later the same year, Frank expanded on the same theme in another civil case:

> As opposed to a judicial system where every technical slipup may be instantly appealed and will be automatically held to be fatal, ours is one in which correction is not ordinarily possible until the conclusion of the litigation, at which time only the seriously prejudicial defects will be dignified by appellate attention. The philosophy behind this practice is that many mistakes, apparently important at the time, will be seen to be trivial from the perspective of a final disposition of the case, and that disputes will therefore be more expeditiously settled. The principle is that of relatively speedy justice.[67]

In several other civil appeals, Frank took the same position.[68] But even in civil cases, Frank was not a consistent supporter of the "harmless error" rule. In an appeal from a jury verdict favorable to a bus company that was sued by a woman for the death of her mother, he dissented from a holding that an error in the trial judge's charge to the jury—which had been corrected at the end of the charge—was harmless. "I find it impossible . . . to decide," he opined, "that the jury were correctly guided. To say that the jurymen were not misled is to indulge in unverified and unverifiable guessing. . . . Who are we that we should so confidently probe the mental interiors of the jurors."[69] Perhaps the explanation for Frank's failure to back up application of "harmless error" in this case is that the party hurt by the mistake was an underdog.

Certainly in criminal law appeals, Frank's intense desire to prevent any miscarriage of justice colored his approach to the doctrine. All of his colleagues strongly favored utilization of "harmless error" analysis in reviewing convictions. Frank believed that the Second

---

[66] *In re* Barnett, 124 F.2d 10005, 10011 (2d Cir. 1942).

[67] Perkins v. Endicott Johnson Corp., 128 F.2d 208, 211–212 (2d Cir. 1942).

[68] For example, Perrone v. Pennsylvania R., 143 F.2d 168 (2d Cir. 1944) and Westchester County Park Commission v. United States, 143 F.2d 688 (2d Cir. 1944).

[69] Keller v. Brooklyn Bus Corp., 128 F.2d 510, 517–18 (2d Cir. 1942).

JUDGES FRANK AND CLARK

Circuit attitude toward the "harmless error" rule amounted to the proposition that the upper court judges would review the trial record and, if they concluded that the convicted man was guilty, they would rule that the defect in the proceedings was harmless. This was wrong, he felt, because "the doctrine of 'harmless error' does not dispense with the necessity of a fair trial of a defendant whom the appellate judges believe to be guilty. . . . As I understand the fundamental principle of the jury system, we appellate judges do not sit as a jury. . . . I cannot subscribe to a rule that what is substantial reversible error depends not on whether it probably affected the jury to the substantial prejudice of the defendant but on whether we appellate judges think the defendant guilty or innocent."[70]

In this criticism of the other members of the Second Circuit, Frank had accurately described how they approached the issue.[71] But by rejecting the common sense conception of "harmless error," Frank left his own position vulnerable. Since he insisted that appellate judges cannot "confidently probe the mental interiors of the jurors,"[72] how can they ever determine that an error was not prejudicial? Moreover, on the relationship of the doctrine to a defendant's guilt, since the question to be decided on appeal was whether the error had led to a denial of substantial justice, how could the subject of guilt be avoided? Short of denying the place of "harmless error" in all criminal cases, Frank would be faced with the same criticism as he directed against his colleagues. His answer was, "I think the correct rule is this: We should reverse where error has been committed, regardless of our belief as to guilt or innocence, unless we conclude that in all probability the error had no effect on the jury; or, to phrase it differently, that the record is such that, if there had been no error, no reasonably sane jury could have acquitted, or that there is no reasonable ground for thinking that the jury was misled by error."[73]

It is immediately apparent that this formulation, while more favorable to defendants, is not without problems.[74] It, too, requires

[70] United States v. Liss, 137 F.2d 995, 1001–2 (2d Cir. 1943). Frank's opinion in this case was his first dissent against the application of the doctrine to criminal law.

[71] In the Liss case, Learned Hand spoke for the majority: "Perhaps all that a court should ever say is that a remote chance of prejudice should not balance the extreme probability that the jury came to the right result" (p. 999).

[72] *Ibid.,* p. 1003.

[73] United States v. Rubenstein, 151 F.2d 915, 924 (2d Cir. 1945).

[74] Frank recognized this, for in Rubenstein he wrote in a footnote to his own approach: "True, even with the rule thus limited, the appeal judges are conjecturing as to whether the evidence affected the jury. But the area of guessing is severely restricted" (p. 922, n. 11).

upper-court examination of the trial record and a judgment by the appellate judges as to guilt. There is no other way to determine whether without the error "no reasonably sane jury could have acquitted." In the final analysis, Frank would balance probabilities, which is really what the majority was doing. True, he insisted on giving a break, or the benefit of the doubt to the defendant, but this alone does not make his approach more logical than the alternative one. However, Frank's position was more consistent with the belief that proof of guilt must be beyond a reasonable doubt.

Although a minority of one on the court, Frank continued to go it alone on this issue, even after the Supreme Court had refused to review "harmless error" cases taken to it from the Second Circuit.[75] "Although usually I concur in the established precedents of this court even when I think them erroneous," he explained in one dissent, "I deem it not improper to continue to dissent in cases of this kind until the Supreme Court tells me that I am wrong."[76]

In this last case, *United States v. Bennett,* Judges Chase and Learned Hand, without referring at all to the "harmless error" principle, upheld a conspiracy conviction, although the judge—over the objection of the defendant's lawyer—had charged the jury: "Did she steal them? Who did if she didn't? You are to decide that." What the judge was saying was that in order for the jury to acquit, it had to determine who else may have committed the crime. This was an error, of course, and a serious one, at that; the majority view is hard to comprehend. Not surprisingly, the Supreme Court accepted the appeal and upset the jury verdict, holding that the error was prejudicial.[77]

This was the High Court's first reversal of the Second Circuit in a "harmless error" case in which Frank had dissented. On the same day, in a more important case from the Second Circuit, *Kotteakos v. United States,*[78] the Supreme Court took a big step toward embracing Frank's conception of "harmless error," though he had not participated when the appeal was heard by the Second Circuit.[79]

[75] However, in United States v. Bramson, 139 F.2d 598 (2d Cir. 1943), he wrote the opinion upholding the conviction, even though a defense witness had been improperly asked whether she was a Communist. Frank wrote that "in the context of this lengthy trial and in the light of the mass of evidence against the defendants, we think it was not so prejudicial as to constitute reversible error" (p. 600).

[76] United States v. Bennett, 152 F.2d 342, 349 (2d Cir. 1945).

[77] Bihn v. United States, 328 U.S. 633 (1946). The vote was 5–3, with Justice Douglas writing the majority opinion and Justice Black speaking for the dissenters.

[78] 328 U.S. 750 (1946).

[79] United States v. Lekacos, 151 F.2d 170 (2d Cir. 1945). The panel upholding the convictions of three men was made up of Judges Learned and Augustus Hand, and Judge Swan.

Even before these two decisions, the Supreme Court had moved toward Frank's view when in *Bollenbach v. United States* it reversed a Second Circuit decision that an erroneous instruction to the jury was insufficient grounds for reversal of a conviction. The judge had told the jurors that they could presume that a person accused of transporting stolen securities in interstate commerce was the thief because they were found in his possession.[80] Once more, the error seems quite important; also, the lower court opinion did not mention the "harmless error" doctrine. All in all, the High Court's reversal in *Bollenbach* taken by itself did not necessarily indicate that it was dissatisfied with the Second Circuit's approach to "harmless error." However, Justice Frankfurter's opinion for the court employed an argument similar to that which had been advanced by Jerome Frank:

> From presuming too often all errors to be "prejudicial," the judicial pendulum need not swing to presuming all errors to be "harmless" if only the appellate court is left without doubt that one who claims its corrective process is, after all, guilty. In view of the place of importance that trial by jury has in our Bill of Rights, it is not to be supposed that Congress intended to substitute the belief of appellate judges in the guilt of an accused, however justifiably engendered by the dead record, for ascertainment of guilt by a jury under appropriate judicial guidance, however cumbersome that process may be.[81]

The *Bollenbach* ruling came down shortly before the Second Circuit began its consideration of *United States v. Antonelli Fireworks Co.*, an appropriately named case because it was the occasion for a major conflict between Clark and Frank over the "harmless error" rule. Before going into this case, it is well to note that up until *Antonelli*, although Frank's dissenting opinions on "harmless error" were as angry as any other that he had written, the four Coolidge appointees who formed the majority and wrote the opinions in most of these cases, did not seem perturbed. For the most part, Clark was on the sidelines, but he was plainly upset over Frank's insistence on pressuring the Second Circuit—and, in effect, the Supreme Court—to adopt his formulation of the doctrine.[82]

[80] United States v. Bollenbach, 147 F.2d 199 (2d Cir. 1945). The opinion was by Learned Hand, who was supported by Augustus Hand and Chase.

[81] Bollenbach v. United States, 326 U.S. 607, 615 (1946). The vote was 7–1; Justice Black alone dissented.

[82] During the 1946 controversy over Antonelli, Clark wrote to Frank: "I had strenuously opposed, as quite unfounded, your charges against the court, even in cases I had not been in, and had taken the somewhat unusual course in connection with one of these cases, I think the Bennett case, of writing you a letter of protest" (May 17, 1946).

On November 21, 1945, eight days after the Supreme Court granted certiorari in the *Kotteakos* case,[83] Clark wrote to Learned Hand: "I am informed from Washington that Jerry has been down lobbying with the Supreme Court law clerks against what he likes to term the dreadful 'Second Circuit rule' of harmless error, and that the law clerks are all emotionally upset—so much so that it is confidently believed the Supreme Court only awaits an appropriate vehicle for Felix to write a scathing condemnation of us for our brutality."[84]

Hand responded diplomatically, deliberately ignoring Clark's allegation of Frank's "lobbying": "What you say about the 'Second Circuit Rule' of harmless error, disturbs me. I am quite aware that Felix is 'hot and bothered' about the way we deal with criminal appeals, and it may be he will be able to get a majority with him; but from what I have heard so far, he was not able to do so."[85] But Hand's tactic only temporarily defused a Clark-Frank clash. In March 1946, the *Antonelli* case came before a Second Circuit panel composed of the Chief Judge and the court's two junior members.

Antonelli is the sort of criminal appeal which in perhaps 99 of 100 cases would be decided without any real difficulty and without dissent. But Jerome Frank was no ordinary judge, and out of his deep concern for criminal justice grew a scathing (and, in some ways, petty) dissent and the disagreement with Clark.

The appeal was taken by a company and a number of its officers, convicted after a six-week trial of conspiracy to defraud the government by producing defective munitions. The evidence, as detailed by Judge Clark in his majority opinion, seems quite substantial and convincing, a conclusion not seriously challenged by Frank's angry words. What caused the disagreement in the appellate court was the concluding sentence of the prosecutor's summation: "I cherish an overwhelming confidence, ladies and gentlemen," said the man from the United States Attorney's office, "in the belief that each one of you, after you have been instructed by the Court, will each render your verdict without malice, but without sympathy, that you will each

[83] The Supreme Court granted certiorari in the Kotteakos (Lekacos) appeal on November 13, 1945, and handed down its decision on June 10, 1946; it agreed to review Bihn (Bennett) on February 11, 1946, and rendered its decision on June 10, 1946, and Bollenbach was decided by the High Court on January 28, 1946. The Second Circuit heard argument in Antonelli in March, 1946; its ruling was made on May 2, 1946.

[84] CEC to LH, November 21, 1945.

[85] LH to CEC, November 27, 1945. As we have seen, less than two months later the Supreme Court reversed the Second Circuit in Bollenbach by a vote of 7–1, with Frankfurter writing the majority opinion.

render a verdict of which you can always be proudly justified in the presence of your fellow men, those here at home who labor and have labored unceasingly in an honest effort to manufacture munitions of war as well as those of us beyond the seas who look to us for the things they need to sustain them in their hour of extreme sacrifice." Following this, the trial judge asked the defense counsel whether they had any exceptions, whereupon objection was made to the appeal to patriotism and several other matters. The following day, while charging the jury, the judge specifically told them to disregard the prosecutor's remarks because "we would do our government a disservice if we allowed the hysteria of war to usurp the place of calm deliberation in deciding this case, and we would do these defendants a great injustice."[86]

Now it is extremely doubtful that after a long trial with much evidence and many witnesses, and the caution by the judge to the jurors, that the zealous prosecutorial comments really prejudiced the defendants' case; one must say, using Frank's own "harmless error' philosophy, that there was "no reasonable ground for thinking that the jury was misled by error." Clark's opinion actually affirmed the jury result without reliance on the doctrine. Then, strangely and disjointedly, since he had just dismissed other assignments of error, Clark decided to say something about "harmless error" just as he was concluding his opinion. Perhaps he had finished most of his opinion when he got Frank's acerbic dissent and he decided to add these words:

> In the review of a criminal conviction after a long and bitterly fought trial, there is considerable incentive for reviewing judges to order reversal. It is comparatively easy to single out particular instances, which, apart from their setting in the total trial, may afford a dramatic basis for appeal to the American spirit of fair play and cherished love of personal liberty. Such an opinion writes itself, chances of reversal and reinstatement of the verdict are remote, and academic claim is assured. . . . Of course we must be acutely sensitive to errors affecting human rights and freedom; but there is an equal demand that the law should have its way when a long and fair trial has proceeded to its natural conclusion.[87]

Frank opened his dissent with a sort of defense for his decision to dissent once more: "I have no respect for the humorless self-righteous sort of person who has a firm conviction that always he alone, of the entire regiment, is in step. Accordingly, when all my colleagues (whom I consider among the ablest of judges) repeatedly

[86] United States v. Antonelli Fireworks Co., 155 F.2d 631, 637–38, 645, n. 5 (2d Cir. 1946).

[87] *Ibid.*, pp. 641–42.

arrive at a certain conclusion, my sense of humor usually downs my doubts and nudges me into acquiescence. But on the subject of 'harmless error' in criminal trials, I find myself, because of the deep seriousness of the matter, unable to follow that course."[88] Frank then tried to show that the majority had distorted the facts, but without much success. His main point, in this regard, was the revelation that the defendants were Italian and that the trial took place shortly after the 1944 Allied landing at Normandy. The bulk of the extremely long opinion consists of a reiteration of the familiar views on "harmless error," judicial fact-finding, and the jury system. All in all, Frank's strenuous effort to demonstrate a reasonable possibility that the accused did not have a fair trial is not convincing. *Antonelli* was probably his weakest dissent on "harmless error," something that he may have recognized, for in the final analysis his case for reversal was posited on the ground that, independent of impact, what the prosecutor said was wrong and prejudicial per se. The prosecutor, he contended, "should not be permitted to summon that thirteenth juror, prejudice. . . . When the government puts a citizen to the hazards of a criminal jury trial, a government attorney should not be allowed to increase those hazards unfairly. When, as here, such an attorney has done so, I, as a government servant am unwilling to approve the result."[89] As a prophylactic, much-needed because United States attorneys frequently employ inflammatory language, he argued that the *attempt* in *Antonelli* should be punished by a reversal, which "might well serve as a deterrent: If it became known that misconduct of a United States Attorney had caused the public the expense of a new trial, his resultant unpopularity might tend to make him subsequently live up to professional standards of courtroom decency."[90]

Although Frank's dissent in *Antonelli* was sharply critical of his colleagues,[91] it was no more so than others he had written on the

88 *Ibid.*, p. 642.

89 *Ibid.*, pp. 659–60.

90 *Ibid.*, pp. 661–62.

91 With or without due respect, Frank included the following in his opinion: "And I think this court needlessly falls far short of it [fairness], if it affirms a conviction of defendants, obtained in marked violation of the rules governing fair trials, merely because the judges of this court believe those defendants guilty. If it does so, it is, I think helping to undermine a basic tenet of the American faith. That seems to me to be dangerous in these days when America is seeking to induce the world to accept its conception of civilization as a pattern of world order. Perhaps my sense of humor has indeed deserted me, and I indulge in exaggeration; but I think not: The courts alone can neither create moral principles nor tear them down, but they can be among the vital agencies which either preserve or corrode them. "Lawyers may talk rhapsodically about JUSTICE. They may, in Bar

same subject. But, unlike the other judges who reacted passively, if at all, Clark was angered by what Frank had written. There was already strong feeling on both sides at the conference after argument and this was carried over into the memoranda exchanged before the decision was issued. The controversy continued for some months, erupting sharply with a post-decision letter from Frank denying Clark's alleged conference suggestion that he "had improperly engaged in propaganda activities with the Supreme Court law clerks." Frank also wanted to dispose of "a rumor to the effect that you were critical of the fact that my next session, in the course on the Judicial Process at Yale Law School, I intend to devote to 'harmless error.' I hope the rumor of your criticism is unfounded. If not, then let me say that you ought to know me well enough to trust that, as a pedagogue, my aim is socratically to bring out all sides of a discussed issue, leaving it to the students to reach their own conclusions."[92]

Clark replied at once, returning the letter, "as I know nothing about the facts to which reference is made." Instead of leaving it at that, he continued, "It is my understanding that you have sent copies of your Antonelli opinion to various persons in or about the Supreme Court, and that this was done in previous cases. This does seem to be inappropriate." Then, in reference to the "harmless error" debate and Yale, he wrote, "I do think that on this particular issue you have made violent, unrestrained personal attacks upon the individual members of this court which are not sustained on the record of our conduct; and it seems to me that carrying this forward to the law schools can only make the situation more distressing."[93]

Predictably, Frank quickly wrote back, denying Clark's charges and accusing his colleague of "personalizing what I said in my dissent in the Antonelli case." He also defended his practice of sending copies of some of his opinions to several Supreme Court justices.[94] On the same day, two more letters were sent: Clark admitting that "in the

---

Association meetings, hymn the pre-eminent virtues of "our Lady of the Common Law," prostrate themselves devotedly before the miracle of the common law's protection of human liberties. But in the last analysis, there is only one practical way to test puddings: If, again and again in concrete instances, courts unnecessarily take the chance of having innocent men sent to jail or put to death by the government because they have been found guilty by juries persuaded by unfair appeals to improper prejudice, then the praises of our legal system will be but beautiful verbal garlands concealing ugly practices we have not the courage, or have grown too callous, to contemplate" (p. 663).

[92] JNF to CEC, May 15, 1946.
[93] CEC to JNF, May 15, 1946.
[94] JNF to CEC, May 16, 1946.

final analysis each of us must be the ultimate judge of what he himself does,"[95] while Frank, in a conciliatory mood, claimed that if he had been told before he filed his opinion that it contained "violent, unrestrained personal attacks upon the individual members of this court,' I would have altered it."[96]

Five letters were exchanged in the first two days of this correspondence war; many more were sent in the following weeks. The conflict over "harmless error" spilled over into other areas of disagreement. Sometime in the summer it petered out. However, Clark never really forgave Frank for the *Antonelli* dissent; it was one of their two substantive disagreements that probably bothered him until his death. Twelve years after the case was decided—and a year after Frank died—he wrote to Professor Edmond Cahn, a close friend of Frank: "Jerry had one unfortunate habit which I steadily criticized, but without effect. That was a tendency to ascribe fairly unconscionable positions to his colleagues against their openly stated views, preparatory to demolition of the straw men thus created. An outstanding (but not sole) example was that of the doctrine, so called, of 'harmless error.' "[97]

Interestingly, while Frank may have "pressured" the Supreme Court to reverse in *Antonelli*—and at the same time that the High Court was critically reviewing two of the lower court's decisions in the same area—certiorari was denied in this case. Still, less than six weeks after the *Antonelli* decision of the intermediate court, the Supreme Court decisively rejected the Second Circuit's doctrine of "harmless error." In *Kotteakos v. United States,* Justice Rutledge wrote for the majority that while the "harmless error" statute "makes no distinction between civil and criminal causes," "this does not mean that the same criteria shall always be applied regardless of this difference."[98] He then elaborated the majority's approach to the issue, and while it is not all that clear, it is certainly closer to that of Frank's than to the view of his colleagues. Judge Frank once again had an influence on the Supreme Court and on American law.[99]

[95] CEC to JNF, May 16, 1946.

[96] JNF to CEC, May 16, 1946.

[97] CEC to Professor Edmond Cahn, February 25, 1958.

[98] 328 U.S. 750, 762 (1946).

[99] The degree of influence can only be guessed at, though there is a tendency to rate it very high and to assume that the Supreme Court accepted all of Frank's position. This was not the case. True, he did call attention to the subject and he did in a considerable way affect the shape of the law in this area. The most direct impact of his "harmless error" polemics was in the publicity he gave to a problem no one cared very much about; without Frank the Supreme Court would not have become as involved as it did. But once the Supreme Court addressed itself to "harmless error," it did so in a context not exactly established by him. Of the three Second Circuit

While Clark and Frank had divergent philosophies toward criminal law, their approaches to civil liberties matters were quite similar. Both judges were of libertarian persuasion, yet, even here, they managed to become embroiled in what probably was their nastiest and most memorable fight of the decade.

In view of his hard-line attitude in criminal appeals, Clark's liberalism on the First Amendment and related issues may come as a surprise. All that this proves is that Clark cannot be easily catalogued as a liberal or conservative; generally a liberal, he cannot be so classified with respect to criminal cases. He resisted stereotyping, something that he recognized in a 1959 letter to John Frank. "I sometimes feel," he wrote, "that my judicial course is nicely attuned to displease everyone—the liberals, by not being easy on the confirmed crooks, and the conservatives, by speaking now and then for minority groups."[100]

As was true of their colleagues, neither Clark nor Frank had much opportunity to speak out via judicial opinions on the important civil liberties and civil rights issues of the past generation. Of the two men, in opinions, memoranda, and extrajudicial writings, Clark was by far the more eloquent and insistent in articulating a libertarian-activist point of view. Throughout the decade, and into the 1950's, Frank, perhaps calculatingly, refrained from going into the crucial First Amendment problems of individual freedom. There is nothing in this area remotely approaching the forcefulness of his advocacy of

---

decisions touching on "harmless error" which were reversed in 1946—Bollenbach, Bihn, and Kotteakos—Frank participated and dissented in one, and this (Bihn) happened to be the least important of the three. In Kotteakos Justice Rutledge, citing the majority and dissenting opinions in Antonelli, wrote: "Discussion, some of it recent, has undertaken to formulate the problem in terms of presumptions. . . . [but] it would seem that any attempt to create a generalized presumption to apply in all cases would be contrary not only to the spirit of . . . [the statute] but also to the expressed intent of its legislative sponsors" (328 U.S. 765). Moreover, as was mentioned above, it is not without significance that certiorari was denied in Antonelli—and, indeed, in most of the other cases on the subject in which Frank dissented.

On the specific "harmless error" issue of inflammatory comments by prosecutors, as in the Antonelli case, neither the Supreme Court nor the Second Circuit has accepted Frank's approach. The lower court, of course, was considerably more cautious after 1946 in upholding convictions where errors had been made in the charge to the jury. Over the second five years of the Learned Hand court, Frank wrote only one "harmless error" dissent, United States v. Farina, 184 F.2d 18, 21 (2d Cir. 1950).

[100] CEC to John Frank, June 25, 1957.

defendants' rights.[101] Even during the McCarthy witch hunts in the late 1940's and early 1950's, when so much was being written about freedom of expression, he concentrated on other questions. In his most direct comment on "the anti-democratic spirit of intolerance generated by the 'McCarthyism' of the early 1950's,"[102] he was far less critical of this spirit than were Judges Learned Hand and Clark in their pronouncements during the same period:

> Someone has mentioned the "paradise of the imagination." But the imagination also has its hell. In that hell are conceived, these days, unfounded calumnies. Without opportunity to prove their innocence, without a court trial conducted according to our Constitution and our traditions of fair play, men, on the basis of such calumnies, are pronounced guilty of grave misconduct. No court enters judgments against them, but the consequences are often penalties stiffer than a court would exact after a trial—dismissals from jobs, the loss of the means of earning a living in occupations for which they were trained. A drop of acid gossip suffices to curdle a reputation irrevocably.
>
> Guilt is imputed to any man who, unknown to him, employed another, later revealed as a spy—as if to say that George Washington should have been suspected of treason because the traitor Benedict Arnold was one of his trusted generals.
>
> Our democracy, we had thought until now, prized a high degree of privacy for the ordinary man, afforded him some shelter from public scrutiny, some insulated enclosure, some enclave, some inviolate place as his castle. Unless we call a halt, such castles may soon be obsolete. Those who speak up for civil liberties are often now regarded as impractical visionaries—or worse.[103]

However, Frank emphasized that it was important that liberals "not fail also to note" that in each past period of repression

> there was some objective justification for the fear which prompted those methods, there were then some persons who deserved not persecution but prosecution and conviction after a fair trial. So in our revulsion against contemporary despicable, fear-stimulated conduct, let us not lose sight of the frightening dangers that warrant some real apprehensions, of the fact that the totalitarian regime, which deems us the enemy, does have some active but secret agents in our midst. Since our "days are danger-ridden" indeed, little wonder that for some of us, "the nightmare rides upon sleep."[104]

[101] In *A Man's Reach*, a collection of Frank's most representative writings on and off the bench, edited by his daughter and subtitled *The Philosophy of Judge Jerome Frank*, there is only one piece touching on freedom of speech.

[102] Kristein, *A Man's Reach*, p. 1. The quotation is from the introductory comments of the editor.

[103] Jerome Frank, "On Holding Abe Lincoln's Hat," in *ibid.*, p. 4.

[104] *Ibid.*, p. 5

Elsewhere in this speech, Frank cautioned liberals to fight "against those who pooh-pooh all talk of real internal dangers,"[105] and placed himself in opposition to "the fashion in pseudo liberal circles [which] dictates severe criticism of the F.B.I."[106]

Frank's reaction to the anti-Communist mood of the postwar period raises certain questions which we shall return to later. For the moment it is enough to note that the conventional image of Frank as a civil libertarian should not be accepted uncritically.

Although in several of his public addresses Clark was rather guarded in his advocacy of judicial activism to preserve personal rights, he could write with a concentrated passion when governmental agencies were engaged in witch hunts or basic freedoms were threatened. In a 1942 paper he identified himself with certain critics of our democratic system:

> Of course, we must expect some delays in the operation of the democratic process, and we must yield to dictatorships the palm for direct and speedy action even in peace and most certainly in war. Even so, we have tolerated certain clogs on that process which appear not merely unnecessary, but also unwise, in a truly democratic organization. There is a gap between the people and their representatives which we do not bridge, and which serves admirably to promote irresponsibility and disunity.[107]

A year earlier, in 1941, his concern for First Amendment freedoms was plainly evident in two opinions. In the first of these, he disagreed with his colleagues' ruling that a congressman could sue a newspaper that allegedly had published false statements about him. Said Clark, in words that bring to mind recent decisions on libel:

> Even more dangerous is the rationale of the decision that a comment leading an appreciable number of readers to hate or hold in contempt the public official commented on is libelous per se. Its broad sweep would take in comments found day after day in the most conservative newspapers. . . . Minority comment on labor, religious and political views and activities of politicians become therefore hazardous. . . . Of course, the uncertain threat of suit, invited by a rule at once so vague and so extensive, is a restriction on freedom of the press almost as direct as a rule of clear liability.
>
> I do not think it an adequate answer to such a threat against public comment, which seems to me necessary if democratic processes are to function, to say that it applies only to false statements.[108]

[105] *Ibid.*

[106] *Ibid.,* p. 7.

[107] Clark, "The Function of Law in a Democratic Society," reprinted in Wright and Reasoner, *Procedure,* p. 166.

[108] Sweeney v. Schenectady Union Publishing Co., 122 F.2d 288, 291–92 (2d Cir. 1941).

The Supreme Court affirmed the Second Circuit by an equally divided court;[109] however, Clark's view was ultimately adopted by the High Court in the historic *New York Times* case.[110]

In the second First Amendment case in 1941, Clark, joined by Swan, ruled unconstitutional a New York City ordinance prohibiting the public distribution of commercial handbills. The measure, which actually was designed to prevent litter, was struck down as violative of the First Amendment, the majority interpreting Supreme Court decisions to mean that no distinction was to be made between commercial and other handbills.[111] Judge Frank dissented on the ground that the case did not present a real free speech issue. His position was unanimously accepted by the Supreme Court.[112] While Clark does seem to have gone too far in stretching First Amendment rights, in his defense it might at least be said that he erred on the side of the angels.

There can be no doubt that Clark and Frank had strong, liberal feelings on the subject of racial discrimination; but Frank, over the entire ten years, did not hear a single appeal in this area, while Clark's participation was limited to one case. There, in an opinion largely relying upon the legislative history of the Selective Service Act, he took issue with his colleagues' affirmation of the trial court's dismissal of a Negro's challenge to his draft call which was based on a racial quota system. Clark believed that separate calls for blacks and whites was a discriminatory practice, but he did not make use of the Fourteenth Amendment's guarantee of equal protection and his opinion was not very inspired.[113] The case did not squarely present any constitutional question, at least not in the context of judicial policy of the early 1940's. Clark's feelings on race relations were expressed more clearly in a "somewhat pessimistic letter" to Professor Howard Odum:

> I have warm friends over various parts of the South and my instinctive feeling after many years is to avoid any discussion of the Negro problem whatsoever just because the gulf seems so wide. A year or so ago I did get into a little dispute down in New Orleans because one of the more intellectual ladies of the place could not let the subject alone, but kept demanding whether I did not know and would not concede that they knew

109 Schenectady Union Publishing Co. v. Sweeney, 316 U.S. 642 (1942).
110 New York Times Co. v. Sullivan, 376 U.S. 254 (1964).
111 Christensen v. Valentine, 122 F.2d 511 (2d Cir. 1941).
112 Valentine v. Christensen, 316 U.S. 52 (1942).
113 United States *ex rel.* Lynn v. Downer, 140 F.2d 397, 401 (2d Cir. 1944).

the Negro problem so much better than we and that our inter-
ference postponed settlements. She kept demanding an outright
answer, and you can imagine what happened when finally I
yielded to the badgering and answered.[114]

Clark's most important civil liberties opinions were written after
the war and were, in large measure, impelled by the atmosphere and
actions provoked by the Cold War. In 1949 he discussed "the dilemma
of American judges" in the pages of the *American Bar Association
Journal*. In this article, which was concerned with the debate over
judicial activism in the First Amendment field, he decried "the present
judicial tendency to avoid invalidation at almost all cost," pointing
out that

> the present negative approach of the judges is, in the light of
> tradition, itself a decision—indeed, as popularly conceived, a deci-
> sion "validating" questioned legislation. The problem is again
> immediately insistent because of the present sharp challenge to
> personal liberties. For once more we find ourselves in an era of
> widespread hysteria, so often the aftermath of war, when suppres-
> sion of opinion and its expression by dissident elements appears to
> be the popular course and only the courts have even seeming
> authority to call a halt. Since, however, this authority turns out
> to be more seeming than actual, the semblance of control tends
> rather to promote than to restrain official irresponsibility while
> the constitutional promise of protection remains unfulfilled.[115]

This is strong stuff, certainly for the *American Bar Association
Journal* in 1949. Yet, for a judge who was trying to make a case for
libertarian activism, Clark's conclusion was strikingly similar to the
position of Learned Hand, who was saying that where liberty is en-
dangered judges alone cannot save it. Clark was at the time a First
Amendment activist, and so it seems that in presenting his views to
a wider audience he was, perhaps unconsciously, influenced by Learned
Hand. None of this should detract from his blast at "the present sharp
challenge to personal liberties," characterized by "widespread hysteria"
and "suppression of opinion." Clark was a civil libertarian and, as

[114] CEC to Howard Odum, April 6, 1951. Later in this letter he wrote,
"We are all so implicated because to the rest of the world our country as a
whole, both North and South, is responsible for the situation."
  More than a year later (December 8, 1952), Clark discussed the same issue
and, again, he was in a pessimistic frame of mind: "Over the entire history
of the [Supreme] Court it can well be repeated that the Fourteenth Amendment designed to protect the Negro has, except for some ten years, protected
everyone else but."
[115] Clark, "The Dilemma of American Judges: Is Too Great 'Trust for
Salvation' Placed in Them?," reprinted in Wright and Reasoner, *Procedure*,
p. 198.

time went on, his addresses more adequately reflected the activist strain in him. In the final year or two of his life he boldly outlined the "limits of judicial objectivity" and expressed "a plea for the unprincipled decision."[116] In these essays Clark specifically rejected Professor Herbert Wechsler's call for "neutral principles" in judicial decision-making; it is noteworthy that Wechsler had taken a moderate position, in rebuttal to the ultra-restraintist approach of Learned Hand in the Holmes lectures. But, argued Clark,

> there is no way that decision can be avoided; there is only a kind of pressure—even presumption—to choose what seems the side closest to precedent and past action. And that means a conservative vote for inaction and the status quo. It is a sad, but little noticed, fact that neutral principles eventually push to re-enforce the dead hand of the law and the rule of the past.
> Here, therefore, is my deeply felt, even if not particularly original argument. We need the unprincipled decision, i.e., the unprecedented and novel decision . . . of the kind in fact which has been a glorious heritage of the [Supreme] Court's history.[117]

Clark then specifically answered Learned Hand:

> Even if I may have erred in this analysis of their [restraintist] views, the obvious cautionary admonition for the justice or judge is clearly there, whatever the explanation of a particular case may be. And that is what I fear the most and why I speak out here once more. It seems that—unlike the thirties—the conservative approach has become the respectable one, even honored by the tribute of the Holmes Lectures. . . . For my part I do not fear to be governed by "Plato's wise men," or even replicas of them. I do fear to be left to the tender mercies of judges who shiver to take the responsibility of forthright decision along lines never before attempted.[118]

While Clark's most activist extrajudicial writings came at the end of his life, many years earlier, as a judge, he took forthright positions in civil liberties appeals. At the height of the Cold War, he was a judicial spokesman for principled decisions against arbitrary governmental action. This was especially true in the area of alien rights, where often at issue was the deportation of allegedly subversive aliens. In one case, involving bail for an alien undergoing deportation proceedings, he went along with a generally liberal opinion by Learned Hand, but added his own views in a separate opinion: "Matters

[116] Clark, "The Limits of Judicial Objectivity," in *ibid.*, p. 227; "A Plea for the Unprincipled Decision," *ibid.*, p. 237.

[117] *Ibid.*, p. 240.

[118] *Ibid.*, pp. 240–41.

involving opinions and personal convictions are prone to bring forth more sharp, if not arbitrary, action than are matters about which we feel less deeply; and, as experience shows, it has been easy in the past at times to forget that our country has grown strong in part because of the tolerance of views it permits and that the danger required in historic phrase by the Supreme Court to justify suppression of beliefs must be at once 'clear' and 'present.' "[119]

Clark was more direct in two memoranda in the same case: "I am bound to say, even if alone, that I think the present attacks on all unordinary beliefs are as shameful as the Palmer raids of 1921, with only this difference, that here the AG [Attorney General] is not the leader, but only a weak appeaser of the weaker elements in Congress. . . . I doubt the capacity of this poor crowd to overturn half so much as the suppressors of opinion now having a field day, with judicial approval."[120] Three months later, when the case still had not been finally disposed of, he wrote:

> As time has gone on I am more than ever convinced that this wave of hysteria is the worst thing facing the country today. I ran into loyalty oaths, required even from college professors, in Ohio, and I understand they are affecting admission to the bar in Indiana, with witch hunts at the University of Washington and a general scare proceeding of scientists all over the country. Indeed, a recent interview an FBI man had with me as to one of the leading scientists at Yale, considering only an advisory position in government service, was one of the most shocking things I had seen in its emphasis upon trivialities or honest beliefs; of course the young fellow who came to see me would, as he pointed out, only pass on the information to other quarters, but it illustrated how easily gossip could be used to smear a distinguished person.[121]

[119] United States *ex rel.* Potash v. District Director of Immigration and Naturalization, 169 F.2d 747, 752–53 (2d Cir. 1948).

[120] Memorandum of March 15, 1948 in U.S. *ex rel.* Potash v. District Director of Immigration and Naturalization.

[121] CEC to ANH, July 27, 1948. In a 1951 memorandum Clark wrote: "I fairly cringe at what things are now being done by patriots in the name of democracy. . . . We are too strong to need such super-patriotism; though it appears to be an easy and a popular course, I think judges should restrain rather than encourage it" (Tucci v. U.S., January 15, 1951). Yet, in this case, he and Frank joined Chase in upholding the denial of citizenship to Tucci because he once had been a member of the Italian Fascist party (Petition of Tucci, 187 F.2d 690 [2d Cir. 1951]). The decision was inevitable under the Subversive Activities Control Act of 1950, and the Second Circuit judges had little choice in the matter.

By the early 1950's Clark fully recognized that, irrespective of his own beliefs, Congress definitely wanted the exclusion and deportation of Communists: "The change in the statute is all toward greater harshness. Such

Judge Clark never trusted the F.B.I. or other governmental snoopers. In ordering the return of illegally seized property, he said for the court: "Aside from the work of the criminal identification division, the Federal Bureau of Investigation is by statute only an organization of 'officials who shall be vested with the authority necessary' 'for the detection and prosecution of crimes against the United States.' "[122]

As a civil libertarian, Clark was most concerned with the conventional First Amendment problems; Frank, as we have seen, concentrated on the criminal law area. But he did not abandon a libertarian position, certainly not in alien cases. In *Repouille v. United States* Frank disagreed with Learned Hand's famous ruling that the requirement that prospective new citizens show "good moral character" during the five years prior to naturalization is to be judged by the moral standards of the community. Applying this standard, Hand and his cousin denied citizenship to a father who had killed his monstrously deformed son. To Frank, the "correct statutory test" was "the attitude of our ethical leaders,"[123] and not public opinion. Interestingly, Frank's dissent was calm, though the issue was of the sort that oridinarily would bring out his passion for fair and humane treatment. Had the majority opinion been authored by Clark, Frank would likely have written at much greater length and with a lot more fervor.

---

cases turn my stomach in the invitation to arbitrary action which the courts are directed not to look at; but I confess myself beaten" (Memorandum in U.S. *ex rel.* Watts for Pavlovich v. Shaughnessy, May 16, 1953).

In one notable opinion during the Second World War, related in a way to the rights of aliens, Clark spoke for the Second Circuit in affirming the treason conviction of Anthony Cramer. A German by birth and a naturalized citizen, Cramer was prosecuted for giving aid and comfort to two of the German saboteurs who were landed by submarine in Florida in 1942. In view of the severity of the charge against Cramer and the specific, stringent requirements of the Constitution for treason prosecutions, the case that the government made does not seem very strong. Eventually, the Supreme Court reversed by a vote of 5–4 (Cramer v. United States, 325 U.S. 1 [1945]). In the lower appellate court, Clark wrote: "When one's country, though adopted, is at war, one cannot, without risk of conviction of giving aid and comfort to the enemy, freely associate even with old friends or assist them even in comparatively small ways . . . once one knows or reasonably suspects them to be here in the role of illegal invaders, whether armed physically or with the more modern, but nontheless destructive weapon of propaganda" (United States v. Cramer, 137 F.2d 888, 893 [2d Cir. 1943]). Similar sentiments appear throughout the opinion; they cannot be easily reconciled—except by reference to the fact that we were at war—with much of what Clark wrote in later years.

[122] Weinberg v. United States, 126 F.2d 1004, 1008 (2d Cir. 1942).

[123] 165 F.2d 152, 154 (2d Cir. 1947).

In fact, in one dispute between Frank and Clark over treatment of an alien, where the latter wrote the majority opinion upholding the exclusion of one Jose Medeiros on the ground that he was not a United States citizen and was in this country illegally, Frank wrote a blistering—and unfair—dissent. The case was a good example of Frank's strategic propensity for erecting straw men.

The evidence in this case, as it appears from both opinions, was overwhelmingly in support of the administrative ruling that Medeiros was born in Bermuda and was not an American citizen. The majority decided that he was not entitled to a judicial trial of the validity of his claim of citizenship. Frank's disagreement was over the procedure to be followed to determine Medeiros' claim. Yet, he unfairly opened his opinion with an assertion that had nothing to do with the case: "Were my colleagues' decision correct, the following rule would now prevail: If a citizen leaves this country and if, upon his return, the immigration officials give him a hearing after which they decide as a fact that he is not a citizen, that decision is final, provided only there was conflicting evidence before those officials as to his citizenship, and the hearing was fair."[124] Having established the straw man that the case somehow involved a bona fide American citizen, Frank continued to berate the majority for participating in a terrible injustice. If the majority is right, *"a person born in the United States, who had lived here continuously, would, by the mere circumstance of taking a voluntary business trip outside this country deprive himself of a judicial determination of his right to return to this country. I am disturbed, indeed, shocked by that conclusion."*[125] Of course, this conclusion was Frank's—not the majority's.

Clark's most publicized expressions of the activist philosophy and his hostility toward the fear that threatened to make "the majestic phrases of the Bill of Rights wither and shrivel to mere copybook epigrams,"[126] came in two dissents in cases involving Communists. In *United States v. Josephson*[127] the issue was a conviction for contempt of Congress resulting from Josephson's refusal to testify before the House Un-American Activities Committee. The court's majority upheld the conviction in an opinion of Judge Chase (joined by Judge Swan), which was examined in Chapter 6. Clark's dissent focused on

[124] United States *ex rel.* Medeiros v. Watkins, 166 F.2d 897, 900 (2d Cir. 1948).

[125] *Ibid.*, p. 901. The emphasis is Frank's.

[126] Clark, "Dilemma of American Judges," in Wright and Reasoner, *Procedure,* p. 205.

[127] 165 F.2d 82 (2d Cir. 1947).

the legality of the Committee itself, an unusual approach in 1947. He began boldly:

> I find it neither easy nor pleasant to disagree on this issue, one of the more momentous which has come before us. Despite hoary precedents, public satisfaction with judicial review of legislative acts has not been such as to invite judges to embark thereon hastily or willingly. Even in the field of civil rights, where we are admonished that the ordinary presumption in favor of constitutionality is either faint or nonexisting, it is not yet clear that the courts can accomplish permanent changes in the ways of men's thinking. Yet the precedents compelling scrutiny are precise and pointed, and the presence before us of one citizen deprived of his liberty and probably of his future livelihood makes it impossible to evade judicial responsibility to serve as that "haven of refuge" which the courts must offer a dissident minority. . . . And the necessity of decision becomes all the more pressing when, as I think it obvious, no more extensive search into the hearts and minds of private citizens can be thought of or expected than that we have before us. If this is legally permissible, it can be asserted dogmatically that investigation of private opinion is not really prohibited under the Bill of Rights. In other words, there will then have been discovered a blank spot in the protective covering of that venerated document.[128]

This strongly libertarian frame of reference was followed by a review of the judicial precedents, which pointed to the conclusion that Congress was not "invested with general power to inquire into private affairs and compel disclosures."[129] Accordingly, the question was whether the authorizing resolution and statute under which the Committee acted transcended constitutional limitations. Because the foundation stone for HUAC's activities was in the concept of "un-American," its powers were suffused with what Clark termed a "dangerous vagueness." "All attempts to explain the meaning of the key word 'un-American,' either on the original creation of the Committee or on its later renewals, have been avoided or opposed."[130] In addition, the House Committee's past activities show that "there are no bounds to its asserted and exerted powers." The Committee

> has never made any secret of its strength and its intent to use that strength to the utmost. Suffice it to say here that its range of activity has covered all varieties of organizations, including the American Civil Liberties Union, the C.I.O., the National Catholic Welfare Conference, the Farmer-Labor party, the Federal Theatre Project, consumers' organizations, various publications from the magazine "Time" to the "Daily Worker," and varying forms and

[128] *Ibid.,* p. 93.
[129] *Ibid.*
[130] *Ibid.,* p. 95

types of industry, of which the recent investigation of the movie industry is fresh in the public mind. While it has avoided specific definition of what it is seeking, it has repeatedly inquired as to membership in the Communist party and in other organizations which it regards as communist controlled or affected. It has claimed for itself the functions of a grand jury to focus the spotlight of publicity on those it considers subversive, in order to drive them from their jobs in private and government employment and their offices in the trade unions. It has gathered a file on over 1,000,000 persons and organizations, claimed to be a "file on every known subversive individual and organization in the United States today," and has submitted lists of allegedly subversive government employees to the Attorney General for investigation. Generally speaking it has avoided the suggestion of legislation. No legislation has come from the Committee itself.[131]

Contemporary thought as to what constitutes "un-American activity" was not any more illuminating, particularly since the term could be taken to apply to all criticism of the "American theory of free enterprise." Clark pointed out that "testimony at the recent movie investigation found the necessary un-American qualities for which the committee was searching in films which placed bankers in an unfavorable light."[132]

The vagueness in HUAC's authorization and activities was sufficient, said Clark, to bar any criminal proceedings against Josephson. But the problem of compatibility with the minimum requirements for a criminal prosecution was secondary to the "major issue whether or not an authorization so broad is compatible with the First Amendment." Without a doubt, legislation formulated in the exact words of the Committee's resolution and statute would be unconstitutional. But, "an argument much stressed is that, since there is an area of legal activity for the Committee within the constitutional limitations, therefore the investigation as a whole is to be supported, and only illegal activities rejected." Clark rejected this view as "logically indefensible in the light of constitutional principles. Of course it is only the *going beyond* the constitutional limitation which ever renders legislative acts improper. True, one can say that the question is, as so generally, one of degree. But the *excess* is the important question here. . . . A doctrine that the lesser legislative power always justifies the exercise of the greater investigative power, including control over opinion, will lead to strange analogies indeed!"[133]

Clark rejected the claim that the contempt conviction should be upheld because, rather than objecting to specific questions which he

[131] *Ibid.,* pp. 95–96.
[132] *Ibid.,* p. 96.
[133] *Ibid.,* p. 98.

regarded as beyond the Committee's competence, Josephson had refused to testify at all. This argument

> is to confuse the issue before us here. We need to keep in mind the character of objections available at the examination proper. They will include personal privileges, such as that against self-crimination, in whatever attenuated form they still exist in legislative investigations, and the pertinency of the question to "the question under inquiry." . . . But if the investigation is as broad as thus assumed, there is no logical or rational way of determining that the question is not pertinent. . . . How can it be said that even the stark question, "Are you a Communist?" is not pertinent to an inquiry into un-American propaganda when the latter may be defined as broadly as it has been in actual Committee experience? The real objection is very clearly to the assumed scope of the investigation.[134]

The dissenting judge conceded that "when we concentrate our gaze solely upon the refusal to testify as to party affiliations, it is hard for us to feel very sympathetic with the refuser. The general feeling that one should stand up and show his true colors, particularly when, as here, the inquiry is given a strong patriotic tinge, has led naturally to the public confusion which mingles strong condemnation of Committee procedures with some belief in its assumed objective."[135] Despite this "quite normal reaction," Clark justified refusal to testify because HUAC was not limited to constitutional objectives.

Clark closed his dissent with the argument that judicial intervention against the Committee would actually further legislative investigations. "Friends and supporters of the congressional power may well fear its present exercise here and find the application of a proper restraint a source of strength in the long run, rather than the reverse. For a widespread belief that the Committee is acting in an un-American way to even an American end will destroy the Committee's usefulness in the eyes of a 'liberty-loving people.' "[136]

All in all, this is a remarkable opinion, certainly so because Clark was a lower-court judge issuing a solitary dissent. It is hard to find any more libertarian expressions or a more direct attack on HUAC in any of the much-quoted dissenting opinions of Justice Black and Douglas. At the time that he wrote, no American judge had as yet expressed so sharp a condemnation of congressional investigations conducted in the name of anti-communism. Several months later, after the Supreme Court turned down Josephson's petition for certiorari, Justice Henry W. Edgerton of the Court of Appeals for the District of Columbia

---

[134] *Ibid.*, pp. 98–99.
[135] *Ibid.*, p. 99.
[136] *Ibid.*, p. 100.

dissented in *Barksy v. United States*,[137] which was similar to *Josephson*, and took an approach paralleling the one advanced by Clark.

The refusal of the Supreme Court to review the Second Circuit's decision[138] killed all legal attempts to check the House Committee during its most active period of Cold War investigations. For a long time, Clark viewed his dissent as "one of the deadest of all judicial adventures"[139] and "certainly not of any particular utility."[140] The Warren court ultimately got around to looking at HUAC and in 1957, in *Watkins v. United States*,[141] the court limited its scope of operations and even cast doubt upon the constitutionality of its statutory authorization. However, the Supreme Court backed away from declaring the Committee, as such, illegal, and it did not reject, as Clark did, the concept of a congressional committee invested with the function of probing for "un-American" activity.[142]

[137] 167 F.2d 241 (D.C. Cir. 1948).

[138] 333 U.S. 838 (1948). There are some puzzling questions about the denial of certiorari in this case. Apparently, the vote against review was 6–3, since Justices Douglas, Murphy, and Rutledge expressly voted to grant certiorari and no justices were announced as not participating in the appeal. Had Justice Black sided with the other libertarians, under the "rule of four" the question of HUAC's authority would have directly confronted the Supreme Court as early as 1948. It is difficult to explain Black's vote, especially in light of his own feelings on First Amendment matters. Moreover, more than ten years later, in a dissenting opinion in Barenblatt v. United States, 360 U.S. 109 (1959), he scathingly denounced the House Committee. Adding to the difficulty in understanding Black is his action in the Barsky appeal from the decision of the District of Columbia Court of Appeals. The Supreme Court denied certiorari, at first without any dissent being noted (334 U.S. 843 [1948]). But two years later—after Justices Murphy and Rutledge had died—the High Court finally got around to denying a rehearing on its refusal to review, and Black joined Douglas in dissent (339 U.S. 971 [1950]).

[139] Letter to Barent Ten Eyck, July 6, 1957.

[140] Letter to John Frank, June 25, 1957.

[141] 354 U.S. 178 (1957).

[142] The belief that Watkins did not go very far in curtailing HUAC is supported in the first instance by the vague language employed by Chief Justice Warren, the spokesman for the court, whenever the question of constitutionality was discussed. Furthermore, subsequent Supreme Court activity cast doubt on the meaning of Watkins and on whether the justices really were serious about challenging HUAC's authority. In Barenblatt v. United States, 360 U.S. 109 (1959), the Supreme Court, by a vote of 5–4, affirmed a contempt conviction resulting from a refusal to answer questions before the Committee. Much of the argument in the opinions in this case concerned the meaning of Watkins, with the majority contending that Warren, who was now a spokesman for the dissenters, did not say two years earlier what he now says he said.

More recently, in the 1968 term, the appeals of Dr. Jeremiah Stamler and two others from their contempt convictions were dismissed. With this action the Supreme Court rejected the best organized and most far-reaching effort to have HUAC declared unconstitutional (89 S.Ct. 395 [1968]).

Whatever the import of Supreme Court activity regarding HUAC, Clark's opinion was one of his finest hours in his quarter of a century on the bench. When the *Watkins* ruling was made, John Frank wrote to Clark: "In one of the most important works of your life you have been entirely vindicated. By being the first prophet to enter this field of thorns, you performed one of your life's public services; indeed, with my own exalted view of the importance of these matters, I am inclined to feel that this must indeed be and should be, one of your proudest days."[143]

Significantly, though Clark employed strong language in his *Josephson* dissent, the case does not seem to have excited him very much. His memoranda to Swan and Chase were not very vigorous and he made little effort to win them over to his point of view. After the conference vote to uphold the conviction, all of the passion in his opinion was directed at HUAC; he was barely critical of the majority. And, after the Second Circuit ruling, the case did not linger in his mind. Clark had written one of his most important opinions and in a case raising one of the few constitutional issues that he was called on to consider as a judge, yet in virtually all respects his attitude was that *Josephson* was an ordinary appeal. I cannot offer any explanation for this casual behavior, except the one that has been suggested previously in other connections: Jerome Frank did not hear the *Josephson* appeal.

Frank did sit in the appeal from the contempt of court convictions adjudged against Harry Sacher and other lawyers for the Communist Party leaders who were found guilty of violating the Smith Act. At the end of the long trial, Judge Medina summarily found Sacher and his colleagues guilty of contempt and sentenced them to prison. The lawyers' appeal to the Second Circuit was heard by Augustus Hand, Clark, and Frank. It was in this case that Clark wrote the second of his important dissents involving Communists; and, quite predictably, in this case Frank and Clark once more became embroiled in conflict, although in an unexpected way.

It is unlikely that the panel composition in *Sacher* was totally accidental, the result of the case being scheduled without considera-tion of who would hear it. In the *Dennis* appeal to the Second Circuit— which was argued after the contempt convictions of the lawyers were upheld—the panel consisted of Learned Hand, Swan, and Chase, the three judges who did not sit in *Sacher*. Since some of the issues in the two appeals overlapped, principally Medina's conduct of the trial, Learned Hand probably wanted two distinctly different panels.

[143] Letter to CEC, June 21, 1957.

The *Sacher* case was argued before the Second Circuit on February 6, 1950. Two days later, Frank's initial memorandum was sent out; its concluding words were, "Tentatively, and most reluctantly, I vote to reverse and remand for a hearing before a judge other than Medina."[144] Frank's preliminary, pre-conference vote was based solely on his belief that the trial judge could not summarily punish for contempt. On the broader, and perhaps more important, question of whether the defense counsel had acted contemptuously, Frank's view was that it was very clear that they had.

Augustus Hand's position, which remained unchanged throughout the subsequent consideration in conference and via memoranda, was that many specific acts of contempt were committed during the trial and Medina was in his rights in convicting and sentencing without a hearing because the acts were committed in his presence, which is what is required by the Federal Rules of Criminal Procedure. Clark, on the other hand, felt that while the lawyers had acted in a disgraceful manner, they were entitled to a hearing. He interpreted the Federal Rules to permit summary punishment for contempt only when it was made immediately after commission of the acts. But Medina had waited until the trial's end, weeks and months too late.

Thus, the first reaction of the panel was to upset the convictions. A reversal of Medina, even by a split vote, would have been embarrassing to the government—and, in a way, to the Second Circuit, also—because the appeals from the Smith Act convictions were then pending before the Second Circuit. There would have been some implication that the trial judge had not conducted a fair trial and by his post-trial summary action had shown vindictiveness against the defense lawyers. On the other hand, Second Circuit affirmance of the contempt judgments would have effectively placed a damper on the contention that was to be made in the *Dennis* appeal that the trial was unfair. Indeed, in his *Dennis* opinion, Learned Hand rejected this contention. "It is not irrelevant," he wrote, "that this court decided that they [defense counsel] so far exceeded the bounds of professional propriety as to deserve a sentence for criminal contempt."[145] All of this suggests that it was an error to allow the contempt appeals to be heard prior to disposition of *Dennis*.[146]

At any rate, Judge Augustus Hand was disturbed over the prospect of reversal. Somehow he was able to persuade Frank to back away from his tentative vote. In the final vote, Frank agreed with

[144] JNF memorandum in U.S. v. Sacher, February 8, 1950.

[145] United States v. Dennis, 183 F.2d 201, 225 (2d Cir. 1950).

[146] It is a safe guess that the Second Circuit heard Sacher first because it was a much less complicated case than Dennis and the appellate lawyers were able to prepare their briefs more quickly than in the latter case.

Hand to affirm the contempt findings, except as to Specification I of the contempt certificate and two other minor points, on which he joined Clark in dissent. However, this very limited reversal of Medina left the prison sentences unchanged and had no practical effect.

Specification I charged that there was "an agreement between these defendants, deliberately entered into in a cold and calculating manner" to disrupt the trial. In effect, it alleged that the lawyers had planned to frustrate the trial; Frank reasoned that if this was true, there was a conspiracy; obviously it was not planned in the presence of the trial judge and for this reason he was not empowered to render a summary verdict. Hand upheld even the first charge and, in a way, his position is more understandable than the one taken by Frank. Medina never said that there was a conspiracy. But if Medina's words are read to mean that the lawyers had entered into a conspiracy, then Clark was right in his belief that the entire judgment of criminal contempt was enveloped in the finding that the lawyers had acted in a calculating manner. It is hard to understand Medina's verdict except in terms of his conviction that the lawyers throughout the trial had deliberately tried to disrupt the proceedings. Specification I really cannot be separated from the rest of the allegations. If Medina was wrong on this point, Frank should have found him wrong on the rest.

Indeed, had Frank followed his own formulation of the "harmless error" doctrine, he would have had little choice other than to vote to reverse the lower court. In the *Sacher* case, Medina's role was comparable to that of a jury in an ordinary criminal trial; even, if in his own mind, as an upper court judge, Frank was convinced that the other specifications could stand separately, he could not be sure that Medina's findings on all specifications were not permeated with the error he had made regarding a conspiracy.

Be this as it may, Frank basically sided with Augustus Hand. Clark did make an attempt—as usual, via a memorandum—to sway his brethren. "My isolation here comes as the harder shock," he informed them, "because I had so convinced myself that the precedents made our immediate course—not necessarily the ultimate conclusion—fairly clear. This, however, is the judicial process which of course I must accept, though no one can be more conscious of the penalty for isolation in this cause celebre than I; but before it is too late, may I urge re-reading of the cases uncited by you."[147]

This plea failed and after each judge had written his opinion— Hand, for the majority; Frank, a concurrence; and Clark, a dissent—

[147] Supplementary memorandum in U.S. v. Sacher. No date is given, though it was probably written between February 15 and February 20.

Hand, apparently because he was concerned over the significance that might be read into the division on the court, made a last ditch effort to change Clark's mind. But Clark was not persuaded, although he admitted that he had "examined the possibility of going along, since I know your persuasive opinion will persuade all but inconsiderable doubters and I see no immediate and perhaps no future results from a dissent." Still, he stood his ground; he wrote, "If I get to relying on such considerations I really will have nothing to tie to during what may still prove to be a long course of future judging."[148]

In this letter to Hand, Clark described his dissent as being on the mild side. This was an accurate characterization.[149] After calling some of the appellant's trial conduct "abominable," the dissenting opinion went on to argue that this "does not of itself prove that they should be imprisoned without a hearing weeks or months after the events. For the law must both appear and be inexorable rather than vindictive; and the constitutional course of due process requires that conviction and sentence come only after orderly hearing upon announced charges and full opportunity to the accused to defend themselves."[150]

The major part of Clark's opinion discussed the statutory requirements and judicial decisions relevant to determining the question whether Medina could punish summarily. There were no angry words addressed to the majority position or to the concurring opinion of Judge Frank. Indeed, from the time that the case was argued until the opinions were issued, Clark and Frank managed to avoid their customary friction. The concurring opinion was about as mild as the dissent; was it that Frank was not wholly convinced that he voted the right way? His strongest words were for those who made a major civil liberties issue out of a justified conviction for contempt. Frank began:

> "Friends of the court" have filed with us a large number of briefs which eloquently recall how, in the past, courageous lawyers have importantly contributed to liberty and democracy by defending unpopular clients, despite the browbeating of tyrannical, domineering, trial judges. In those briefs, fear is expressed that, if we affirm any of the contempt orders in this case, lawyers for labor unions or for minority groups or for unpopular persons will, in the future, be intimidated or throttled.

[148] CEC to ANH, March 30, 1950.

[149] In responding to a letter from Max Lerner commending his dissent, Clark wrote: "When, at length, I realized I was to be alone I had a problem whether to make a reasoned statement on legal grounds or to indulge in a vigorous and detailed attack. While my present impression is that the former course, which I chose, has not been oversuccessful, yet I still feel that the latter held no more promise of persuasion to the unpersuaded and would merely have added to bitterness" (April 15, 1950).

[150] United States v. Sacher, 182 F.2d 416, 463 (2d Cir. 1950).

The eloquence is misplaced. The fears are unfounded. We affirm the orders punishing these lawyers not because they courageously defended their clients, or because those clients were Communists, but only because of the lawyers' outrageous conduct—conduct of a kind which no lawyer owes his client, which cannot ever be justified, and which was never employed by those advocates, for minorities or for the unpopular, whose courage has made lawyerdom proud. The acts of the lawyers for the defendants in this trial can make no sensible man proud.

What they did was like assaulting the pilot of an aeroplane in flight, or turning out the lights during a surgical operation. To use homelier words, they tried to throw a wrench in the machinery of justice. Whatever may have been their purpose, their acts *might* have made a trial impossible. Not to punish such behavior summarily, but, instead, to require a long trial of these lawyers, might well be to encourage that sort of behavior. The summary punishment here will tend to deter imitation of that behavior in other trials. If it is not deterred, the administration of justice in our courts is highly likely to break down.

The basis of our decision is as simple as that. We affirm these orders, not because the personal "dignity" of the trial judge, or of the judiciary in general,[151] was affronted; for such dignity, when it exists, manifests itself, needs no punitive safeguards. We affirm for the plain reason that the crude antics of these lawyers, if copied by lawyers in other cases, would almost surely disrupt trials.

Here we come to the heart of the matter: Preservation of the liberties of citizens, when on trial for crimes charged against them, demands order in the court-room. Absent such order, no trial can be fair. More important, if criminal trials cannot go on in orderly fashion, then the defendants, if unpopular or if members of minority groups, may become the victims of that monstrous substitute for trials—mob violence. The gravest danger to those minorities, on whose behalf the "friends of the court" have spoken, could easily result from a denial of the power of a trial judge to deal with trial-disrupters as the judge has dealt with the lawyers here. In short, the protection of civil liberties calls for sustaining the contempt judgments in this case.[152]

In the remainder of his opinion, Frank defended the right of Medina to punish the lawyers as he did, except as to the first specification.

[151] Frank's final revision of his opinion omitted the phrase "or of the judiciary in general." Conceivably, the change was made because the original language gave credence to the argument that the alleged contemptuous actions of the lawyers were directed against the entire judicial system and hence were of such a nature as not to be punishable summarily by the trial judge.

[152] These paragraphs are from the slip opinion. The comparable passages, with few revisions, are found at 182 F.2d 453–54.

After the Second Circuit upheld the convictions, counsel for the appellants petitioned for a rehearing, a not unusual procedure. Accompanying the petition was a new brief, which clearly was directed at Frank's vote and opinion. Predictably, the court denied a rehearing, with Clark voting to grant it. As far as the Second Circuit was concerned, the matter should have ended. However, Frank took the rare step of withdrawing his original opinion and writing a new one.[153] His motive, judging by the changes that were made, seems to have been to bolster his rejection of the key contention that if Medina had any authority to punish summarily it could be exercised only by rendering judgment immediately after commission of the acts and not much later when the trial was concluded. Frank added many paragraphs on this point.

Significantly, though, while the appellants included this issue in their petition for rehearing, it was far from being their major argument. In fact, it occupied a considerably more important place in Clark's dissent. Also supporting the impression that Frank's aim was to answer Clark and not the new petition was his inclusion in the first draft revision of direct quotations from the dissenting opinion, something that he had not done originally. For this reason—and also because in general Clark was disturbed over Frank's decision to "re-open" the case—Clark reacted angrily to the new opinion. "Of course I would be less (or more) than human if I could say that I was wholly insensible to the direct attack you are now making upon me,"[154] he wrote after receiving Frank's first draft revision. Clark believed that the new opinion spoofed and made foolish his position, which deserved "more than caricature and ridicule."

In his not too conciliatory reply, Frank defended his revision, denying the "implications you have read into it." He went on:

> Nor do I think you're justified. A dissenting opinion is inevitably a criticism of the majority opinion. One could phrase the matter by saying that the dissenter is making "a direct attack" upon the majority, that when a dissenter argues that the majority opinion has relied on dicta, he is unpleasantly personal in suggesting something improper, etc., etc. Your position seems to be this: The dissenter is free to differ with the majority opinion, giving it an interpretation with which the majority may not agree,

---

[153] While, as was explained in Chapter 3, it is not unusual in the Second Circuit for revisions to be made in the court's opinion as a result of a petition for rehearing, it is virtually unheard of for this to happen with a concurring opinion. I am unaware of a similar incident in the entire ten years.

[154] CEC to JNF, May 11, 1950. None of the draft revisions are available, except for the final one, which is of course published in the *Federal Reporter*.

and he may try to use a *reductio ad absurdum* argument against a "juridical position" which the majority "thought of some importance"; but those in the majority must not endeavor, in a similar manner, to show that the dissenter is in error.

Nonetheless, he agreed to "remove any phrases indicating that I am replying to you."[155]

Frank's response to Clark and his actions after the original opinions were filed were wrong on at least three grounds. In the first place, Clark's dissent was in no way a personal attack on the majority. It dealt calmly with the issues, as did the majority opinion. Secondly, Frank was not the spokesman for the court in *Sacher;* he wrote a concurring opinion, not the majority opinion. Thirdly, and of greatest importance, is the questionable practice of revising an opinion after it has been issued to include a more direct reply to colleagues with whom one disagrees. If Frank thought that he should strongly criticize Clark, he should have done so originally, not later on through a reply to a petition for rehearing. The Second Circuit gets many such petitions; unlike the Supreme Court, which either grants them (rarely) and orders reargument or summarily rejects them, the practice on the lower court has been to utilize the request as an opportunity to correct errors or misunderstandings pointed out by counsel. It would be a disruptive practice and harmful to intracourt relations if judges made a habit of accompanying denials of requests for rehearing with new opinions which included their post-decision reactions to the opinions of their colleagues. In sum, Frank's action with respect to Clark was improper. Even without their prior record of disagreement, it was provocative.

Clark was not satisfied with the deletions from Frank's concurrence: "I do not believe any real change is made in the straw men you set up to knock over by ascribing them formally to 'applicants,' rather than directly to me."[156] Frank then decided on additional revisions, so as to employ the "locutions" of the appellants. But he concluded this letter to Clark with the sarcastic, "I therefore thank you for helping me to improve my revised concurring opinion."[157]

In none of their many battles of the preceding nine years did Frank seem to be more in the wrong than he was in *Sacher.* This judgment has nothing to do with his vote: the legal questions presented were tough ones, with few and not too enlightening precedents to go by. After it first denied review from the Second Circuit holding, the

---

[155] JNF to CEC, May 12, 1950. There is a strong tinge of sarcasm, totally gratuitous, in this answer. Each of the three phrases in quotation marks was included in Clark's letter of the preceding day.

[156] CEC to JNF, May 13, 1950.

[157] JNF to CEC, May 15, 1950.

Supreme Court granted certiorari in *Sacher* and affirmed by a vote of 5–3.[158] Frank's error was in his conduct after the petition for rehearing was filed. No matter how his revised opinion now reads in the *Federal Reporter*—even after the final deletions it can be read as Clark read it—it remains that Frank intended to answer Clark.

Why did he pursue this extraordinary course? No doubt, apart from the controversy over the decision, Frank's vote was the subject of a great deal of unfavorable discussion in liberal legal circles and at the Yale Law School. The decision was made at the height of the Cold War, at a time when Senator Joseph McCarthy was first appearing ominously on the national scene. If ever a libertarian decision could be expected at this time from the Second Circuit—or perhaps from any federal appellate court—it was from a panel on which Clark and Frank sat. Yet, the latter sorely disappointed many of his friends and admirers, including some in New Haven. Two years after Clark's death, Professor Fred Rodell of Yale, a friend of both judges, wrote in a warm tribute to Clark that "in a tough fight against long odds and rough opposition it would be Charlie Clark I would rather have on my side" than Jerome Frank. This was so,

> For it was Charlie who, among all our judges, stood up first, and at first stood up alone, against the indecencies of the post-war "loyalty" and "security" laws and procedures, against the McCarthy-style witch-hunt even before McCarthy became the hunter, against the travesties of the Constitution that court majorities, high and low, were writing into law; especially notable were his opinions—both of them significantly one-man dissents—in the *Josephson* and *Sacher* cases. . . . Clark remained the unheeded conscience of the Second Circuit.[159]

At the time of the *Sacher* controversy, while Frank was still revising his revised opinion, Clark wrote from New Haven to Augustus Hand: "With reference to *United States v. Sacher,* I suppose I should not feel annoyed that Jerry takes out his guilt complex on me. But I do find it irritating. Although I have not participated in a single discussion up here, I know that he has been involved in some very vigorous discussions with the Yale Law faculty, of whose good opinion he is most avid, and has felt the need of self-justification, which I am quite sure is finding expression here."[160]

Of course, this is but an antagonist's gloss on the dispute, written at the height of the battle, and so it cannot be accepted uncritically.

---

[158] Sacher v. United States, 343 U.S. 1 (1952).

[159] Rodell, "For Charles E. Clark: A Brief and Belated But Fond Farewell," *Columbia Law Review,* 65 (1965), 1328.

[160] CEC to ANH, May 13, 1950.

But it is not unreasonable to interpret Frank's rewriting of his opinion, making it stronger, as an attempt to answer his critics and to justify his vote, while still being beset by self-doubt. This interpretation gains added credence from Frank's strange letter to Clark shortly after the revised opinion was filed, which was quoted in the opening lines of Chapter 7. "I admire you as a person," he wrote to Clark, "and consider you one of the very ablest judges. But somehow you seem to have obtained the impression that I'm antagonistic to you. Through some fault of mine, I got off on the wrong foot with you. I'd like to start again. I hope that, during next year, you'll let me try."[161]

Frank's action in *Sacher* poses the still more speculative question of how he would have voted in the *Dennis* case had he been on that panel. Because of his great reputation as a spokesman for unpopular causes, it is generally assumed that his position would have been to reverse the Smith Act convictions. As one writer puts it:

> Judge Frank believed that the federal courts should actively defend the civil liberties of individuals against the illegal encroachments of governmental authority. He never had the opportunity as a judge to express his thoughts on the legality of laws such as the Smith Act. . . . It can be inferred, however, from other evidence that he considered the Smith Act to be unconstitutional and believed that the courts should not approve this legislative invasion of the right of free speech guaranteed by the First Amendment.[162]

The "other evidence" is not disclosed and we are left with the writer's hunch. Actually, Judge Frank once demurred from an opportunity to give his views on *Dennis:* "I shall not express my own views of the *Dennis* decision. But I do feel that it is absurd to say, as some have said, that only Communist sympathizers will disagree with that decision."[163]

Sacher, and Frank's votes in several other "Communist" cases, support the speculation that his position in *Dennis* would have been to sustain the Smith Act and the convictions obtained under it. Furthermore, Frank's actions in several cases involving real or alleged Communists pose some hard questions to answer. Charles Clark touched on this subject in a letter in 1958 to Frank's friend and admirer, Professor Edmond Cahn of New York University. "In any complete critique of Jerry's generally useful career," he wrote, 'it

[161] JNF to CEC, June 1, 1950.

[162] Walter E. Volkomer, "The Constitutional Ideas of Judge Jerome N. Frank," *New York Law Forum*, 7 (1961), 46.

[163] Jerome Frank, "Some Reflections on Judge Learned Hand," *University of Chicago Law Review*, 24 (1957), 696.

would be necessary to consider his troublesome lack of forthrightness in the political or so-called 'Communist' cases."[164] There was no vindictiveness on Clark's part in raising the issue and, in any case, it deserves to be considered, since others, such as Rodell, have at least indirectly touched on the same question.

Apart from *Sacher,* the 1941–51 period provides little clue to Frank's attitude toward Communists. Perhaps there is no significance to it, but in an obscure criminal appeal decided in 1943, *United States v. Bramson,* he wrote the court's opinion upholding the conviction. One of the errors asserted as a ground for reversal is discussed in the following part of the opinion:

> Yetta Land, Bramson's sister, a lawyer, was asked by government counsel whether she represented "a great many Communists." Objection was made to this question but at once withdrawn. The witness, having answered that she represented "a lot of Communists, like Republicans and a lot of Democrats," was then asked "Are you a Communist?" The witness inquired of the judge whether he desired her to answer this question which she considered improper; the judge replied that it was a matter of indifference to him, but that, if an objection were made, he would sustain it. Objection was made and no answer to the question was given. No motion was made by defendants that the court instruct the jury to disregard this question. It was, of course, improper; but, in the context of this lengthy trial and in the light of the mass of evidence against the defendants, we think it was not so prejudicial as to constitute reversible error.[165]

This attitude comes close to the Second Circuit's "harmless error" doctrine, which Frank had been so much against. In other criminal appeals where he dissented, the errors did not seem any more prejudicial and the evidence against the accused was about as substantial as it was in this case. Interestingly, nine years later Frank wrote that the Second Circuit and other courts "have recognized that the Communist label yields marked ill-will for its American wearer."[166]

These last words are from Frank's opinion for the Second Circuit affirming the convictions of Julius and Ethel Rosenberg. (Frank disagreed with his colleagues and voted to give a new trial to Morton Sobell, the Rosenbergs' co-defendant. In his opinion he dwelt at length on the imposition of the death sentences, indicating that while they could not be reversed he had some reservations as to whether they were justified. However, he was not as enthusiastic on this point as some of his admirers believe.)

[164] CEC to Edmond Cahn, February 25, 1958.
[165] United States v. Bramson, 139 F.2d 598, 600 (2d Cir. 1943).
[166] United States v. Rosenberg, 195 F.2d 583, 596 (2d Cir. 1952).

Since the most basic points raised in the appeal concerned the sufficiency of the evidence, an area where the appellate court has only a limited review, Frank's vote is understandable. On the other hand, using the "harmless error" standard of Frank, there were grounds for reversal. The evidence against the Rosenbergs was not so overwhelming to totally shunt aside errors made by the trial judge. It cannot be denied that Judge Irving R. Kaufman (now of the Second Circuit) played an aggressive role against the defendants. In many ways he indicated support for the government's position. True, in his final instructions to the jury he cautioned them to utterly disregard any impression they may have gotten of his views on the guilt or innocence of the accused. Yet it is doubtful, even without Frank's exacting interpretation of "harmless error," that after a long trial it is possible for jurors to rid themselves of notions resulting from the trial judge's behavior. Certainly, the prejudicial effect on the jurors was far greater than it could have been in *Antonelli*.

More important than any of the "Communist" cases discussed so far was Frank's position in *United States v. Ullmann,* which involved the constitutionality of an immunity statute as applied to a Communist who refused to testify before a grand jury. Ullmann claimed that the grant of immunity did not deprive him of his constitutional privilege against self-incrimination. Frank's opinion for the court, upholding the trial judge's order that the witness testify, consisted of a few words accepting the ruling of the district court, and the following:

> It is well to add a few words about defendant's contention concerning the doctrine of Brown v. Walker . . . which held that the Fifth Amendment privilege against self-incrimination relates solely to testimony that might lead to defendant's prosecution for a crime. Defendant asks us to modify this doctrine in the light of new circumstances which have since arisen. We are not prepared to say that this suggestion lacks all merit. But our possible views on the subject have no significance. For an inferior court like ours may not modify a Supreme Court doctrine in the absence of any indication of new doctrinal trends in that Court's opinions, and we perceive none that are pertinent here. Accordingly, the argument must be addressed not to our ears but to eighteen others in Washington, D.C.[167]

This modest position would not have been extraordinary for any lower court judge other than Jerome Frank. It is difficult, however, to reconcile it with Frank's frequent advocacy in many of his essay-opinions of the abandonment or modification of long-held judicial doctrines. As Thurman Arnold wrote in 1957: "When forced by *stare*

[167] United States v. Ullmann, 221 F.2d 760, 761 (2d Cir. 1955).

decisis to reach what he considered an undesirable result he would write a concurring opinion analyzing the problem and plainly suggesting that either the Supreme Court or Congress do something about it. It was a unique and useful technique whereby a lower court judge could pay allegiance to precedent and at the same time encourage the processes of change."[168]

For some reason, Frank was unwilling to follow this technique in *Ullmann*. Perhaps the explanation for this and his action in other "Communist" cases is rooted in his experiences during the early years of the New Deal. While he was General Counsel of the Agriculture Adjustment Administration, the agency was, in effect, the locus for Communist infiltration in government. Frank recruited for his staff Lee Pressman, John Abt, Nathan Witt, and Alger Hiss—all of whom were, as things eventually turned out, admitted or accused Communists.

Frank's social liberalism and his encouragement of economic experimentation could have accounted for the presence of a sort of Communist cell in his agency, although in the view of New Deal historian Arthur Schlesinger, Jr., these people were in the A.A.A. "not because of any planned Communist infiltration of the Agriculture Department, but because of the accident that Jerome Frank had jobs to fill." But Schlesinger also writes that "the social militance of the office of General Counsel provided a cover behind which operated more than simply the reformist liberalism of Jerome Frank. The smoldering discontent on the farm belt had long attracted the solicitous concern of the American Communist Party." It is apparent that Frank, who "was both philosophically and practically opposed to Communism,"[169] was puzzled, embarrassed, and even hurt when it came out that there were Communists in the A.A.A. No doubt he felt duped and deceived.[170] His name was brought up in the Alger Hiss case before

[168] Arnold, "Judge Jerome Frank," *University of Chicago Law Review*, 24 (1957), 633.

[169] This quotation and the two previous ones in this paragraph are from Arthur M. Schlesinger, Jr., *The Coming of the New Deal* (Boston: Houghton Mifflin Co., 1959), pp. 49–52.

[170] In the early 1950's Frank gave several interviews for the Oral History Project at Columbia University. The interviews dealt almost exclusively with his work with the A.A.A.; while he discussed the question of Communist influence and infiltration, what he said was not very enlightening. He stressed that "there wasn't the slightest reason to suspect that these boys were Communists" (p. 133 of the transcript) and he could not understand "how they could have at that particular time become Communists" (p. 136). Also: "In view of the fact that you had these fellas that were Communists in the Department . . . the impression could be created that that's all you had and that's the kind of fellow I brought in there. It would be very unfair to a hundred thirty men to say that, because there were really distinguished fellows of all kinds in there" (p. 147).

and during the first perjury trial. While of course the evidence is tenuous, it is reasonable to conclude that Frank's unwillingness to take civil libertarian positions (in court or on the outside) on Communist matters was related to his New Deal experiences. Whatever the explanation, he did not speak out in any significant way against the climate of accusation that developed following the Second World War.

Frank's views and votes in this area hardly detract from his truly momentous contributions to the cause of justice. His role in the civil liberties field was, in any case, a severely limited one, and no matter how he would have reacted to the few opportunities that came his way, the impact on law and society would have been minimal. But he transformed the area of criminal law, where with virtually no exceptions lower-court judges are passive, into a forum for the advocacy of fairness and justice. Through pioneering opinions in this field and others he brought new ideas to courts and judges and he stimulated many on and off the bench to think anew about the administration of justice. An iconoclast, yes, but even in his lifetime—indeed during the decade of the Learned Hand court—as illustrations in this chapter and the data to be presented in Chapter 10 show, he profoundly influenced the Supreme Court. What is remarkable, almost incredible, about his judicial accomplishments is that they all came during an era of strict statutory law when the zone of individuality and creativity available to an inferior judge had been sharply narrowed. So, it is not too much to say that there has never been in this country an "inferior" judge like him, and in certain ways his equal has yet to serve on the Supreme Court. Vulnerable as he was and still is in the obviously risky combat of jurisprudential polemics, Jerome Frank's place as a giant among lawyers and judges is secure.

But what will be the historical judgment of Judge Clark? No doubt, as was true during their lifetimes, far less attention will be paid to Clark than to Frank; in fact, it is hard to say that very many, including much of the legal profession, will remember his contributions. This is unfortunate in view of the truly major impact he had on our legal institutions, but it is also understandable: except to a select few, judicial procedure is not a very exciting subject. Clark's fate is inextricably tied to the inferior position of the court on which he sat. The Learned Hand court may have been the outstanding American tribunal of its time, still it was not the Supreme Court of the United States. High Court justices and the rulings they make get attention, which is not true of the lower-court judges. Accordingly, there is nothing surprising about the probability that only a handful will know of Charles Clark; the extraordinary thing is that Learned

Hand and Jerome Frank overcame their place in the judicial hierarchy to achieve relatively lasting fame.

When Clark dissented in *Sacher,* wrote John Frank a year after the decision, he "probably kissed all his Supreme Court chances goodby."[171] Not long before he died, Clark, in an interview, dismissed this contention. At any rate, the 1952 election of Eisenhower ruled out any thoughts Clark may have entertained about this promotion.

If the *Sacher* case had no real effect on his Supreme Court prospects, it does seem to have been a crucial point of sorts in Clark's judicial career. Twice in 1950, with *Sacher* apparently in mind, he wrote to Learned Hand indicating that he felt depressed about his work.[172] Both times Hand wrote back in an effort to cheer him up; while no doubt under the circumstances Hand's replies were inevitably generous, his estimation of Clark as a judge was a fair one. Unique in so many ways, Clark brought to the bench a sort of intensity that is often lost in the "committee" atmosphere that too often pervades appellate courts. He conceived his role as a judge in personal terms that were derived from his own experiences fighting for judicial reform. A number of his separate opinions seem frivolous today, and this is the way they probably appeared when they were published, but it is of note that they were inspired by an independence that bespoke great character. From this same source sprang his important achievements as Dean at Yale, judicial reformer, and ultimately chief judge of the Second Circuit, and his lone dissents in such cases as *Josephson* and *Sacher.* Surely, then, Learned Hand's praise was not undeserved. This is what he wrote to his colleague:

> I have your letter of the 30th, and I hasten to answer that I think you quite misconceive your position. As I told you when you dissented in the contempt case, you showed an admirable courage in a situation where concurrence would have been much the easier course. I tried to tell you then that I admired you for it. You are also right in saying that the position of a judge in these times is a trying one; he can have no solace in the approval of the great sum of those who learn of his work. They cannot understand it and would not try to do so, if they could; he is expected to arrive at the result in any given case which is the desired one. The notion that he may feel himself constrained to do otherwise is put down as a dishonest subterfuge. This was always true, but during the last twenty years or so it has grown stronger, being indeed a part of the gospel of many in the profession itself. I

[171] John Frank, "The Top U.S. Commercial Court," *Fortune* (January 1951), pp. 108–9.
[172] Copies of these letters were not found among Clark's papers.

don't see what we can do but to try to forget all this, and content ourselves, so far as we can, with the belief that we have done our duty as we saw it. Nobody in this world should expect real justice, in the sense of a detached and adequately informed opinion of his work. At least, he ought not to expect it save in rare and exceptional circumstances. I know that you have nothing to look back upon of which you are ashamed; moreover, you ought to be, if you are not, conscious of a large body of professional opinion which puts you high among judges. Surely you will agree that it is just at such periods as these that a brave attitude— mens cerscia recti—is most needed, if we are not to dissolve into a society of mutual hate and suspicion.

Please try to take a friendlier view of yourself and your position.[173]

This was the second of the letters; earlier in the year Hand had written:

We all get the feeling that we are beating our wings ineffectively in the void, and I know of no way to prevent that mood coming on us from time to time. I should like to say, however, for whatever it may be worth, that we all think of you as one of the outstanding judges on the federal bench, or any other bench. Of course, we have positive differences; we should not be worth our salt if we did not; but these do not, I hope, prevent us from realizing one another's merits and being glad of our association, so far then as your discouragement may come from our disagreements, pray don't let it put you down. Between ourselves we may say, what I think we all believe in secret, that we have a fine court and that each of us contributes to it a part which would make the sum much poorer if it were absent.

But if you ever say that I boasted of us even among ourselves, into the Aeecenias Club you go. Courage, mon ami, le Diable est mort.[174]

Clark must have been very pleased to learn that his independence and frequent disagreements with the members of his court did not undermine their estimation of him.

[173] LH to CEC, September 1, 1950.
[174] LH to CEC, February 23, 1950.

9

The Business of the Court

DURING THE TEN-YEAR PERIOD THAT MARKS THE ZENITH FOR LEARNED
Hand and the Second Circuit, the six judges kept up with a heavy case
load and disposed of more cases than any of the other courts of
appeals, although some of them had more judges than the Second
Circuit. In this period 4,268 cases were commenced in the Second
Circuit and 4,281 were terminated.[1] The next busiest circuit was the
Fifth Circuit with 3,719 new cases and 3,576 terminations. Third was
the Court of Appeals for the District of Columbia with 3,371 cases
commenced and 3,230 disposed of. It is also significant that during
these busy years the Second Circuit made very infrequent use of
district court judges and judges from other courts of appeals,[2] a practice prevalent in many circuits and relied upon with increasing
frequency by the Second Circuit after Learned Hand's retirement.

[1] The data in this section are taken from the annual reports of the
Director of the Administrative Office of the United States Courts for the
fiscal years 1942 to 1951. The period covered by these reports is July 1, 1941,
to June 30, 1951. Jerome Frank took the judicial oath on May 5, 1941, and
Learned Hand retired on June 1, 1951, so that these ten reports correspond
closely to the period when the six judges served together.

[2] The Second Circuit, 1941–51, had no senior (retired) judges to use to
ease the burden on the regular judges.

Of course, raw statistics of cases begun and terminated shed light on only one dimension of a court's performance. Yet, the figures in this section indicate that despite its heavy work load the administrative performance of Learned Hand's court compares most favorably with the records of the other courts of appeals. And, while the numbers of cases commenced and terminated are not wholly accurate indicators of the size of a court's volume of business—up to a dozen or more appeals may involve the same set of facts and require only a single opinion[3]—these figures do allow for some measurement of the work being done by the judges.

Table 7. The Business of the Second Circuit, Fiscal Years 1942–51

	Cases		
Year	Commenced	Terminated	Pending at Year's End
1942	501	471	172
1943	499	504	167
1944	595	547	215
1945	466	520	161
1946	425	450	136
1947	378	386	128
1948	381	378	131
1949	344	351	124
1950	318	355	87
1951	361	319	129
Totals	4,268	4,281	

Table 7 gives the number of cases commenced, terminated, and pending in the Second Circuit for each of the ten years. The statistics become meaningful, and show how busy the court was when they are placed in relation to the business of the eleven courts of appeals. In 1941 the Second Circuit had six, or 10.5 per cent, of the fifty-seven circuit judges. During the next ten years Congress occasionally authorized new judges in several of the circuits and by 1951 there were sixty-five such judges, with the Second Circuit having 9.2 per cent of the total.[4] Yet, the judges of the Second Circuit did substantially more than 10 per cent of the business of the courts of appeals, as is indicated in Table 8.

Each year the Second Circuit disposed of between 2 and 8 per cent more appeals than its allotment would be if the number of cases

[3] Admiralty cases often illustrate this point.

[4] If not in 1941, then almost certainly by 1951, the average age of the Second Circuit judges was greater than that for any other circuit.

Table 8. Second Circuit's Share of Business of Courts of Appeals

	Cases		Cases Filed per Judge	
Year	Commenced	Terminated	Second Circuit	All Circuits
	%	%		
1942	15.5	15.7	83.5	56.6
1943	16.1	15.8	83.2	53.3
1944	19.4	18.0	99.2	53.0
1945	16.7	18.2	77.7	46.2
1946	16.2	17.2	71.0	44.5
1947	14.5	14.5	63.0	44.2
1948	13.8	14.7	63.5	46.9
1949	11.5	12.7	57.3	50.7
1950	11.2	11.5	53.0	43.5
1951	12.1	11.3	60.2	45.9

handled were based on the size of the court's bench. The greatest disparity was in the five years between 1942 and 1946. In the second five years the court disposed of considerably fewer cases than it had earlier and its share of the business of the eleven courts was not too disproportionate.

The final two columns of Table 8 reveal that in terms of individual case load the Second Circuit judges were substantially busier than their counterparts in the other circuits. Only in 1949 did the number of cases filed per judge on the Second Circuit fall below ten more than the average for all circuits. In the 1942–46 period, the yearly average of filings in the Second Circuit was 71.9 per judge, while for all circuit judges it was 48.9. This means that each of the judges on the Second Circuit was given 22.2 more cases to deal with during each of the five years than the average given to all judges in all circuits. Obviously, the disparity would be even greater if the national average excluded cases from the Second Circuit.

It might be expected that, in view of their heavy case load and the advanced age of three judges, the members of the Second Circuit would have had much unfinished business at the end of each term. Actually, as Table 9 shows, the court kept abreast of its docket throughout the decade, with the exception of the year ending June 30, 1944, when 215 cases were pending. In that year, the court experienced a sharp rise (96) in the number of cases commenced. For each of the other years, the Second Circuit's share of cases pending in all of the circuits was below its percentages of circuit judges and cases commenced and terminated.

Apart from being the busiest court of appeals, the Second Circuit also handled its work in an expeditious fashion. This is demonstrated by the small number of cases pending at year's end and more impor-

Table 9. The Second Circuit and Its Docket, 1942–51

Year	Cases Pending at End of Year	
	Second Circuit	All Circuits
		%
1942	172	10.0
1943	167	10.4
1944	215	13.1
1945	161	10.6
1946	136	8.9
1947	128	8.6
1948	131	7.8
1949	124	6.5
1950	87	5.2
1951	129	7.1

tantly by the time required to dispose of its cases. In this respect, the record of the Second Circuit, relative to the performance of the other circuits that were less burdened, was truly outstanding. The data presented in Table 10 show that from the filing of the record below to final disposition it regularly took the Second Circuit two to three months less time than the other circuits to conclude appeals. Apart from the fact that the Second Circuit was the busiest court of appeals, this record is remarkable because, unlike other circuits, it did not decide many appeals through the time-saving device of per curiam opinions; additionally, as we have seen, the Second Circuit employs the memorandum system and this could be expected to add up to two weeks to the time required to dispose of cases. Apparently, these time-consuming features of the court's decision-making process were more than offset by the enviable work habits of the judges.

Table 10. Time Taken to Dispose Cases, Second Circuit
and All Circuits, 1942–51

Year	Median Time Interval from Filing of Record to Final Disposition		Rank of Second Circuit
	Second Circuit	All Circuits	
	months	months	
1942	3.9	7.7	1
1943	3.3	6.5	1
1944	4.5	6.5	2
1945	4.3	7.0	2
1946	3.7	6.8	2
1947	3.8	6.9	1
1948	3.5	6.3	1
1949	3.6	7.1	2
1950	3.3	7.1	1
1951	3.3	6.7	1

The strictly quantitative evidence presented so far supports the view that the Learned Hand court was an exceptional tribunal; from the administrative standpoint, perhaps the nation's outstanding court of appeals. The annual reports of the Administrative Office of United States Courts also give some idea about the qualitative aspect of cases decided by the Second Circuit.

As is true of all the courts of appeals, the bulk of the Second Circuit's business comes from the federal district courts located within the circuit. The large majority of these appeals—as high as 80 per cent or more—present no difficult problems and can be handled rather quickly. From 1941 to 1951 the Second Circuit got many of its cases from the Tax Court of the United States, the National Labor Relations Board, and other federal administrative agencies. Few cases from these sources can be disposed of summarily; many require the reading of voluminous records or involve novel questions of law.[5] Often it is necessary to choose between conflicting interpretations of a federal statute where the intent of Congress has not been spelled out clearly.

Thus it is significant that in these ten years the Second Circuit heard 675 Tax Court and 221 N.L.R.B. appeals, accounting for 21.3 per cent and 13.1 per cent, respectively, of all such cases commenced in the eleven courts of appeals during this period. The data included in Table 11 on the source of cases filed in the Second Circuit disclose, then, a qualitative burden on the 1941–51 judges. The six district courts within the circuit accounted for 75.2 per cent of the appellate

Table 11. Sources of Cases Commenced in the Second Circuit, 1942–51

Year	Total Commenced	District Court	Tax Court	N.L.R.B.	Other Administrative Agencies	Original
1942	501	349	104	27	17	4
1943	499	341	75	52	25	6
1944	595	435	106	36	16	2
1945	466	378	58	8	21	1
1946	425	326	80	12	7	0
1947	378	307	49	17	5	0
1948	381	271	80	6	5	19
1949	344	283	37	14	4	6
1950	318	262	32	18	5	1
1951	361	255	54	31	12	9
Total	4,268	3,207	675	221	117	48

[5] Our period commenced a few years after the adoption of important New Deal legislation and shortly after a major revision of the Internal Revenue Code. As the data presented later in this chapter show, a substantial number of dissenting opinions in Second Circuit cases, 1941–51, involved taxation questions and administrative agencies.

court's business, the Tax Court for 15.8 per cent, the N.L.R.B. for 5.2 per cent, other administrative agencies for 2.7 per cent, and original proceedings for 1.1 per cent.

The six district courts serve the District of Connecticut, the Northern District of New York, the Eastern District of New York, the Southern District of New York, the Western District of New York, and the District of Vermont. The Southern District—easily the largest district in the country in the number of judges and volume of business—is the single greatest supplier of cases to the Second Circuit. This fact, in turn, provides some additional qualitative evidence on the types of cases coming to the Second Circuit.

It has long been recognized by the Judicial Conference of the United States and the judiciary committees of both houses of Congress that the Southern District has the largest number of complicated lawsuits of any of the district courts. The one year for which we have detailed information is 1959. In that year the Southern District had:

33 government antitrust cases, or over one-third of all such cases pending in the country;

237 patent suits, constituting almost one-fifth of all such cases in the United States;

2,376 admiralty proceedings (exclusive of Jones Act personal injury cases) representing two-fifths of all admiralty matters on file in the federal courts;

117 private antitrust suits, or about 20 per cent of all such litigation in the federal courts, and approximately 25 Robinson-Patman Act cases.[6]

There is no reason to believe that the business for 1959 departed from the normal pattern in that the cases coming to the Southern District were more difficult than those of preceding years. Moreover, because of the important stakes involved in the outcome of antitrust, patent, and other commercial law litigation, almost all of them are appealed, and at the appellate level they remain more complicated than other cases.

The breakdown of appeals from the six district courts is given in Table 12. Of all such cases, 3.8 per cent were from Connecticut, 2.9 per cent from the Northern District, 22.4 per cent from the Eastern District, 64.9 percent from the Southern District, 5.0 per cent from the Western District, and 1.0 per cent from Vermont. This pre-

---

[6] U.S., Congress, House, Committee of the Judiciary, *Hearings Before Subcommittee No. 5,* 87th Cong., 1st sess., 1961, p. 247. The complexity of the judicial business of the Southern District was described at length in the course of these hearings, pp. 230–59.

Table 12. Distribution of Cases from the District Courts,
Second Circuit, 1942–51

Year	Conn.	Northern N.Y.	Eastern N.Y.	Southern N.Y.	Western N.Y.	Vt.
1942	7	12	90	210	23	7
1943	16	11	74	218	19	3
1944	10	9	107	280	25	4
1945	13	12	117	226	8	2
1946	16	3	75	213	13	6
1947	10	7	76	199	14	1
1948	9	8	56	185	13	0
1949	13	18	41	187	21	3
1950	16	7	34	186	15	4
1951	11	5	49	177	11	2
Total	121	92	719	2,081	162	32

ponderance of cases coming from New York City (Eastern and Southern Districts) almost certainly was maintained in cases coming from the Tax Court and the administrative agencies.

A third indication of the complexity of the appeals handled by the Second Circuit is provided by a breakdown of the cases terminated. The statistics in Table 13 show that a relatively small percentage of the total terminations—516, or 12.1 per cent of the total—were criminal appeals. This is significant because it is generally recognized that criminal cases are usually easier to dispose of than other types of cases. A perusal of the *Federal Reporter* demonstrates that many

Table 13. Nature of Cases Terminated, Second Circuit, 1942–51

Year	Total Terminated	Criminal	U.S. Civil	Private Civil	Bankruptcy	Administrative Appeals	Original and Miscellaneous
1942	471	38	44	225[a]		164	not used[a]
1943	504	47	63	177	69	142	6
1944	547	94	76	174	49	152	2
1945	520	74	89	163	83	110	1
1946	450	71	99	129	34	117	0
1947	386	58	120	111	21	76	0
1948	378	45	112	105	20	77	19
1949	351	28	108	112	25	73	5
1950	355	39	106	115	27	66	2
1951	319	22	87	103	21	77	9
Total	4,281	516	904	1,763		1,054	44

[a] Until fiscal year 1943 private civil and bankruptcy cases were reported together and there was no category for original and miscellaneous cases.

criminal appeals are decided by brief opinions.[7] During these ten years, 1,054 administrative appeals were terminated, representing 24.6 per cent of the total. As has already been noted, normally these cases cannot be disposed of quickly. The same is true of many of the 904 appeals in the United States civil category, constituting 21.1 per cent of the total.

To summarize, the data presented in this section, insofar as they are meaningful, support three conclusions. First, between 1941 and 1951 the Second Circuit had a disproportionately large share of the cases decided by the federal courts of appeals. Second, despite being overburdened, the court operated at a high level of efficiency. Finally, it appears that a relatively large number of appeals to the Second Circuit were of the types that ordinarily present complications and cannot be decided with dispatch. All in all, from the administrative standpoint the acclaim accorded to Learned Hand's court was merited.

Of the 4,281 cases terminated by the Second Circuit in the period from July 1, 1941, to June 30, 1951, there were 1,169 terminated without a hearing or submission to the court, and 3,112 were concluded after a hearing or submission. Presumably, only the latter (comprising 72.7 per cent of the total) required written opinions by the judges. In fact, during this decade the Second Circuit decided nearly 3,000 appeals with opinions.

Cases decided by the Second Circuit after Judge Frank joined it until the retirement of Judge Learned Hand are contained in Volumes 120 through 189 of the *Federal Reporter 2d*.[8] These seventy volumes give an almost complete picture of the Second Circuit's work during these years. All of the court's cases included in these reports have been read and analyzed. Data on the number and kinds of opinion are presented in Table 14.

If we disregard the summary opinions—the one- or two-line opinions that do not require additional effort after argument (many simply indicate affirmance in open court)—the judges wrote, on the average, about 250 opinions (excluding concurrences and dissents) each term. The percentage disposed of summarily is extraordinarily low for an intermediate appellate court and is believed to be signifi-

---

[7] Chief Judge Lumbard of the Second Circuit is of the opinion that an even larger percentage of criminal appeals should be disposed of immediately after argument with per curiam opinions ("Appellate Advocacy," mimeographed [New York: Institute of Judicial Administration, 1962], pp. 10–11).

[8] There may be a handful of cases included in the first and last of these volumes that were decided when the six judges did not serve as regular members of the Second Circuit.

Table 14. Opinions of the Second Circuit Included in the
Federal Reporter 2d, Volumes 120–89

Total number of decisions	2,831
Number of summary opinions	244
Number of full opinions	2,587
Percentage of decisions with full opinion	91.4
Number of concurring opinions	126
Percentage of decisions with concurring opinions	4.4
Number of dissenting opinions	311[a]
Percentage of decisions with dissent	11.0[b]

[a] Partial dissents are recorded as dissenting opinions.
[b] This figure is not wholly accurate because in a small number of cases two of the three judges on the panel dissented in part in separate opinions.

cantly below the average for all of the federal courts of appeals during the same period.[9] However, a large number of the full opinions were quite brief, consisting of a short review of the important facts (possibly extracted from the briefs) and a quick disposal of the crucial points of law. The typical opinion was two to three pages long;[10] only in extraordinary cases or when Judge Frank became "essayistic" did the opinions exceed ten pages.

The small number of concurring opinions, only 126 for the full ten years, is not surprising in view of the panel system. Moreover, the attitude on the Second Circuit has not been very favorable toward concurring opinions. The judges either settle their differences or, failing this, dissent.[11] A review of the work of the court makes it clear that partial dissents were often preferred over concurring opinions. An interesting relationship between concurring and dissenting opinions is that only 21 concurrences came in cases with dissenting opinions.

The relatively large number of dissents effectively demonstrates the individualism of the judges and the encouragement of expressions of dissent that generally prevailed while Learned Hand was chief judge. Moreover, dissents in a lower appellate court such as the Second Circuit can serve an immediate function in our judicial system. While dissenting Supreme Court justices appeal to posterity (actually to a future Supreme Court), dissenting intermediate judges announce to a higher court their disagreement with their colleagues and invite reversal of the decision. A study of the certiorari jurisdiction of the Supreme Court demonstrates that dissent in the lower court serves as

[9] This was discussed in Chapter 3.
[10] There are two columns to each *Federal Reporter* page and the type is comparatively small.
[11] There is reason to believe that this is also true of judges on the other courts of appeals.

a positive "cue" to the Supreme Court justices when they quickly decide whether to grant certiorari.[12]

Yet, the rate of dissent does seem high when considered in terms of the total business of the Second Circuit. The accepted view on the court is that roughly between 70 and 80 per cent of appeals are frivolous and that only about 10 per cent pose hard-to-resolve questions.[13] It stands to reason that dissents occur in the tough cases and, accordingly, it appears that in a distinct majority of these cases the three judges serving on the panel were not able to agree.[14]

After the dissenting opinions are read, however, it does not seem that the rate of disagreement is unjustifiably high. In every case, the differences on the court were real, even when they were over procedural matters, and it makes little sense to argue that some of the separate opinions should not have been written. Likewise, where unanimity prevailed because a judge withheld his dissents and later the Supreme Court reversed, it makes no sense to say that the doubting judge should have publicly registered his disagreement. In the final analysis, the decision when to dissent is mostly a matter of judicial style and personality. The distribution of opinions among the judges of the Learned Hand court is given in Table 15. Despite its heavy case load, the Second Circuit in the 1940's did not rely much on outside judges and almost 99 percent of the court's full opinions were written by the regular members. But it is not possible to determine exactly how many of the court's opinions were authored by each judge, since 440

[12] J. Tanenhaus, M. Schick, M. Muraskin, and D. Rosen, "The Supreme Court's Certiorari Jurisdiction: Cue Theory," in Glendon A. Schubert (ed.), *Judicial Decision-Making* (Glencoe, Ill.: Free Press, 1963), p. 111. Statistics regarding the outcome in the Supreme Court of 1941–51 dissenting opinions in the Second Circuit are given in the next chapter.

[13] "Judge Clark, in a subjective test covering 300 appeals on which he has sat during the last two years, found clear one-way cases comprised at least 70 per cent, while around 10 per cent were highly original cases giving scope to the methods of social values. In the remaining 20 per cent the outcome actualy proved certain, but counsel might be forgiven for thinking they had a bare chance of success" (Charles E. Clark and David M. Trubek, "The Creative Role of the Judge: Restraint and Freedom in the Common Law Tradition," *Yale Law Journal*, 71 [1963], 256).

[14] In the 1941–51 period Judge Clark led the Second Circuit with 88 dissents. If we assume that under the panel system Judge Clark heard about one-half of the court's appeals, then he participated in about 1,415 decisions and his rate of dissent was about 6.2 per cent. Since in many cases in which he participated he was in the majority and one of the other judges dissented, it is obvious that the rate of dissent in cases which he heard was close to 10 per cent and perhaps above that in cases where the panel consisted of Judges Learned Hand, Clark, and Frank—the Second Circuit's most frequent dissenters.

Table 15. Writers of Opinions[a] in the Second Circuit, 1941–51

Judge	Full Opinions[c]		Concurrences[d]		Dissents[d]	
	No.	Per Cent	No.	Per Cent	No.	Per Cent
L. Hand	406	15.7	39	30.9	57	18.3
Swan	356	13.8	12	9.5	42	13.5
A. Hand	311	12.0	5	4.0	11	3.5
Chase	331	12.8	6	4.8	30	9.7
Clark	352	13.7	33	26.2	88	28.3
Frank	355	13.8	30	23.8	76	24.4
Per curiam	440	17.1	0	0.0	0	0.0
Other[b]	36	1.1	1	0.8	7	2.3
Total	2,587	100.0	126	100.0	311	100.0

[a] A judge is credited with a full opinion whenever his opinion announced the court's decision and presented the facts of the case. Because of the Second Circuit's procedure and the publicized fact that not infrequently votes are changed after assignment (and even writing) of opinions, the opinion for the court on a number of occasions served also as a dissenting opinion.
[b] District court judges within the Second Circuit and circuit judges from other circuits on assignment with the Second Circuit.
[c] Excludes summary opinions, all of which are per curiam.
[d] The headings "concurrences" and "dissents" are not designated as "opinions" because in some instances (very rare, though) the concurrence or dissent was without opinion. Also, as indicated, a number of dissents were expressed in the opinions written for the court.

(17.1 per cent of the total) of the full opinions were handed down per curiam. These per curiams were nominally the responsibility of one of the panel members, although it is probable that, quite often when decisions were made in this fashion, the memoranda of the other judges and the work of the law clerks contributed substantially to the final product. The choice of the per curiam form may have been due to the brevity of the opinion or the unimportance of the case or because the judge who wrote it did not care to be identified.

It is very unlikely that the greater number of opinions attributed to Judge Learned Hand or the relatively small number credited to Judge Augustus Hand resulted from the former's infrequent reliance on per curiams as compared to his cousin's frequent use of them. For one thing, the procedure on the Second Circuit seems to be that the chief judge or whoever presides has the responsibility of preparing a large number of the per curiam opinions. In fact, quite a few per curiams of 1941–51 read as if they were written by Learned Hand. With respect to Augustus Hand, it is true that "he was absolutely without vanity, and his opinions show no trace of a desire to shine."[15]

[15] Thomas W. Swan, "Augustus Noble Hand," Memorial Book, 1955, Association of the Bar of the City of New York, p. 36.

Still, he was the oldest member of the court (he served from the age of seventy-two to eighty-one) and his colleagues may have eased the burden on him by making him responsible for fewer opinions.

Except for the Hands there is no appreciable difference in the number of full opinions written by any of the judges. The same does not hold true for the concurring and dissenting opinions. Three judges—Learned Hand, Clark, and Frank—accounted for four out of five of the concurrences and more than 70 per cent of the dissents. That the bulk of concurring opinions were written by the most frequent dissenters indicates that the same factors that led the three judges to dissent so often were also responsible for their tendency (relative to their colleagues) to concur separately. Accordingly, we will consider the two types of opinions together.

The most striking aspect of the distribution of dissenting and concurring opinions is that Learned Hand and the Roosevelt appointees were the more liberal members of the court while the other three judges were more conservative in their views. This suggests that the Second Circuit, as a whole, during these years tended toward conservative results.[16] If this is true,[17] it raises an interesting question: since the liberals were equal in number to the conservatives, why the conservative tendency? Presumably, when Charles Clark and Jerome Frank sat on the same panel their liberal views prevailed in much the same way that any two of the conservatives sitting together were able to control the outcome. That this was not the case was, as we have seen in preceding chapters, the result of the lack of cohesion among the court's liberals as compared to the unity of Swan, Augustus Hand, and Chase.

The data on cohesion are presented in the next section of this chapter. There are two explanations for the low degree of liberal cohesiveness. First, the commitment to a liberal decision, as distinguished from a personal libertarian philosophy, was not equally strong among the liberals. Illustrative of this is Learned Hand's votes in naturalization and deportation cases, where his restraintist attitude more than counterbalanced his personal views. Second, one or more of the three judges explicitly rejected the liberal position in one or more areas. Examples are Hand's refusal to upset "harmless error" convictions and Clark's unwillingness to reverse convictions in criminal cases when the matter relied upon on appeal was procedural.

[16] Once more it is necessary to caution that the labels "conservative" and "liberal" are used only to denote the relative position or tendencies of courts and judges and nothing more. It is in this sense that the terms are applied here; the Second Circuit tended toward conservative results, but it was relatively more liberal than all of the other federal courts of appeals.

[17] In 1951 John Frank wrote that "where pure policy must take over judgment, highly conservative results are likely" ("The Top U.S. Commercial Court," *Fortune* [January 1951], p. 108).

At the same time, the conservatives were generally of one mind in cases where there was a possibility for a liberal-conservative division.[18]

Cohesion (or lack of it) alone does not account for the disproportionate distribution of dissenting and concurring opinions. The vast majority of appeals coming to the Second Circuit do not deal with questions that ordinarily contribute to a judge's acquiring a reputation as a liberal or a conservative. Indeed, analysis of the more than three hundred cases with dissenting opinions (Tables 22 and 23) makes it clear that dissenting opinions were written in virtually all types of cases confronting the Second Circuit. In about one half of the cases with dissents the issues in question usually would not involve divisions between liberals and conservatives. Even if we assume, as was often true of Jerome Frank's dissents, that key questions are recast by the dissenting judge to fit into a liberal-conservative mold, we still find a large number of dissenting opinions that had nothing to do with liberalism and conservatism, and we still find that the same judges were the most frequent dissenters.

A second factor accounting for the distribution of dissents was the personality of the judges. The judges who were conservative were also individuals who, apart from the issues, were not much given to dissent. They dissented or concurred with rare exceptions only when they felt quite strongly about a case and after they failed to reconcile their differences with the majority. We have seen that this was characteristic of Judge Augustus Hand, but it was also true of Judge Swan and Judge Chase. As a group, the three conservatives were not dogmatic or fiery judges. They were conservatives in personality as well as on the issues that came to their court.

Learned Hand, Clark, and Frank were as different from their colleagues in temperament and personality as they were in outlook. Each was strong-willed and iconoclastic, more given to dissent than amenable to persuasion. Rather than go along meekly with the majority, they usually preferred to express themselves in dissent or concurrence. This was especially true of Judge Clark, who dissented more often than any of his colleagues. He firmly believed that a judge should dissent whenever he did not agree with the decision that was to be made.

In addition to the liberal-conservative division on the court and the personality of the judges, the literary abilities of the liberals may have contributed to their writing many separate opinions. Of course this suggestion is highly speculative, yet it is known that the three dissenters were gifted writers and Frank and Clark were able to pro-

[18] Of course, as we saw in Chapter 6, cohesion among the conservatives was not perfect.

duce opinions and extrajudicial writings with considerable facility. The other judges were less noted for their literary skill and wrote much shorter opinions. Nor did they find the time or have the inclination to write speeches and law review articles. The more painstaking writers were reluctant to write separately while faced with the task of keeping up with a heavy case load.

Not unrelated to this question is the memorandum system, which in the discussion of the Second Circuit's decisional process was suggested as a probable contributing factor to the large number of dissents on the court. Judge Clark's memoranda, "it is rumored," wrote John Frank toward the end of Learned Hand's era, "are frequently completely documented and ready to be published as opinions," while Jerome Frank's are "on occasion astonishingly erudite." These two judges dissented most frequently. On the other hand, the memoranda of Augustus Hand are "usually terse."[19] Presumably, the more developed memoranda are almost ready for use as opinions, if not majority opinions, then concurring or dissenting.

The very large number of appeals decided each year by the Second Circuit (or any other of the courts of appeals) makes it difficult to discover patterns of agreement and disagreement among the judges. It is not merely a question of numbers but, more importantly, of finding meaningful relationships on a court when the vast majority of cases are one-sided and decided by a unanimous bench. Of the 2,831 decisions handed down by the Second Circuit in the period studied and included in the *Federal Reporter,* almost 90 per cent were unanimous. In terms of the alignment of the judges, this means that the lowest rate of agreement between any two members of the court in all the cases in which they participated together was not much lower than 90 per cent. This point can be illustrated by reference to the record of disagreement between Judges Swan and Clark, the two judges who opposed each other most frequently in the cases with dissenting votes. In the ten years they disagreed in a total of 66 cases, Clark dissenting 46 times when Swan was in the majority and Swan dissenting 20 times when Clark was in the majority. The six judges who constituted the Second Circuit formed twenty different panel combinations, with Swan and Clark together on four of them. If we assume that (1) panels with Swan, Clark, and a third judge actually comprised one-fifth of the panels sitting in the ten years, and (2) panels with Swan and Clark together actually decided approximately one-fifth of all appeals, then panels with these judges handed down

[19] John Frank, "Top U.S. Commercial Court," p. 95. Actually, the memoranda of Judges Swan and Chase were also "usually terse."

approximately 565 decisions. Swan and Clark disagreed in 66 of these and were on the same side in about 500, making their over-all percentage of agreement more than 88 per cent. Even if the two assumptions are partially incorrect and Swan and Clark participated together in fewer cases, their rate of agreement would not be much lower.

When we apply this same formula to Judges Augustus Hand and Chase, whose disagreements totaled eleven, fewest on the Learned Hand court, we find that they agreed in approximately 98 per cent of the cases they heard together. All in all, the six judges form fifteen pairs (see Table 21) and if their rates of agreement were based on all decisions, the range would be narrow, only 10 percentage points separating the most cohesive pair from the most divided pair. Thus the total number of decisions does not encourage analysis of the voting records of the judges. However, if we use only the cases with dissent most of the obstacles are overcome. The data presented in this section are derived from the votes in all cases with dissenting opinions. First, some qualifications on their use should be specified.

The most important limitation is the panel system, which in every single case decided in the ten years intervened to prevent the judges from registering their views in all cases decided by the court. Clearly, had the six judges sat in every case the number of dissents would have been much higher than 311 and, probably not too infrequently, judges in the minority under the panel system would have been in the majority.

Moreover, the panel system contributes to a somewhat blurred picture of judicial attitudes because of the problem of circuit precedent and conflict of panels. As we saw in Chapter 4, there are no hard and fast rules requiring intermediate appellate judges to abide by long-standing precedents of their own court, decisions in other circuits, or rulings by other panels within the circuit. The problem is least acute when two or more circuits are in conflict for, then, if the disagreement is overt and persistent, the Supreme Court is virtually certain to grant certiorari and resolve the issue and this will bind the lower judges. When there is intracircuit conflict, the judges, at least on the Second Circuit, generally tend to follow precedent and previous panels, though the advent of en banc proceedings makes it easier to overrule precedents and theoretically does away with the problem of conflict between panels. However, during the chief judgeship of Learned Hand, the Second Circuit obstinately refused to hear cases en banc, so that the judges at times were squarely faced with the question of whether to adhere to earlier decisions that they disagreed with.

Learned Hand was "conscientious in abiding by a precise precedent cited from either a higher court or a court composed of his brethren."[20] In one case he wrote, "having taken part in that decision and my notions being then overruled, I regard it as authoritative."[21] The three conservatives regularly adhered to decisions of other panels, though for them this was not very difficult since the precedents tended toward conservative results and, in any event, during the 1940's their views usually prevailed. Judge Clark, on the other hand, felt strongly that judges should not be too afraid of reversing other panels, for to defer completely to earlier decisions would be to allow minority rule to prevail on the court.[22] Judge Frank was not very consistent in his position; at times he went along with precedent, while at other times he would dissent and refuse to accept previous decisions of his own court.[23] Thus, there was no single pattern on the Learned Hand court; what is certain, however, is that to the extent that the judges did follow Second Circuit precedents their views were distorted by the panel system.

The fact that intermediate judges, with rare exceptions, follow the rulings of the Supreme Court also contributes to the inability to discern, at times, their true opinions through their votes.

Finally, there is need for caution in analyzing the statistics derived from dissent because the raw vote, independent of the substance of the disagreement, gives us only one dimension of the conflict on the bench. All dissents are considered to be of equal significance, even the partial dissents which constitute a substantial number of the total. In reality, the gulf between the majority and the dissenter was not very wide in some of these cases. An analytical study of the cases with dissenting opinions based on the text of the opinions would probably alter the picture presented on these pages, based as it is on only the votes.

After all these points are considered it remains valid that while all important and contentious cases did not conclude in a split court, and that some disagreements were obscured by a veil of unanimity, all of the cases with dissents were sources of conflict on the court. Through study of the votes in these cases we get a better understanding of the Second Circuit during its great period.

[20] Charles E. Wyzanski, Jr., "Judge Learned Hand's Contribution to Public Law," *Harvard Law Review,* 60 (1947), 368.

[21] Phelps Dodge Corp. v. National Labor Relations Board, 113 F.2d 202, 207 (2d Cir. 1940). See also his concurring opinion in Molnar v. Commissioner of Internal Revenue, 156 F.2d 924, 926–27 (2d Cir. 1946).

[22] Interview with Judge Charles E. Clark, December 17, 1962. For his views in an opinion, see his dissent in Zalkind v. Scheinman, 139 F.2d 895, 905 (2d Cir. 1943).

[23] This was notably true in "harmless error" cases. In one of these he dissented, saying that he would continue to do so until the Supreme Court told him he was wrong (United States v. Bennett, 152 F.2d 342, 349 [2d Cir. 1945]).

Table 16. Action of Second Circuit Judges, Cases with Dissent

Judge	Total No. of Cases	With Majority		No. of Dissents	Con-curring Opinions	Majority Opinions
		No.	Per Cent			
L. Hand	155	98	63.2	57	8	44
Swan	161	119	74.0	42	0	49
A. Hand	103	92	89.3	11	0	39
Chase	135	105	77.8	30	1	46
Clark	182	94	51.6	88	4	55
Frank	161	85	52.7	76	8	35
Other				7	0	5
Per curiam						8

The basic information included in Table 16 reveals again the strength of the conservative judges. In particular, Augustus Hand's record of being with the majority in 90 per cent of the split decisions in which he participated is remarkable and may be unmatched by any other recent federal appellate judge. It is quite apparent that on the issues that divided the court Hand exerted a decisive influence as his vote usually determined the outcome.

A revealing sidelight is that eight of the dissents came in cases where the majority opinion was per curiam, apparently indicating that the majority did not regard the case as very important or think too highly of the contentions of the dissenter.

The raw data on dissents in Table 16 shed insufficient light on the alignment of the judges and of the relative cohesion of the conservatives and liberals. The nonsupportive interactions of the judges in cases with dissent—that is, the number of times each judge disagreed with each of his colleagues—are presented in Tables 17 and 18.

Table 17. Interactions of Judges in Cases with Dissent

With Majority	L. Hand, Dissent From	Swan, Dissent From	A. Hand, Dissent From	Chase, Dissent From	Clark, Dissent From	Frank, Dissent From
L. Hand		22	6	14	33	24
Swan	27		2	11	46	31
A. Hand	14	11		8	39	24
Chase	30	6	3		28	34
Clark	26	20	4	10		36
Frank	16	25	7	15	22	
Total[a]	113	84	22	58	168	149

[a] Because each dissent is a disagreement with two colleagues, the total for each judge should be roughly double the number of dissents by each. It would be exactly double were it not for the occasional participation by outside judges.

Table 18. Total Disagreements of the Judges

Judge	L. Hand	Swan	A. Hand	Chase	Clark	Frank
L. Hand		49	20	44	59	40
Swan	49		13	17	66	56
A. Hand	20	13		11	43	31
Chase	44	17	11		38	49
Clark	59	66	43	38		58
Frank	40	56	41	49	58	

The boxed area in each table isolates the interactions of the three conservative judges. It is clear that their disagreements with one another were not frequent. The three dissented 83 times and had 164 disagreements with colleagues; only 41 of the disagreements, or one-fourth, were with conservatives. Judge Swan's 42 dissents were directed most often against Frank and Learned Hand in that order; Augustus Hand's 11 were primarily against Learned Hand and Frank; and Chase's 30 dissents found Frank and Learned Hand most often with the majority. However, because Clark's dissents were so often against majorities that included Swan, Augustus Hand, and Chase, he did not have a high rate of agreement with the conservatives. It is significant that more of Frank's dissents were directed against fellow New Dealer Clark than against any other judge, a statistic that highlights the poor relationship between them that was discussed previously. Moreover, Frank and Learned Hand were involved in more disagreements with Clark (58 and 59, respectively) than with any of the conservatives. Clearly, the figures in the two tables confirm the cohesion of the conservatives and show how badly divided the liberals were.

Tables 17 and 18 give but part of the whole picture: how often the members of the Second Circuit disagreed with one another. Nonsupportive interactions alone are not fully indicative of the alignment of the judges. We must also know how often they were in agreement. Then, on the basis of the total number of interactions—supportive and nonsupportive—we can calculate the rates of agreement of all of the judges. The number of supportive interactions is shown in Table 19. By combining the figures in Tables 18 and 19 we are able to compute the percentages of agreement among all of the judges, as is shown in Table 20. Another way of looking at the data in this table is to treat the judges in pairs and to rank the fifteen pairs in the order of the solidarity of their members. This is done in Table 21.

The data in Tables 20 and 21 modify only slightly the conclusions that were drawn when only the disagreements of the judges were considered. At first glance, it may appear that the rate of agreement

Table 19. Supportive Interactions of Judges in Cases with Dissent[a]

Judge	L. Hand	Swan	A. Hand	Chase	Clark	Frank
L. Hand		28	19	12	9	23
Swan	28		16	31	27	10
A. Hand	19	16		27	18	11
Chase	12	31	27		13	12
Clark	9	27	18	13		18
Frank	23	10	11	12	18	

[a] Except where it is clear from the text that the two judges are in complete agreement, concurring votes in separate opinions are not regarded as supportive actions.

Table 20. Rate of Agreement of Judges in Cases with Dissent

Judge	L. Hand	Swan	A. Hand	Chase	Clark	Frank
L. Hand		36.4	48.7	21.4	13.2	36.5
Swan	36.4		55.2	64.5	29.0	15.2
A. Hand	48.7	55.2		71.1	29.5	26.2
Chase	21.4	64.5	71.1		25.5	19.7
Clark	13.2	29.0	29.5	25.5		23.7
Frank	36.5	15.2	26.2	19.7	23.7	

Table 21. Solidarity of Judges According to Pairs

Rank	Judges	Agreement
		%
1	A. Hand–Chase	71.1
2	Swan–Chase	64.5
3	Swan–A. Hand	55.2
4	L. Hand–A. Hand	48.7
5	L. Hand–Frank	36.5
6	L. Hand–Swan	36.4
7	A. Hand–Clark	29.5
8	Swan–Clark	29.0
9	A. Hand–Frank	26.2
10	Chase–Clark	25.5
11	Clark–Frank	23.7
12	L. Hand–Chase	21.4
13	Chase–Frank	19.7
14	Swan–Frank	15.2
15	L. Hand–Clark	13.2

of the three conservatives—who form the three highest-ranking pairs in Table 21—is not too high, ranging from 71.1 per cent for Augustus Hand-Chase to 55.2 per cent for Swan-Augustus Hand. We must remember that we are concerned here only with the 10 per cent of the Second Circuit's decisions made by a divided court and that in each of these cases there are three judges on the panel and three interactions, one supportive and two nonsupportive. Accordingly, any rate of agreement in cases with dissent above 50 per cent must be regarded as high. In addition, it should be kept in mind that while in the 311 cases with dissent, Swan, Augustus Hand, and Chase did not disagree with one another often, the number of supportive interactions is kept low because usually the decision was unanimous when they were on the panel together. This explains why in the 311 cases, Swan actually voted more often with Learned Hand than he did with Augustus Hand, though the percentage of agreement of the Learned Hand-Swan pair is 36.4. When Swan and Augustus Hand were on the panel there was considerably less likelihood of dissent, regardless of who the third judge was, than when Learned Hand, Swan, and another judge comprised the panel.

Tables 20 and 21 substantiate the lack of cohesion among the three liberals. The highest percentage of agreement of any liberal pair is between Learned Hand and Frank, only 36.5 per cent. Almost amazingly, Learned Hand and Clark rank last, agreeing in only about 13 per cent of their interactions in cases with dissent.

In Table 22, the cases with dissenting opinions have been arranged according to subject matter. Clearly, there is a preponderance of

Table 22. Subject Matter of Dissents

Subject Matter	No.	Per Cent
Taxation	59	19.0
Bankruptcy	27	8.7
Patents[a]	30	9.7
Admiralty and shipping	32	10.3
Regulation of economic life[b]	33	10.6
Criminal prosecutions	32	10.3
Private, diversity	33	10.6
Private, federal question[c]	24	7.7
Miscellaneous, U.S. government[d]	10	3.2
Wartime economic regulation	3	1.0
State taxation	2	0.6
Aliens	12	3.8
Selective Service	8	2.6
Civil liberties[e]	4	1.3
Court martial	2	0.6
Total	311	100.0

[a] Includes copyright and trademark cases.
[b] Consists primarily of appeals from federal administrative agencies and from lower-court decisions where the United States government as a party was seeking to enforce New Deal legislation.
[c] Included Federal Employers' Liability Act, Fair Labor Standards Act, Jones Act, and antitrust cases.
[d] Civil suits with government as a party.
[e] First Amendment cases.

cases in the various economic categories, and this supports the view that the Second Circuit is one of the leading commercial courts in the nation. Only 58, or less than 1 out of 5, of the dissents are in categories (criminal, alien, selective service, court martial, and civil liberties) that are readily subject to liberal-conservative analysis. However, many of the dissents in the regulation of economic life, patent, and several other categories did involve differences between nominally liberal and conservative approaches. Illustrative of this are most of Frank's dissents in patent law appeals and Swan's dissents in cases concerned with the regulation of economic life. On the other hand, few of the 59 dissents in taxation cases had anything to do with liberalism or conservatism; this was also true of admiralty and shipping appeals. These two categories alone accounted for about 30 per cent of all dissents.

A breakdown of the various categories according to each judge, as is shown in Table 23, reveals a number of interesting points about the Second Circuit and its members. Learned Hand's 21 dissents in tax cases reflect, perhaps, his irritation over the complexity and confused language of the Internal Revenue Code,[24] which was revised in the late 1930's. This major revision explains the large number of disagreements over taxation matters.

For Judge Swan, the two most significant groupings are regulation of economic life and private federal questions. His dissents were primarily directed against antibusiness decisions of administrative agencies and pro-employee interpretations of the Fair Labor Standards Act and the Federal Employers' Liability Act. In these dissents, the picture of Swan as a conservative comes through quite clearly.

Because Judge Augustus Hand dissented so infrequently, there are too few dissents in all to provide any pattern. Eight of his eleven dissents involved questions not germane to conservative or liberal positions.

Most noteworthy about Judge Chase's record is that fully one-half of his dissents came in cases where the court divided along liberal-conservative lines, and in virtually all of these he took a conservative position. As was shown in Chapter 6 he differed with his colleagues' generally liberal attitude in Selective Service appeals and this is registered by his 5 dissents in that area.

Judge Clark's dissents were not concentrated in a few areas; rather, he disagreed with his colleagues in virtually all types of cases, revealing the importance he attached to procedural matters, irrespective of substantive questions. While it is considerably more difficult to

[24] Learned Hand, "Thomas Walter Swan," in Irving Dilliard (ed.), *The Spirit of Liberty* (New York: Vintage Books, 1959), p. 161.

Table 23. Dissents of Judges According to Subject Matter

Judge	Tax	Bankruptcy	Patents	Admiralty	Regulation of Economic Life	Criminal	Private Diversity	Private Federal	Aliens	Selective Service	Miscellaneous, U.S.	Civil Liberties	State Tax	Court Martial	Wartime Economic Reguation	Total
L. Hand	21	5	4	8	3	4	7	1	0	0	3	0	1	0	0	57
Swan	8	2	2	2	9	1	3	8	4	1	1	0	1	0	0	42
A. Hand	3	0	0	2	0	1	3	1	1	0	0	0	0	0	0	11
Chase	7	0	2	3	2	3	2	3	1	5	1	0	0	0	1	30
Clark	8	10	10	10	15	8	12	5	3	2	2	2	0	0	1	88
Frank	9	10	11	7	4	15	5	5	3	0	3	2	0	2	0	76
Other	3	0	1	0	0	0	1	1	0	0	0	0	0	0	1	7
Total	59	27	30	32	33	32	33	24	12	8	10	4	2	2	3	311

generalize about his dissents than about those of the other judges, the regulation of economic life and criminal law dissents demonstrate the split among the court's liberals and Clark's refusal to go along with the liberal position in certain areas. When it came to the power of the federal government to regulate economic affairs, he advocated the liberal line, favoring the administrative agencies and the New Deal. But almost every one of the eight dissents in the criminal category is against a majority decision reversing a conviction.

The outstanding aspect of Jerome Frank as a dissenting judge is the large number of his dissents in criminal cases. In several of these he disagreed with the reversal of convictions; most of them, however, came during his first half-dozen years on the bench when he fought a single-handed and eventually winning battle for a more restrictive application of the harmless error rule in criminal appeals. Frank's dissents in the bankruptcy and patent law areas were, for the most part, expressions of his concern for small businessmen.

In large measure, the data included in Tables 22 and 23 are not relevant to the questions raised throughout much of this chapter. Where they do touch on such matters as alignment and cohesion of the Second Circuit's judges, however, the pattern that emerged earlier is again supported.

10

The Second Circuit
and the Supreme Court: 1942-51

WE HAVE PREVIOUSLY NOTED ON A NUMBER OF OCCASIONS THE OUTCOME
of Second Circuit rulings that were appealed to the Supreme Court.
Since our focus is on the Second Circuit, this treatment of interaction
with the nation's highest court has been sketchy. This chapter is an
attempt to more systematically trace the fate of Second Circuit rulings
in the Supreme Court. This effort consists principally of establishing
statistical relationships between both courts. However, interpretation
of the data generally is hampered because there is little basis for
comparison with the other courts of appeals and their judges, which
have not been subjected to the same kind of study.

The first step in the relationship between the Supreme Court and
the courts of appeals after the lower-court ruling has been made is the
petition for the writ of certiorari. Except in rare cases, appeals from the
intermediate appellate courts must take the certiorari route to the
Supreme Court, which exercises a discretionary jurisdiction. Unless the
petitioner wins the support of four of the justices, the prospects for
reversal of the lower court are dead.

In fact, the majority of cases terminated by the courts of appeals
do not even reach the certiorari stage. The exact percentage for any
court or year cannot be determined because many times the courts

of appeals refer cases back to the district courts and administrative agencies where they originated, and it is some time before they climb again in the federal judicial system toward the Supreme Court. For what it is worth, according to the statistics of the Administrative Office of the United States Courts, in the years 1942–51 there were 28,581 terminations in the eleven courts of appeals. During the years 1943–52 there were 6,296 petitions for certiorari from the courts of appeals, a ratio of less than one filing for certiorari to every four terminations.[1]

Apart from those cases where no appeal is possible to the Supreme Court until the lower courts decide once more, the probable reason why the losing parties do not request certiorari is that they or their counsel recognize that there is little prospect that the Supreme Court will entertain their appeals.

It is extremely doubtful that at this initial stage of certiorari the Supreme Court's attitude toward the lower court, even if it is known, plays any part in the decision whether to take a case to the High Court. In any event, where certiorari is not requested, there is no interaction between the Supreme Court and the courts of appeals. We cannot conclude on the basis of a number or percentage of cases not appealed further that the Supreme Court does or does not have confidence in a particular court of appeals and its judges.

Because the Second Circuit was the busiest court of appeals during the ten years studied, it is not surprising that more petitions for review came from it and that the Supreme Court heard more appeals from it than from any of the other circuits. There were 1,022 certiorari petitions from the Second Circuit in this period, of which 155 were granted. Table 24 shows that the Second Circuit's share of the certiorari business from the courts of appeals was about the same as its share of cases terminated in these courts. The court had 15.0 per cent of all terminations and 15.2 per cent of all petitions of certiorari granted in appeals from the courts of appeals.

Conceivably, the fact that the Learned Hand court got a disproportionately large share of the nation's important commercial and governmental civil litigation might have resulted in certiorari being requested and granted in a larger proportion of its cases than in those of the other circuits. It could be expected that in these cases the stakes are so high that the losing parties would carry the battle all the way to the Supreme Court. In addition, these cases involved large financial

---

[1] Throughout this chapter, the ten-year period for terminations is from July 1, 1941, to June 30, 1951 (fiscal years 1942–51), while for certiorari the period is from July 1, 1942, to June 30, 1952. The reason for this is that it usually takes the better part of a year after the lower-court decision for the Supreme Court to act on a certiorari petition.

Table 24. Terminations and Petitions for Certiorari Filed and Granted,
All Courts of Appeals and Second Circuit

	All Circuits	Second Circuit	
		No.	Per Cent of Total
Cases terminated	28,581	4,281	15.0
Petitions for certiorari	6,296	1,022	16.2
Ratio of petitions to terminations	.220	.239	
Certiorari granted	1,019	155	15.2
Percentage of petitions granted	16.2	15.2	
Ratio of certiorari granted to terminations	.036	.036	

interests and often affect many people, factors that could influence the prospects for High Court review.

In fact, as Table 24 indicates, the cases terminated–certiorari filed ratio and certiorari filed–certiorari granted relationship for Second Circuit appeals were about the same as they were for the other courts of appeals. In part, this may have been due to the large number of administrative appeals heard by the Second Circuit. As the data in Table 25 reveal, although administrative appeals accounted for almost one-fourth of the Court's 4,281 terminations, they accounted for only 103 of the 1,022 petitions coming from it. Despite the obvious importance of this type of litigation, certiorari was requested in only about 10 per cent of administrative appeals terminations. This contrasts with the over-all rate of almost 25 per cent over the ten-year period for all Second Circuit cases, and a rate of close to 30 per cent (921 of 3,227) if the administrative cases are left out. The explanation for the low number of certiorari petitions in administrative appeals is that in many of these cases, after the court of appeals ruling, the case is returned to the administrative agency where it orginated for further

Table 25. Termination—Certiorari Relationship According to
Subject Matter, Second Circuit

	Criminal	U.S. Civil	Administrative Appeals	All Other
Cases terminated	516	904	1,054	1,807
Petitions for certiorari	172	332	103	415
Ratio of petitions to terminations	.333	.367	.098	.229
Certiorari granted	25	61	27	42
Percentage of petitions granted	14.5	18.4	26.2	10.1
Ratio of certiorari granted to terminations	.048	.067	.026	.023

proceedings. Significantly, when certiorari was requested in administrative appeals, it was granted at a higher rate (26.2 per cent) than in any other category of appeals.

Inasmuch as the certiorari record of the Second Circuit closely parallels that of the other courts of appeals, we cannot conclude that counsel often did not apply for certiorari or the Supreme Court did not grant it because of the prestige of the Second Circuit bench or because of the high regard in which it was held by the justices in Washington.[2] In short, interactions between the Supreme Court and the courts of appeals at the certiorari stage do not permit any conclusions regarding the attitude of the High Court toward any of the circuits or their judges.

The most important steps in the Supreme Court's decisional process occur after it has agreed to hear an appeal. The opposing parties write briefs and present oral argument and the justices consider, question, confer, and write opinions which are announced in open court. Until the decision is announced the public has no knowledge of what the outcome of an appeal will be.

Accordingly, the grant of a writ of certiorari is primarily an indication that at least four justices believe, after a quick review, that a case is worthy of further consideration on the merits. But is it true, as some justices have from time to time stated, that the decision whether to grant review has nothing to do with the merits?

As far as the denial of certiorari is concerned, the justices have generally maintained that it "imports no expression of opinion upon the merits of the case"[3] and only means "that fewer than four members of the Court deemed it desirable to review a decision of the lower court."[4] Logically, what is true of refusals to review lower-court rulings must also be true of decisions to grant certiorari, namely, that they are made apart from any opinion on the issues raised on appeal.

However, the disclaimers of the justices notwithstanding, there are reasons to believe that the certiorari decision is related to judicial views on the substantive questions posed by a case. Occasionally a

[2] This judgment is not disturbed by a statement made by Justice Harlan in a tribute to Judge Learned Hand: "May I say that when you read in Monday's *New York Times* 'Certiorari Denied' to one of your cases, then despite the usual teachings, what the notation really means is 'Judgment Affirmed'" (*Proceedings of a Special Session of the United States Court of Appeals for the Second Circuit to Commemorate Fifty Years of Federal Judicial Services, by the Honorable Learned Hand,* April 10, 1959, 264 F.2d, p. 23).

[3] Justice Holmes in United States v. Carver, 260 U.S. 472, 490 (1923).

[4] Justice Frankfurter in Maryland v. Baltimore Radio Show, 338 U.S. 912, 917 (1950).

denial of certiorari is accompanied by a dissenting opinion, which goes to the merits of the case. More significantly, while it is not often spelled out in their opinions, lower-court judges tend to regard denials of certiorari in appeals from their rulings as indicating that the Supreme Court goes along with their holdings. As Judge Swan said in one case: "This is precisely the same situation as this court passed upon in *United States* ex rel. *Eichenlaub v. Watkins.* . . . But our construction of the statute was not so plainly erroneous as to induce the Supreme Court to grant certiorari."[5]

Observers of the Supreme Court have generally interpreted refusals to review as expressions on the merits. Fowler Harper, in particular, regularly attacked the Supreme Court's certiorari performance on the ground that the court was deliberately reaching certain results through the guise of refusing to hear cases.[6] He pointed out that over a three-year period (1949–51), the lower-court decision was reversed in 62 per cent of the appeals from federal courts and 68 per cent of the state cases in which certiorari was granted. These figures supported the conclusion that "since the grants of certiorari came most often in cases where the Court disapproved of the decision below, the denial of certiorari may imply at least some degree of approval of the decision below."[7] While Harper's argument probably has some validity when applied to Supreme Court action in the civil liberties field and in cases that achieve notoriety, it makes little sense in the context of more than 3,000 certiorari rulings made each year. Most of these decisions are made so quickly by the justices that it is apparent that there cannot be real consideration of the issues. Even in the relatively small number of cases in which certiorari is granted, often the court acts without paying much attention to the merits. This is true of appeals involving tax laws and the interpretation of other congressional statutes, where the decision to review is based on a conflict between circuits, or the novelty of the questions presented, or the importance of the litigation in terms of the number of people affected by it, and the justices voting to review have given little thought to how they will eventually vote.

[5] United States *ex rel.* Willumeit v. Watkins, 171 F.2d 773, 775 (2d Cir. 1949).

[6] Fowler V. Harper and Alan S. Rosenthal, "What the Supreme Court Did Not Do in the 1949 Term—An Appraisal of Certiorari," *University of Pennsylvania Law Review,* 99 (1950), 293; Harper and Edwin D. Etherington, "What the Supreme Court Did Not Do During the 1950 Term," *University of Pennsylvania Law Review,* 100 (1951), 351; Harper and George C. Pratt, "What the Supreme Court Did Not Do During the 1951 Term," *University of Pennsylvania Law Review,* 101 (1953), 439.

[7] Harper and Pratt, *ibid.,* pp. 445–46.

Yet, if the decision on certiorari is not in itself a judgment on the holding below, how do we explain the high percentage of reversals after certiorari has been granted? The "cue theory of certiorari," proposed by Joseph Tanenhaus, helps to explain this pattern of judicial behavior. According to this theory, the presence of any of three cues (there may be others not tested by Tanenhaus)—the federal government's seeking review, dissension in the court below or disagreement between two or more courts or agencies, and the salience of a civil liberties issue—

> would warn a justice that a petition deserved scrutiny. If, on the other hand, no cue was present, a justice could safely discard a petition without further expenditure of time and energy. Careful study by a justice of the petitions containing cues could then be made to determine which should be denied because of jurisdictional defects, inadequacies in the records, lack of ripeness, tactical inadvisability, etc., and which should be allotted some of the limited time available for oral argument, research, and preparation of full opinions.[8]

To be sure, the cue theory avoids the question whether during the "careful study" of the petitions containing cues the justices go into the merits. However, the theory could easily be expanded to provide for such a preliminary examination and this, then, would account for the large number of reversals. Even without including any substantive evaluation in the search for cues, the theory offers an explanation for the high percentage of reversals of lower courts after certiorari is granted. We can say that where certiorari is obtained, there is a better than even chance of reversal for the very same reasons that prompted the justices to hear the appeal. In other words, when the government asks for reversal or there is dissension below or a civil liberties issue is at stake, there is a strong likelihood that when the justices get to the merits they will vote to reverse.

Over the ten years in question, the Supreme Court handed down 145 decisions after certiorari was granted in cases coming from the Second Circuit. Of these, 129 were with full opinion while 16 were memorandum decisions. The nature of these 16 decisions is given in Table 26. Generally, these cases do not give any clear indication whether the Supreme Court was or was not satisfied with the lower court's rulings. This is obviously true of the three affirmances by an equally divided court and the two moot cases. In two of the "vacated and remanded" cases, the federal government, which was the winning

<hr/>

[8] J. Tanenhaus, M. Schick, M. Muraskin, and D. Rosen, "The Supreme Court's Certiorari Jurisdiction: Cue Theory," in Glendon A. Schubert (ed.), *Judicial Decision-Making* (Glencoe, Ill.: Free Press, 1963), pp. 129–30.

Table 26. Memorandum Decisions of the Supreme Court
in Cases from the Second Circuit

Affirmed by equally divided court	3
Vacated and remanded	9
Reversed	2
Vacated; case is moot	1
Dismissed; case is moot	1

party in the court of appeals, concurred in the Supreme Court's action, while in at least two others the remand was to allow the intermediate court to consider a particular question.

In the 129 cases with full opinion, the Supreme Court affirmed the Second Circuit in 71 and reversed (including reversed in part and vacated and remanded) in 58. This comes to a reversal rate of 45.0 per cent, significantly below the expected reversal rate of around 60 per cent. The Second Circuit's reversal rate is still below 50 per cent when all but the two mootness memorandum holdings are included in the totals; the record is then 74 Second Circuit decisions affirmed and 69 reversed.

It is interesting to compare the record of the Second Circuit with Supreme Court action during the same years in cases coming from all the courts of appeals that were decided by full opinion. As the data in Table 27 reveal, only the First and Second Circuits were reversed in less than 50 per cent of the full opinions in cases coming from them. For all circuits, including the First and Second, 800 appeals were heard by the Supreme Court, of which 452, or 56.5 per cent, culminated in

Table 27. Supreme Court Actions in Cases from the Courts of
Appeals Decided by Full Opinion, 1941–51

Court	No.	Affirmed	Reversed No.	Reversed Per Cent
District of Columbia	87	30	57	65.5
First Circuit	22	16	6	27.2
Second Circuit	129	71	58	45.0
Third Circuit	89	41	48	53.9
Fourth Circuit	46	22	24	52.2
Fifth Circuit	96	36	60	62.5
Sixth Circuit	65	25	40	61.5
Seventh Circuit	88	35	53	60.2
Eighth Circuit	37	13	24	64.9
Ninth Circuit	88	35	53	60.2
Tenth Circuit	53	24	29	54.7
All courts	800	348	452	56.5

the lower court's being overturned. The outstanding record of the First Circuit, maintained at least well into the 1950's, may have been due to its being the least busy of the intermediate courts and perhaps also to the high regard in which it was held by the Supreme Court while Calvert Magruder was its chief judge.[9]

If we use the rate of reversal by the Supreme Court as a measure of the effectiveness and the quality of a lower court, the Second Circuit under Learned Hand must be regarded as a very good and strong court. Although it was faced with a very large case load and a good deal of complex litigation, it was more often affirmed than reversed by the Supreme Court in cases in which the Supreme Court had granted certiorari. What is especially significant is that in 33 of the 129 cases decided with full opinion, the Supreme Court explained that certiorari had been granted because of a conflict between the Second Circuit and one or more other circuits. Each of these 33 appeals from the Second Circuit was decided together with one or more other cases. In these instances of intercircuit conflict involving the Second Circuit, the Supreme Court supported the Second Circuit in 23 (69.7 per cent) and reversed in 10 (30.3 per cent). Obviously, between 1941 and 1951, the Second Circuit fared very well in the Supreme Court.

The major problem posed by these data is that they do not provide any easy explanation for the fine performance of the Second Circuit in the Supreme Court. While we can confidently conclude that this record was not happenstance, it is difficult to attribute it to any single cause or cluster of causes. However, two plausible, and closely related, explanations merit consideration. These are that (1) the record was due to the excellence of the lower court's members and (2) it was the result of Supreme Court deference to the views of the Second Circuit.

The first explanation is partly predicated on the assumption that a reversal by the Supreme Court generally means that the inferior court has misinterpreted or ignored a previous Supreme Court ruling. Of course, often this cannot be the case, as when the High Court refuses to follow its own precedents or when the lower courts are presented with novel questions not ruled on by the Supreme Court. But over a large number of appeals, the difference between a high rate of reversal (55 per cent and above) and a low rate of reversal (45 per cent and below) can be attributed to some extent to the way lower judges treat Supreme Court rulings.

From the opinions expressed by those who paid attention to the Learned Hand court and from our own analysis of the work of the six

[9] Felix Frankfurter, "Calvert Magruder," *Harvard Law Review,* 72 (1959), 1202.

members of the court, the conclusion is justified that during the 1940's the Second Circuit bench was outstanding. Individually, the judges were regarded as men of great intellect and integrity. Two qualities that make for a good intermediate appellate judge should be mentioned here. The first is the intellectual strength to understand fully and apply correctly in all their ramifications the relevant decisions of the nation's highest tribunal. The second is the detachment which allows the judge to accept his inferior position in the judicial hierarchy and therefore to follow Supreme Court rulings dutifully.

These two qualities were possessed in abundance by the members of the Second Circuit; the intellectual detachment was manifested particularly in economic decisions, such as appeals from the National Labor Relations Board, where the holdings of the Roosevelt court were accepted by the more conservative lower-court judges. Presumably, this fidelity, translated as it was into decisions in harmony with the views of the Supreme Court, helps us to understand why the Supreme Court did not find it necessary to reverse the Second Circuit in the majority of appeals coming from it which were decided by full opinion.

The second reason given for the Second Circuit's record—deference to it by the justices in Washington—is related to the one just discussed. Because the Second Circuit was so highly thought of by just about everyone who observed its operations and its members were known to try to interpret Supreme Court decisions properly, the High Court was more willing to go along with its views than with those of the other intermediate courts.

If there is any validity to this interpretation of the data favorable to the Learned Hand court, likely two patterns should have emerged in the relationship between the two courts. The first is that in cases that represented intercircuit conflict involving the Second Circuit, the Supreme Court supported the Second Circuit substantially more often than it did the other circuits. Even if the Supreme Court's rate of approval in all appeals was higher for the Second Circuit than it was for the other courts of appeals, it is unlikely that there was any deference to the lower court unless it was strongly supported in the conflict cases. As a rule, these appeals involve issues, for instance tax law, that do not greatly excite the interests or passions of the justices and likely certiorari would not have been granted were it not for disagreement in the lower judiciary. Under these conditions the members of the Supreme Court might be influenced by their attitudes toward inferior courts and judges. Accordingly, with respect to the Learned Hand court, the fact that it was supported in twenty-three of its thirty-three conflicts with other circuits suggests that it was accorded a high degree of respect in Washington.

The second relationship between the two courts that ought to exist if the "deference theory" is to be given serious consideration, is that in cases in which the major function of both courts was the interpretation of congressional statutes, the Supreme Court gave substantial support to the Second Circuit. In these cases, both the intermediate and Supreme appellate courts are primarily concerned with determining legislative intention, somewhat apart from doctrinal considerations, with the lower court having the added task of discerning on the basis of past decisions how the Supreme Court would view the litigation. When we note the acclaim accorded to the two Hands and Swan for their performance in interpreting statutes and also the faithfulness of the Second Circuit to the Supreme Court, there is good reason to expect that in this type of appeal the Supreme Court was willing to defer to the lower court's judgment.

Even before the statutory interpretation appeals were analyzed, it was reasonable to believe that the Second Circuit's interpretation usually prevailed on appeal. This was based on the court's record in intercircuit conflicts, since these conflicts tend to arise when the courts of appeals are required to interpret recently enacted legislation. Table 28 demonstrates that in the overwhelming majority of statutory interpretation appeals, the Second Circuit was affirmed. Fifty-four cases—the

Table 28. Supreme Court Decisions in Cases with Full Opinion from the Second Circuit, According to Subject Matter

	No.	Reversed
Criminal	22	15
Tax	20	7
Federal regulation of economic life	16	6
Fair Labor Standards Act	10	2
Bankruptcy	8	2
Trading with the Enemy Act	8	2
Seamen and longshoremen legislation	6	5
Private, diversity	6	4
Private, federal question[a]	5	3
Aliens	5	1
Patents and copyrights	5	2
Admiralty	5	2
Selective Service	3	2
Federal Tort Claims Act	3	1
State tax	2	2
Contempt of court	2	0
Court martial	1	1
Civil liberties	1	1
Intergovernmental immunities	1	0
Totals	129	58

[a] Includes antitrust and Federal Employers' Liability Act cases.

appeals involving tax law, Fair Labor Standards Act, Trading with the Enemy Act, bankruptcy law, admiralty law, and the Federal Tort Claims Act—in which the principal function of the Supreme Court was regarded to be the determination of congressional intent, were included in this category. The Second Circuit was affirmed in thirty-eight of these and reversed in the remaining sixteen, a support rate of 70.4 per cent. Actually, other appeals also required the interpretation or application of federal law, such as those involving the Federal Employers' Liability Act and Selective Service law; they were not considered, however, because in these cases the votes of the judges are not infrequently colored by doctrinal attitudes. In the seventy-five cases not regarded as requiring statutory interpretation, the Supreme Court affirmed in only 33 (44 per cent), just about the affirmance rate for all courts of appeals during this period. In summary, the success of the Second Circuit in intercircuit conflict and statutory interpretation cases lends credence to the view that the Supreme Court deferred to its judgments.

The breakdown of the Supreme Court decisions according to subject matter (Table 28) also sheds some light on the first explanation offered for the good record before the Supreme Court, namely, that the six judges exercised such great care in following prior Supreme Court rulings that they reduced the possibility of reversal on appeal. As we have said, the cases involving application of federal statutes also may require the analysis of past Supreme Court decisions; thus, the lower court's success in these cases gives support to this explanation, too. On the other hand, the Second Circuit was reversed in fifteen of twenty-two (68.2 per cent) criminal appeals. More than anywhere else, it was in this area that the Second Circuit—on "harmless error" and on other questions—resisted Supreme Court rulings. In these cases, with the exception of Jerome Frank, the judges did not bring to their decision-making the qualities of detachment and fidelity which generally characterized their work.

Of course, it must be emphasized that the data only substantiate the possible validity of the two explanations advanced for the high rate of affirmance in appeals from the Second Circuit. However, when we consider the data together with the enthusiastic evaluations of the 1941–51 court and its judges that have been offered by Supreme Court justices and others, these explanations become quite plausible.

So far we have been concerned with the over-all relationship between the Supreme Court and the Second Circuit. Little has been said of the interactions between the judges of the two courts, though interactions occurred in each of the 129 appeals from the Second Circuit in which the Supreme Court handed down a full opinion. Through the

Table 29. Outcome of Dissents by Second Circuit Judges in the
Supreme Court after Certiorari Was Granted

Dissenting Judge	No. of Dissents	Supreme Court	
		Affirmed	Reversed
L. Hand	57	3	3
Swan	42	4	6
A. Hand	11	1	2
Chase	30	2	2
Clark	88	9	4
Frank	76	3	8
Totals	304	22	25

tabulation of the votes of the members of both courts in these cases, we can discern patterns of agreement and support and arrive at some conclusions about the judges of the Second Circuit.

Before getting to this, it is well to consider what happened to the cases with dissent in the Second Circuit that were reviewed by the Supreme Court. As is shown in Table 29, a total of 47 such cases reached the final decisional stage in the Supreme Court.[10] This represents more than one-third of appeals from the Second Circuit accepted by the High Court and 15 per cent of the 311 dissents in the intermediate appelate court over the ten-year period. This contrasts with the over-all rate of 3.6 petitions for certiorari granted for every 100 terminations by the Second Circuit (Table 24). While it is almost certain that the rate of appeal to the Supreme Court was considerably higher in the cases with dissent than in those decided unanimously, since often the losing party in the intermediate court was encouraged by the dissent to continue the battle, it is improbable that certiorari was requested in more than half of the cases with intracircuit division. Actually, one of the key reasons why certiorari is not requested is applicable both to split and unanimous decisions. That is, in a large number of cases, particularly administrative appeals, referral for further proceedings is made by the court of appeals to the body where the litigation originated. If we assume that the losing party petitioned the Supreme Court for review in about 150 cases decided with dissent, then the acceptance rate by the Supreme Court comes to about 30 per cent. Of course, we do not have exact figures to work with here, but the

[10] All but two of the forty-seven cases were decided by the Supreme Court with full opinion. The two memorandum decisions were in cases in which Charles Clark was the dissenting judge. In one, an equally divided Supreme Court affirmed; in the second, the Second Circuit's ruling was vacated and remanded.

fact that so many of the appeals from the Second Circuit reviewed by the Supreme Court were where there was disagreement below suggests rather conclusively that such disagreement is often a decisive factor at the certiorari stage.

The breakdown in Table 29 of the forty-seven cases according to the members of the Second Circuit reveals that only six, or 10.5 per cent, of Learned Hand's dissents reached the decisional stage in the Supreme Court, a somewhat surprising figure in view of the customary evaluations of this famed judge's influence on the Supreme Court. The percentages for all the other judges are higher: Swan 23.8 per cent; Augustus Hand 27.3 per cent; Chase 13.3 per cent; Clark 14.8 per cent; and Frank 14.5 per cent. Apparently, a dissent by the Chief Judge was not a special cue to the nine justices to take a closer look at the lower-court ruling.

In terms of actual success in the Supreme Court, the best records were achieved by Judge Swan, who saw six of his forty-two dissents vindicated, and Judge Augustus Hand, who was upheld in two of his eleven dissents. Judge Frank also did well, while Judge Clark was perhaps the most disappointed member of the court. The Second Circuit's most frequent dissenter saw only four of his eighty-eight dissents win the approval of a Supreme Court majority.

Interestingly, the data in Table 29 show that where the Supreme Court agrees to hear an appeal, the likelihood for reversal is significantly higher if there was a dissenting opinion below. In 53.2 per cent (25 of 47) of the appeals with dissent in the Second Circuit,[11] the Supreme Court reversed. As we saw, the over-all reversal rate in Second Circuit cases was a low 45.0 per cent; the figure for cases in which the Second Circuit was unanimous was 40.5 per cent.

The following six tables (30–35) indicate the support given to each member of the Learned Hand court by the justices of the Supreme Court who served during the same period. The data are derived from the votes of the justices in the 129 cases with full opinion and the votes in the same cases in the court of appeals. An interaction consists of the votes of a Second Circuit judge and a Supreme Court member in a single case. A supportive interaction is any one in which the two judges voted for the same outcome: both were in the majority when the Supreme Court affirmed; both dissented when the Supreme Court affirmed; and the Supreme Court justice was with the majority in a case reversed by the Supreme Court in which the Second Circuit judge dissented. A nonsupportive interaction is any in which the two judges voted for different outcomes. No attempt has been made to dis-

---

[11] This includes the two memorandum decisions. If they are left out, the reversal rate in cases with dissent was 53.3 per cent.

Table 30. Supreme Court Interaction with Judge Learned Hand

	Interactions			Support	
	Total No.	Supportive	Non-supportive	Per Cent	Rank
Stone	36	19	17	52.8	8
Vinson	34	15	19	44.1	11
Roberts	30	14	16	46.7	9
Black	74	41	33	55.4	7
Reed	75	44	31	58.7	4
Frankfurter	75	47	28	62.7	2
Douglas	69	32	37	46.4	10
Murphy	58	34	24	58.6	5
Byrnes	7	4	3	57.1	*
Jackson	64	37	27	57.8	6
Rutledge	51	31	20	60.8	3
Burton	43	27	16	62.8	1
Clark	14	6	8	42.9	*
Minton	15	7	8	46.7	*

* Too few cases for purposes of ranking.

tinguish between degrees of support or disagreement. Only the votes were considered. Accordingly, concurring opinions or votes in both courts are recorded as votes with the majority and dissents in part are recorded as dissents.

Of the fourteen justices who served during the decade, only five— Hugo Black, Stanley Reed, Felix Frankfurter, William Douglas, and Robert Jackson—were members of the court throughout the ten years.

Table 31. Supreme Court Justices' Interactions with Judge Swan

	Interactions			Support	
	Total No.	Supportive	Non-supportive	Per Cent	Rank
Stone	30	19	11	63.3	1
Vinson	36	21	15	58.3	4
Roberts	31	15	16	48.4	10
Black	68	33	35	48.5	9
Reed	66	40	26	60.6	3
Frankfurter	67	41	26	61.2	2
Douglas	59	29	30	49.2	7
Murphy	50	23	27	46.0	11
Byrnes	7	3	4	42.9	*
Jackson	56	32	24	57.1	5
Rutledge	43	21	22	48.8	8
Burton	41	21	20	51.2	6
Clark	10	4	6	40.0	*
Minton	16	10	6	62.5	*

* Too few cases for purposes of ranking.

Table 32. Supreme Court Justices' Interactions with Judge Augustus Hand

	Interactions			Support	
	Total No.	Supportive	Non-supportive	Per Cent	Rank
Stone	35	17	18	48.6	7
Vinson	26	17	9	65.4	1
Roberts	27	12	15	44.4	11
Black	67	34	33	50.7	5
Reed	65	41	24	63.1	3
Frankfurter	66	31	35	47.0	9
Douglas	58	30	28	51.7	4
Murphy	53	24	29	45.3	10
Byrnes	7	4	3	57.1	*
Jackson	54	26	28	48.1	8
Rutledge	44	22	22	50.0	6
Burton	37	24	13	64.9	2
Clark	5	3	2	60.0	*
Minton	11	7	4	63.6	*

* Too few cases for purposes of ranking.

Table 33. Supreme Court Justices' Interactions with Judge Chase

	Interactions			Support	
	Total No.	Supportive	Non-supportive	Per Cent	Rank
Stone	31	15	16	48.4	7
Vinson	21	15	6	71.4	1
Roberts	24	11	13	45.8	8
Black	55	27	28	49.1	5.5
Reed	53	30	23	56.6	3
Frankfurter	55	27	28	49.1	5.5
Douglas	50	22	28	44.0	9
Murphy	43	16	27	37.2	11
Byrnes	6	4	2	66.7	*
Jackson	43	24	19	55.8	4
Rutledge	34	13	21	38.2	10
Burton	31	20	11	64.5	2
Clark	8	5	3	62.5	*
Minton	11	8	3	72.7	*

* Too few cases for purposes of ranking.

But Justice Jackson, as a result of his service at the Nuremberg Trial of the major Nazi leaders, was away from the Supreme Court during the middle years of this period. Justice James Byrnes served only for one year and Justices Tom Clark and Sherman Minton were appointed late in 1949. These three participated in too few of the 129 cases to permit any meaningful analysis of their relationships with the Second Circuit judges.

Table 34. Supreme Court Justices' Interactions with Judge Clark

	Interactions			Support	
	Total No.	Supportive	Non-supportive	Per Cent	Rank
Stone	21	10	11	47.6	7
Vinson	28	14	14	50.0	5.5
Roberts	18	6	12	33.3	11
Black	52	29	23	55.8	3
Reed	53	28	25	52.8	4
Frankfurter	53	19	34	35.8	9
Douglas	47	27	20	57.4	2
Murphy	39	18	21	46.2	8
Byrnes	6	4	2	66.7	*
Jackson	46	16	30	34.8	10
Rutledge	30	19	11	63.3	1
Burton	34	17	17	50.0	5.5
Clark	9	5	4	55.5	*
Minton	13	6	7	46.2	*

* Too few cases for purposes of ranking.

Table 35. Supreme Court Justices' Intearctions with Judge Frank

	Interactions			Support	
	Total No.	Supportive	Non-supportive	No.	Rank
Stone	27	15	12	55.5	8.5
Vinson	27	15	12	55.5	8.5
Roberts	22	8	14	36.4	11
Black	57	42	15	73.7	2
Reed	59	40	19	67.8	4
Frankfurter	59	34	25	57.6	7
Douglas	49	32	17	65.3	6
Murphy	44	31	13	70.5	3
Byrnes	5	4	1	80.0	*
Jackson	52	28	24	53.8	10
Rutledge	35	28	7	75.0	1
Burton	36	24	12	66.7	5
Clark	10	5	5	50.0	*
Minton	14	10	4	71.4	*

* Too few cases for purposes of ranking.

Learned Hand received generally good support from most of the justices. His highest rates of agreement were with Justices Harold Burton and Frankfurter. Actually, if we take Frankfurter at his word, the support percentage of 62.7 may be low. At a ceremony honoring Hand when he stepped down as chief judge in 1951, Frankfurter said: "Speaking for myself, the only gain possibly to be had from his retirement from the Court of Appeals is that hereafter I shall feel freer to act on my belief that a decision of the Circuit Court of the Second Circuit might give occasion for review by the Supreme Court, and I might even perchance at times feel that an opinion which he wrote might be wrong."[12] Apart from Frankfurter's readiness to disagree with Learned Hand in more than one-third of their interactions, it is of some note that Hand's long friendship with Chief Justice Stone does not seem to have had any effect on their voting relationship.

While there are significant differences with respect to individual justices, in terms of range and degree of support, the interaction patterns for Judges Swan and Augustus Hand resemble that of Learned Hand.

Judge Chase, as we shall see (Table 38), was only a little less successful in the Supreme Court than the other three Coolidge appointees. But his support from individual members varied a great deal, ranging from agreement in almost three out of every four interactions with Chief Justice Vinson to disagreement in almost two-thirds of the interactions with Justice Rutledge. Chase, the most conservative member of the Learned Hand court, fared most poorly with the three most notable Supreme Court liberals of the 1940's—Justices Douglas, Murphy, and Rutledge.

Of the six judges, Judge Clark was the least successful before the Supreme Court. Excluding Justices Byrnes and Clark, he received support in a majority of his interactions with only four members of the High Court. Justice Rutledge alone agreed with him in more than 60 per cent of interactions and he fared very poorly with Justices Frankfurter and Jackson, two members of the court whom he knew well.

Even a cursory glance at the figures in Table 35 would show how well Judge Frank was received in the Supreme Court. Only Justice Owen Roberts supported him in fewer than half of the interactions, while three members went along with Frank in more than 70 per cent of the cases in which they reviewed him. Without a doubt his boldness in challenging both Second Circuit and Supreme Court precedent and long-standing judicial dogma did not put him in any Supreme Court doghouse. He did not always win before the Supreme Court, but he came just about as close to complete success in this regard as any lower-court judge can be expected to come. He may well have been the most successful and influential inferior-court judge of his time. He may not have had much of a direct impact through his extrajudicial writings on courthouse justice or on the legal profession, yet it cannot be gainsaid that he was taken seriously in Washington.

[12] "A Great Judge Retires: American Law Institute Honors Learned Hand," *American Bar Association Journal,* 37 (1951), 503.

Table 36. Supreme Court Justices' Percentage of Agreement
with Second Circuit Judges

	L. Hand	Swan	A. Hand	Chase	Clark	Frank
Stone	52.8	63.3	48.6	48.4	47.6	55.5
Vinson	44.1	58.3	65.4	71.4	50.0	55.5
Roberts	46.7	48.4	44.4	45.8	33.3	36.4
Black	55.4	48.5	50.7	49.1	55.8	73.7
Reed	58.7	60.6	63.1	56.6	52.8	67.8
Frankfurter	62.7	61.2	47.0	49.1	35.8	57.6
Douglas	46.4	49.2	51.7	44.0	57.4	65.3
Murphy	58.6	46.0	45.3	37.2	46.2	70.5
Byrnes	57.1	42.9	57.1	66.7	66.7	80.0
Jackson	57.8	57.1	48.1	55.8	34.8	53.8
Rutledge	60.8	48.8	50.0	38.2	63.3	75.0
Burton	62.8	51.2	64.9	64.5	50.0	66.7
Clark	42.9	40.0	60.0	62.5	55.5	50.0
Minton	46.7	62.5	63.6	72.7	46.2	71.4

The percentages of support given to each of the Second Circuit judges by the members of the Supreme Court are collected from the six tables and presented in Table 36. The data in this table reveal some of the patterns of agreement within the Supreme Court that have inspired wide comment.[13] The strong cohesion of Justices Murphy and Rutledge is evident, except in their interactions with Judge Clark, where there is great disparity in their support scores. Perhaps this deviation from the expected pattern was more the product of erratic voting behavior on Clark's part than of any substantial differences between the two justices. The data also corroborate the cohesion of two other pairs of justices: Black with Douglas, and Frankfurter with Jackson.

As was noted in the previous chapter, the case load of the Second Circuit includes a large number of appeals that do not lend themselves to analysis along liberal-conservative lines. The subject matter breakdown in the intermediate court is reflected generally in the cases from it decided by full opinion by the Supreme Court. More than one-sixth of the 129 appeals from the Second Circuit involved tax law. Accordingly, there are definite limits to any evaluation of the interactions between judges on both courts to determine whether there was cohesion between the liberals or conservatives on the two bodies.

However, examination of the interrelationships between the two levels of federal judges reveals that by and large the liberal justices supported the liberals on the Second Circuit at a considerably higher

[13] See, particularly, the two studies by C. Herman Pritchett, *The Roosevelt Court: A Study in Judicial Politics and Values, 1937–1947* (New York: Macmillan Co., 1948), and *Civil Liberties and the Vinson Court* (Chicago: University of Chicago Press, 1954).

rate than they did the conservatives on the lower court. At the same time, the conservative justices were in greater agreement with the conservative judges than with the liberal ones.

These patterns become clearer when we place the Supreme Court justices who served during these years into three groups, as follows:

Liberal	Moderate	Conservative
Black	Stone	Vinson
Douglas	Reed	Roberts
Murphy	Frankfurter	Byrnes
Rutledge	Jackson	Burton
		Clark
		Minton

Of course, there were important disagreements among the justices within each of these groups that were liberal-conservative in nature, and some observers of Supreme Court affairs would disagree with the placement of particular justices. Still, the above division conforms to the generally accepted view of the Supreme Court in 1942–51.

Table 37 gives the percentage of support received by each Second Circuit judge from each of the three groups.

Table 37. Percentages of Support of Second Circuit Judges by Supreme Court Justices, According to Group

	Liberal	Moderate	Conservative
L. Hand	54.8	58.8	51.0
Swan	48.2	60.3	52.8
A. Hand	49.5	52.3	59.3
Chase	42.8	52.7	62.4
Clark	55.4	42.2	48.1
Frank	71.9	59.4	57.9

Judge Learned Hand, a moderate with liberal tendencies, received his greatest support from the four justices constituting the moderate group. Next in order were the liberals, with the lowest rate of support coming from the conservative justices. The general pattern is as expected. Judge Swan's record is more puzzling. Since he was regarded as a conservative, we should expect that he received the greatest support from the conservatives and least support from the liberals. In his interactions with the Supreme Court he was most in agreement with the moderate group. It might be possible to explain the lower rate of support from the conservatives by reasoning that the Supreme Court justices were more conservative than Swan. This, in turn, would account for the low rate of support given by Justice Roberts to all six Second Circuit judges. The difficulty with this interpretation is that it does not hold true for the interaction patterns of the other two conservatives, Judges Augustus Hand and Chase. Judge Hand received support from the three groups as follows: conservatives, 59.3 per cent; moderates, 52.3 per cent; and liberals, 49.5 per cent. The interactions of Judge Chase, more than those of any of his colleagues, substantiate the existence of a relationship between the two courts along liberal-conservative lines. His support rates were: conservatives, 62.4 per cent; moderates, 52.7 per cent; and liberals, 42.8 per cent.

It is virtually impossible to detect any liberal-conservative pattern in Judge Clark's interactions. He was the only member of the Learned Hand court who did the poorest with the Supreme Court moderates. But what we know of his views and voting record enables us to explain his relationships with members of the Supreme Court. It is possible that Clark's support record was due to his clearcut liberalism in certain areas (for instance, appeals involving seamen or aliens) and his general conservatism in others (for instance, criminal law). In these areas, depending on his vote, he received a fair measure of support from either the liberal or conservative group, but relatively little support from the moderates. As Table 38 indicates, when interactions with all justices are calculated, Judge Clark ranked lowest in support from the Supreme Court. The data plainly suggest that the justices agreed less with his views than with those of any of the other Second Circuit judges.

Table 38. Second Circuit Judges' Interactions with the
Supreme Court, All Justices

	Interactions			Support	
	Total No.	Supportive	Non-supportive	Per Cent	Rank
L. Hand	645	358	287	55.5	2
Swan	575	312	263	54.3	3
A. Hand	555	292	263	52.6	4
Chase	465	237	228	51.0	5
Clark	449	218	231	48.6	6
Frank	496	316	180	63.7	1

Each of the four members appointed by President Coolidge received just about the same degree of support. Clearly the most successful member of the Learned Hand court was Jerome Frank. He received substantial support from all groups of justices, but most outstandingly from the liberals, who, as a group, voted with him in almost three out of four interactions. There is little doubt that Frank was the Second Circuit judge most often vindicated in the Supreme Court. During the 1940's—and of course before and after—Learned Hand was more famous. But he was not more influential than the junior member of the court over which he presided.

11

The Stature of a Court

THE VIRTUES OF THE SECOND CIRCUIT UNDER LEARNED HAND HAVE BEEN
sung by nearly everyone who has written about the court. Professor
Kurland's judgment that "we are not likely to see its equal for many a
year"[1] is widely shared. So universal is the admiration for the Learned
Hand court that it seems unnecessary to conclude this work with
another evaluation of its importance and stature. Yet, despite the
general agreement that between 1941 and 1951 the Second Circuit was
a great court—and there are some who would include many more years
in this evaluation[2]—this estimate ought not to be accepted uncritically.
It is fitting to conclude this study with the question: how justified is
the reputation of the 1941–51 Second Circuit?

[1] Philip B. Kurland, "Jerome N. Frank: Some Reflections and Recollections of a Law Clerk," *University of Chicago Law Review,* 24 (Summer, 1957),
661.

[2] "The Second Circuit Court of Appeals probably already stood first
among the eleven such courts when he [Learned Hand] was appointed to it,
and he has not been alone in adding to its luster" (Whitney North Seymour,
in *Proceedings of a Special Session of the United Court of Appeals for
the Second Circuit to Commemorate Fifty Years of Federal Judicial Service,
by the Honorable Learned Hand,* April 10, 1959. 264 F.2d. p. 34).

But how are we to measure greatness in a court or even in a judge, particularly one who occupies an inferior position in the judicial hierarchy? What standards of measurement are to be used? A noted foreign observer was right to add to his expression of high regard for the Second Circuit the footnote that "assertions of the legal preeminence of this sort are hard to document and even harder to prove."[3] And in his tribute to Augustus Hand, Judge Swan commented that "it is not always easy to determine what causes a judge to stand out above his fellow judges and be acclaimed as a 'great' judge."[4] Greatness in the judiciary is often nothing more than a reputation of greatness; judges, or courts, are "great" because they have been proclaimed to be so. In the absence of recognizable objective standards, estimates of judges tend to be repetitions of earlier subjective analyses.[5] Accordingly, a judge is great simply because he is great. Worse, yet, "among lawyers and certainly among laymen, judicial stature has tended to be equated with quotability."[6]

Professor Willard Hurst, after bemoaning the lack of "a norm by which to weigh the quality of the judge's work,"[7] suggests that the components of judicial eminence are intellectual integrity, learning, craftsmanship, and wisdom. But these criteria not only do not have any set meaning, they also require the use of other norms. Hurst says of wisdom:

> On what bases shall we judge wisdom? . . . I will make only two suggestions. The work of judges must be subjected to two tests that apply sharply to all men who have the responsibility of power. First, they will be measured by their knowledge of what they are doing, by their sense for the secondary and more remote conse-

[3] Edward McWhinney, "A Legal Realist and a Humanist—Cross Currents in the Legal Philosophy of Judge Jerome Frank," *Indiana Law Journal*, 33 (1957), 115, n. 8.

[4] Thomas W. Swan, "Augustus Noble Hand," *Memorial Book, 1955*, Association of the Bar of the City of New York, p. 36.

[5] William Hurst has summed up the problem: "Now, in what consists greatness in the doing of his [the appellate judge's] job? What are the most important ways in which the appellate judge may affect his times? Here is our central question, but despite its importance it is almost unexplored. What makes a 'great' judge? You will search the books and learned journals and come up only with scraps of analysis of this question, the answer to which should provide the whole framework for judicial biography. . . . We have failed to develop a comprehensive, explicit statement of a norm by which to weigh the quality of the judge's work. By what criteria do we single out Shaw, and the rest?" ("Who Is the 'Great' Appellate Judge?," *Indiana Law Journal*, 24 [1949], 397).

[6] Charles A. Horsky, "Augustus Noble Hand," *Harvard Law Review*, 68 (1955), 1118.

[7] Hurst, "Who Is the 'Great' Appellate Judge?," p. 397.

quences of their decisions. For the judge, this means not only awareness of the choices he makes, but also of their significance in the life of his community. Mr. Justice Holmes cautioned that judges need a touch of Mephistopheles. Second, the wisdom of the great judge consists in a grasp both of the potentialities and the limitations of the kind of power that he wields.[8]

Perhaps Hurst's formula provides a reliable yardstick of judicial stature; without the criteria he put forth, judicial eminence cannot be achieved; with them there is the potential for greatness. Still, the qualities he stresses may not be enough. A tribunal is the product of the attitudes and actions of the men who sit on it. But it is a lot more. Somehow, wisdom and learning and the rest do not ensure that a court will merit the accolade "great." The Supreme Court of the early 1940's comes to mind. Chief Justice Stone and at least also Justices Frankfurter, Douglas, Black, Jackson, and Rutledge were men of considerable stature, yet there was much lacking and no one considers it an outstanding court.

This search for standards is complicated further by the seeming paradox whereby two judges of sharply divergent temperaments and conceptions of the judicial function are placed in the first ranks. Thus historians are likely to regard both Justice Black and Justice Frankfurter as great judges even though they held different views on many important questions decided by the Supreme Court during the past generation. Or, to return to the Second Circuit, both Learned Hand and Jerome Frank have been acclaimed as belonging among our very best jurists,[9] though the attributes found so commendable in Judge Hand—his disinterestedness and self-restraint—were not possessed by Judge Frank. Still, the evaluations of both judges may be valid.

In a speech about the Second Circuit, Judge Medina pointed out another flaw in the search for judicial eminence. To him, "the idea of going down into history as a great judge—oh, what a myth! How impossible! Think of all the great judges and great lawyers when I was a boy and the young people never heard of. They are gone with the wind and disappeared with the mist."[10] The lesson is clear: How-

---

[8] *Ibid.*, p. 399.

[9] Judge Clark called Frank "a great judge" (Charles E. Clark, "Jerome N. Frank," Memorial Address at a Special Meeting of the New York County Lawyers Association and the Association of the Bar of the City of New York, May 23, 1957. On p. 1 of the *Proceedings*.) Justice Black said of Frank, "I rate him as one of the great judges" (Edmond Cahn, "Fact-Skepticism and Fundamental Law," *New York University Law Review*, 33 [1958], 10).

[10] Harold R. Medina, "The Decisional Process in the United States Court of Appeals, Second Circuit—How the Wheels Go Around Inside—with Commentary." Address at the New York County Lawyers' Association, Forum Evening, April 26, 1962 (typed), p. 20.

ever great our enthusiasm for a contemporary court or judge, we should not forget that judicial styles are subject to change.[11] History often does not deal kindly with—and at times even ignores—those to whom previous generations have ascribed greatness.

In view of these caveats, the difficulties of evaluating the Learned Hand court are thus evident. Of course, if some evaluation is needed, the Second Circuit's reputation for greatness can be used to reach a conclusion about the court, in much the same way that certain social scientists rely on a reputational yardstick to measure power.

Nevertheless, I think that there is a good deal of evidence to support the assertion that a number of the 1941–51 judges were exceptionally able and that, as a whole, the court was a remarkable institution. It is less certain, however, whether during this or any other period the Second Circuit could justifiably be called "great." The question of a court's eminence might best be approached by distinguishing between the "internal" and "external" conditions which permit a tribunal to achieve greatness and by determining whether these conditions were present at the time that a court's stature is being measured.

"Internal" conditions refer to those organizational, administrative, and personal factors that would permit a court to operate at a high level of creativity and efficiency. "External" conditions refer to those factors that determine the impact of a court on the law, on other courts, and on other social and political institutions. Clearly, if they were not present, the court can not have achieved greatness.

With respect to the "internal" conditions, various circumstances permitted the Second Circuit to function more effectively than the other courts of appeals. The Association of the Bar of the City of New York, perhaps the most highly regarded bar association in the country, and other lawyer groups in the area have exerted a good influence on appointments to the federal courts in the city. With all of the qualms about the decline in the quality of advocacy, it is still certain that the lawyers who practice before the Second Circuit are generally more talented than those found elsewhere, with the possible exception of the District of Columbia. The Second Circuit is also aided by the high quality of work done by the Southern District, which is its major supplier of appeals. In addition, a fairly large number of important cases regularly come to the Second Circuit.

These inputs were converted by the Learned Hand court into first-rate judicial performances. Although the court was faced with

---

[11] An English appraisal of Learned Hand says of the views he expressed in his Holmes Lectures at Harvard, "And even while he lectured in 1958 Judge Hand knew that the tide of opinion was against him" (D. W. M. Waters, "Judge Learned Hand," *The Solicitor Quarterly*, 1 [1962], 37).

the heaviest case load of any of the intermediate federal courts, it regularly disposed of its business more quickly than did any of the other courts, and the opinions gave evidence of the highest standard of judicial craftsmanship. The memorandum system, which might have worked for delay, guaranteed appropriate consideration of all aspects of an appeal and care in preparation of opinions. Even the virtually uninterrupted strife between Judges Clark and Frank did not have an adverse effect on the court's efficient functioning; indeed, at least with respect to the combatants, it contributed to the greater exertion of intellectual and physical energy, with the result that the Second Circuit was a place of some intellectual excitement.

Furthermore, in the 1940's the Second Circuit was called on to interpret major legislation such as the revised Internal Revenue Code, the Fair Labor Standards Act, the National Labor Relations Act, and the Securities and Exchanges Act.[12] The Supreme Court heard a fairly large number of appeals from the Second Circuit and affirmed the decision below in an unusually high percentage of cases.

The judges of the Learned Hand court were men of learning, intellectual integrity, craftsmanship, and wisdom. Their opinions gave evidence of their awareness of the consequences of their actions and all of them were conscious of the power they wielded. In them was "placed the greatest confidence as judges," for they inspired in the legal community the "conviction that the decision of every question, the weighing of every argument, the resolution of every discretionary issue" was made "selflessly, fearlessly, wisely" insofar as wisdom was given to them.[13]

[12] Cf. with the following by Judge Wyzanski: "These ideas [of economic and social experimentation] expressed in enactments by the body politic have come to him [Learned Hand] for interpretation almost always before the Supreme Court has acted, and often before any so-called 'constitutional court' has acted. They have but partly emerged from a fiery furnace of public controversy to test both his character and his intellectual capacity" (Charles E. Wyzanski, Jr., "Judge Learned Hand's Contribution to Public Law," *Harvard Law Review*, 60 [1947], 359).

[13] Horsky, "Augustus Noble Hand," p. 1119. Horsky presented the following yardstick of judicial greatness:

"In the ultimate sense, the greatest of judges are those in whom is placed the greatest confidence as judges. And this confidence goes to the judge who inspires in his brethren on the bench, at the bar, and among the public whom he serves the conviction that the decision of every question, the weighing of every argument, the resolution of every discretionary issue, will be made selflessly, fearlessly, wisely insofar as wisdom is given to him, and to the best of his understanding of the law which binds him as well as the litigants.

"This conviction must be inspired by the whole man, but it is possible to name some of the predominant elements. One of them is suggested by the

Accordingly, there is support for the conclusion that between 1941 and 1951 the Second Circuit was an excellent court and did its work as well, if not better, than any of the other circuit courts. In terms of internal criteria of measurement there is, in short, justification for rating the court's performance as great.

Conceivably, many lawyers will be satisfied that these essentially administrative accomplishments and personal qualities are sufficient to establish and maintain the reputation of the Learned Hand court. They may be right, but some political scientists who stress power and authority will not accept the self-contained, internal path to greatness. To them, the focus must be on the influence that it exerted on other courts.[14]

It is true, of course, that in more than 95 per cent of the appeals taken to them the intermediate appellate courts are the courts of final decision. In private law disputes the figure is above 99 per cent. From the perspective of most litigants in the federal district courts and agencies, the courts of appeals are more important than the nation's highest court. Moreover, since they are not strictly bound by Supreme Court precedents, in a large number of cases the courts of appeals have considerable decisional leeway. Also, as N.L.R.B. and school desegregation cases illustrate, the courts of appeals are often able to evade or slow down the effects of High Court rulings.

However, their partial freedom in making decisions and the finality of most of their rulings are not manifestations of the ability to influence in a significant way the course of law and politics. This freedom does not undermine the power and authority of the Supreme Court, for when it is petitioned for review, that tribunal can review and reverse the lower federal courts. The inferior courts operate within definite limits, and while most often what they decide is not disturbed, they are subject to Supreme Court direction and rebuke. The courts of appeals plainly are incapable of effecting major changes in the political or social fabric of the nation as the Supreme Court did through the reapportionment and school desegregation rulings. In fact, the bolder

---

word 'selflessly.' The greatest enemy of disinterestedness is the ego. Its presence or absence is detected at once. Its absence carries the assurance that the judge has his whole mind on the task of judging and is not affected by the image of himself as judge. Along with selflessness goes discipline, the discipline of self to the rule of the law which he must apply. And with both of these goes courage, the fortitude to decide as disciplined mind, disinterested conscience, and that elevated common sense which we call wisdom show the way."

[14] What Professor Hurst noted about the great judge applies to the great court: "The 'great' judge's impact is felt on the law, on politics, and on the history of ideas" ("Who Is the 'Great' Appellate Judge?,") p. 400.

the decision of a lower court, the greater the likelihood of Supreme Court intervention to settle the matter.

The impotence of the courts of appeals is, in some respects, more evident in the Second Circuit than in a number of the other circuits. Since the Second Circuit is the "top commercial court" in the United States by virtue of the scope and volume of the litigation affecting important economic interests which come before it, this situation is paradoxical. Yet, economic questions do not constitute an area in which the judicial policy-making function has been prominent during the past generation. In many commercial law areas, courts now follow the landmark decisions of the nineteenth and early twentieth centuries. Judge Wyzanski pointed out in 1947 that "what is significant is that during Judge [Learned] Hand's period of service the balance in American jurisprudence has shifted from a predominantly common-law to a predominantly statutory basis."[15] Common-law judges and courts have had opportunities to influence the law that are not available nowadays when the primary judicial function involves statutory interpretation.

A second shift that has undermined the influence of the lower federal courts, particularly the Second Circuit, occurred around 1937 when the Supreme Court's previous concern with property was pushed into the background by its increasing preoccupation with individual rights. Since the late 1930's there has been a Supreme Court-directed expansion of the rights and privileges afforded by the Bill of Rights and the Due Process and Equal Protection clauses of the Fourteenth Amendment. Most of the noteworthy cases involving individual rights have come from the state courts; the percentage is very high when we consider only first amendment and criminal law appeals. Nor has the Second Circuit been occupied with these issues to the same extent as several of the other courts of appeals, notably the Court of Appeals for the District of Columbia.[16] As Judge Wyzanski wrote, the Second Circuit "has not been faced with the 'civil liberties' issues raised so frequently in the last thirty volumes of Supreme Court reports."[17]

In a handful of cases, the Learned Hand court ruled on important constitutional law questions. But the significance of the issues raised in these appeals encouraged High Court review, thereby vitiating the intermediate court's holdings, giving them only interim impact until the Supreme Court reviewed the same questions. Despite Chief Justice Vinson's borrowing of Learned Hand's reformulation of the "clear and

[15] Wyzanski, "Hand's Contribution to the Public Law," p. 358.

[16] See Eleanor Bontecou (ed.), *Freedom in the Balance: Opinions of Judge Henry W. Edgerton Relating to Civil Liberties* (Ithaca, N. Y.: Cornell University Press, 1960), esp. pp. 5–6.

[17] Wyzanski, "Hand's Contribution to the Public Law," p. 354.

present danger" test in the *Dennis* case, it is apparent that the Supreme Court would in any case have reached the same result and almost certainly by the same vote.

The Second Circuit's influence on law during the Learned Hand period was severely restricted by its general unwillingness to be bold about personal liberties. The court may not have been behind the times, but it definitely was not ahead of them and, as such, it was in no position to affect the development of law. Orrin Judd noted in 1947 that, in the criminal law area, "under the influence of recent rulings of the Supreme Court, the Court presided over by Judge Hand is now, perhaps, giving the defendant a little more benefit of the doubt as to what effect erroneous rulings may have had on the jury."[18]

In his Holmes Lectures at Harvard in 1958, Learned Hand seemed uneasy over the school desegregation decisions and unhappy over the Warren court's civil liberties rulings. Years before, his memorial to Chief Justice Stone contained one of the sharpest attacks ever made on the libertarian-activist position. During a period when the Supreme Court was not especially dedicated to the libertarian creed, Judge Wyzanski wrote that "we should expect that he [Learned Hand] would be slower than most of the present Justices of the Supreme Court to invalidate a statute on the ground it violated civil liberties."[19]

Far more significant than these limitations on the Second Circuit's influence in the civil rights and civil liberties area, is the absence of reliable evidence of influence on the courts outside the circuit. There is a belief that because of the fame of Learned Hand and his court, courts of appeals and district courts throughout the country looked to the courthouse at Foley Square for legal guidance. Impressive as are the reputations of Learned Hand and his colleagues, the available evidence suggests that this belief is a legacy of the myth of Learned Hand. Courts of appeals usually rely on the decisions of their fellow courts to back up rulings which they have reached on their own.

For these reasons, even under Learned Hand, the Second Circuit was not capable of attaining greatness in the sense of the capacity to influence other courts and judges. Perhaps this should be the conclusion of this study. But a final word of caution should be noted. The "external" criterion may not be relevant to the measurement of a court such as the Second Circuit. By defining greatness in terms which are alien to the nature and authority of the tribunal, it robs the quest for judgment of any meaning. Greatness may consist of doing greatly what a court is capable of doing. In this sense, the Learned Hand court was truly outstanding.

[18] Orrin C. Judd, "Judge Learned Hand and the Criminal Law," *Harvard Law Review*, 60 (1947), 410.

[19] Wyzanski, "Hand's Contribution to the Public Law," p. 355.

Bibliography

THE FEDERAL JUDICIARY

Books and Monographs

Clark, Charles E. "Experience Under the Federal Rules of Civil Procedure: Reporter's Summary of Suggestions, Criticisms and Published Discussions." Mimeographed. United States Supreme Court Committee on the Rules of Civil Procedure, 1953.

Frankfurter, Felix, and Landis, James M. *The Business of the Supreme Court.* New York: Macmillan Company, 1927.

Hart, Henry M., Jr., and Wechsler, Herbert. *The Federal Courts and the Federal System.* Brooklyn: Foundation Press, 1953.

Karlen, Delmar. *Appellate Courts in the United States and England.* New York: New York University Press, 1963.

Peltason, Jack W. *Federal Courts in the Political Process.* New York: Random House, 1955.

————. *Fifty-Eight Lonely Men.* New York: Harcourt, Brace and World, 1961.

Wiener, Frederick Bernays. *Effective Appellate Advocacy.* New York: Prentice-Hall, 1950.

————. *Briefing and Arguing Federal Appeals.* Washington: The Bureau of National Affairs, 1961.

Articles

Chandler, Henry F. "Some Major Advances in the Federal Judicial System, 1922–1947," 31 *Federal Rules Decision,* 307.

Clark, Charles E. "The Influence of Federal Procedural Reform," *Law and Contemporary Problems,* 13 (1948), 144.

————, and Trubek, David M. "The Creative Role of the Judge: Restraint and Freedom in the Common Law Tradition," *Yale Law Journal*, 71 (1961), 255.

Dobie, Armistead. "A Judge Judges Judges," *Washington Law Quarterly*, 3 (1951), 471.

Frank, John P. "Historical Bases of the Federal Judicial System," *Law and Contemporary Problems*, 13 (1948), 3.

Frankfurter, Felix. "Distribution of Judicial Power Between United States and State Courts," *Cornell Law Quarterly*, 13 (1928), 499.

Friendly, Henry J. "Reactions of a Lawyer Newly-Become Judge," *Yale Law Journal*, 71 (1961), 218.

Hart, Jr., Henry M. "The Time Chart of the Justices," *Harvard Law Review*, 73 (1959), 84.

Llewellyn, Karl N. "How Appellate Courts Decide Cases," *Pennsylvania Bar Association Quarterly*, 16 (1945), 220.

Lumbard, J. Edward. "The Responsibility of the Bar for the Performance of the Courts," *New York State Bar Journal*, 34 (1962), **169**.

Murphy, Walter F. "Lower Court Checks on Supreme Court Power," *American Political Science Review*, 53 (1959), 1017.

Wyzanski, Jr., Charles E. "A Trial Judge's Freedom and Responsibility," *Atlantic Monthly*, 190 (July 1952), 55.

THE UNITED STATES COURTS OF APPEALS

Monographs

"Appellate Courts—Internal Operating Procedures; Preliminary Report." Mimeographed. New York: Institute of Judicial Administration, 1957.

"Appellate Courts—Internal Operating Procedures; Summary and Supplement." Mimeographed. New York: Institute of Judicial Administration, 1959.

Dorsen, Norman. "Law Clerks in the Appellate Courts in the United States." Mimeographed. New York: Institute of Judicial Administration, 1962.

Articles

Clark, Charles E. "The Role of the United States Courts of Appeals in Law Administration," *Conference on Judicial Administration*, Conference Series No. 16, The Law School, University of Chicago. Chicago: The University of Chicago Press, 1957, p. 87.

Evans, Evan A. "Fifty Years of the United States Circuit Courts of Appeals," *Missouri Law Review*, 9 (1941), 189.

————. "The Course of an Appeal to the United States Circuit Courts of Appeals," *Missouri Law Review*, 10 (1945), 29.

Goldman, Sheldon. "Voting Behavior on the United States Courts of Appeals, 1961–1964," *American Political Science Review*, 60 (1966), 374.

————. "Judicial Appointments To the United States Courts of Appeals," *Wisconsin Law Review* (Winter 1967), 186.

Green, Milton D. "The Next Step: Uniform Rules for the Courts of Appeals," *Vanderbilt Law Review*, 14 (1961), 947.

Loeb, Louis S. "Judicial Blocs and Judicial Values in Civil Liberties Cases Decided by the Supreme Court and the United States Court of Appeals for the District of Columbia Circuit," *American University Law Review,* 14 (1965), 146.

Lumbard, J. Edward. "The Place of the Federal Judicial Councils in the Administration of the Courts," *American Bar Association Journal,* 47 (1961), 169.

Magruder, Calvert. "The Trials and Tribulations of an Intermediate Appellate Court," *Cornell Law Quarterly,* 44 (1958), 1.

Manton, Martin T. "Organization and Work of the United States Circuit Court of Appeals," *American Bar Association Journal,* 12 (1926), 41.

Maris, Albert P. "Hearing and Rehearsing Cases In Banc; The Procedure of the United States Court of Appeals for the Third Circuit," 14 *Federal Rules Decisions,* 91.

Note. "En Banc Procedure in the Federal Courts of Appeals," *University of Pensylvania Law Review,* 111 (1962), 220.

Parker, John J. "Improving Appellate Methods," *New York University Law Review,* 25 (1950), 1.

Prettyman, E. Barrett. "The Duties of a Circuit Chief Judge," *American Bar Association Journal,* 46 (1960), 633.

Richardson, Richard J., and Vines, Kenneth N. "Review, Dissent, and the Appellate Process: A Political Interpretation," *Journal of Politics,* 29 (1967), 597.

Rosenzweig, Simon. "The Opinions of Judge Edgerton—A Study in the Judicial Process," *Cornell Law Quarterly,* 37 (1952), 149.

Short, Charles F., Jr. "Traveling in Circuit; A Commentary on the Rules of Practice of the United States Court of Appeals," 28 *United States Code Annotated, Volume on Rules* (1956).

Stern, Robert L. "Changes in the Federal Appellate Rules," 41 *Federal Rules Decisions,* 277.

Sunderland, Edson R. "Improvement of Appellate Procedure," *Iowa Law Review,* 26 (1940), 3.

Vines, Kenneth N. "The Role of the Circuit Courts of Appeal in the Federal Judicial Process: A Case Study," *Midwest Journal of Political Science,* 7 (1963), 305.

Wright, Charles Alan. "The Interlocutory Appeals Act of 1958," 23 *Federal Rules Decisions,* 202.

THE UNITED STATES COURT OF APPEALS FOR THE SECOND CIRCUIT

Books and Monographs

Friendly, Henry J. "How a Judge of the United States Court of Appeals Works." Mimeographed. New York: Institute of Judicial Administration, 1962.

Hough, Charles M. *The United States District Court for the Southern District of New York.* New York: Maritime Law Association, 1934.

Lumbard, J. Edward. "Appellate Advocacy." Mimeographed. New York: Institute of Judicial Administration, 1962.

Articles

Frank, John P. "The Top U.S. Commercial Court," *Fortune* (January 1951), p. 92.

Karlen, Delmar. "The United States Court of Appeals for the Second Circuit," *Record of the Association of the Bar of the City of New York,* 17 (1962), 505.

Medina, Harold R. "Some Reflections on the Judicial Function at the Appellate Level," *Washington University Law Quarterly,* 2 (1961), 148.

————. "The Decisional Process," *Bar Bulletin, New York County Lawyers' Association,* 20 (1962), 94.

————. "The Decisional Process in the United States Court of Appeals, Second Circuit—How the Wheels Go Around Inside—with Commentary," An Address at the New York County Lawyers' Association Forum Evening, April 26, 1962. Typed.

Note. "The Second Circuit: Federal Judicial Administration in Microcosm," *Columbia Law Review,* 13 (1963), 874.

LEARNED HAND

Books and Monographs

Breuer, Ernest H. "Learned Hand Bibliography." Mimeographed. New York State Library, Albany, N. Y., 1964.

Dilliard, Irving (ed.). *The Spirit of Liberty; Papers and Addresses of Learned Hand.* New York: Vintage Books, 1959.

Hand, Learned. *The Bill of Rights.* Cambridge: Harvard University Press, 1958.

Proceedings of a Special Session of the United States Court of Appeals for the Second Circuit to Commemorate Fifty Years of Federal Judicial Service, by the Honorable Learned Hand, April 10, 1959. 264 F.2d.

Shanks, Hershel (ed.). *The Art and Craft of Judging; The Decisions of Judge Learned Hand.* New York: Macmillan Co., 1968.

Articles

"A Great Judge Retires: American Law Institute Honors Learned Hand," *American Bar Association Journal,* 37 (1951), 503.

Burlingham, Charles C. "Judge Learned Hand," *Harvard Law Review,* 60 (1947), 330.

Cahn, Edmond. "Authority and Responsibility," *Columbia Law Review,* 51 (1951), 838.

Cound, John J. "Learned Hand," *Minnesota Law Review,* 46 (1961), 217.

Cox, Archibald. "Judge Learned Hand and the Interpretation of Statutes," *Harvard Law Review,* 60 (1947), 370.

Frank, Jerome N. "Some Reflections on Judge Learned Hand," *University of Chicago Law Review,* 24 (1957), 666.

Frankfurter, Felix. "Judge Learned Hand," *Harvard Law Review,* 60 (1947), 325.

————. "Learned Hand," *Harvard Law Review,* 75 (1961), 1.

Freund, Paul A. "Learned Hand: A Tribute," *Harvard Law Record,* 33 1961), 11.

Friendly, Henry J. "Learned Hand: An Expression from the Second Circuit," *Brooklyn Law Review,* 29 (1962), 6.

Hervey, John J. "'Learned Hand: Law Teacher Unsurpassed," *Brooklyn Law Review,* 29 (1962), 16.

Judd, Orrin G. "Judge Learned Hand and the Criminal Law," *Harvard Law Review,* 60 (1947), 405.

"Learned Hand:. Senior Judge–Second Circuit," *American Bar Association Journal,* 33 (1947), 869.

"Learned Hand Memorial Issue," *New York State Bar Journal,* 33 (1961), 405–28.

Mendelson, Wallace. "Learned Hand: Patient Democrat," *Harvard Law Review,* 76 (1962), 322.

Moore, Leonard P. "Learned Hand: An Appreciation," *Brooklyn Law Review,* 29 (1962), 2.

Pepper, George Wharton. "The Literary Style of Learned Hand," *Harvard Law Review,* 60 (1947), 333.

Philbin, Stephen. "Judge Learned Hand and the Law of Patents and Copyrights," *Harvard Law Review,* 60 (1947), 394.

Ribble, F. D. G. "In Memoriam: Judge Learned Hand," *Virginia Law Review,* 47 (1961), 925.

Waters, D. W. M. "Judge Learned Hand," *Solicitor Quarterly,* 1 (1962), 30.

Wyzanski, Jr., Charles E. "Judge Learned Hand's Contribution to Public Law," *Harvard Law Review,* 60 (1947), 348.

————. "Learned Hand," *Atlantic Monthly,* 208 (December 1961), 55.

THOMAS W. SWAN

Articles

Corbin, Arthur L. "The Yale Law School and Tom Swan," *Yale Law Report,* 4 (1958), 2.

Hand, Learned. "Thomas Walter Swan," *Yale Law Journal,* 57 (1947), 167.

AUGUSTUS N. HAND

Articles

Clark, Charles E. "Augustus Noble Hand," *Harvard Law Review,* 68 (1955), 1113.

————. "Augustus Noble Hand," An Address at a Special Memorial Meeting of the New York County Lawyers' Association and the Association of the Bar of the City of New York, May 4, 1955.

Hand, Augustus N. "A Sketch of Constitutional Law In America," in *Lectures on Legal Topics.* vol. 3, New York: Macmillan Co., 1926, p. 367.

————. "The Practice of Law—Then and Now," *Proceedings of the Vermont Bar Association,* 34 (1940), 76.

————. "Lawyers in a Revolutionary Age," *Pennsylvania Bar Association Quarterly,* 18 (1946), 46.

Horsky, Charles A. "Augustus Noble Hand," *Harvard Law Review,* 68 (1955), 118.

Swan, Thomas W. "Augustus Noble Hand," *Memorial Book, 1955,* p. 36. Association of the Bar of the City of New York.

Wyzanski, Jr., Charles E. "Augustus Noble Hand," *Harvard Law Review,* 61 (1948), 573.

————. "Augustus Noble Hand," An Address Before a Special Memorial Meeting of the New York County Lawyers' Association and the Association of the Bar of the City of New York, May 4, 1955.

CHARLES E. CLARK

Books and Monographs

Proceedings of a Special Session of the United States Court of Appeals, Second Circuit, in Memoriam to Judge Charles E. Clark, 328 F.2d.

Wright, Charles Alan, and Reasoner, Harry M. (eds.). *Procedure—The Handmaid of Justice.* St. Paul, Minn.: West Publishing Company, 1965.

Articles

Clark, Charles E. "Law and Its Uses in Modern Society," *Yale Alumni Week,* October 21, 1934.

————. "The Function of Law in a Democratic Society," *University of Chicago Law Review,* 9 (1942), 393.

————. "The Dilemma of American Judges: Is Too Great 'Trust for Salvation' Placed in Them?" *American Bar Association Journal,* 35 (1949), 8.

————. "Federal Procedural Reform and States' Rights; To a More Perfect Union," *Texas Law Review,* 40 (1961), 211.

————. "The Limits of Judicial Objectivity," *American University Law Review,* 12 (1963), 1.

"Charles Edward Clark Memorial Issue," *Connecticut Bar Journal,* 38 (1963).

Douglas, William O. "Charles E. Clark," *Yale Law Journal,* 73 (1963), 3.

Frank, John P. "For Maintaining Diversity Jurisdiction," *Yale Law Journal,* 73 (1963), 7.

Medina, Harold R. "Remarks," *Record of the Association of the Bar of the City of New York,* 15 (1960), 12.

Rodell, Fred. "For Charles E. Clark: A Brief and Belated But Fond Farewell," *Columbia Law Review,* 65 (1965), 1328.

Rostow, Eugene V. "Judge Charles E. Clark," *Yale Law Journal,* 73 (1963), 3.

JEROME FRANK

Books

Frank, Jerome N. *Law and the Modern Mind.* New York: Coward-McCann, 1930.

————. *Courts on Trial.* Princeton, N. J.: Princeton University Press, 1949.

————, and Frank, Barbara. *Not Guilty.* Garden City, N. Y.: Doubleday and Company, Inc., 1957.

Kristein, Barbara Frank (ed.). *A Man's Reach.* New York: Macmillan Co., 1965.

Paul, Julius. *The Legal Realism of Jerome N. Frank.* The Hague, Netherlands: Martinus Nijhoff, 1959.

Articles

Arnold, Thurman, "Judge Jerome Frank," *University of Chicago Law Review,* 24 (1957), 633.

Beatty, Sam A. "On Legal Realism—Some Basic Ideas of Jerome Frank," *Alabama Law Review,* 11 (1959), 239.

Brown, Brendan F. "Jerome Frank and the Natural Law," *Catholic Lawyer,* 5 (1959), 133.

Cahn, Edmond N. "Judge Frank's Fact Skepticism and Our Future," *Yale Law Journal,* 66 (1957), 824.

————. "Fact-Skepticism and Fundamental Law," *New York University Law Review,* 33 (1958), 1.

Clark, Charles E. "Jerome N. Frank," *Yale Law Journal,* 66 (1957), 817.

————. "Jerome N. Frank," An Address at a Special Memorial Meeting of the New York County Lawyers' Association and the Association of the Bar of the City of New York, May 23, 1957.

Davis, Sidney M. "Jerome Frank—Portrait of a Personality," *University of Chicago Law Review,* 24 (1957), 617.

Douglas, William O. "Jerome N. Frank," *University of Chicago Law Review,* 24 (1957), 626.

————. "Jerome N. Frank," An Address at a Special Memorial Meeting of the New York County Lawyers' Association and the Association of the Bar of the City of New York, May 23, 1957.

Frank, Jerome N. "Are Judges Human?" *University of Pennsylvania Law Review,* 80 (1931), 17, 233.

————. "What Courts Do in Fact," *Illinois Law Review,* 26 (1932), 645.

————. (Anon. Y. Mous). "The Speech of Judges: A Dissenting Opinion," *Virginia Law Review,* 29 (1943), 625.

————. "Words and Music: Some Remarks on Statutory Interpretation," *Columbia Law Review,* 47 (1947), 1259.

————. "Say It With Music," *Harvard Law Review,* 61 (1948), 921.

————. " 'Short of Sickness and Death': A Study of Moral Responsibility in Legal Criticism," *New York University Law Review,* 26 (1951), 545.

————. "A Conflict with Oblivion: Some Observations on the Founders of Legal Pragmatism," *Rutgers Law Review,* 9 (1954), 425.

————. "The Lawyer's Role in Modern Society," *Journal of Public Law,* 4 (1955), 8.

————. "Civil Law Influences on the Common Law—Some Reflections on 'Comparative' and 'Contrastive' Law," *University of Pennsylvania Law Review,* 104 (1956), 887.

————. "Today's Problems in the Administration of Criminal Justice," 15 *Federal Rules Decisions,* 95.

Frankfurter, Felix. "Jerome N. Frank," *University of Chicago Law Review,* 24 (1957), 625.

Hamilton, Waldo H. "The Great Tradition—Jerome Frank," *Yale Law Journal,* 66 (1947), 167.

Kessler, Friedrich. "In Memoriam: Jerome Frank," *Natural Law Forum,* 2 (1957), 1.

Kurland, Philip B. "Jerome N. Frank: Some Reflections and Recollections of a Law Clerk," *University of Chicago Law Review,* 24 (1957), 661.

McWhinney, Edward. "Judge Jerome Frank and Legal Realism: An Appraisal," *New York Law Forum,* 3 (1957), 113.

————. "A Legal Realist and a Humanist—Crosscurrents in the Legal Philosophy of Judge Jerome Frank," *Indiana Law Journal,* 33 (1957), 115.

Rodell, Fred. "Jerome Frank: In Remembrance," *Yale Law Report,* 3 (1957), 3.

Rostow, Eugene V. "Jerome N. Frank," *Yale Law Journal,* 66 (1957), 819.

Rovere, Richard H. "Jerome N. Frank," An Address at a Special Memorial Meeting of the New York County Lawyers' Association and the Association of the Bar of the City of New York, May 23, 1957.

Rumble, Jr., Wilfrid E. "Jerome Frank and His Critics: Certainty and Fantasy in the Judicial Process," *Journal of Public Law,* 10 (1961), 125.

Volkomer, Walter E. "The Constitutional Ideas of Judge Jerome N. Frank," *New York Law Forum,* 7 (1961), 17.

Index

Abruzzo, Matthew T., 137–38
Administrative Office of the United States Courts, 69

Betts, Samuel R., 41
Biddle, Francis, 16
Biggs, John, 79
Black, Hugo, 192
Blatchford, Samuel: as circuit judge, 50; as reporter, 44, 50
Borchard, Edwin, 124, 126n, 228–29
Burlingham, Charles C.: and Learned Hand, 14, 17; on Judge Hough, 61
Byrnes, James, 18

Cahn, Edmond, 171–72, 174: on Jerome Frank, 252
Chafee, Zechariah, 178
Chase, Harrie Brigham: biography of, 26–29; conservatism of, 29, 325; in *Dennis* case, 204–5; on Federal Employers' Liability Act, 202–3; on First Amendment, 181n, 204-7; in immigration and naturalization cases, 216–17; on National Labor Relations Board, 200; in patient appeals, 101, 189n, 197; in selective service cases, 211–12; and Supreme Court, 152, 342, 344, 346–47
Circuit Courts of Appeals. *See* United States Courts of Appeals
Clark, Charles E.: and administrative agencies, 247, 248; appointment of, 9; biography of, 29–32; as chief judge, 32; and civil liberties, 277, 279–84, 285–90; correspondence of, 75, 100, 222, 242; on criminal rights, 266–67; and dissenting opinions, 110–11, 112n, 314n, 317, 320; as district court judge, 77n; on en banc proceedings, 105–6, 116, 120–22; on Fair Labor Standards Act, 247; on federalism, 250–51; and Federal Rules of Civil Procedure, 31, 223–24; and Justice Frankfurter, 239–40; and Learned Hand, relations with, 139–41, 239–40, 303–5, 324; on harmless error rule, 267–68, 272–73; on House Un-American Activities Committee, 285–90; in immigration and naturalization cases, 283–85; and judicial reform, 30–31, 223; on memoran-

dum system, 98–99; and National Labor Relations Board, 248–49; and procedural cases, 105–6, 110–11, 224n, 228n, 246; in selective service cases, 211; and Supreme Court, 151–52, 343, 344, 346–47; in *United States v. Sacher,* 290–97; and Yale Law School, 30: *See also* Clark-Frank relationship

Clark-Frank relationship, 32. 219–23, 322, 350n: Clark memorial to Frank, 221, 225; colleagues' attitude toward, 130, 236, 240–45, 242–43n; communication between Clark and Frank, 75–76, 219–20n, 220n, 222n, 222–23n, 243; consultation with non-sitting judges, 103–5; consultation with outside experts, 126–29; declaratory judgments, 227–29; extrajudicial writings, 226, 227n; Learned Hand's attitude toward, 128, 129, 232, 235–37; harmless error rule, 143–44, 267–76; interlocutory appeals, 229–39; judicial procedure, 223–26, 245–46; special verdicts, 227; summary judgments, 127–28, 227; *United States v. Antonelli,* 271–76; *United States v. Sacher,* 200, 290–98; Yale Law School, 124, 126, 129n, 143, 222, 226, 228-29n, 275, 297

Commerce Court, 59

Coolidge, Calvin, 7

Cooper, Frank, 138

Corbin, Arthur, 124, 125, 129

Countryman, Vern, 124

Coxe, Alfred Conkling, 56

District courts (federal): and courts of appeals, relations with, 133–34; and courts of appeals, service of judges on, 77; names of judges in opinions, 138–40

Eastern District Court of New York, 45

Edgerton, Henry W., 288–89

Evans, Evan, 80–81

Evarts Act (Court of Appeals Act of 1891), 52–53, 54

Fair Labor Standards Act, 194, 202, 247

Federal Employers' Liability Act, 193, 202–3

Federal Rules of Appellate Procedure, 86–89, 113, 119

Federal Rules of Civil Procedure, 8, 85: and Judge Clark, 31, 223–24; and Judge Frank, 224–25

Feinberg, Wilfred, 67

Frank, Jerome N.: and administrative agencies, 81–82, 247–48; appointment of, 9–10; and bankruptcy law, 257–59; biography of, 32–38, 301–2; and civil liberties, 277–79, 298; in "Communist" cases, 270n, 298–302; and criminal rights, 261–66, 268–76, 327; and dissenting opinions, attitude toward, 108n, 112n; "fact-skepticism" of, 252–54; and Fair Labor Standards Act, 247; and Learned Hand, 13, 170n, 185–86, 237n, 244–45; and harmless error rule, 268–76, 299–300; in immigration and naturalization cases, 216–17n, 284–85; and Indian rights, 255; on interlocutory appeals, 230–39; and judicial function, 253–55, 269; jurisprudence of, 10, 32–33, 222, 224–26; and jury system, 253; opinions of, 35–38, 108; and patent law, 259–60; and protection of underdogs, 254–59, 261–62, 268; and rights of seamen, 256; on self-incrimination, 263–64, 300; on special verdicts, 227; style of, 223, 242–43; and Supreme Court, 142, 143–44, 150, 153, 300–301, 302, 343, 344, 346–47; on trademarks, 260–61; *United States v. Sacher,* 290–98; and Yale Law School, 55n, 226. *See also* Clark-Frank relationship

Frank, John P., 11, 194–95n, 221, 290

Frankfurter, Felix, 157, 158–61, 192, 193, 224n, 271; and Judge Clark, 224n, 239–40; and Learned Hand, 13, 17, 18, 19, 142, 154n, 157, 170n, 171, 187; and judicial restraint, 159–61; on rehearings, 113–14; 20, 113n, 117; and Second Circuit, 77n, 91n

Freund, Paul, 189

Friendly, Henry J., 66, 90–91, 99

Galston, Clarence, 140

Hand, Augustus Noble, 70: on administrative agencies, 195–96, 197n; attitude toward dissent, 23, 26, 110, 196, 198; and bankruptcy law, 258; biography of, 24–26; on civil rights, 208–9; and criminal rights, 267; on Federal Employers' Liability Act, 202; in immigration and naturalization cases, 199, 215–16; influence on colleagues, 23, 26, 198–200, 321; philosophy of, 195, 196; in selective service appeals, 101, 209–11; style of, 23, 197–98n; and Supreme Court, 146n, 342, 344, 346–47; and Judge Swan, 26; in *United States v. Sacher,* 207, 291

Hand, Learned: on administrative agencies, 168–70; and bankruptcy law, 258; biography of, 13–19; as chief judge, 83n, 84n, 94, 188n; and Judge Clark, 303–5; and criminal law, 182–

83n, 265; in *Dennis* case, 180–81, 291; and en banc proceedings, 105; and Federal Employers' Liability Act, 202, 203; and Judge Frank, 262; and freedom of speech, 176–80, 183–84; and harmless error rule, 182n, 269n, 270; Holmes Lectures of ("Bill of Rights"), 17, 156, 162–63, 355; in immigration and naturalization cases, 171–75, 316; influence of, 19, 155, 187–89; on interlocutory appeals, 232, 234–35; on Internal Revenue Code, 8; and Manton case, 6n; in *Masses* case, 176–78; on the New Deal, 167–68; in patent cases, 101, 166–69, 189n, 197; philosophy of, 17, 160–61, 162–66, 167, 174, 183–87, 191; on precedent, 114–15; reputation of, 12–13, 16–17, 156–57, 187–91; and statutory interpretation, 162–63n, 189–90; on Justice Stone, 160–61; style and temperament of, 15, 16n, 92n, 189; and Supreme Court, 142, 147, 150, 151, 340–41, 343–44, 346; Supreme Court, aspirations for appointment to, 6–7, 15, 17n; in *United States v. Aluminum Company of America*, 170–71
Harlan, John Marshall, 16, 66
Harmless error rule, 143–44, 267–76
Harper, Fowler, 332
Hart, Henry M., Jr., 69–70
Hays, Paul R., 67
Hincks, Carroll C., 66
Holmes, Oliver Wendell, Jr., 13, 17, 157–59, 178n, 179, 187, 197
Horsky, Charles A., 352–53
Hough, Charles Merrill, 24, 60–62: on early history of Second Circuit, 42, 47, 50
House Un-American Activities Committee, 206–7, 285–90
Hunt, Ward, 43
Hurst, Willard, 349–50
Hutcheson, Joseph, 81–82, 145n, 146, 198
Hyneman, Charles S., 4

Immigration and naturalization appeals, 101, 171–75, 199, 215–17, 283–85, 316
Inch, Robert, 138
Interlocutory appeals, 229–39

Johnson, Alexander Smith, 48
Judicial councils, 83–84, 138
Judiciary Act of 1787, 39–40
Judiciary Act of 1801, 41–42
Judiciary Act of 1869, 46–47

Karlen, Delmar, 93
Kaufman, Irving R., 19, 67
Knapp, Martin A., 59

Kurland, Philip B.: evaluation of Second Circuit, 11, 348

Lacombe, Emile Henry, 51, 54–55, 57
Law clerks, 106–8
Livingston, Brockholst, 43
Llewellyn, Karl, 10, 20, 60–61, 187–88
Lumbard, J. Edward, 66: on advocacy, 91–93; as chief judge, 82; on en banc proceedings, 120; on per curiam opinions, 94, 312n

McReynolds, James C., 198
Magruder, Calvert, 80, 133–34, 144–45, 149, 335
Maltbie, William M., 131–32
Manton, Martin T., 5–6, 7, 62–63
Marshall, Thurgood, 67
Mayer, Julius M., 60, 63–64
Medina, Harold R., 66, 207, 290–93: on assignment of opinions, 100–101, 101n; on memorandum system, 97; on reading of briefs, 90n
Moore, James W., 124–26, 129, 230, 234, 236, 238
Moore, Leonard P., 66
Moore's Federal Practice, 124, 229
Moscowitz, Grover, 136–37
Murphy, Walter F., 146–47

National Labor Relations Board, 200, 248–49, 336
Nelson, Samuel, 43, 44, 47
New York Court of Appeals, 94–95
Noss, Luther, 126–28
Noyes, Walter Chadwick, 57, 59

Paine's Reports, 43, 44
Parker, John, 85, 101, 111, 148–49
Patterson, Robert P., 9, 135

Removal Act of 1875, 46
Report of the Attorney General, 48, 58
Rifkind, Simon, 135
Roberts, Owen, 202
Rodell, Fred, 124, 253n, 297
Rogers, Henry Wade, 59, 179n
Roosevelt, Franklin D., 7, 8, 18
Rutledge, Wiley, 10

Schlesinger, Arthur, Jr., 301
Second Circuit. *See* United States Court of Appeals for the Second Circuit
Shapiro, Martin, 2, 180, 181n
Shipman, Nathaniel, 54–55
Simons, Charles C., 81
Smith, J. Joseph, 67
"Society of Jobbists," 158–59
Southern District of New York: history of, 41, 43, 44; importance of, 46, 310–11; relations with Second Circuit, 134; reputation of, 24, 60

Stone, Harlan Fiske, 164–65: and Learned Hand, 17, 160–61

Supreme Court of Errors of Connecticut, 130–31

Swan, Thomas Walter: and administrative agencies, 21; biography of, 19–23; in *Dennis* case, 204; on dissenting opinions, 109–10; Fair Labor Standards Act, 202; Federal Employers' Liability Act, 203–4; and Augustus Hand, 20; Learned Hand on, 22–23, 190n; and immigration and naturalization cases, 101, 212–15, 216, 217–18; and National Labor Relations Board, 200–201; and New Deal, attitude toward, 21; style of, 19–21; and Supreme Court, 340–41, 344, 346; and Yale Law School, 20

Taft, William Howard, 14–15, 18, 63

Tanenhaus, Joseph, 333

Thompson, Smith, 43, 44

Townsend, William, 56

United States Court of Appeals for the District of Columbia, 138, 140, 289, 354

United States Court of Appeals for the Eighth Circuit, 96n

United States Court of Appeals for the First Circuit, 334–35

United States Court of Appeals for the Second Circuit: and bankruptcy law, 257–59; business of, 7, 10, 58, 65, 68–72, 305–12, 354–55; as a conservative court, 194–98, 316–17; and dissent, attitude toward, 109, 313–14; and district courts, relations with, 134–41; and First Amendment, 194; history of, 1789–1791, 41–52; 1891–1941, 54–66; 1951–, 66–72; and immigration and naturalization cases, 212–18; and interlocutory appeals, dispute over, 229–39; intracircuit conflict, 110, 114–15, 117, 319–20; and judges, cohesion of, 74–75, 100; and judges, disqualification of, 88–89n; judges from other courts on, 77–82; judicial conference of, 84n; judicial council of, 83n; and National Labor Relations Board, 16–17n, 169–70 194; New Deal, attitude toward, 7, 10; reputation of, 5, 10, 11–12, 348–49, 355; rules of, 86; and selective service law, 209–12; and Supreme Court, anticipation of, 150–53; and Supreme Court, defiance of, 146–48; and Supreme Court, relationship with, 13, 141–53, 329–31, 334–38

United States Court of Appeals for the Second Circuit, decision-making process: advocacy before, 87n, 89–93; bargaining, 100, 102; briefs, 90–91; concurring opinions, 108, 313; conferences, 99–100; consulation with nonsitting judges, 102–5; dissenting opinions, 108–12, 313, 316–18, 319–20, 339–40; and en banc proceedings, 115–22; law clerks, 99, 106–8; memorandum system, 80, 96–99, 101, 102, 109n, 219–20n, 318; opinions, 73n, 94–96, 100–101, 102, 113, 308–9; panel schedule, 6, 76, 82, 88–89, 102, 193–94, 290, 319; per curiam opinions, 94–96, 308–9, 315, 321; rehearings, 113–14, 296; sessions, 76

United States Court of Appeals for the Sixth Circuit, 57n

United States Courts of Appeals: appointments to, 134–35n; bargaining on, 75; chief judges of, 82, 83–84; and district courts, attitude toward, 133–34; en banc proceedings in, 115–20; finality of rulings, 1, 353; formation of, 52–53; intercircuit relations, 80–82, 132–33, 336–37; judges, intercircuit assignment of, 45, 78–82; jurisdiction of, 53n, 193; litigation before, 3–4, 353–54; neglect of, 1–4; prior to 1891, 39–52; rules of procedure, 85–86; and state courts, relations with, 130–31; and Supreme Court, relations with, 141–53, 193, 328–31

United States Supreme Court: attention to, by constitutional scholars, 2; certiorari jurisdiction, 95–96, 112, 193, 328–333; circuit riding of justices, 40, 41, 42, 43, 52n, 77n; and en banc proceedings in courts of appeals, 115, 117–18; and harmless error rule, 267, 271–72, 276–77n; importance of, 2, 241

Wallace, James William, 50–51, 52, 55

Ward, Henry Galbraith, 57

Waterman, Sterry R., 66

Wechsler, Herbert, 166

Woodbury, Peter, 79, 148–49n

Woodruff, Lewis B., 47

Wyzanski, Charles E., Jr.: and Augustus Hand, 25, 26, 196, 198; and Learned Hand, 19, 159n, 160, 168, 178n, 189n, 352n, 355; on Judge Hough, 60; on Second Circuit, 11, 354

Index of Cases

Adams-Mitchell Co. v. Cambridge Distributing Co., 259
Aero Spark Plug Co. v. B. G. Corporation, 260
Allen Bradley Co. v. Local Union No. 3, 248n
American Communication Association v. Douds, 179
Arnstein v. Porter, 127–28, 129
Associated Industries v. Ickes, 259n
Audi Vision Inc. v. R.C.A. Manufacturing Co., 230

Baird v. Franklin, 249
In re Barnett, 255, 268
Barnett v. Texas and Pacific Ry., 209
Barnette v. West Virginia State Board of Education, 148–49
Barsky v. United States, 289
P. Beiersdorf & Co. v. McGohey, 234n, 251
Benjamin v. Jaspan, 249
Bihn v. United States, 270
Bollenbach v. United States, 271
Borella v. Borden Co., 202

Brooklyn National Corp. v. Commissioner of Internal Revenue, 169n
Buck v. Bell, 158
Bush v. Order of United Commerical Travellers, 249

Callus v. 10 East Fortieth Street Building, 202
Chandler v. Judicial Council of the Tenth Circuit, 84n
Christensen v. Valentine, 280
Clark v. Taylor, 233–34n, 255
Cohen v. Jeskowitz, 258
Colonie Fibre Co. v. National Labor Relations Board, 248
Corning Glass Works v. National Labor Relations Board, 104–5n
Cover v. Schwartz, 227–28
Cramer v. United States, 284n

Dennis v. United States, 181
Dickinson v. Mulligan, 233–34n
Douds v. Local 1250, Retail, Wholesale Department Store Union, 249n
Duquesne Warehouse Co. v. Railroad Retirement Board, 81–82

Erie v. Tompkins, 8, 130, 250
Erie Railroad Co. v. The Cornell No. 20, 254–55

Flegenheimer v. General Mills, Inc., 235–36
Fleming v. Arsenal Building Corporation, 202
Fred Fisher Music Co. v. M. Witmark & Sons, 257n
In re Fried, 265–66

Gardella v. Chandler, 152–53
Gitlow v. New York, 204
Ex parte Green, 255

Hammond-Knowlton v. United States, 254–55n
Herring v. Luckenbach S.S. Co., 203n
Herzfeld v. Federal Trade Commission, 168
In re Herzog, 249
Hoffman v. Palmer, 103–4n
Hume v. Moore-McCormack Lines, 256

Keller v. Brooklyn Bus Corp., 268
Kirsch Manufacturing Co. v. Gould Mersereau Co., Inc., 167n
Korte v. New York, New Haven & Hartford R., 203
Kotteakos v. United States, 267, 276

La Touraine Coffee Co. v. Lorraine Coffee Co., 254n
Libby-Owens-Ford Glass Co. v. Sylvania Industrial Corp., 232–33n
Lopinsky v. Hertz Drive-Ur-Self System, 236–37
In re Luma Camera Service, 258–59

McComb v. Frank Scerbo & Sons, 164n
MacDonald v. Du Maurier, 224
Maggio v. Zeitz, 259
Malman v. United States, 129
Masses Publishing Co. v Patten, 176–78, 179
Mastrapasqua v. Shaughnessy, 217
Meyer v. Nebraska, 158, 161
Morris v. Pennsylvania R., 203, 227n
Mostyn v. Delaware, Lackawanna & Western R., 203–4

National Labor Relations Board v. Dadourian Export Corp., 201n
National Labor Relations Board v. National Broadcasting Company, 249n
National Labor Relations Board v. Universal Camera Corp., 169
Newman v. Clayton F. Summy Co., 257n
New York Times Co. v. Sullivan, 206
North American Co. v. Securities & Exchange Commission, 200

Old Colony Bondholders v. New York, New Haven & Hartford R. Co., 248

Pabellon v. Grace Line, Inc., 235
Paetau v. Watkins, 215
Parke, Davis & Co. v. H. K. Mulford Co., 166n
Perkins v. Endicott Johnson Corp., 150n, 268
Picard v. United Aircraft Corporation, 259–60
In re P–R Holding Corporation, 124–25

Repouille v. United States, 173, 244n, 284
Republic Aviation Corporation v. National Labor Relations Board, 201
Republic of China v. American Express, 234n
Ricketts v. Pennsylvania R., 204, 256
Rieser v. Baltimore & Ohio R., 226n, 237n, 239n
Robbins v. Gottbetter, 258

In re Sandow, 257n
Schenck v. United States, 178n, 179
Schirrmeister v. Watkins, 215n
Schmidt v. United States, 173
Security Exchange Commission v. Long Island Lighting Co., 81
Seligson v. Goldsmith, 258n
Shaughnessy v. United States ex rel. Mezei, 176n
Skidmore v. Baltimore & Ohio R., 227
Spector Motor Service v. O'Connor, 131, 151–52
Spector Motor Service v. Walsh, 130, 131, 151
Stewart v. Baltimore & Ohio R., 203
Sweeney v. Schenectady Publishing Co., 206, 283

10 East Fortieth Street Building v. Callus, 202
Textile Mills Security Corp. v. Commissioner, 115
Toolson v. New York Yankees, Inc., 153
Triangle Publications, Inc. v. Rohrlich, 260–61

United States ex rel. Adams v. McCann, 146–47
United States v. Aluminum Company of America, 170–71
United States v. Antonelli Fireworks Co., 271–75
United States v. Bennett, 270
United States ex rel. Beye v. Downer, 211–12
United States ex rel. Bradley v. Watkins, 215

United States v. Bramson, 270n, 299
United States v. Caffey, 171
United States v. Carolene Products, 160–61n, 164, 165
United States v. Cohen, 81
United States v. Dennis, 180–81, 204–6, 291
United States ex rel. D'Esquiva v. Uhl, 214
United States v. Di Re, 266–67
United States v. Ebeling, 262–63
United States v. Forness, 255
United States v. Francioso, 172
United States v. Girouard, 149–50n
United States ex rel. Gregoire v. Watkins, 214n
United States ex rel. Hirshberg v. Malanaphy, 212, 214n
United States v. Hoffman, 212n
United States v. Johnson, 263n
United States v. Josephson, 206–7, 285–89
United States ex rel. Kaloudis v. Shaughnessy, 174
United States v. Kauten, 209–10
United States ex rel. Knauff v. McGrath, 216–17
United States ex rel. Knauff v. Shaughnessy, 216
United States v. Liss, 269
United States ex rel. Ludecke v. Watkins, 215–16
United States ex rel. Ludwig v. Watkins, 215
United States ex rel. Lynn v. Downer, 208, 280
United States v. Marzano, 136

United States ex rel. Medeiros v. Watkins, 285
United States ex rel. Mezei v. Shaughnessy, 175–76
United States ex rel. Phillips v. Downer, 211
United States ex rel. Potash v. District Director of Immigration and Naturalization, 199, 216, 282–83
United States v. Rosenberg, 299–300
United States v. Rubenstein, 269
United States v. Sacher, 110, 200, 207, 290–98
United States v. St. Pierre, 263–64
United States v. Schenck, 197
United States ex rel. Schleuter v. Watkins, 215
United States ex rel. Schwarzkopf v. Uhl, 213–14
United States v. Seeger, 210
United States v. Sotzek, 217n
United States v. Ullmann, 300–301
United States ex rel. Zdunic v. Uhl, 213
Universal Camera Corp. v. National Labor Relations Board, 170

Watkins v. United States, 207, 289
Welsh v. United States, 210
West Virginia State Board of Education v. Barnette, 149, 161
Western Pacific R.R. Corp. v. Western Pacific R.R. Co., 117–18, 119–20
Willis v. Pennsylvania R., 253
M. Witmark & Sons v. Fred Fisher Music Co., 256–57

Zalkind v. Scheinman, 231–32

THE JOHNS HOPKINS PRESS

Designed by Arlene J. Sheer

Composed in Baskerville text with Baskerville display
by Baltimore Type and Composition Corporation

Printed on 60 lb. Warren 1854 Regular
by Universal Lithographers, Inc.

Bound in Interlaken Arco Vellum
by L. H. Jenkins, Inc.

DISCARD